The Sword of Ambition

Letter from the General Editor

The Library of Arabic Literature series offers Arabic editions and English translations of significant works of Arabic literature, with an emphasis on the seventh to nineteenth centuries. The Library of Arabic Literature thus includes texts from the pre-Islamic era to the cusp of the modern period, and encompasses a wide range of genres, including poetry, poetics, fiction, religion, philosophy, law, science, history, and historiography.

Books in the series are edited and translated by internationally recognized scholars and are published in parallel-text format with Arabic and English on facing pages, and are also made available as English-only paperbacks.

The Library encourages scholars to produce authoritative, though not necessarily critical, Arabic editions, accompanied by modern, lucid English translations. Its ultimate goal is to introduce the rich, largely untapped Arabic literary heritage to both a general audience of readers as well as to scholars and students.

The Library of Arabic Literature is supported by a grant from the New York University Abu Dhabi Institute and is published by NYU Press.

Philip F. Kennedy
General Editor, Library of Arabic Literature

تجريد سيف الهمّة
لاستخراج ما في ذمّة الذمّة

لأبي عمرو عثمان بن ابرٰهيم النابلسيّ المصريّ

LIBRARY OF
المكتبة
ARABIC
العربية
LITERATURE

The Sword of Ambition

Bureaucratic Rivalry in Medieval Egypt

Abū ʿAmr ʿUthmān ibn Ibrāhīm
al-Nābulusī al-Miṣrī

Edited and translated by
Luke B. Yarbrough

Foreword by
Sherman ʿAbd al-Ḥakīm Jackson

Volume editor
Devin J. Stewart

NEW YORK UNIVERSITY PRESS
New York

NEW YORK UNIVERSITY PRESS
New York

Library of Congress Cataloging-in-Publication Data

Names: Nabulusi, Uthman ibn Ibrahim, active 1235, author. | Yarbrough, Luke B., editor translator. | Nabulusi, Uthman ibn Ibrahim, active 1235. Luma al-qawanin al-mudiyah fi dawawin al-diyar al-Misriyah. | Nabulusi, Uthman ibn Ibrahim, active 1235. Luma al-qawanin al-mudiyah fi dawawin al-diyar al-Misriyah. English.
Title: The sword of ambition: bureaucratic rivalry in medieval Egypt / Abu Amr Uthman ibn Ibrahim al-Nabulusi al-Misri; edited and translated by Luke B. Yarbrough.
Description: New York: New York University Press, 2016. | In Arabic with English translation. | Includes bibliographical references and index.
Identifiers: LCCN 2016007041| ISBN 9781479889457 (cl : alk. paper) | ISBN 9781479839087 (e-book) | ISBN 9781479842575 (e-book)
Subjects: LCSH: Administrative agencies--Egypt--Early works to 1800. | Egypt--Politics and government--640-1882--Early works to 1800.
Classification: LCC JQ3831 .N3313 2016 | DDC 320.962/09022--dc23
LC record available at http://lccn.loc.gov/2016007041

New York University Press books are printed on acid-free paper, and their binding materials are chosen for strength and durability.

Series design by Titus Nemeth.

Typeset in Tasmeem, using DecoType Naskh and Emiri.

Typesetting and digitization by Stuart Brown.

Manufactured in the United States of America
c10 9 8 7 6 5 4 3 2 1

Table of Contents

Letter from the General Editor iii
Foreword xii
Abbreviations xv
Acknowledgments xvi
Introduction xviii
A Note on the Text xxxiii
Ayyubid Cairo xxxviii
The Central Near East in the 7th Century xxxix
Notes to the Introduction xl

The Sword of Ambition 1

The First Chapter, On the Reprehensibility of Employing Dhimmis for the Muslims' Jobs, in Fifteen Sections 10
The First Section: The Testimony of the Illustrious Book 10
The Second Section: The Example of the Messenger of God 12
The Third Section: The Testimony of the Ancient Authorities 12
The Fourth Section: The Example of Imam Abū Bakr al-Ṣiddīq, God Be Pleased with Him 14
The Fifth Section: The Example of Imam ʿUmar ibn al-Khaṭṭāb 16
The Sixth Section: The Example of ʿAbd al-Malik ibn Marwān 20
The Seventh Section: The Deeds of al-Ḥajjāj 22
The Eighth Section: The Example of ʿUmar ibn ʿAbd al-ʿAzīz, God Be Pleased with Him 22
The Ninth Section: The Events That Took Place in the Days of Caliph al-Manṣūr 26
The Tenth Section: The Events That Took Place in the Days of Caliph al-Mahdī 30
The Eleventh Section: The Events That Took Place in the Days of Caliph Hārūn al-Rashīd 32
The Twelfth Section: The Events That Took Place in the Days of Caliph al-Maʾmūn 34

The Thirteenth Section: The Events That Took Place in the Days of al-Mutawakkil 38
The Fourteenth Section: The Events That Took Place in the Days of Caliph al-Muqtadir Bi-llāh 48
The Fifteenth Section: Examples of the Jews' Ignominy, Wickedness, and Trickery 50

The Second Chapter, A Description of the Copts and Their Perfidies, in Fifteen Sections 54
The First Section: A General Description of Them 54
The Second Section: Why the Copts Specialize as Secretaries and Neglect Other Professions 54
The Third Section: Concerning Their Pervasive yet Imperceptible Influence in the Land of Egypt 56
The Fourth Section: How Aḥmad ibn Ṭūlūn Discovered Their Notorious Malfeasance, and How He Resolved to Act toward Them 58
The Fifth Section: What Befell Them at the Hands of Muḥammad ibn Sulaymān 60
The Sixth Section: The Events That Took Place in the Days of al-Ḥākim bi-Amr Allāh 62
The Seventh Section: The Events That Took Place in the Days of al-Āmir, and the Confiscations Carried Out by the Accursed Monk 66
The Eighth Section: Their Perfidy in the Story of ʿArīb the Singer 68
The Ninth Section: Their Scheming in the Days of al-Ḥāfiẓ, Their Perfidy during His Regime, and the Way in Which They Corrupted Aspects of His Life Which Had Otherwise Been Righteous 70
The Tenth Section: Their Shameless Testimony in Court Cases Involving Muslims 74
The Eleventh Section: Concerning Their Scheming in Carrying Out the Cadastral Survey, and Their Shamelessness in Causing Harm, with No Concern for God, Be He Exalted, No Fear of Scandal from the Discovery of Their Disgrace, and No Regard for Consequences 78

The Twelfth Section: Their Scheming against a Certain Judicial Witness Who Was in Their Company, and How They Cannot Be Restrained from Malfeasance 80
The Thirteenth Section: Concerning a Calculated Stratagem Carried Out by a Christian against His Jewish Associate, a Shocking Act That Only Someone of That Accursed Community Would Dare to Commit 82
The Fourteenth Section: Their Disgraceful Deeds in the Days of al-ʿĀḍid, When al-Malik al-Ṣāliḥ Ṭalāʾiʿ ibn Ruzzīk Was Sultan 84
The Fifteenth Section: Why It Is That When One of Them Converts to Islam Due to Some Predicament or Calamity, He Becomes Even More Miserable and Dishonest than He Had Been Formerly, and Even More Insolent 90

The Third Chapter, A Description of Secretaries and Their Art, in Three Sections 98
The First Section: A Description of the Secretarial Art 98
The Second Section: An Account of Those Men Who May Properly Be Called Secretaries, along with Some of Their Achievements in Prose, Though It Be but a Single Phrase to Demonstrate the Excellence of Each One 98
The Third Section: Examples of the Poetry Produced by the Most Excellent Secretaries, Though It Be but a Single Line Each 136

The Fourth Chapter, An Account of the Ignorant Men Who Have Unworthily Donned the Garments of the Secretaries, in Three Sections 154
The First Section: Poetry Composed about Such Men in Former and More Recent Times 154
The Second Section: Concerning Amusing Aspects of Their Vulgar Expression, and Their Foolishness 160
The Third Section, From Which Our Book Gets Its Title: What Should Be Done with Them, Namely, Taking Back the Property They Have Skimmed for Themselves from Public Funds Rightfully Belonging to the Muslims 176
A Section with Which I End This Book, Explaining My Reason for Composing It 188

Notes	193
The Fatimid Caliphs in Egypt	210
The Ayyubid Sultans in Egypt	211
Glossary of Names and Terms	212
Bibliography	234
Further Reading	245
Index	247
About the NYU Abu Dhabi Institute	262
About the Typefaces	263
Titles Published by the Library of Arabic Literature	264
About the Editor–Translator	266

D.B.G.

Foreword

A prominent scholar of Islamic history once wrote, "Ulamalogy is a noble science—at least we have to think so, because it is almost all the Islamic social history we will ever have." This sentiment about ulama—religious scholars and jurists—underscores a perduring tension in the study of premodern Islam, between the ideal theories and prescriptions laid down by those writers on the one hand and quotidian reality on the other. Even the descriptive efforts of premodern Muslim historians afford scant insight into social trends, attitudes, actors, or movements. And it is in this context that the value of the present work is thrown into bold relief.

The Sword of Ambition (*Tajrīd sayf al-himmah li-stikhrāj mā fī dhimmat al-dhimmah*) might be described as a social polemic packaged in the language of Islamic law. Its author, ʿUthmān ibn Ibrāhīm al-Nābulusī (d. 660/1262), a noted official in the Ayyubid state, sets out to undermine the legitimacy of non-Muslims serving in positions of political authority. Not only are non-Muslims untrustworthy in Ibn al-Nābulusī's view, for him the very fact of their functioning in any official capacity in a Muslim state violates the ideal Islamic social order, which, he intimates, is supposed to reflect the absolute supremacy of Islam and the subordination of all other religions. Thus, Ibn al-Nābulusī is relentless in adducing Qur'anic verses, Prophetic hadiths, statements and actions of the prophet Muhammad's Companions, the early caliphs, governors, scholars, and even poets, to substantiate both the impermissibility and the impropriety of non-Muslims serving in Muslim government.

We must be careful, however, as we negotiate the ferocity of Ibn al-Nābulusī's invective, not to be seduced into overestimating or underestimating its value or meaning. Ibn al-Nābulusī clearly casts his arguments in explicitly legal terms, as he wants to convey the sense that he is motivated not by personal bias but by piety and an assiduous commitment to the ideals and interests of Islam. Yet, by de-contextualizing scripture, conflating its general descriptions with specific identities, by suppressing countervailing texts and historical examples, and by imputing to early generations the authority to hand down permanently binding findings of fact, Ibn al-Nābulusī ultimately tips his hand. To take just a couple of examples, he completely suppresses Qur'anic statements that speak to the trustworthiness of Jews and Christians, for example: «And among the People of the Book are those whom if you entrust them with an entire treasure, they will promptly return it to you. . . .» (Q Āl ʿImrān 3:75). Meanwhile, he leaves us to assume that a Jew's or a Christian's commission of this or that indiscretion as a matter of *fact* translates into a permanent, inextricably inherent character trait of all Jews and Christians.

But rather than dismiss Ibn al-Nābulusī's campaign as a simple expression of prejudice, we must remain open to the possible degree of factual veracity it contains and to what his manner of proceeding tells us about the broader sociopolitical reality and perceptions prevailing at the time. The fact, in other words, that Ibn al-Nābulusī loathes the idea of non-Muslims serving in government should not be taken as proof that all of the infelicities, ruses or moral failings he attributes to individual Jews and Christians are necessarily factually false. Indeed, to dismiss him in this manner would be to forfeit the value of *The Sword of Ambition* as a source for social history. For Ibn al-Nābulusī's attitudes, the facts and nonfacts he tells about Jews and Christians, why he recounts these, the perceived need to write such a tract, why and how he couches his arguments in explicitly legal language, why his recriminations seem to be directed almost solely at non-Muslims and not at the rulers or high officials who appoint them, and how the contents of this work compare with what the historical record tells us about the actual reality of Jews and Christians serving in Muslim government—all of this provides invaluable insight into the sociopolitical and, indeed, sociopsychological realities of the time.

Of course, beyond social history per se (or perhaps we should say in addition to social history) this tract provides valuable insight also into how extralegal, pre-rational mindsets and experiences inform the deployment of legal sources and arguments, and thus influence the substance and contours of the law. In the modern West, movements such as legal realism and critical legal studies have tracked this relationship between interpretive presuppositions and the conclusions claimed to be grounded solely in the sources to very useful ends in their analyses of Western law. Ibn al-Nābulusī's text both underscores the potential value of applying such approaches to Islamic legal history and provides a useful specimen on the basis of which to proceed in this regard.

We are all in debt to the translator for providing us with such an informed rendering of *Tajrīd sayf al-himmah li-stikhrāj mā fī dhimmat al-dhimmah*. We must hope that the interpretive strategies that we as readers employ in studying this text are sophisticated and imaginative enough to recognize its full value, enabling us to derive from it the fullest benefit and most meaningful insights.

Sherman ʿAbd al-Ḥakīm Jackson
University of Southern California

Abbreviations

See the Bibliography for full information.

In the endnotes to the translation:

Aḥkām	Ibn Qayyim al-Jawziyyah, *Aḥkām ahl al-dhimmah*
EI2	*The Encyclopaedia of Islam, Second Edition*
EI3	*The Encyclopaedia of Islam, Three*
Madhammah	Ibn al-Naqqāsh, *Kitāb al-Madhammah fī stiʿmāl ahl al-dhimmah*
Radd	Ghāzī ibn Aḥmad ibn al-Wāsiṭī, *Radd ʿalā ahl al-dhimmah wa-man tabiʿahum*
Yatīmah	al-Thaʿālibī, *Yatīmat al-dahr*

In the footnotes to the edition:

الأحكام	Ibn Qayyim al-Jawziyyah, *Aḥkām ahl al-dhimmah*
الذيل	al-Yūnīnī, *Dhayl mirʾāt al-zamān*
فتوح البلدان	al-Balādhurī, *Futūḥ al-buldān*
فتوح مصر	Ibn ʿAbd al-Ḥakam, *The History of the Conquest of Egypt*
المواعظ	al-Maqrīzī, *al-Mawāʿiẓ wa-l-iʿtibār fī dhikr al-khiṭaṭ wa-l-āthār*
الوافي	al-Ṣafadī, *Kitāb al-Wāfī bi-l-wafayāt*
اليتيمة	al-Thaʿālibī, *Yatīmat al-dahr*

Acknowledgments

I am grateful for the generous financial and logistical support this project received from four institutions in particular: the Herbert D. Katz Center for Advanced Judaic Studies at the University of Pennsylvania, the Mellon Faculty Development Grant of Saint Louis University, Saint Louis University, and Princeton University. A visit to manuscripts in 2014 was made possible by practical support from the Centre d'Études Maghrébines à Tunis, the Centre d'Études Maghrébines en Algérie, and their respective directors, Laryssa Chomiak and Robert Parks. In this connection, too, I am supremely grateful to the Kacimi Library of Zawiyat El Hamel, Algeria and, above all, to Muhammad Foued Kacimi al-Hasani al-Sharif for his intellectual generosity, personal sincerity, and warm hospitality. For access to images of manuscripts I thank M. Şükrü Hanioğlu, the Süleymaniye Library, the Bibliothèque Nationale de Tunisie, the British Library, and the Widener Library of Harvard University.

Numerous individuals have given generously of their time and expertise to assist me in this project. They include Mark Cohen, Michael Cook, Matthew Gordon, Hannah-Lena Hagemann, Kamel Hameidia, Andras Hamori, Alaa Kacimi, Amr Osman, Thomas Madden, Johannes Pahlitzsch, Alex Petras, Marina Rustow, Adam Sabra, Samir Khalil Samir, S.J., Uri Shachar, Rebekah Sheldon, Damian Smith, Daniel Stolz, Mark Swanson, Alexander Treiger, Elizabeth Urban, Joseph Witztum, Oded Zinger, and my colleagues at Saint Louis University and at the Fall 2012 seminar of the Katz Center. Particular thanks are due Amr Osman, Torki Fahad Al Saud, Yossef Rapoport, and Christian Sahner for reading and critiquing large parts of the book, and especially to Andras Hamori, who gave exceedingly generous and learned assistance with the poetry. Project Editor Devin Stewart deserves special thanks, too, for providing steady guidance and correcting countless errors while reading multiple drafts of the manuscript. I am also grateful to the other editors of the Library of Arabic Literature for further corrections and for their vision and faith in this project. It is fitting, too, that I acknowledge my debt to the late Claude Cahen for his pioneering work, without which this volume could not have come to be.

I wish finally to extend warmest thanks to my family. My wife Aubrey has lent encouragement and support in countless ways, notably by critiquing a draft of the translation. My parents, too, extended moral support and frequent hospitality. The labor in these pages is dedicated to my grandmother, D.B.G., whose kindness, curiosity, and wit are a legacy to her family. I alone bear responsibility for the book's shortcomings.

Luke Yarbrough

Introduction

> The malfeasance of rural and Coptic officials is incalculably vast and gravely pernicious. I have surveyed this topic elsewhere, however: in a book that I wrote and presented to the prosperous royal treasuries of Sultan al-Malik al-Ṣāliḥ. Entitled *The Book of Unsheathed Ambition to Take Back What is in the Dhimmis' Possession*,[1] it shows how incredible it is that the rustics and the Copts should be trusted or exercise leadership, for the simple reason that meanness and perfidy are ingrained in their natures.
>
> —ʿUthmān ibn Ibrāhīm al-Nābulusī, *A Few Luminous Rules for Egypt's Administrative Offices*[2]

Thus did our author, ʿUthmān ibn Ibrāhīm al-Nābulusī, describe *The Sword of Ambition* some time after he composed it, at a low point in his life, around the year 640/1242. In the book's conclusion (§4.4.2), he unburdened himself to the reader—whom he envisioned as no less a personage than the Ayyubid sultan himself—of some piteous personal information. He and his fifty-two children and grandchildren were dependent on the dwindling rent from a dilapidated property that his father had left them.[3] Social conventions in Cairo obliged them to put on a cheerful face for friends and neighbors, but within their own walls the mood was grim.[4] They were down to just two Greek slaves—low-grade slaves at that—and three bedraggled riding animals. Yet Ibn al-Nābulusī eagerly informed the sultan that his prospects had not always looked so bleak. At one time, when he had been overseer of the tax offices in all the land of Egypt, his household had enjoyed the services of ten slaves and sixteen horses and mules. He had spent lavishly on them as well as on clothing, as befitted a high official. In order to sustain this lifestyle without compromising his professional integrity, he had been obliged to sell family property in Syria for the hefty sum of five thousand gold coins. After such sacrifices, he bitterly concluded, the reason for his current poverty was that he had remained honest when handling money.

Ibn al-Nābulusī's account of his own career contrasted sharply with the patterns that he observed in the careers of the Coptic Christian (and convert) officials employed by the Ayyubid state. Whereas he had been powerful and ended up poor, it seemed to him that even the pettiest Coptic bureaucrat rapidly amassed wealth to spare. The explanation for the contrast was clear to him: the Coptic officials were corrupt. No less clear was the remedy: the Copts should be dismissed from their positions and stripped of their ill-gotten wealth. At the same time, he should be granted an official position and a stipend to match. It was to these ends that Ibn al-Nābulusī directed his literary energies, interweaving his own exhortation with a curious assortment of excerpts from earlier sources to compose the present book, to which he gave the rhyming title *Tajrīd sayf al-himmah li-stikhrāj mā fī dhimmat al-dhimmah* – *The Sword of Ambition*, or, more literally, *Unsheathing Ambition's Sword to Extract What the Dhimmis Hoard*.

The Author

Ibn al-Nābulusī's full name, according to one of his students, a certain al-Dimyāṭī, was ʿAlāʾ al-Dīn Abū ʿAmr ʿUthmān ibn Ibrāhīm ibn Khālid ibn Muḥammad ibn al-Salm[5] al-Qurashī, al-Nābulusī (of Nablus) by extraction (*al-maḥtid*), al-Miṣrī (of Cairo) in birth, life, and death. The same source reports that he was born on the nineteenth of Dhū l-Ḥijjah 588 [December 26, 1192]—thus he wrote *The Sword of Ambition* at the age of about fifty.[6] His connection to the city of Nablus in Palestine was through his father's family. Although we cannot be certain when they moved to Egypt, it seems likely to have been during his father ʿAlam al-Dīn Ibrāhīm's life, inasmuch as Ibn al-Nābulusī's name meant "son of the man from Nablus,"[7] and since he still maintained control of property in Syria. We know little about his father, who is described in the sources as a judge (*qāḍī*), an honorific title that should not necessarily be taken literally; we can be certain only that he was a professional witness or notary (*ʿadl*). Ibn al-Nābulusī's maternal grandfather, the Ḥanbalī jurist and preacher Zayn al-Dīn ʿAlī ibn Ibrāhīm ibn Najā al-Anṣārī (508/1114–1115 to 599/1203), known as Ibn Nujayyah, is better known.[8] He, too, had come to Egypt from Syria and, like his grandson Ibn al-Nābulusī, made it his business to exhort Egypt's military rulers to godliness.[9] Ibn Nujayyah served as an ambassador to Baghdad on behalf of the Zangid ruler Nūr al-Dīn in 564/1168–69. In *The Sword of Ambition* (§2.14.3), we find him remonstrating with the Fatimid vizier Ṭalāʾiʿ ibn Ruzzīk about a Christian official called Ibn Dukhān, who in addition to being corrupt and seditious also happened to be obstructing the payment of Ibn Nujayyah's government stipend. From other sources, we learn that Ibn Nujayyah played a leading role in sniffing out the conspiracy to restore the Fatimid dynasty in which the famous poet ʿUmārah ibn Ḥamzah was involved (one of ʿUmārah's many poems against Ibn Dukhān features in *The Sword of Ambition*, §2.14.4). After pretending to go along with the plot, Ibn Nujayyah reported it to Saladin, with whom he enjoyed considerable influence, in exchange for the property of one of the conspirators. ʿUmārah and the others were executed.[10]

Ibn al-Nābulusī had, then, a family heritage that was noteworthy for its ties to both Islamic scholarship and state power. According to his own testimony in *The Sword of Ambition* (§3.2.34), he spent his youth pursuing a law-college (*madrasah*) curriculum that must have focused on Islamic law, quite possibly in the very Nābulusiyyah Madrasah that his father had established.[11] His student, al-Dimyāṭī, notes that he followed the Shāfiʿī legal rite (*madhhab*). We also know that he heard and later narrated Prophetic Hadith; al-Dimyāṭī reproduces a hadith that he transmitted.[12] The same passage of *The Sword of Ambition* that alludes to his law-college education strongly implies that he and his contemporaries did not view it as a springboard to state service, but on the contrary as quite distinct from the formation expected of a secretary (*kātib*), though it was of course standard for a judge (*qāḍī*), mosque preacher (*khaṭīb*), or other holder of an overtly religious office.[13] Nevertheless, early in the reign of the Ayyubid sultan al-Malik al-Kāmil (r. 615–35/1218–38), through the intercession of a patron and thanks to his own talents and his show of reluctance to accept employment, Ibn al-Nābulusī became a state official. One office that he mentions explicitly from this period of his life is the directorship of the Royal Guesthouse (*dār al-ḍiyāfah*).[14] Sultan al-Kāmil promoted him to a series of progressively more important posts. Eventually, according to his own report as well as that of al-Maqrīzī,[15] he became overseer or auditor (*nāẓir*) of the tax administration in virtually all of Egypt, a position that he had urged his patron to create. In about 634/1237, however, he fell out of favor with al-Kāmil. This event, as he tells it, was due to the machinations of an Ayyubid emir who coveted a house that he owned beside the Nile in Giza.[16] The house, called Dār al-Malik (or al-Mulk), was part of the property that had been granted to his maternal grandfather, Ibn Nujayyah, by Saladin.

It is to the subsequent nadir in Ibn al-Nābulusī's career that we owe *The Sword of Ambition*. Another of his works, *Lumaʿ al-qawānīn al-muḍiyyah fī dawāwīn al-diyār al-miṣriyyah* (*A Few Luminous Rules for Egypt's Administrative Offices*, cited at the beginning of this Introduction), was drafted some time afterward and offers additional biographical clues to the context of *The Sword of Ambition*.

For instance, it is evident from information in the *Luminous Rules* that Coptic Christians or converts played prominent roles in the real-estate dispute in which Ibn al-Nābulusī lost his high post in the administration, not to mention his riverfront estate. Our author tells the story in his typical wounded way. As he engaged in reluctant negotiations with the powerful emir Nūr al-Dīn over the price of the estate, which the latter had espied and sworn to possess, a powerful converted Copt, al-As'ad al-Fā'izī, sided vocally with Nūr al-Dīn.[17] Later, after Ibn al-Nābulusī and then Nūr al-Dīn himself had lost control of the property, the same al-As'ad purchased it from its shadow owner for a song and transferred it to the charitable endowments of the deceased sultan al-Kāmil.[18] Ibn al-Nābulusī later implored the current sultan, al-Malik al-Ṣāliḥ (r. 637–47/1240–49), to return the estate to him, describing the hardships that its loss had inflicted upon his family. Having lost their spot on the water, they suffered the indignity of day-tripping: "Now the children and I have no vantage point from which to view the river. When they want to behold the Nile, that great work of God, they have to set up a tent outside the city. Then at the end of the day they have to leave."[19]

Ibn al-Nābulusī thus had enemies among the converted Copts in the administration; it is not unreasonable to suppose that this factored in his decision to write *The Sword of Ambition*, a book against Coptic officials that contains strident, thinly veiled personal polemic against those of them who had converted outwardly to Islam (§§2.15.1–3, 4.2.2). The tone of the *Luminous Rules*, too, reflects Ibn al-Nābulusī's zeal to denounce fellow administrators whom he judged to be incompetent, corrupt, impious, or dull. This might justly be called the central theme of the book, to the degree that in its introduction the author was at pains to distinguish between sincere advice (*naṣīḥah*) and self-serving slander of rivals (*si'āyah*). His own book, naturally, was *naṣīḥah*, but he nevertheless confessed that he hesitated to write it, so much did he worry that he might be suspected of harboring ulterior personal motives (*aghrāḍ*) against his colleagues. Perhaps this hesitation arose from his intention to level a string of savage accusations at his fellow officials, several of whom he named in the work.[20] As in *The Sword of Ambition* and indeed in his work on the Fayyūm (see below), he evinced marked antipathy not only to Copts but also to rural Muslims, undereducated Muslims, and even, in one passage of our work (§§4.2.32–36) ignorant Muslim judges. We may thus characterize our author as well-bred, educated, and professionally accomplished, yet at this point in his life also embittered and envious.

It is evident from Ibn al-Nābulusī's third and final surviving work that he found his way for a time into the graces of al-Malik al-Ṣāliḥ, the last independent Ayyubid sultan in Egypt. The *Luminous Rules* and/or *The Sword of Ambition*, which were directed to al-Ṣāliḥ, may thus indirectly have had their desired effect. This third work, *Iẓhār ṣanʿat al-Ḥayy al-Qayyūm fī tartīb bilād al-Fayyūm* (*A Presentation of the Living, Eternal God's Work in Regulating the Fayyūm*), has recently been described as "the most detailed tax survey to have survived from any region of the medieval Islamic world, a Domesday Book for the medieval Egyptian countryside."[21] It is a detailed report on conditions in the fertile Fayyūm oasis of Egypt—whither Ibn al-Nābulusī was dispatched as an inspector in 642/1245—insofar as these are relevant to tax administration, touching for instance upon demography, land tenure, and sources of revenue. This work constitutes the last indication we have of the author's life until he died, in relative obscurity, at Cairo on 25 Jumādā I 660 [April 17, 1262], a Monday evening. He was buried at the foot of the Muqaṭṭam heights to the east of the city.

Ibn al-Nābulusī composed at least three other works, none of which seems to have survived. One is known only from an allusion in *The Sword of Ambition* (§1.1.4), and had a theme similar to that of the present work. Its title—*Taṣrīḥ al-Qurʾān bi-l-naṣr ʿalā man istaʿāna bi-kuffār al-ʿaṣr* (*The Qurʾan's Assurance of Victory over Those Who Seek Aid from the Infidels of This Age*)—indicates that it used scriptural exegesis to demonstrate that allying or cooperating with non-Muslims is forbidden and will lead to the downfall of the Muslim who indulges in it. The work might possibly have been a polemic against the Ayyubid rivals of al-Malik al-Ṣāliḥ Najm al-Dīn, namely al-Ṣāliḥ ʿImād al-Dīn and al-Ṣāliḥ Ismāʿīl, who at various times allied with the Franks against their kinsman.[22] Another of his works, mentioned in the book on the Fayyūm, was probably a panegyric to the Ayyubid sultan; its title is *Ḥusn al-sulūk fī faḍl malik Miṣr ʿalā sāʾir al-mulūk* (*A Seemly Demonstration of the Superiority of Egypt's King over All Others*).[23] Ibn al-Nābulusī showed elsewhere that he was prepared to praise the sultan in effusive (not to say sycophantic) terms.[24] The final composition attributed to Ibn al-Nābulusī—*Ḥusn al-sarīrah fī ttikhādh al-ḥiṣn bi-l-Jazīrah* (*The Excellent Idea of Establishing the Island Fortress*)—appears to have praised al-Malik al-Ṣāliḥ's decision to build a citadel on the Nile island of al-Rawḍah to serve as a base for his large corps of *mamlūk* ("owned") Turkic military slaves.[25] It was they, of course, who would soon supplant the Ayyubids as rulers of Egypt. For more than a century the Mamluk rulers would be known as the *baḥrī* or "river" dynasty because of their ties to this fortress.

Ibn al-Nābulusī earned very minor repute as a poet. The account by his student al-Dimyāṭī preserves five lines of his verse. It is fitting that they should express the author's preoccupation with hierarchy, railing eloquently against the elevation of low-class people (*al-asāfil*) at the expense of the high-born (*al-aʿālī*).[26]

The Work

In *The Sword of Ambition*, Ibn al-Nābulusī explains the circumstances and motives of the work's composition, announcing in its introductory section that he has been inspired by a recent edict that imposed traditional discriminatory restrictions on non-Muslims, notably the distinctive clothing they were required to wear (the *ghiyār*; see §0.2).[27] He also expresses confidence that this measure is only a first step in the right direction, and hope that the present book will encourage the sultan to finish the job, as it were, by dismissing and cashiering his Coptic officials. In the conclusion, Ibn al-Nābulusī gives three reasons for having composed the work. The third and most important of these is his straitened financial condition, which contrasts to the opulence his Coptic colleagues allegedly enjoyed. The other two reasons he provides are his ardent zeal for the money of the Muslim community and his love for the sultan.

The Sword of Ambition resists precise dating. Other works by Ibn al-Nābulusī may have been composed and redacted in stages, so that no single date can be assigned to them.[28] While there are no definite indications that this was the case for the work at hand, neither is it possible to accept the estimate of ca. 638/1240 given by Claude Cahen, on the basis of the dating of the edict concerning non-Muslim clothing.[29] That edict should probably instead be dated to 640/1242 (see §0.2 of the Translation). A handful of passages found in some manuscripts, however, refer to events that occurred long after this date, but within the lifetime of the author (e.g., §4.2.7, which mentions the year 660/1261–62). Ibn al-Nābulusī might conceivably have produced multiple recensions of the work, or early copyists might have added to it.

The perspicuous "table of contents" (§§0.3–6) presents the work's rather stiff structure, relieving us of the need to detail its contents and organization here. Taken together, its four chapters, each of which comprises either three or fifteen sections, give the impression that the author drew on all available arguments to make the point that Coptic Christians (and converts), as well as Jewish, rural, and otherwise disreputable individuals, were unfit for state service and should therefore be dismissed. Some (and only some) of the sources used to back up these arguments were: Qur'anic exegesis; hadith of the Prophet; historical accounts of Muslim rulers' dealings with non-Muslim officials; demonstration of the perfidy and sedition inherent in Copts and Jews; poetry mocking incompetent officials; jokes about bumbling and illiterate Copts and other despicable persons; and both poetry and prose demonstrating the excellence of *real* secretaries (*kuttāb*), whom the author contrasted to the loathsome pretenders who were laying claim to that sublime title. The work's eclectic angles of attack must be read in their full variety to be appreciated.[30] The character of its intended audience, namely the Sultan al-Malik al-Ṣāliḥ himself, may have shaped the author's decisions about its content. The sources depict al-Malik al-Ṣāliḥ as proud, acquisitive, sober, taciturn, and aloof, an inspirer of reverence and dread. Although he did not impress his contemporaries as particularly bookish, he was known as a patron of scholars.[31] These aspects of the sultan's character might have simultaneously emboldened Ibn al-Nābulusī to beg for employment and led him to keep the sections of his work brief and vivid in order to hold the attention of his royal audience. There is some evidence that *The Sword of Ambition* was intended more to entertain than to bear learned scrutiny. For example, much of the poetry in the third chapter seems to have been borrowed without acknowledgment from the works of al-Thaʿālibī (d. 429/1038), but carelessly attributed to the wrong poets in the course of the borrowing process. Similarly, a passage concerning Ibn Ṭūlūn's rule in Egypt (§2.4.1) ascribes certain past misdeeds of the government to the Copts, where in other sources, the same misdeeds are ascribed to Muslim administrators. A learned reader would have noted such discrepancies, which the sultan, by contrast, could have been expected to overlook. Ibn al-Nābulusī thus probably did not mean *The Sword of Ambition* to be a resource for serious scholars. He seems rather to have intended to entertain an audience that was unlikely to have had deep prior familiarity with his material.

What sort of book is this? Its multifarious contents and disparate registers make it a poor fit for any one genre. It would be unsatisfying to classify it as exegesis (*tafsīr*), history (*tārīkh*), law (*fiqh*), polemic (*jadal*), or, save in the broadest sense, belles lettres (*adab*), though it contains elements of all these. I would suggest, however, that it was not *sui generis*. Rather, it was intended to be read (or listened to) as a representative of the established Arabic genre of advice literature (*naṣīḥah*).[32] While its form is not typical of "mirrors for princes," *The Sword of Ambition* qualifies as *naṣīḥah* in that it, like standard examples of that genre, was directed to a ruler in the hope of convincing him to bring his wayward conduct into line with certain principles. Unlike many *naṣīḥah* works, *The Sword of Ambition* does not present a comprehensive ethical vision for the ruler's conduct. Instead it is concerned with a specific issue, namely the ongoing employment of Copts and other undesirables. In this it stands as an early example of a small cluster of anti-Copt treatises that were composed in Egypt between the late twelfth and mid-fourteenth centuries. It drew on the same sources as some other works in the cluster did, and served as a source for others.[33] *The Sword of Ambition* is also closely comparable to Ibn al-Nābulusī's own *Luminous Rules*, which was written, as we have seen, around the same time, and which declares itself openly to be a work of *naṣīḥah*. Both works, no matter how far they digress, circle relentlessly back to the problem of socially marginal and unqualified men who receive stipends and administrative posts, while the deserving few (notably the author himself) are left in the cold.

Only a portion of *The Sword of Ambition* represents what a modern reader would call Ibn al-Nābulusī's original work. The author, like most of his compeers in the Arabic literary heritage, makes liberal use of the sources available to him. Only in a few instances, however, does he name his sources. From a literary perspective, a work like this one would have been judged not for its originality or meticulousness, but for its artful arrangement of engaging selections of poetry and prose, interspersed with apposite remarks and digressions by the author himself. Parts of the work can be traced (or, rarely, are openly credited) to such earlier works as *The Life of ʿUmar ibn ʿAbd al-ʿAzīz* (*Sīrat ʿUmar ibn ʿAbd al-ʿAzīz*) attributed to ʿAbdallāh ibn ʿAbd al-Ḥakam (d. 214/829); *The Conquest of Egypt* (*Futūḥ Miṣr*) by the latter's son ʿAbd al-Raḥmān Ibn ʿAbd al-Ḥakam (d. 257/871); *The Book of Songs* (*Kitāb al-aghānī*) of Abū l-Faraj al-Iṣbahānī (d. 356/967); unnamed writings of the well-known Fatimid official al-Muwaffaq ibn al-Khallāl (d. 566/1171); *The Eternally Incomparable* (*Yatīmat al-dahr*) and *Inimitability and Pithiness* (*al-Iʿjāz wa-l-ījāz*) of al-Thaʿālibī; and (for most of the historical accounts in the first and some in the second chapter) an as-yet-unidentified work against non-Muslim officials composed around the time of Saladin's accession in Egypt (ca. 567/1171). This last source also influenced many, though not all, of the polemical works composed against Christian and Jewish officials in later medieval Egypt.[34]

The Sword of Ambition has greater value as an historical source for the late Ayyubid period and for inter-communal relations over the *longue durée* than as a work of literature *per se*. As a source, it is an intriguing inventory of the ideational resources available to Muslim polemicists in Egypt in the seventh/thirteenth century, and a clue to the potential methods by which, and conditions under which, these were deployed. For example, the stories about inept and illiterate Copts and others (§4.2.1 and following) might serve as a source for the social history of popular stereotypes and of humor in medieval Egypt. The work also reflects changes in the composition and self-conception of the Egyptian state's administrative corps, given its numerous and vivid incidental references to conditions among both religious specialists (*ʿulamāʾ*) and secretaries (*kuttāb*), particularly as these groups related to state power. It is, for instance, instructive to observe the author as a liminal figure, trained as a scholar but employed as a state secretary in an age when membership in these groups increasingly overlapped (more on this below). In his capacity as a scholar-bureaucrat, Ibn al-Nābulusī uses the issue of Coptic officials to mount subtle critiques of state power, as where (§2.4.1) he attributes the standing state monopoly on the mineral natron to a Coptic plot that dated from Abbasid times, implying that this un-Islamic monopoly should be rescinded. Finally, the work is of value in that it preserves numerous earlier passages, some of which have been lost or survive only in much later sources. For example, Ibn al-Nābulusī includes long and entertaining anecdotes in §§2.9.1–3 that preserve parts of the work of al-Muwaffaq ibn al-Khallāl, otherwise found only later and in different forms in the works of the official Ghāzī ibn Aḥmad ibn al-Wāsiṭī (d. 712/1312) and the historian al-Maqrīzī (d. 845/1442).

In *The Sword of Ambition*'s anthologizing portions, the author's choices were guided by subject matter rather than literary artistry; even in sections (notably Chapter Three) that present outstanding examples of poetry and prose produced by secretaries, these appear invariably in the vein of *bons mots*. This is not surprising in view of Ibn al-Nābulusī's professional background. Although he wrote in praise of refined literature (*adab*, §3.2.1), Ibn al-Nābulusī was in fact a bureaucrat and religious scholar of ordinary rank who does not seem to have been much noted as a *littérateur*. Ibn al-Nābulusī's lifelong involvement in the competitive worlds of scholarship and court life, along with his weighty family responsibilities, may have forced him to subordinate his literary aspirations to the more quotidian tastes of the audience he needed to sway.

It will be worthwhile briefly to consider *The Sword of Ambition* alongside other premodern literary productions of a similar stripe. To the classicist, for example, it may recall the polemics of the Neo-Platonist philosopher and Christian bishop Synesius of Cyrene (d. ca. AD 414) against politically influential "barbarians," primarily Goths, in *De Regno* and *De Providentia*. Synesius's opposition to powerful Gothic generals and courtiers did not arise from Roman chauvinism alone; it had an additional, ideational aspect. "Let all be excluded from magistracies," Synesius wrote in *De Regno*, "and kept away from the privileges of the council who are ashamed of all that has been sacred to the Romans from olden times, and has been so esteemed. Of a truth both Themis, herself sacred to the Senate, and the god of our battle-line must I think, cover their faces when the man with leather jerkin marches in command of those that wear the general's cloak, and whenever such a one divests himself of the sheepskin in which he was clad to assume the toga."[35] Ibn al-Nābulusī's own invective urges the exclusion of officials who spurned symbols revered by Muslims (the Pilgrimage rites, for example, in §2.15.2) and mocks pretenders who dared don the cowl or *ṭaylasān*, the garment that marked Muslim secretaries and scholars (e.g., §4.2.9).

Well after Ibn al-Nābulusī's lifetime, we find another point of comparison in the work of the Ottoman official and historian Muṣṭafā ʿĀlī (d. 1008/1600), who in his book of advice, *Nuṣḥatü s-selāṭīn*, plainly intended to secure the dismissal of his rivals by invoking their ethnicity and alleged unsuitability for employment. His larger corpus of writings, like Ibn al-Nābulusī's, evinces a petulant preoccupation with the sagging standards of state officialdom. Muṣṭafā ʿĀlī's modern biographer, Cornell Fleischer, has described him as "able, well-educated and far more outspoken than most of his peers," but also "an embittered bureaucrat . . . a disappointed man who felt that his abilities had gone unrewarded."[36] *Mutatis mutandis*, the characterization holds for Ibn al-Nābulusī, who, though a lesser intellect than Muṣṭafā ʿĀlī, channeled his disappointment into similar literary productions.

Notwithstanding its similarity to works of other times and places and its liberal use of earlier sources, *The Sword of Ambition* is very much the product of a particular moment in the history of Egypt, and indeed of Islamic societies more broadly. It should be noted that Ibn al-Nābulusī's preoccupation with non-Muslim state officials was widely shared in certain Muslim circles in thirteenth- and fourteenth-century Egypt, and that it was a recurrent issue in Islamic history. It has often been pointed out that Muslim rulers sometimes preferred to hire non-Muslims for certain positions; those employees' relative weakness and lack of connections to powerful Muslim factions tended—in the eyes of some Muslim employers, at least—to make them more trustworthy. This phenomenon can be traced from the Syrian Umayyad court, where a Christian progenitor of John of Damascus oversaw the empire's finances, to Islamic Spain, where Jewish officials, such as the tenth-century figure Hasdai ibn Shaprut, occasionally served as the Muslim ruler's right-hand men, to the very eve of modernity. When Napoleon invaded Egypt, he found the financial administration in the hands of a Copt, Jirjis al-Jawharī, whom the French preserved in office.[37] Muslim religious elites regularly objected to the empowerment of non-Muslims. Their complaints form a continuous discourse that runs throughout Islamic history, and in which *The Sword of Ambition* participates.[38] The fact that Muslim rulers regularly perceived non-Muslims as especially trustworthy was the hidden counterargument that Ibn al-Nābulusī, like other figures who contributed to the discourse, sought to discredit.

We may briefly consider two major ways, however, in which the work reflects more particularly the social, religious, and political developments of its day. Both relate to what may be called the "Sunni shift," a series of momentous changes in the relation of emergent Sunni Islam to state power in the eleventh through thirteenth centuries.[39] The Sunni shift saw the accession of a number of powerful dynasties, from Afghanistan to North Africa, that relied for their legitimacy upon the established Sunni religious elites who already functioned as foci for popular support in their capacity as scholars, preachers, judges, and local notables. The religious elites who supported these dynasties were rewarded with unprecedented patronage, notably via such novel institutions as the *madrasah* for legal scholars and *khānqāh* for Sufis, both of which were supported by the expanded use of *waqf* (charitable endowment) as a means for transmitting wealth and social power. The rapprochement between military rulers and Sunni religious elites tended to benefit both parties, faced as they were with the religio-political challenges of Shiʿite-leaning states with heritages dating to the tenth century, of the European Crusading movement that challenged Muslim ascendancy in Egypt and greater Syria from the early twelfth century until the late thirteenth and even beyond, and finally of the Mongol storm that broke across the region in the mid-thirteenth century.

In adducing the Crusades, we in fact identify the first major way in which *The Sword of Ambition* most pervasively reflects its historical moment. The work may be read, with considerable justification, as representative of the Muslim "counter-crusade" by which militant sentiment against the European Crusaders contributed to significant change within Islamic societies, notably by generating pressure upon marginal elements to conform to an ideal of comprehensive Muslim ascendancy as articulated and advocated by certain Sunni religious elites.[40] In such a climate, native Christians and Jews, especially when seen to exercise undue power, could more easily find themselves in conflict with Muslims who saw non-Muslim power as an implicit challenge to their vision of the properly ordered Islamic society. In practical terms, non-Muslims, especially Christians, could come under suspicion as a fifth column for Crusader designs on Muslim territory. This fear is clearly visible in *The Sword of Ambition*, as both an historical "fact" (as in §2.14.4, the case of the disloyal Christian Ibn Dukhān) and a present danger. Sultan al-Malik al-Kāmil is made to remark in a timeless tone (§3.2.37) that when Copts become too wealthy, their incorrigible tendency to conspire with foreign enemies poses a grave threat to the security of the Egyptian state.

Although it is plain that the idea of "counter-crusade" resonates strongly with particular passages in *The Sword of Ambition*, the currency of counter-crusade ideology in the mid-thirteenth century does not explain why Ibn al-Nābulusī should have found it expedient to invoke that ideology, in a limited way, in his screed against Coptic officials, or indeed why he set out to write the screed at all. The more finely grained problem of authorial motivation and strategy highlights the second major way in which *The Sword of Ambition* most pervasively reflects its historical moment, namely as a symptom of a set of social and political developments that are relatively detached from the counter-crusade and more firmly internal to the Islamic sphere. In the period following the Sunni shift in Egypt, for reasons that cannot be developed here, the state both increased its control over economic activity in Egypt and expanded its patronage of Sunni urban religious elites (*ʿulamāʾ*), generating heightened competition for state patronage among those elites and between them and other competitors, such as Christians, Jews, and (Ibn al-Nābulusī would remind us) Muslim rural elites.[41] As S.D. Goitein argues, "from the thirteenth century on, . . . when the economy became increasingly monopolized by the state, the clamoring of Muslim candidates for government posts became ever stronger, and the minority groups had to give way."[42] The clamoring arose as the *madrasah* was increasingly utilized by the Ayyubids to make the military-patronage state the primary source of economic support for Sunni religious elites, cementing ties between them and the Sunni rulers.[43] Beginning in the late twelfth century, it became increasingly common for state officials to be drawn from the ranks of *madrasah*-trained religious elites. In earlier centuries, by contrast, administrative personnel had traditionally represented a more eclectic and less uniformly orthodox cross section of the population. The secretaries (*kuttāb*) of the Abbasid period were famed not only for their literary virtuosity, much celebrated in *The Sword of Ambition*, but also for their moral laxness and their frequent dissent from law- and tradition-centered Islam of the kind that would become dominant in the Ayyubid and Mamluk periods. After the disintegration of the Abbasid empire in the ninth and tenth centuries, the Fatimids and their deputies and allies who ruled Egypt and much of Syria employed a motley assortment of non-Muslims, converts, foreign Muslims, Shiʿites (both Ismaʿili and Twelver), military men (who might also be of foreign origin and/or converts), and local Sunnis. Under the Ayyubids, however, as under their ideological progenitors, the Seljuq Turks, it was the Sunni scholars who increasingly received the bulk of the state's patronage, in the form of official employment and stipends for scholars and students. Ibn al-Nābulusī was fully immersed in these currents. *Madrasah*-educated, with no specific training for government service (see §§3.2.34–35), he nonetheless came to depend on the state for his income. Competition from his peers, whom he portrayed as undeserving of employment because of their religious affiliation, level of education, or regional and class origin, provoked him to marshal his *madrasah*-honed linguistic and literary skills in support of his own cause. Michael Chamberlain has described the culture of *fitnah*—disapproved but ubiquitous conflict for patronage and power—that prevailed among the urban learned classes in Ayyubid and Mamluk domains of the thirteenth and fourteenth centuries. Ibn al-Nābulusī's shrill critique of his competitors, both in *The Sword of Ambition* and in the *Luminous Rules*, is a typical product of this competitive culture.

The Sword of Ambition has seen sporadic use by modern scholars since its rediscovery and partial transcription by Claude Cahen in 1960 (on Cahen's published transcriptions, see "The Arabic Text" below).[44] These scattered references to the work may be placed into two broad categories. First, the simple fact of the work's composition is cited as a symptom of anti-dhimmi sentiment in thirteenth-century Egypt, or as another iteration of the regular calls for enforcement of the theoretical *dhimmah* regulations that rigorists believed should govern the lives of non-Muslims under Islamic rule (on the term *dhimmah*, see

"Pact of Security" in the Glossary).[45] While it is perfectly defensible to use the work in this way, there is at the same time a certain risk in extrapolating from a few works of this nature to larger cultural trends without also highlighting the personal circumstances and motivations of the authors. Similarly, although Ibn al-Nābulusī does make passing reference to legal aspects of the *dhimmah* arrangement in *The Sword of Ambition*, it is not primarily a legal work and makes scarcely any mention of the "conditions" (*shurūṭ*) that many jurists thought should lie at the heart of that arrangement. Indeed, putative rules concerning the employment of non-Muslims as state officials are not, strictly speaking, part of the *dhimmah*; the obvious awkwardness of requiring non-Muslims to refuse offers of employment from Muslim leaders generally prevented Muslim elites from proposing such a requirement. It is telling that in the best-known work in the legal discourse on the *dhimmah*, *Aḥkām ahl al-dhimmah* by Ibn Qayyim al-Jawziyyah (d. 751/1350), the chapter against non-Muslim officials features only the same string of Qur'ānic admonitions and cautionary anecdotes that we find in *The Sword of Ambition*, probably culled from the same (unidentified) source.[46] The goal of these selections was to dissuade powerful Muslims from employing non-Muslims, not to dilate upon a law that non-Muslims themselves were meant to observe.

Second, modern scholars have used *The Sword of Ambition* in passing references that are of particular relevance to their own research. Thus, for example, Josef van Ess has used the work as evidence for chiliastic expectations surrounding the Fatimid caliph al-Ḥākim; Joseph Sadan has studied passages relevant to Jews; Brian Catlos has examined the extended anecdote involving the author's grandfather, Ibn Nujayyah, and the Christian Ibn Dukhān; and Hassanein Rabie has used the work for evidence concerning the *iqṭāʿ*.[47] The present publication of a full edition and translation will, it is hoped, make it easier for more scholars to use the work in similar ways.

The publication of *The Sword of Ambition* at the present moment poses certain challenges, however. There is, for instance, the current predicament of non-Muslim populations in many countries in the Middle East, Egypt among them.[48] Inasmuch as *The Sword of Ambition* contains hostile denunciations of Christians and Jews, might it not lend support to those today who advocate the harsh subordination of non-Muslims? Conversely, virulent hostility toward Islam and Muslims is alive and well in Europe and North America. A work like this one could help to confirm the dark aspersions of intolerance that are regularly hurled at "Islam." Indeed, I do not believe that either fear can be dispelled. *The Sword of Ambition* may really provide material for polemicists. It is in the nature of historical data to be available for a wide variety of narrative agendas.

However, there are also many reasons that favor bringing the work to light. These may even help to redeem its less appealing aspects. Most obviously, several historical works closely comparable to *The Sword of Ambition* in tone and subject matter are already available on bookstands in Arabic-speaking countries and online. At least one of these, which in fact drew on the present work, was translated into English long ago.[49] Equally evident is the precept of modern scientific historiography according to which all evidence must be considered, no matter how marginal or unsavory it might appear. The precept is particularly important in the case of premodern history, where scarcity imbues all written sources with significance, particularly those that, like *The Sword of Ambition*, vividly represent aspects of contemporary life and abound with pungent anecdotes. Polemical literature has enriched our knowledge of other historical figures and their societies. How much the poorer would the study of early Christianity be if the polemics of Tertullian, Celsus, and Chrysostom were excised from it, much as these might still embolden Christian supremacists, militantly intolerant atheists, and anti-Semites?[50] The history of medieval Islam deserves no less. Indeed, in the light of contemporary trends it may deserve more. *The Sword of Ambition* affords us an unusual opportunity to situate virulent religious polemic in the particular historical context that generated it, allowing us to see such antagonism as circumstantially conditioned. The author's patent desperation and autobiographical candor make it clear that the project was not suggested to him by sacred texts or abstract reflection alone, but instead was inspired by historically specific, self-interested motives, however sincerely he meant it. For obvious reasons, polemicists tend not to reveal such contingent and personal aspects of their writings. It may be hoped that the present work's manifest contingency will dull its edge among Islam's militant supporters and its militant opponents alike. Both may in fact glimpse in it their own reflections.

A Note on the Text

The Arabic Text

The edited text below represents the *editio princeps* of the work as a whole. This is not, however, the first time that significant portions of it have appeared in print. More than half a century ago, the French Arabist Claude Cahen published a transcription of most of the second chapter from a microfilm of one manuscript, as well as short excerpts from the third and fourth chapters in a separate publication (the only previous efforts toward an edition of the work that have been undertaken).[51] The transcribed text Cahen published, however, in addition to drawing on only one of the four manuscripts that are now known to exist, was marred by numerous printing errors, was only occasionally corrected for textual problems, and in general was intended to offer a kind of first glimpse rather than a reliable edition. Its utility has thus remained limited, while the publication of a part of it led many historians to believe that the work had been published in full. A passing remark made by Cahen indicates that Moshe Perlmann (d. 2001) intended a complete edition, but it does not appear that Perlmann ever carried this project to completion.[52]

The present edition is based upon the four manuscript witnesses (existing handwritten copies of the book) known to the editor.[53] In the footnotes to the edition, each witness is designated by an Arabic letter. The description that follows employs those letters' Roman equivalents.

Witness ب (= B) is the last of several works contained in British Library Add. 23,293, all of which are in the same *naskhī* hand. This codex has suffered water damage and the lower portions of many folios are partially illegible. Each folio bears approximately 17 lines per side at an average of 13 words per line. *The Sword of Ambition* occupies folios 175 r.–223 v. The other works are on topics in Sufism (chiefly sayings of Abū l-Ḥasan al-Shādhilī) and history (the *Mukhtaṣar* of Abū l-Fidā). In B, *The Sword of Ambition* lacks its introduction and the first five sections of its first chapter, apparently because a number of folios were removed from the manuscript prior to its (modern) foliation. On an earlier folio the completion of a different work is dated 18 Rabīʿ I 749 [June 16, 1348]. It would be surprising if *The Sword of Ambition* had not been copied at about the same time.

Witness ت (= T) is the lone work found in Tūnis Jāmiʿ al-Zaytūnah, IV 74, 1922, the more recent shelfmark of which is Dār al-Kutub al-Waṭaniyyah/Bibliothèque Nationale de Tunisie 08802. This complete, undated copy in a single *naskhī* hand takes up 93 folios, averaging 13 lines of text per side, about 10 words per line. On paleographical grounds it appears to be a relatively early copy, certainly pre–tenth/sixteenth century, but no earlier than the eighth/fourteenth, since in §3.2.37 the copyist (who is not named) erroneously supplies the century of an event in the author's life as "seven hundred" rather than the correct "six hundred." This error could scarcely have been committed by a copyist of the seventh/thirteenth century; he would have had to mistakenly write the date of a future century (imagine absentmindedly writing "2116" for "2016"). Several faint and partly effaced ownership statements are found on the first folio. Marginal notes in the same hand as one of these statements appear on the early folios of the text and sporadically thereafter; these notes are in the vein of earnest summary. Despite some insect damage, the manuscript is legible in its entirety. A later trimming of the pages has, however, clipped some of the marginal notes. Chapter, section, and subsection headings are in red ink.

Witness ج (= J) is Maktabat Zāwiyat al-Hāmil, Algeria, 1/14 ن. It is the second of two works in the manuscript; the first is the *Natījat al-ijtihād fī l-muhādanah wa-l-jihād*, an account of a trip to Spain by a twelfth/eighteenth century Moroccan ambassador named Aḥmad ibn al-Mahdī al-Ghazzāl al-Fāsī. *The Sword of Ambition* occupies 21 folios, which average approximately 28 lines per side at 14 words per line. The manuscript was copied in a mediocre *maghribī* hand by a certain Muḥammad ibn al-Ṭayyib. It is dated 2 Rajab 1290 [August 26, 1873]. In this manuscript, the work bears a different *incipit*/*taḥmīd* and is missing part of its final section. Witness J appears to descend from an intermediary that was copied in Egypt shortly after 767/1365, since it alone makes passing reference to the Alexandrian Crusade of that year (§2.6.3). Chapter, section, and subsection headings are in red ink.

The fourth and final witness is د (= D), which is the lone work in Süleymaniye Library, Dāmād Ibrāhīm Pāshā 273, an undated manuscript the copyist of which is not indicated. Here *The Sword of Ambition* takes up 37 folios, averaging 21 lines per side, 13 words per line. Copied in a *naskhī* hand, this manuscript is in excellent condition, complete (save for certain passages that are also missing from other witnesses, as we shall see), and fully legible. Its divisions are indicated by the use of red ink.

The edited Arabic text in this volume is based upon T. This means that it follows T except where otherwise noted. There are several reasons that I have privileged T. Foremost among these is that it is generally the most complete and correct of the witnesses. For example, the vivid autobiographical plea with which the work concludes in T is lacking in the other manuscripts. There are also indications that T maintained a certain proximity to the original, preserving, for example, pious invocations on behalf of the Ayyubid sultans that the other manuscripts omit. With the exception of poetry, where the other manuscripts offer many superior readings, T tends to be more persuasive in the numerous instances where the other manuscripts disagree with T on a word or phrase. However, there are several short passages and one long one that are lacking in T, and which I have supplied from the other manuscripts. A table of correspondences between the edition and T is to be posted on the website of the Library of Arabic Literature (www.libraryofarabicliterature.org).

The other three manuscripts—B, J, and D—belong to a different "family"; they have a pronounced tendency to agree with one another against T. Of these, B and D are nearest to one another. J is closer to both B and D than it is to T, and to B than to D, but surprisingly shares a substantial number of readings with T against both B and D. A speculative transmission stemma such as the following, where "?" represents hypothetical, lost intermediaries and a dotted line indicates that other such intermediaries are likely to have intervened, could account for these affinities.

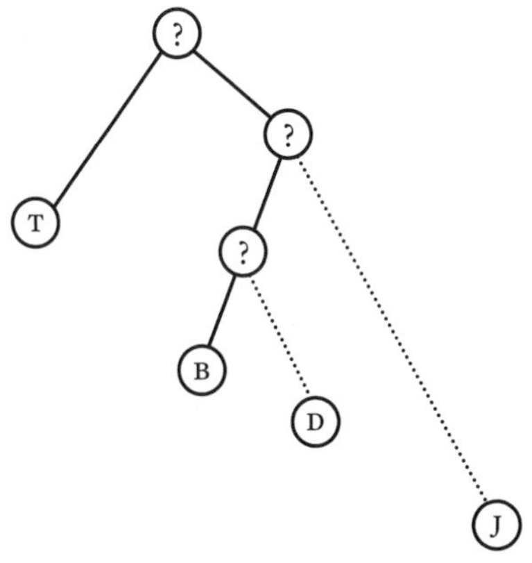

In preparing the text, I first produced a full critical edition, noting all variants in the four manuscripts. The exception was J, which departs so often and so freely from the other witnesses that it seemed inadvisable to note its countless unique variants. With very few exceptions, note was made of J only where it corroborated other witnesses or supplied a uniquely superior reading.

Due to practical limitations and the conventions of the Library of Arabic Literature, the apparatus is minimal, giving only crucial variants from the manuscripts. An edition with critical apparatus is to be made available on the Library's website. Thus for example grammatical errors, orthographical variants, disparate conjunctions, trivial omissions, disagreements in pious blessings, and other banal discrepancies are not noted. Orthography follows the conventions of classical literary Arabic, not those of the manuscripts, which of course frequently differ among themselves. Punctuation conforms to the conventions of the Library of Arabic Literature in that it, too, is extremely minimal. Thus conjunctions take on a primary role in the present edition, much as they did in premodern classical literary Arabic before the widespread adoption of European-style punctuation relegated them to a subordinate position.

I have sought to balance two opposing ideals in producing this edition. The first is a thoroughgoing critical edition that reconstructs the best possible urtext, the second a faithful representation of the surviving manuscript tradition, unburdened by the potentially quixotic search for a pristine original. In privileging T, which could in principle be reconstituted in its entirety from the apparatus to the online edition, I have inclined toward the latter ideal. But because all significant variants found in the other manuscripts are noted in the online apparatus, it is also possible for the reader who is eager to recover the author's original composition to go some distance toward doing so.

The Translation

The Arabic of *The Sword of Ambition* alternates among registers of formality and sophistication, from poetry of considerable complexity, to humorous and ribald tales, to occasional phrases that betray colloquial influence and apparently represent direct speech. These registers only intermittently intrude on a large middle ground that may be characterized, broadly, as classical literary Arabic. My translation represents an attempt to convey the fluctuating tenor of the original. Thus when the Arabic rings high and ancient, as in poetry and hoary aphorisms, I have not resisted the attraction of archaic English. In conversation and where the text implies a conspiratorial understanding between narrator and reader, I have searched for a vernacular English voice in which contractions and folk idioms are at home. For the predominant linguistic middle ground, I have aimed for what seemed to me an economical English equivalent to Ibn al-Nābulusī's proficient but unadorned Arabic style. I have everywhere shrugged off any constraint of Arabic verb tense, mood, idiom, semantic range, and syntax that seemed, when construed strictly, to distort the sense of the original. My goal has been to translate concepts as faithfully as possible, with far less regard for literal forms, which the most keenly interested readers can consult easily enough on the facing page.

Although *The Sword of Ambition* is not a particularly difficult work, it has presented the usual scattering of interpretive problems, not all of which I have succeeded in solving to my own satisfaction. This applies above all to poetry, which I have handled with considerable trepidation, particularly inasmuch as the manuscripts give numerous variants; published editions of other works that contain the same poems have been of only sporadic assistance in selecting among those variants. In general, in both edition and translation, I have adopted a minimally invasive approach that seeks to reproduce for modern readers of *The Sword of Ambition* something of their premodern forebears' experience. I have not, for instance, aggressively emended the edition to produce a text that is as easy to read as possible, or attempted to efface genuine ambiguities when translating. Points of obscurity are part of the author's work as it came down to all of its readers in the manuscript tradition. In the same spirit, I have tried to minimize clutter in the translation by making the Glossary, and not the notes, the repository of most information regarding the many proper names that appear in the text, including the Introduction. Thus readers in search of brief explanations for unfamiliar people, places, and other entities should refer first to the Glossary.

A point remains regarding my use of other English translations. For the Qur'an, I have used A. J. Arberry's *The Koran Interpreted*, with occasional adjustments. Short passages from *The Sword of Ambition* have been translated in two published articles, by Joseph Sadan and Brian Catlos.[54] I have consulted these, but in no instance is my translation based on them. In the notes I have given prominence to translations of Arabic sources, when these exist, over Arabic editions of the same works.

In spite of the shortcomings that undoubtedly remain in this book, it is my hope that readers will look upon it with greater approval than may be reasonably expected from the shade of Ibn al-Nābulusī himself.

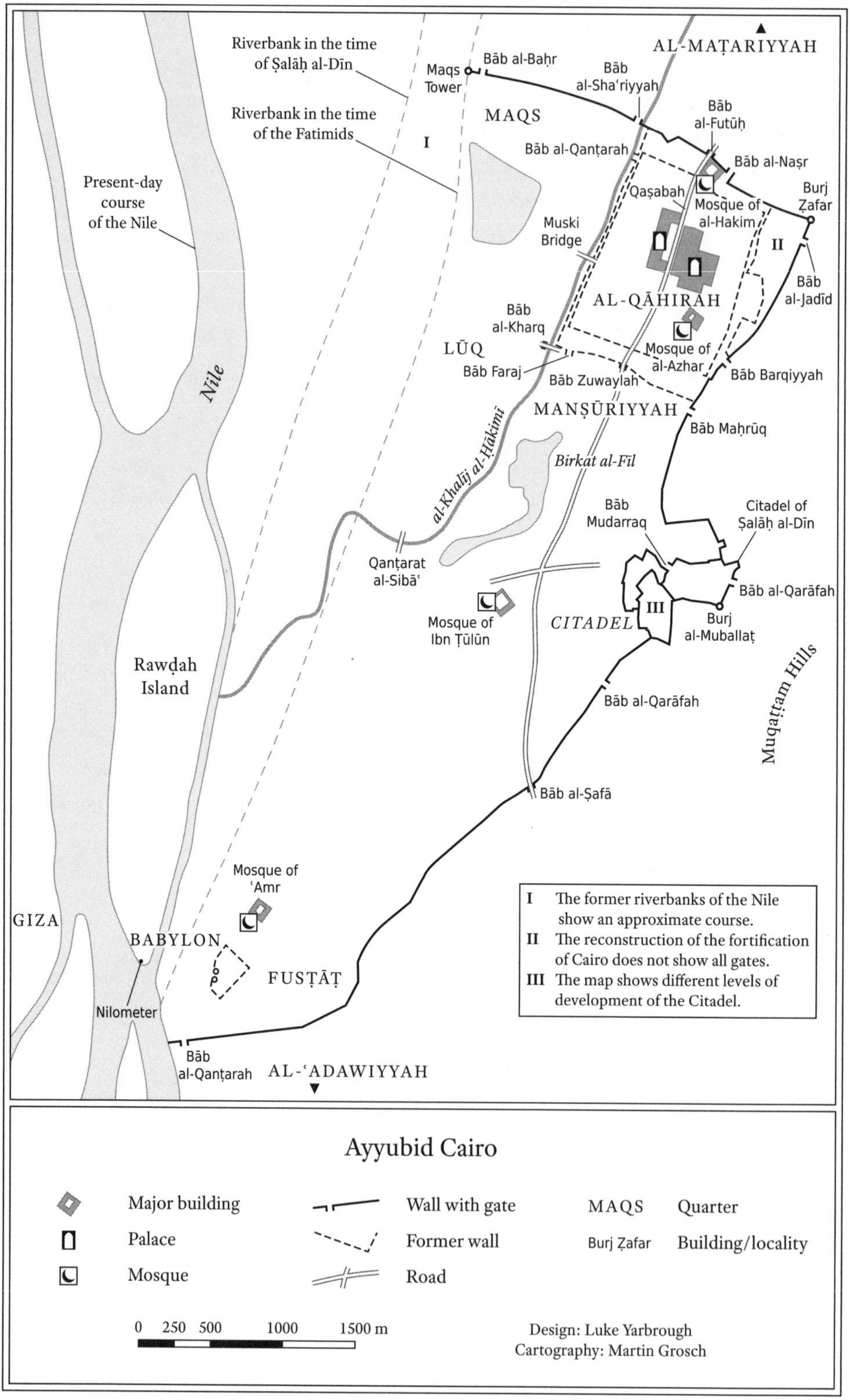
Riverbank in the time of Ṣalāḥ al-Dīn
Riverbank in the time of the Fatimids
Present-day course of the Nile
Nile
Maqs Tower
Bāb al-Baḥr
Bāb al-Sha'riyyah
AL-MAṬARIYYAH
MAQS
I
Bāb al-Qanṭarah
Bāb al-Futūḥ
Bāb al-Naṣr
Qaṣabah
Mosque of al-Hakim
Burj Ẓafar
II
Muski Bridge
Bāb al-Jadīd
AL-QĀHIRAH
Bāb al-Kharq
LŪQ
Mosque of al-Azhar
Bāb Faraj
Bāb Zuwaylah
Bāb Barqiyyah
MANṢŪRIYYAH
Bāb Maḥrūq
Birkat al-Fīl
al-Khalīj al-Ḥākimī
Bāb Mudarraq
Citadel of Ṣalāḥ al-Dīn
Qanṭarat al-Sibā'
Bāb al-Qarāfah
Mosque of Ibn Ṭūlūn
III
CITADEL
Burj al-Muballaṭ
Rawḍah Island
Bāb al-Qarāfah
Muqaṭṭam Hills
Bāb al-Ṣafā
Mosque of 'Amr
GIZA
BABYLON
FUSṬĀṬ
Nilometer
Bāb al-Qanṭarah
AL-'ADAWIYYAH
I The former riverbanks of the Nile show an approximate course.
II The reconstruction of the fortification of Cairo does not show all gates.
III The map shows different levels of development of the Citadel.
Ayyubid Cairo
Major building
Palace
Mosque
Wall with gate
Former wall
Road
MAQS Quarter
Burj Ẓafar Building/locality
0 250 500 1000 1500 m
Design: Luke Yarbrough
Cartography: Martin Grosch

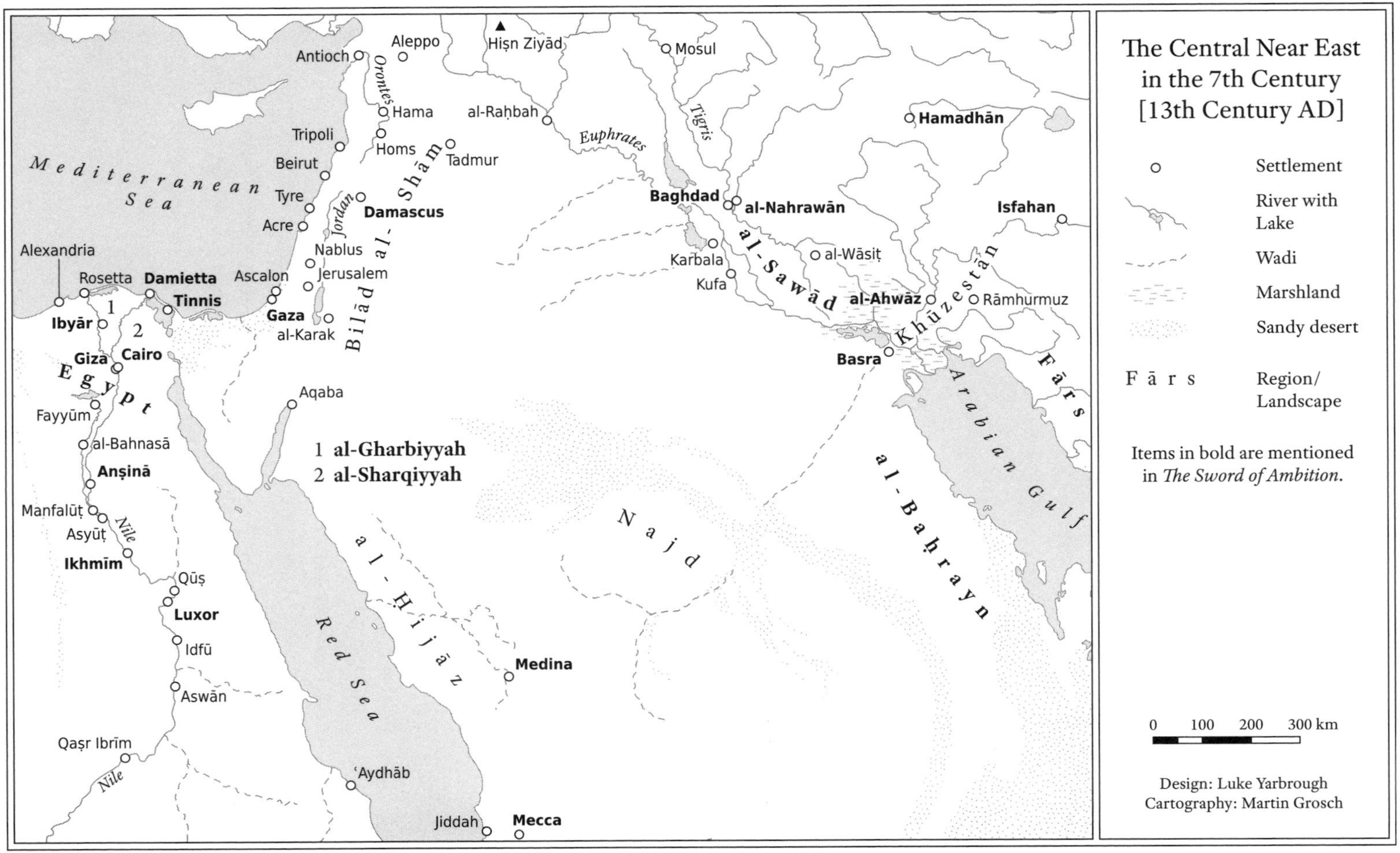
The Central Near East
in the 7th Century
[13th Century AD]
Settlement
River with Lake
Wadi
Marshland
Sandy desert
Fārs
Region/ Landscape
Items in bold are mentioned in The Sword of Ambition.
0 100 200 300 km
Design: Luke Yarbrough
Cartography: Martin Grosch
Mediterranean Sea
Red Sea
Arabian Gulf
Egypt
Bilād al-Shām
al-Ḥijāz
Najd
al-Sawād
Khūzestān
al-Baḥrayn
Fārs
1 al-Gharbiyyah
2 al-Sharqiyyah
Alexandria
Rosetta
Damietta
Tinnis
Ibyār
Giza
Cairo
Fayyūm
al-Bahnasā
Anṣinā
Manfalūṭ
Asyūṭ
Nile
Ikhmīm
Qūṣ
Luxor
Idfū
Aswān
Qaṣr Ibrīm
Antioch
Aleppo
Orontes
Hama
Homs
Tripoli
Beirut
Tyre
Acre
Jordan
Damascus
Tadmur
Nablus
Jerusalem
Ascalon
Gaza
al-Karak
Aqaba
'Aydhāb
Jiddah
Mecca
Medina
Ḥiṣn Ziyād
al-Raḥbah
Euphrates
Mosul
Tigris
Baghdad
al-Nahrawān
Karbala
Kufa
al-Wāsiṭ
al-Ahwāz
Rāmhurmuz
Basra
Hamadhān
Isfahan

Notes to the Introduction

1 This title differs in minor respects from that given in the manuscripts of *The Sword of Ambition.*

2 Cahen and Becker, "Kitāb lumaʿ al-qawānīn," 61.

3 Possibly the income-bearing property of the Nābulusiyyah Madrasah established by ʿUthmān's father (al-Maqrīzī, *al-Mawāʿiẓ*, vol. 4, pt. 2, p. 678). I owe this reference to Yossef Rapoport.

4 On hiding one's poverty in medieval Egypt, see Cohen, *Poverty and Charity,* 43, 49–51.

5 Modern historians, notably Claude Cahen, have read this name as "Muslim," but the manuscript of the work containing his earliest (and principal) prosopographical entry is quite clear at this point. This manuscript—the *Muʿjam al-shuyūkh* of ʿAbd al-Muʾmin ibn Khalaf al-Dimyāṭī—was copied during the lifetime of its author. Parts of it were read out loud to him (Dār al-Kutub al-Waṭaniyyah al-Tūnisiyyah, 12909: fol. 75r). For a summary in French, see Vajda, *Le Dictionnaire des Autorités,* 146. For Cahen's use of this source, see Cahen and Becker, "*Kitāb lumaʿ al-qawānīn,*" 120ff. Brief notices on Ibn al-Nābulusī in later works confirm the name "al-Salm" or "Salm" (al-Dhahabī, *Tārīkh al-Islām,* 14:936; al-Ḥusaynī, *Ṣilat al-takmilah,* 1:470; al-Maqrīzī, *al-Mawāʿiẓ*, vol. 4, pt. 2, p. 678).

6 Much of the material presented here is derived from the manuscript source cited in the previous note and from Cahen and Becker, "*Kitāb lumaʿ al-qawānīn,*" 120ff. The latter study depended primarily on information gleaned from the author's own works. I have presented some of this material previously (Yarbrough, "ʿUthmān b. Ibrāhīm al-Nābulusī"). See also Catlos, "To Catch a Spy"; Owen, "Scandal in the Egyptian Treasury." I have benefited, too, from the work of Yossef Rapoport, who generously shared a draft of his introduction to the author's life.

7 Also pronounced "Ibn al-Nābulsī." This title could also of course refer to a still earlier forebear. Al-Dimyāṭī's text refers to our author as "Abū ʿAmr ʿUthmān ibn al-Nābulusī" and "al-ʿAlāʾ ibn al-Nābulusī," indicating that he was in fact known as Ibn al-Nābulusī. Claude Cahen consistently called him "al-Nābulusī" and virtually all subsequent historians (my own earlier publications included) have followed this convention, which should now be abandoned.

8 The prosopographical literature informs us that he was wealthy (perhaps fantastically so) and well connected as well as pious and learned. See al-Dhahabī, *Siyar aʿlām al-nubalāʾ*, 21:393–396, no. 199; Ibn Rajab, *al-Dhayl ʿalā Ṭabaqāt al-Ḥanābilah*, 2:528–38, no. 233.

9 His emigration may have coincided with that of a large number of refugees who fled Frankish rule at around this time (see Sivan, "Réfugiés syro-palestiniens"; Talmon-Heller, "Arabic Sources on Muslim Villagers Under Frankish Rule").

10 For this account, see Ibn Rajab, *al-Dhayl*, 2:532–34. For Ibn Nujayyah's influence over Saladin, who allegedly referred to him as ʿAmr ibn al-ʿĀṣ and acted on his advice, see Ibn Rajab, *al-Dhayl*, 2:531.

11 For various views on the content of *madrasah* curricula, see Makdisi, *Rise of Colleges*; Chamberlain, *Knowledge and Social Practice*; Stewart, "Doctorate of Islamic Law."

12 It concerns the Prophet's preferred supplicatory prayer (*duʿāʾ*) and is found in the canonical books of al-Bukhārī and Muslim (e.g., Muslim, *Ṣaḥīḥ*, 4:2070).

13 Also suggesting an uneasy relationship between *madrasah* training and state employment is the slanderous accusation leveled at Ibn al-Nābulusī by his rival in a real-estate dispute (on which more below): that he was absent from work, without leave, because he was off studying in one *madrasah* after another. Muslim officials with scholarly backgrounds had their vulnerabilities, too.

14 Cahen and Becker, "Kitāb lumaʿ al-qawānīn," 59, drawn to my attention by Yossef Rapoport.

15 Al-Maqrīzī, *al-Mawāʿiẓ*, vol. 4, pt. 2, p. 678, drawn to my attention by Yossef Rapoport.

16 For this information and what follows, see Cahen and Becker, "Kitāb lumaʿ al-qawānīn," 36–44.

17 On al-Asʿad: Cahen and Becker, "Kitāb lumaʿ al-qawānīn," 40 n. 15. He was to become vizier to the first Mamluk sultan, al-Muʿizz. This Nūr al-Dīn was the son of the high emir Fakhr al-Dīn ibn al-Shaykh (d. 647/1250).

18 For a strikingly similar administrative maneuver performed against a Muslim by a Christian official, supposedly in the early Abbasid period, see below in *The Sword of Ambition*, §1.9.1.

19 Cahen and Becker, "Kitāb lumaʿ al-qawānīn," 43.

20 Cahen and Becker, "Kitāb lumaʿ al-qawānīn," 61–64.

21 "Rural Society in Medieval Islam," by Yossef Rapoport and Ido Shahar, accessed July 29, 2014, http://www2.history.qmul.ac.uk/ruralsocietyislam. For a full study of this work we must await the forthcoming publication by Yossef Rapoport.

22 My hypothesis seems the most plausible way to construe the notion, conveyed in the title, of "victory over" certain other Muslims who ally with non-Muslims. The term

istiʿānah is used most often in the context of alliance in warfare. For administrative employment the terms *istiʿmāl* and *istiktāb* are more common. See al-Maqrīzī, *A History of the Ayyubid Sultans of Egypt*, 262–64.

23 Cahen and Becker, "Kitāb lumaʿ al-qawānīn," 31–34.

24 See, e.g., Cahen and Becker, "Kitāb lumaʿ al-qawānīn," 34, and below in *The Sword of Ambition*, §0.3.

25 Al-Maqrīzī, *al-Mawāʿiẓ*, 1:231; 2:112.

26 These lines of poetry were reproduced by al-Yūnīnī in his entry on Ibn al-Nābulusī, which is dependent upon that of al-Dimyāṭī: al-Yūnīnī, *Dhayl mirʾāt al-zamān*, 1:504–5. For another brief sample of Ibn al-Nābulusī's poetry, see al-Madanī, *Anwār al-rabīʿ*, 5:251–2.

27 On the *ghiyār*, see Yarbrough, "Origins of the ghiyār."

28 On possible layers in the *Lumaʿ*, see Cahen and Becker, "Kitāb lumaʿ al-qawānīn," 122f. For the same in the *Iẓhār*, see the editor Moritz's introduction to Ibn al-Nābulusī, *Description du Faiyoum*, ii (not paginated).

29 Cahen, "Histoires coptes," 134.

30 As Cahen wrote, "Il est surtout amusant de voir comment l'auteur utilise pour les besoins de sa cause n'importe quel épisode" ("It is above all amusing to see how the author cites all manner of episodes to make his case.") ("Histoires coptes," 134).

31 Al-Maqrīzī, *History of the Ayyubid Sultans*, 294–95; al-Makīn, *Chronique*, 85.

32 For an example of a passage in an advice work against non-Muslim officials being read out loud to a Mamluk sultan about fifty years later, see Yarbrough, "A Rather Small Genre." The *Luminous Rules*, written shortly after *The Sword of Ambition* and for the same patron, was expressly presented as *naṣīḥah*.

33 On these works, their interrelationship, and the milieus that produced them, see el-Leithy, "Sufis, Copts, and the Politics of Piety"; Yarbrough, "A Rather Small Genre."

34 For the unidentified source and its heirs, see Yarbrough, "A Rather Small Genre."

35 Synesius, *Essays and hymns*, 2:135. A general study is Cameron and Long, *Barbarians and Politics*.

36 ʿĀlī, *Nuṣḥatü s-selāṭīn*; Fleischer, *Bureaucrat and Intellectual*, 8–9.

37 A few of the relatively recent studies of non-Muslim state officials and doctors are: Abele, *Der politisch-gesellschaftliche Einfluss der nestorianischen Ärzte*; Cabrol, *Les secrétaires nestoriens à Bagdad*; Cheikho and Héchaïmé, *Wuzarāʾ al-Naṣrāniyyah*; Hutait, "The Position of the Copts in Mamluk Administration"; Mazor, "Jewish Court Physicians in the Mamluk Sultanate"; Samir, "The Role of Christians in the Fāṭimid

Government Services"; Sirry, "The Public Role of *Dhimmīs*"; Stillman, "The emergence . . . of the Sephardi courtier class."

38 For the beginnings of this discourse, see Yarbrough, "Upholding God's Rule."

39 This phase is traditionally known as the "Sunni revival." This term has been criticized for presuming a continuity between late-medieval Sunni Islam and the pre–tenth-century ideological progenitors to which it traced its own genealogy. See for example Berkey, *The Formation of Islam*, 189–202.

40 For a rich selection of studies on this development, see Stewart, "The *Maqāmāt*," 232 n. 43. See also Hillenbrand, *The Crusades: Islamic Perspectives*; Mallett, *Popular Muslim Reactions*.

41 For these developments in general, see Chamberlain, *Knowledge and Social Practice in Medieval Damascus*; Ephrat, *A Learned Society*.

42 Goitein, *Mediterranean Society*, 2:375.

43 Leiser, "The *Madrasa* and the Islamization of the Middle East"; Yarbrough, "The *Madrasa* and the Non-Muslims of Thirteenth-Century Egypt."

44 For a near-comprehensive list of modern scholarship that refers to the work, see Yarbrough, "ʿUthmān b. Ibrāhīm al-Nābulusī." To this list should be added a few works in Arabic, including: Sayyid, *al-Dawlah al-Fāṭimiyyah fī Miṣr*, 240; Cheikho and Héchaïmé, *Wuzarāʾ al-Naṣrāniyyah*, 31.

45 Examples of modern works that have cited works like *The Sword of Ambition* in this way (there are many) include Cohen, *Under Crescent and Cross*, 229 n. 101; Sivan, "Notes sur la situation des chrétiens à l'époque ayyubide," 119–20.

46 On the theoretical *dhimmah* system developed by Muslim jurists, parts of which were sporadically enforced by Muslim rulers, usually at the behest of religious elites, see (inter alia) Fattal, *Le statut légal*; Cahen, art. "Dhimma," *EI2*; Bosworth, "The Concept of Dhimma"; Cohen, *Under Crescent and Cross*; Friedmann, *Tolerance and Coercion*; Papaconstantinou, "Between *Umma* and *Dhimma*"; Wasserstein, "Conversion and the *ahl al-dhimma*"; Levy-Rubin, *Non-Muslims in the Early Islamic Empire*; Emon, *Religious Pluralism and Islamic Law*. The well-known "Pact of ʿUmar" (*shurūṭ ʿUmar*) was sometimes accorded a certain authority in premodern thought concerning the *dhimmah* system; the most important recent studies of it are Cohen, "What was the Pact of ʿUmar?"; Noth, "Problems of Differentiation"; Levy-Rubin, *Non-Muslims in the Early Islamic Empire*, chap. 2 and 4.

47 Van Ess, *Chiliastische Erwartungen*, 13 n. 38; Sadan, "Some Literary Problems," 365–70; Catlos, "To Catch a Spy"; Rabie, "The Size and Value of the *Iqṭāʿ* in Egypt," 131 n. 8.

48 For accessible introductions to the current predicament of certain non-Muslim populations, see Sennott, *The Body and the Blood*; Dalrymple, *From the Holy Mountain.*

49 Available in Arabic: *Aḥkām*; *Madhammah*; *Radd*; Ibn al-Durayhim, *Manhaj al-ṣawāb*; Ibn Taymiyyah, *Mas'alah*; idem, *Iqtiḍā'*. Modern-day compilations available online: al-Shuʿaybī, *al-Qawl al-mukhtār*; al-Yāfiʿī, *Ḥukm tawliyat ahl al-dhimmah.* Translated into English: Gottheil, "An Answer to the Dhimmis."

50 On Tertullian, see Stroumsa, "Tertullian on idolatry and the limits of tolerance"; on Celsus, Chadwick, *Origen: Contra Celsum*; on Chrysostom, Wilken, *John Chrysostom and the Jews.*

51 Cahen, "Histoires coptes"; Cahen and Becker, "*Kitāb lumaʿ al-qawānīn.*"

52 Cahen and Becker, "*Kitāb lumaʿ al-qawānīn,*" 122; Schmidtke, "Moshe Perlmann (1905–2001): A Bibliography."

53 Three of these have been used before. Claude Cahen based his transcriptions on T. Moshe Perlmann used B in an article published in 1942, though without stating its title or author. D has been used by Joseph Sadan in more recent work (Perlmann, "Notes on Anti-Christian Propaganda"; Sadan, "Some Literary Problems"). So far as I am aware, J has not been mentioned in modern scholarship.

54 Sadan, "Some Literary Problems"; Catlos, "To Catch a Spy."

تجريد سيف الهمّة
لاستخراج ما في ذمّة الذمّة

The Sword of Ambition

بسم الله الرحمن الرحيم

الحمد لله الذي رفع[1] دين الإسلام على سائر الأديان وخفض أهل الشرك وعبدة الصلبان أحمده على ما يكون من قضائه وقدره وما كان وأشهد أنّ لا إلٰه إلّا الله وحده لا شريك له في السرّ والإعلان وأشهد أنّ محمّدًا عبده ورسوله المبعوث إلى الأحمر والأسود والإنس والجانّ صلّى الله عليه وعلى آله وصحبه والتابعين لهم بإحسان صلاةً تبقى ويفنى دونها الزمان. ١،٠

وبعد فإنّه لمّا بلغني أنّ مولانا السلطان الأعظم مالك رقاب الأمم وسيّد ملوك العرب والعجم ملك البرّين والبحرين حامي حوزة الدين قاصم الطغاة والمتمرّدين مرغِم آناف الملحدين قامع الكفرة والمشركين محيي العدل في العالمين سلطان الإسلام والمسلمين نجم الدنيا والدين أيّوب ولد مولانا السلطان السعيد الشهيد الملك الكامل ناصر الدنيا والدين محمّد ولد مولانا السلطان السعيد الشهيد الملك العادل سيف الدنيا والدين أبي بكر ولد مولانا السيّد السعيد الشهيد العظيم الشأن نجم الدين أيّوب عظّم الله شانه وقوّى سلطانه وأذلّ عدوّه وأهانه خرج أمره المطاع أنفذه الله في مشارق الأرض ومغاربها بأن ترفع الذمّة العذب وتشدّ الزنّار وأن يُمنعوا من التشبّه بالمسلمين فيلبسوا الغيار وأن يلفعوا بأبراد الخزي والهوان والصغار وأن ينزلوا حيث أنزلهم الله من وهاد الذلّ ومهابط الاحتقار علمت أنّ هذه الحركة السعيدة والمقاصد الشريفة السديدة مقدّمات تنتج البشرى بالنصر على أعداء الدين وتبهج بالبشر[2] وجوه الإسلام والمسلمين. فأحببت أن أخدم الخزانة الشريفة بكتاب أصنّفه في الذمّة ٢،٠

---

١ كذا في د؛ و في ت: وقع. ٢ كذا في المخطوطتين، ولعلّ الصواب هو: البشّ.

In the name of God, the Merciful and Compassionate:

Praise God, who has elevated the religion of Islam above all other religions while demoting the cross-worshippers and those who associate partners with Him.[1] *I give Him praise for his Eternal Decree concerning what will be and what has come to pass. I testify, both openly and in my heart, that there is no god but Him alone, Who has no partner. I testify, too, that Muḥammad is his devoted servant and messenger, sent to the Arabs and the non-Arabs, to humans and jinn alike.*[2] *May God bless him along with his family, his Companions, and their upright Followers with an enduring blessing that outlasts Time itself.* 0.1

I learned recently that a command had been issued by our lord the supreme sultan, who is master of the nations and chief among the kings of the Arabs and all peoples, king of both continents and both seas, protector of the domain of the true religion, shatterer of tyrants and rebels, bane of heretics, subduer of infidels and unbelievers, reviver of justice among mankind, the sultan of Islam and the Muslims, Star of this world and of the faith, Najm al-Dīn Ayyūb. He is the son of our lord the blessed, martyred sultan, al-Malik al-Kāmil, Nāṣir al-Dīn Muḥammad, Champion of this world and of the faith, who was the son of our lord the blessed, martyred sultan, al-Malik al-ʿĀdil, Sayf al-Dīn Abū Bakr, Sword of this world and of the faith, who was the son of our lord the eminent and blessed martyr, the great Najm al-Dīn Ayyūb, may God glorify his estate, strengthen his authority, and humiliate and abase his enemy. This universally obeyed command—God hasten it forth to East and West—decreed that the dhimmis must remove the fringes from their clothing, wear their distinguishing belts, and be forbidden to resemble Muslims in their outward aspect.[3] Instead they were to wear their distinguishing garb and to wrap themselves in the garments of shame, degradation, and ignominy. They were to occupy the debased position in which God has placed them: the lowest pits and the depths of abjection. 0.2

When I heard news of this edict, I knew that such an auspicious policy and the noble, well-aimed intentions that lay behind it had to portend something even greater. I knew that in time they would produce good news of victory

وتأليف أؤلّفه شكرًا لهذه النعمة فألّفت هذا الكتاب وسمّيته تجريد سيف الهمّة لاستخراج ما في ذمّة الذمّة وبنيت المقصود منه على قواعد وأصول وجعلته أربعة أبواب يشتمل كلّ باب منها على فصول.

الباب الأوّل في كراهية استعمال الذمّة في أشغال المسلمين وفيه خمسة عشر فصلاً ٣،٠

الفصل الأوّل فيما ورد في الكتاب العزيز في ذلك

الفصل الثاني فيما ورد عن رسول الله صلّى الله عليه وسلّم في ذلك

الفصل الثالث فيما ورد من كلام الحكماء المتقدّمين في ذلك

الفصل الرابع فيما ورد عن الإمام أبي بكر الصدّيق في ذلك

الفصل الخامس فيما ورد عن الإمام عمر بن الخطّاب في ذلك

الفصل السادس فيما ورد عن عبد الملك بن مروان في ذلك

الفصل السابع فيما جرى من الحجّاج في ذلك

الفصل الثامن فيما جاء عن عمر بن عبد العزيز في ذلك

الفصل التاسع فيما جرى أيّام الخليفة المنصور في ذلك

الفصل العاشر فيما جرى أيّام الخليفة المهديّ في ذلك

الفصل الحادي عشر فيما جرى أيّام الخليفة هارون الرشيد في ذلك

الفصل الثاني عشر فيما جرى أيّام الخليفة المأمون في ذلك

الفصل الثالث عشر فيما جرى أيّام الخليفة المتوكّل في ذلك

الفصل الرابع عشر فيما جرى أيّام المقتدر بالله في ذلك

الفصل الخامس عشر في ذكر لمعة من خزي اليهود ومكرهم وخبثهم

الباب الثاني في وصف الأقباط وخياناتهم ويشتمل على خمسة عشر فصلاً ٤،٠

الفصل الأوّل في وصفهم بما اشتملوا عليه من حيث الجملة

over the enemies of the faith, brightening the face of Islam and of Muslims with gladness. I therefore desired to serve the noble government by writing a book on the dhimmis. It would be an expression of gratitude for the benefaction of this edict applying to them. The result is this book, which I have entitled *Unsheathing Ambition's Sword to Take Back What the Dhimmis Hoard*. I have grounded the message of my work upon firm bases and foundations, dividing it into four chapters, each of which is comprised of sections.

The first chapter, on the reprehensibility of employing dhimmis for the Muslims' jobs, in fifteen sections: 0.3

The first section: the testimony of the Illustrious Book on this matter;[4]

The second section: the sayings passed down from the Messenger of God, God bless and keep him;

The third section: the testimony of the ancient authorities;

The fourth section: the sayings passed down from Imam Abū Bakr al-Ṣiddīq;

The fifth section: the sayings passed down from Imam ʿUmar ibn al-Khaṭṭāb;

The sixth section: the sayings passed down from ʿAbd al-Malik ibn Marwān;

The seventh section: the deeds of al-Ḥajjāj;

The eighth section: the sayings passed down from ʿUmar ibn ʿAbd al-ʿAzīz;

The ninth section: the events that took place in the days of Caliph al-Manṣūr;

The tenth section: the events that took place in the days of Caliph al-Mahdī;

The eleventh section: the events that took place in the days of Caliph Hārūn al-Rashīd;

The twelfth section: the events that took place in the days of Caliph al-Maʾmūn;

The thirteenth section: the events that took place in the days of Caliph al-Mutawakkil;

The fourteenth section: the events that took place in the days of Caliph al-Muqtadir bi-llāh;

The fifteenth section: examples of the Jews' ignominy, cunning, and wickedness.

The second chapter, a description of the Copts and their perfidies, in fifteen sections: 0.4

The first section: a comprehensive and general description of them;

الفصل الثاني في ذكر سبب اشتغالهم بالكتابة دون بقيّة الحِرَف
الفصل الثالث في عموم تصرّفهم من حيث لا يُشعر بهم في الديار المصريّة
الفصل الرابع فيما اطّلع عليه أحمد بن طولون من خيانتهم المشهورة وما اعتمده فيهم
الفصل الخامس فيما جرى لهم مع محمّد بن سليمان
الفصل السادس فيما جرى أيّام الحاكم بأمر الله في ذلك
الفصل السابع فيما جرى في ذلك أيّام الآمر وما جرى للملعون الراهب من المصادرة
الفصل الثامن فيما جرى من خيانتهم في أمر عريب المغنيّة
الفصل التاسع فيما جرى من تميمهم أيّام الحافظ
الفصل العاشر فيما جرى من إقدامهم على الشهادة في حجج المسلمين
الفصل الحادي عشر فيما جرى من تميمهم في المساحة
الفصل الثاني عشر فيما جرى من تميمهم على مرافقيهم من العدول وأنّه لا يمكن ضبطهم عن الخيانة
الفصل الثالث عشر فيما جرى من تدقيق الحيلة من نصرانيّ على رفيق له يهوديّ ممّا هو من العجائب التي لا يُقدِم عليها إلّا هذه الطائفة الملعونة
الفصل الرابع عشر فيما جرى من مخازيهم أيّام العاضد حين كان السلطان الملك الصالح طلائع بن رزّيك
الفصل الخامس عشر في ذكر السبب الذي لأجله صار إذا أسلم أحد منهم لكائنة أو جائحة حصلت له جاء أنحس ممّا كان وأكثر خيانةً وأقلّ أمانةً وأشدّ قِحّة

الباب الثالث في وصف الكتابة والكتّاب وفيه فصول ثلاثة ٥،٠
الفصل الأوّل في وصف الكتابة وذكر من تزيّا بها من غير أهلها وباشر جليل شغلها
الفصل الثاني في ذكر من يجوز أن يوصف بالكتابة ويقال له كاتب وذكر شيء من محاسنهم وما لهم من النثر ولو كلمة واحدة لكلّ واحد ليُعرف بها فضله

The second section: why they specialize as state secretaries and neglect other professions;

The third section: their pervasive yet imperceptible influence in the land of Egypt;

The fourth section: how Aḥmad ibn Ṭūlūn discovered their notorious malfeasance, and how he resolved to act toward them;

The fifth section: what befell them at the hands of Muḥammad ibn Sulaymān;

The sixth section: the events that took place in the days of al-Ḥākim bi-Amr Allāh;

The seventh section: the events that took place in the days of al-Āmir, and the confiscations carried out by the accursed Monk;

The eighth section: their perfidy in the story of ʿArīb the singer;

The ninth section: their scheming in the days of al-Ḥāfiẓ;

The tenth section: their shameless testimony in court cases involving Muslims;

The eleventh section: their scheming in carrying out the land survey;

The twelfth section: their scheming against a certain judicial witness who was in their company, and how they cannot be restrained from malfeasance;

The thirteenth section: a calculated stratagem carried out by a Christian against his Jewish associate, a shocking act that only someone belonging to that accursed community would dare to commit;

The fourteenth section: the disgraceful things they did in the days of al-ʿĀḍid, when al-Malik al-Ṣāliḥ Ṭalāʾiʿ ibn Ruzzīk was sultan;

The fifteenth section: why it is that, when one of them converts to Islam due to some predicament or calamity, he becomes even more miserable and duplicitous than before, less trustworthy and more insolent.

The third chapter, a description of secretaries and their art, in three sections: 0.5

The first section: a description of the secretarial art, with an account of certain unworthy men who have pretended to it and thereby occupied themselves with its sublime offices;

The second section: an account of those men who may properly be called secretaries, along with some of their achievements and examples of their prose, though it be but a single phrase to demonstrate the excellence of each one;

الفصل الثالث في ذكر شيء من أشعار الكتّاب الفضلاء ولو بيت واحد

الباب الرابع في ذكر الجهّال الذين تزيّوا بزيّ الكتّاب وليسوا منهم وفيه فصول ثلاثة ٦،٠
الفصل الأوّل في الأشعار التي قيلت فيهم قديماً وحديثاً
الفصل الثاني في عامّيّة ألفاظهم وجهلهم
الفصل الثالث وبمعناه سمّي الكتاب فيما يحسن سلوكه بهم ومعهم من أخذ الأموال التي اختزلوها من أموال المسلمين.

The third section: examples of the poetry produced by the most excellent secretaries, though it be but a single line.

The fourth chapter, an account of the ignorant men who have unworthily donned the garments of the secretaries, in three sections: 0.6

The first section: poetry composed about such men in former and more recent times;

The second section: concerning the vulgarity of their expression and their ignorance;

The third section, from which the book gets its title: what should be done with them, namely, taking back the wealth that they have skimmed for themselves from public funds properly belonging to the Muslims.

الباب الأوّل في كراهية استعمال الذمّة في أشغال المسلمين وفيه خمسة عشر فصلاً

الفصل الأوّل فيما ورد في الكتاب العزيز في ذلك

١،١،١ قال الله سبحانه وتعالى في كتابه العزيز الذي ﴿لَا يَأْتِيهِ الْبَاطِلُ مِنْ بَيْنِ يَدَيْهِ وَلَا مِنْ خَلْفِهِ﴾ ﴿تَرَىٰ كَثِيرًا مِنْهُمْ يَتَوَلَّوْنَ الَّذِينَ كَفَرُوا ۚ لَبِئْسَ مَا قَدَّمَتْ لَهُمْ أَنْفُسُهُمْ أَنْ سَخِطَ اللَّهُ عَلَيْهِمْ وَفِي الْعَذَابِ هُمْ خَالِدُونَ وَلَوْ كَانُوا يُؤْمِنُونَ بِاللَّهِ وَالنَّبِيِّ وَمَا أُنْزِلَ إِلَيْهِ مَا اتَّخَذُوهُمْ أَوْلِيَاءَ﴾.

٢،١،١ قلت فأخبر الله سبحانه أنّ من يتولّاهم سخط الله عليه وأنّه بئس ما قدّمت له نفسه. ومفهوم هذه الآية أنّ مَن تولّاهم ليس بمؤمن بالله ولا رسوله ولا ما أُنزل إليه وأيّ خطر أعظم من تمكّنهم من التصرّف في أعمال المسلمين واستئمانهم على أموال ربّ العالمين؟

٣،١،١ وقال الله سبحانه وتعالى ﴿يَا أَيُّهَا الَّذِينَ آمَنُوا لَا تَتَّخِذُوا الْيَهُودَ وَالنَّصَارَىٰ أَوْلِيَاءَ ۘ بَعْضُهُمْ أَوْلِيَاءُ بَعْضٍ ۚ وَمَنْ يَتَوَلَّهُمْ مِنْكُمْ فَإِنَّهُ مِنْهُمْ﴾ وفي هذه الآية ما يدلّ على كراهية استعمالهم وفيها ما هو أشدّ تصريحاً من الآية التي قبلها.

٤،١،١ وقال سبحانه وتعالى ﴿يَا أَيُّهَا الَّذِينَ آمَنُوا لَا تَتَّخِذُوا عَدُوِّي وَعَدُوَّكُمْ أَوْلِيَاءَ تُلْقُونَ إِلَيْهِمْ بِالْمَوَدَّةِ وَقَدْ كَفَرُوا بِمَا جَاءَكُمْ مِنَ الْحَقِّ﴾[1] وفي هذا التصريح مقنع وكفاية في الدلالة بل لو أراد الفقيه أن يستدلّ بهذه الآيات الشريفات[2] على أنّ استعمالهم حرام بالنصّ

---

[1] كذا في ت؛ والآية ساقطة في ج،د. [2] كذا في ت؛ وفي ج،د: بهاتين الآيتين.

The First Chapter, On the Reprehensibility of Employing Dhimmis for the Muslims' Jobs, in Fifteen Sections

The First Section: The Testimony of the Illustrious Book

God, be He glorified and exalted, said in his Illustrious Book—«falsehood comes not to it from before it nor from behind it»[5]—«Thou seest many of them making unbelievers their friends. Evil is what they have forwarded to their own account, that God is angered against them, and in the chastisement they shall dwell forever. Yet had they believed in God and the Prophet and what has been sent down to him, they would not have taken them as friends.»[6] 1.1.1

My own view is that God, be He glorified, informs us in this verse that the person who makes unbelievers his friends provokes God's anger. In acting thus that person has indeed forwarded evil to his own account. The broader meaning of the verse is that whoever takes them as his friends is not really a believer in God or in his Prophet and what was revealed to him. For what peril could be graver than for unbelievers to gain control over the Muslims' own administration, or that they should be entrusted with the properties that rightfully belong to the Lord of the Worlds? 1.1.2

God, be He glorified and exalted, said, «O believers, take not Jews and Christians as friends; they are friends of each other. Whoso of you makes them his friends is one of them.»[7] This verse clearly demonstrates that it is reprehensible to employ them. In fact, it is even more explicit in this regard than the previous verse. 1.1.3

God, be He glorified and exalted, said, «O believers, take not my enemy and your enemy for friends, offering them love, though they have disbelieved in the truth that has come to you.»[8] This statement by itself contains sufficient evidence to prove the point. Thus Muslim jurists are justified in citing these noble verses to show that it is forbidden to employ non-Muslims, according to the text of Revelation itself. I would add, too, that the introduction to the book I presented to the noble government—the one entitled *The Qur'an's Assurance* 1.1.4

لا ستدلّ. قلت وقد مضى في مقدّمة كتابي الذي خدمت به الخزائن الشريفة[1] المسمّى بتصريح القرآن بالنصر على من استعان بكفّار العصر ما يغني عن إعادته هنا.

الفصل الثاني فيما ورد عن رسول الله صلّى الله عليه وسلّم في ذلك

١،٢،١ قلت وقد ورد أنّ رسول الله صلّى الله عليه وسلّم لمّا خرج إلى غزاة بدر وكان في عدّة قليلة وهي ثلاثمائة وثلاثة عشر رجلاً ما فيهم سوى فارسين وكان الكفّار أضعافاً مضاعفة وفي جمع كثير من الخيل والرجل فتبعه رجل من المشركين فقال إنّي أريد أن أتبعك فأصيب معك قال تؤمن بالله ورسوله قال لا قال له ارجع فلن أستعين بمشرك فلحقه إلى موضع آخر فرآه أصحاب رسول الله صلّى الله عليه وسلّم فساعدوه وكان فيه قوّة وشجاعة وشدّة فقال يا رسول الله جئت لأتبعك فأصيب معك فقال تؤمن بالله ورسوله قال لا فقال له ارجع فلن أستعين بمشرك. ثمّ لحقه على ظهر بالبيداء فقال له كالقول الأوّل يا رسول الله جئت لأتبعك فأصيب معك فقال تؤمن بالله ورسوله فقال نعم فلمّا أسلم استعان به. وهذا أصل قويّ يُعتمد عليه في أنّه لا يستعان بمشرك.

الفصل الثالث فيما ورد من كلام الحكماء المتقدّمين في ذلك

١،٣،١ قلت ولم تزل الحكماء والعلماء والعقلاء والفضلاء يحرّضون على الاستعانة بالأولياء المخلصين الصادقين ويحذرون من الأعداء والثقة بهم وينهون عن الاستعانة بهم والاستكانة إليهم خلفاً بعد خلف وسلفاً بعد سلف.

٢،٣،١ فمن قولهم في ذلك من استعمل عدوّه وترك وليّه شغل قلبه وأغضب ربّه وتلف

[1] كذا في ت؛ والعبارة من (الذي) ساقطة في ج،د.

of Victory over Those Who Seek Aid from the Infidels of this Age—contains demonstration enough to this effect. There is no need to repeat it here.[9]

The Second Section: The Example of the Messenger of God

1.2.1 I would recount here how it is told that the Messenger of God, God bless and keep him, went out to fight the Battle of Badr with a very small force: three hundred and thirteen men, only two of them mounted. The infidels arrayed against them were many times their number, a great multitude of horses and men. On that day a certain polytheist followed the Prophet as he was going out to battle and said to him, "I want to follow you and raid with you." The Prophet asked, "Do you believe in God and his Messenger?" "No," he replied. The Prophet said, "Then go back, for I will not accept the aid of a polytheist." The man, however, caught up to him again at another place. The Companions of the Messenger of God, God bless and keep him, saw the man and gave him encouragement, for he was powerful, full of bravery and vigor. He said to the Prophet, "Messenger of God, I have come to follow you and raid with you." The Prophet asked, "Do you believe in God and his Messenger?" "No," he replied. "Then go back," the Prophet said, "for I will not accept the aid of a polytheist." After this he caught up to him once more upon the heights of al-Baydāʾ. He said to him, as he had before, "Messenger of God, I have come to follow you and raid with you." "Do you believe in God and his Messenger?" the Prophet asked. "Yes," he replied. Only after he had converted did the Prophet accept his aid.[10] This is strong evidence that can be relied upon to show that the aid of polytheists is not to be accepted.

The Third Section: The Testimony of the Ancient Authorities

1.3.1 Here I would observe that people of wisdom, learning, reason, and virtue have always urged that aid be sought from friends who are sincere and honest. The same authorities have, by contrast, cautioned against trusting enemies. One after another, from age to age, they have consistently advised against accepting enemies' aid and submitting to their power.

1.3.2 One such authority has said the following concerning this issue: "He who seeks aid from his enemy while neglecting his friend only troubles his heart and angers his Lord. His wealth is dissipated, his affairs disturbed,

ماله واختلّت أحواله وكان من أمر غده على خطر ومن فعله على غرر.[1] وقال بعض الحكماء المسلمين العجب من مؤمن يستخدم كافرًا يخالفه في رأيه ويضادّه في دينه واعتقاده. وقال آخر العجب كلّ العجب ممّن يطرح وليًّا مؤمنًا عاقلًا كافيًا ويستكفي عدوًّا كافرًا جاهلًا. وقال آخر لا تصطنع من خالفك في الدين ولا تستخدم من عدم اليقين. وقال بعض الحكماء من اعتمد على كفاة السوء لم يخلُ من رأي فاسد. وقال آخر أعجب الناس إليّ المعتمد على عدوّ لا يرجو خيره ولا يأمن شرّه. وقال آخر لا ضرر أعظم من استخبار من لا يصدق إذا خبّر ولا أشدّ من استكفاء من لا ينصح إذا دبّر.

٣،٣،١ وقال بعض الحكماء المسلمين أربعة لا تنتصف من أربعة: شريف مِن دنيّ ورشيد[2] من غويّ وبرّ من فاجر ومنصف من جائر فالمسلم شريف والكافر دنيّ والمسلم رشيد[3] والكافر غويّ والمسلم برّ والكافر فاجر والمسلم منصف والكافر جائر. وقال آخر في المسلم أربع خصال لا توجد في غيره: حسن العفاف وكثرة الإنصاف والرقّة على أهل الدين وإنصاف المسلمين. وفي المشرك أربع خصال: قلّة الديانة وكثرة الخيانة وغشّ المسلمين وإبعاد أهل الدين.

الفصل الرابع فيما ورد عن الإمام أبي بكر الصدّيق رضي الله عنه في ذلك

١،٤،١ قلت وقد جاء عن الإمام أبي بكر رضي الله عنه أنّه خطب الناس فقال معاشر المسلمين رحمكم الله بلغني رجوع قوم من المشركين عن دين الإسلام بعد دخولهم فيه واستعمالهم في مصالحه اغترارًا بالله وجهلًا به وطاعةً للشيطان واقتداءً به. وقد

---

١ كذا في ت؛ وفي ج،د زيادة: بل ذلك ممّا يعزّ توقيه ويفوت تداركه وتلافيه. ٢ كذا في د؛ وفي ت: سيّد. ٣ كذا في د؛ وفي ت: سيّد.

his future endangered, and his deeds imperiled." A Muslim authority has said, "How astonishing it is that a believer should employ an infidel who disagrees with his views and opposes him in his religion and creed." Another has said, "How utterly astonishing that a man should discard a believing friend who is intelligent and capable while placing boundless confidence in an infidel enemy who is ignorant." Another has said, "Do not choose to raise up someone who disagrees with you in religion, and do not employ someone who is devoid of conviction." A certain authority has said, "He who relies upon men skilled in wickedness will not lack for unsound advice." Another has said, "No one astounds me more than a person who relies upon an enemy from whom no good can be hoped and no evil prevented." Another has said, "There is no harm greater than accepting the testimony of someone who bears false witness, or more dire than trusting someone who means no good in what he devises."[11]

A certain Muslim authority has said, "There are four kinds of people who 1.3.3
get no justice from four others: a noble person from a lowly one; a rightly guided person from an erring one; a righteous person from a sinner; a fair person from a tyrant." Observe that the Muslim is noble, the infidel lowly; the Muslim is rightly guided, the infidel errant; the Muslim is righteous, the infidel a sinner; the Muslim is fair, the infidel a tyrant. Another has said, "The Muslim has four traits that exist in no one else: proper integrity, abundant fairness, graciousness toward pious people, and fairness toward Muslims. The unbeliever, too, has four traits: scant devotion to religion, abundant perfidy, guile toward Muslims, and ill-treatment of pious people."

The Fourth Section: The Example of Imam Abū Bakr al-Ṣiddīq, God Be Pleased with Him

I would cite here the report about Imam Abū Bakr, God be pleased with 1.4.1
him, who addressed the people, saying, "All you Muslims! God have mercy on you! Word reached me that a group of polytheists, who had entered Islam and secured employment in its administration, had gone back to their old religion. In their ignorance of God they imagined that He was heedless of what they had done when they obeyed the Devil and followed after him. Therefore I dispatched Khālid ibn al-Walīd and commanded him to fight them. He did so, and forbad their employment in the Muslims' administration. For I do not

بعثت خالد بن الوليد وأمرته بقتالهم فقاتلهم ومنع من استعمالهم في مصالح المسلمين فلا أرى استعمال مشرك في أمور المسلمين ومصالحهم.

الفصل الخامس فيما ورد عن الإمام عمر بن الخطّاب رضي الله عنه في ذلك

١،٥،١ قلت ولمّا قدم على عمر بن الخطّاب رضي الله عنه بعض المهاجرين بمال من البحرين رقي المنبر فحمد الله وأثنى عليه وصلّى على محمّد نبيّه صلّى الله عليه وسلّم ثمّ قال معاشر المسلمين رحمكم الله قد جاءنا مال كثير فإن شئتم كلنا كيلاً وإن شئتم وزنّا وزنًا وإن شئتم عددنا عدّاً فقام إليه رجل وقال يا أمير المؤمنين قد رأينا الأعاجم يدوّنون دواوين فأمر عمر بوضع الدواوين في الأعمال وكتب إلى عمّاله أن لا يستخدموا كافرًا يهوديًا كان أو نصرانيًا.

٢،٥،١ وكتب أبو موسى الأشعريّ إلى عمر بن الخطّاب رضي الله عنه في سنة سبع عشرة من الهجرة إنّ المال قد كثر وليس يحصيه إلّا الأعاجم يشير إلى الذمّة فإنّهم كانوا ضربوا على أهل البلاد التي فتحوها الجزية وسأله أن يكتب إليه بما يرى فكتب إليه عمر لا تُدخِل هذا الأمر في دينكم ولا تسلّموا إلى أعدائكم فيه ما منعهم الله عنه ولا تأمنوهم على أموالكم وتعلّموا الكتابة فإنّما هي حلية الرجال.[١] والمعنى الذي ذهب إليه عمر رضي الله عنه أنّ كلّ فضيلة يضع المسلمين أيديهم فيها يتقنونها ويجمعون فنونها ويظهرون مكنونها فالفضائل بهم حسنت ومنهم استحسنت وعنهم أُخذت وفيهم وُجدت وإذا كان الأمر بهذه المثابة فلا حاجة إلى غير المسلمين في شغل من الأشغال لا سيّما في أجلّ الصنائع وأشرف المراتب وهي الكتابة.

٣،٥،١ وعمر بن الخطّاب رضي الله عنه هو الذي أرّخ بالهجرة فإنّه سئل بِمَ تؤرّخ؟ وكانت العرب تؤرّخ بعام الفيل فقال عمر رضي الله عنه أرّخوا بالهجرة فإنّها فرق بين

---

١ في سائر المخطوطات: تعلّموا فإنّما هي الرجال؛ والزيادة من الأحكام، ١:٢١١.

approve of the employment of a polytheist in the administrative affairs of the Muslims."[12]

The Fifth Section: The Example of Imam ʿUmar ibn al-Khaṭṭāb

Here I would tell how when one of the Emigrants came before ʿUmar ibn 1.5.1
al-Khaṭṭāb, God be pleased with him, with wealth from al-Baḥrayn, the caliph ascended the pulpit. He praised and extolled God, asked his blessing upon Muḥammad his Prophet, God bless and keep him, and said, "All you Muslims! God have mercy on you! A great sum has come to us. If you wish, we shall measure it out by volume, or by weight if you prefer that, or we could count it out." Then a man stood up and said, "Commander of the Believers, we have observed that the Persian foreigners make records in registers." Upon hearing this, ʿUmar commanded that registers be made for the various administrative regions. He also wrote to his agents not to employ any infidel, whether Jew or Christian.[13]

Abū Mūsā al-Ashʿarī wrote the following lines to ʿUmar ibn al-Khaṭṭāb, God 1.5.2
be pleased with him, in the year 17 of the Emigration [ca. AD 638]: "Our tax receipts have increased mightily, and no one is able to count them but the Persian foreigners." By this last phrase he meant the dhimmis, for the Muslims would impose the poll tax upon the people in the lands they conquered. Abū Mūsā asked ʿUmar for his view on the matter. ʿUmar wrote to him, "Do not embroil your religion in this affair, and do not hand over to your enemies in religion that which God has forbidden them. Do not entrust your property to them, but instead learn to write, for writing is the glory of men."[14] ʿUmar's central message here, God be pleased with him, is that Muslims should apply themselves to every virtuous pursuit, master it, gather its disparate arts, and make manifest its hidden secrets. For all virtues are most properly expressed and most commendable in Muslims; it is from Muslims that they should be derived and among them that they should be found. This being the case, there is no need whatsoever for non-Muslims in any task, particularly in that loftiest of crafts and noblest of ranks: the secretarial art.

It was in fact ʿUmar ibn al-Khaṭṭāb, God be pleased with him, who began 1.5.3
the practice of dating according to the Calendar of the Emigration. Someone asked him, "How should we calculate dates?" At that time, the Arabs calculated

الحقّ والباطل فقالوا بِمَ نبدأ من الشهور؟ فقال بعض الحاضرين بشهر رمضان فإنّه أُنزل فيه القرآن فقال عمر لا بل بالمحرّم فإنّه منصرف الناس من حجّهم.

٤،٥،١ وكتب عمر إلى عمّاله أمّا بعد فإنّه من كان قبله كاتب من المشركين فلا يعاشره ولا يوازره ولا يقرّبه ولا يأتمنه ولا يعتضد برأيه ولا يجالسه ولا يستعمله فإنّ رسول الله صلّى الله عليه وسلّم لم يأمر باستعمال المشركين ولا أذن فيه ولا خليفته من بعده. وهذا كتابي آمر بما أمر به رسول الله صلّى الله عليه وسلّم ناهٍ عمّا نهى عنه فلينته إليّ ما رسم فيه وليحذر من تجاوزه وتعدّيه.

٥،٥،١ وكتب معاوية بن أبي سفيان إلى عمر رضي الله عنه بما نسخته أمّا بعد يا أمير المؤمنين فإنّ في عملي كاتباً نصرانياً لا يتمّ أمر الخراج إلّا به وكرهت أن أستخدمه دون أمرك. فكتب إليه عمر رضي الله عنه عافانا الله وإيّاك قرأت كتابك في أمر النصرانيّ والجواب أمّا بعد فإنّ النصرانيّ قد مات والسلام.

٦،٥،١ ودخل عليه أبو موسى الأشعريّ وهو في مسجد رسول الله صلّى الله عليه وسلّم فسلّم وجلس ثمّ قال ائذن لكاتبي يا أمير المؤمنين. فقال وما منعه من الدخول معك أجنب هو؟ فقال إنّه نصرانيّ فتغيّر وجه عمر وقال أتتّخذ على المسلمين كاتباً ذمّيّاً يستحلّ دماءهم وأموالهم هل لا اتّخذت حنيفاً مسلماً يأمر بالعدل والإحسان؟ فقال لي كتابته وعليه[١] وزره فقال عمر يجب عليك أن لا تقرّبه إذ أبعده الله ولا تعزّه إذ اذلّه الله ولا تكرّمه إذ أهانه الله ولا تحبّه إذ أبغضه الله عملاً بقول الله سبحانه ﴿وَمَنْ يُهِنِ اللَّهُ فَمَا لَهُ مِنْ مُكْرِمٍ﴾.

١ كذا في ت؛ وفي د: عليّ.

from the Year of the Elephant [ca. 570]. ʿUmar, God be pleased with him, said, "Calculate from the Emigration, for it is the divide between Truth and Falsehood." Those present asked, "With what month should we begin?" One of the people said, "With the month of Ramadan, in which the Qur'an was revealed." But ʿUmar said, "Nay, rather with the month of Muharram, for it is the month in which the people return from their Pilgrimage."[15]

ʿUmar wrote to his agents, "If anyone has a secretary who is an unbeliever, let him not empower him, include him, trust him, have recourse to his opinion, sit with him, or indeed employ him at all. For the Messenger of God, God bless and keep him, did not command anyone to employ unbelievers; neither he nor his caliph after him gave anyone permission to do so. This is my edict, commanding what the Messenger of God, God bless and keep him, commanded, and forbidding what he forbad. Therefore let me be informed how he has instructed his subordinates in this matter, and let him beware lest they violate and transgress it."[16] 1.5.4

Muʿāwiyah ibn Abī Sufyān wrote the following letter to ʿUmar, God be pleased with him: "O Commander of the Believers, there is a Christian secretary in my district without whom we are unable to collect the land tax. Yet I have been loath to employ him without your command." ʿUmar, God be pleased with him, wrote to him, "God save us both! I have read your letter concerning the matter of the Christian. Here is the reply: Consider the Christian dead. Farewell."[17] 1.5.5

Abū Mūsā l-Ashʿarī came to ʿUmar in the Mosque of the Messenger of God, God bless and keep him, greeted him, and sat down. After sitting for a moment, he said, "Please permit my secretary to come in, Commander of the Believers." ʿUmar said, "What prevented him from coming in with you? Is he ritually impure?" "He is a Christian," Abū Mūsā replied. Then ʿUmar's expression changed and he said, "Do you appoint over the Muslims a dhimmi secretary, who deems it lawful for himself to spill Muslim blood and take Muslim property? Could you not have appointed a pious Muslim, one who commands justice and righteous deeds?" Abū Mūsā said, "His secretarial skills belong to me, but he is responsible for his own evil deeds."[18] ʿUmar replied, "You must not include him when God has excluded him, uphold him when God has humbled him, honor him when God has reviled him, or love him when God has declared his hatred for him. In this you must act according to what God, be He glorified, has said: «And whom God abases, there is none to honor him»."[19] 1.5.6

وكتب إلى أبي هريرة أمّا بعد فإنّ للناس نفرةً عن سلطانهم فأعوذ بالله أن تدركني ٧،٥،١
وإيّاك ثمّ أوصاه فقال في وصيّته[1] أبعد أهل الشرك وأنكر أفعالهم ولا تستعن في أمر من أمور المسلمين بمشرك. ولم ينقل أنّه استُعمل مشرك من المشركين في عمل من الأعمال زمنَ النبيّ صلّى الله عليه وسلّم ولا زمن أبي بكر ولا زمن عمر ولا زمن عثمان ولا زمن عليّ بن أبي طالب رضي الله عنهم أجمعين.

الفصل السادس فيما ورد عن عبد الملك بن مروان في ذلك

قلت وممّا جرى لبعض النصارى أنّ سرجون بن منصور النصرانيّ كان يتولّى لعبد ١،٦،١
الملك بن مروان ديوان ماله[2] فأمره بأمر فخان[3] فيه فبلغ عبد الملك ذلك وعظم عليه. وقال ذلك لأبي ثابت سليمان بن قضاعة وكان يتولّى ديوان الرسائل والخاتم فقال له إن أراد أمير المؤمنين رجلاً فاضلاً مسلماً فعليه بمحمّد بن يزيد الأنصاريّ.

واتّفق أن عرضت وهما يتخاطبان في ذلك رقعة وفيها شعر وهو [البسيط]

بَنِي أُمَيَّةَ كُفُّوا أَلْسُنَ ٱلْغَلَفَا   كَذَاكَ سَنَّ رَسُولُ ٱللهِ وَٱلْخُلَفَا
لَا تَرْضَوا ٱلرُّومَ كُتَّاباً لِدَوْلَتِكُمْ   فَإِنَّ فِي ذٰلِكَ ٱلْعُدْوَانَ وَٱلْجَنَفَا
فَأَنْتُمُ لِلْهُدَى نُورٌ يُضِيءُ بِهِ   بِكُمْ عَلَى نَهْجِهِ يَجْرِي إِذَا وَقَفَا

فأمر بصرف النصرانيّ المذكور للوقت وولّى محمّد بن يزيد الأنصاريّ. وكانت دواوين الشام يُكتب فيها بالروميّ فنقله إلى العربيّ ومن ذلك الوقت استُخدم المسلمون عوضاً عن النصارى وذلك في سنة ثمانٍ وسبعين للهجرة.

---

١ يبدأ نصّ مخطوطة ب من هاهنا. ٢ كذا في ت؛ وفي ب،د: الشام. ٣ كذا في ت؛ وفي ب:فخاف؛ ج: حاف على الناس؛د:فخالف.

'Umar also wrote to Abū Hurayrah, "The people have an aversion to their rulers. I beseech God lest it be directed at us." Continuing, he offered him wise counsel in the following words: "Exclude the polytheists, condemn their deeds, and seek not the aid of an unbeliever in any of the Muslims' affairs." 1.5.7

In conclusion, there is no indication in the sources that any unbeliever was hired for any job in the time of the Prophet, God bless and keep him, or that of Abū Bakr, or that of 'Umar, or that of 'Uthmān, or that of 'Alī ibn Abī Ṭālib, God be pleased with all of them.[20]

The Sixth Section: The Example of 'Abd al-Malik ibn Marwān

Here I would tell of what befell a certain Christian. Sarjūn ibn Manṣūr the Christian had charge of the financial office of 'Abd al-Malik ibn Marwān. The caliph gave him a command, but he carried it out in a dishonest manner. When news of this reached 'Abd al-Malik, he was deeply troubled. He confided this to Abū Thābit Sulaymān ibn Quḍā'ah, who had charge of the offices of the chancery and the seal. Abū Thābit said to him, "If the Commander of the Believers seeks a virtuous Muslim, then the man for the job is Muḥammad ibn Yazīd al-Anṣārī." 1.6.1

At the very moment they were engaged in this discussion, it so happened that a petition arrived on which some poetry was written. This is what it said:

> Sons of Umayyah! Stop the tongues of these uncircumcised men,
> following the example of the Messenger of God and the caliphs.
> Favor not the Greeks as secretaries of your state,
> for it will only bring enmity and wrong.
> Your clan is a light unto Guidance itself, by which it casts light;
> by you alone it now runs upon its course.[21]

Then 'Abd al-Malik commanded the immediate dismissal of the Christian and appointed Muḥammad ibn Yazīd al-Anṣārī to replace him. In those days, Greek was used in the financial administration of Syria; al-Anṣārī, however, changed it over to Arabic. From that time forth, Muslims were employed instead of Christians. This was in the year 78 of the Emigration [697–98].[22]

الفصل السابع فيما جرى من الحجّاج في ذلك

١،٧،١ قلت ولمّا ولي الحجّاج بن يوسف العراق كان به ديوانان أحدهما بالعربيّ وهو الذي وضعه أمير المؤمنين عمر بن الخطّاب رضي الله عنه والآخر بالفارسيّة وكان متقلّده صالح بن عبد الرحمن فقال للحجّاج يوماً كثر همّي من قبل هؤلاء النصارى وإقدامهم وخياناتهم فإن أمرني الأمير وساعدني نقلت ديوان العراق إلى العربيّ واسترحت من جناية هؤلاء الكفرة وخياناتهم وتسويفهم وإقدامهم على ما يوجب قطع أيديهم بما يعتمدونه في وضعهم الحساب الذي وضعه الله للحقّ فوصلوا به إلى الباطل وحرّفوا أقلامهم فيه إلى أغراضهم ومقاصدهم. فساعده الحجّاج على ذلك فنقله وصرف النصارى ونقش سكّة الدنانير والدراهم بالعربيّ وكان منقوشاً على الدنانير بالروميّ وعلى الدراهم بالفارسيّ.

٢،٧،١ ولو أخذت أعدّ مثالب المذكورين لضاق العمر عن بعض الواقع واتّسع الخرق على الراقع وأين هؤلاء السفلة الأراذل الأسقاط المذكورون في هذا الباب من السادة المتقدّمين من الوزراء والكتّاب الذين لو أخذت أصف كلّ واحد منهم بكلمة من محاسنه خرج الكتاب عن القصد فيه وأفنيتُ العام وما يليه.

الفصل الثامن فيما ورد عن عمر بن عبد العزيز رضي الله عنه في ذلك

١،٨،١ قلت وكتب عمر بن عبد العزيز رضي الله عنه إلى عمّاله في الآفاق أمّا بعد فإنّ عمر يقرأ عليكم السلام ويقرأ عليكم كتاب الله المبين ﴿يَا أَيُّهَا الَّذِينَ آمَنُوا إِنَّمَا الْمُشْرِكُونَ نَجَسٌ﴾ جعلهم الله ﴿حِزْبَ الشَّيْطَانِ﴾ وجعلهم الأخسرين ﴿أَعْمَالاً الَّذِينَ ضَلَّ سَعْيُهُمْ فِي الْحَيَاةِ الدُّنْيَا وَهُمْ يَحْسَبُونَ أَنَّهُمْ يُحْسِنُونَ صُنْعاً﴾ أولئك ﴿عَلَيْهِمْ لَعْنَةَ

The Seventh Section: The Deeds of al-Ḥajjāj

When al-Ḥajjāj ibn Yūsuf took charge in Iraq, there were two offices there. 1.7.1
One was in Arabic—this was the one that had been established by the Commander of the Believers ʿUmar ibn al-Khaṭṭāb, God be pleased with him—and the other was in Persian. The official in charge of the Persian office was Ṣāliḥ ibn ʿAbd al-Raḥmān. One day he said to al-Ḥajjāj, "I am growing worried about these Christians, with all their shameless malfeasance. If the emir were to give me a mandate and assist me, I would change over the administrative records of Iraq to Arabic. This would relieve me of the crimes of these infidels, of their malfeasance, their procrastination, and their effrontery. They even dare to commit acts for which their hands ought to be severed.[23] They sanction the falsification of arithmetic itself, which God established for the sake of truth. Far from seeking truth, they employ their devious pens to make arithmetic serve their own goals and devices." Al-Ḥajjāj gave him the support that he had requested and he changed the records to Arabic, dismissed the Christians, and engraved the dies for striking gold and silver coins in Arabic. The gold coins had previously been engraved in Greek, and the silver coins in Persian.[24]

If I undertook to enumerate the faults of these people, a lifetime would not 1.7.2
suffice to convey even a portion of them. The hole would be too wide for the mender to patch.[25] How can one even begin to compare the base and wicked refuse discussed in this chapter to our lordly forebears among the viziers and secretaries? Yet if I undertook to describe the merits of these latter men, devoting but a word to each one of them, the book would depart from its purpose and I would have squandered the whole year, and the next one as well.

The Eighth Section: The Example of ʿUmar ibn ʿAbd al-ʿAzīz, God Be Pleased with Him

I would tell here how ʿUmar ibn ʿAbd al-ʿAzīz, God be pleased with him, wrote 1.8.1
the following letter to his agents in every part of the empire: "ʿUmar recites to you greetings, and recites to you the Clear Book of God: «O believers, the idolaters are indeed unclean.»[26] God has made them «Satan's Party»[27] and «the greatest losers in their works: those whose striving goes astray in the present life, while they think that they are working good deeds.»[28] These are the ones of whom He said, «there shall rest on them the curse of God and of the angels and of men.»[29] Know that the reason that those who preceded you

اللَّهِ وَٱلْمَلَائِكَةِ وَٱلنَّاسِ أَجْمَعِينَ﴾ واعلموا أنّه لم يهلك من قبلكم إلّا بمنعه الحقّ وبسطه يد الظلم وقد بلغني عن قوم من المسلمين فيما مضى إذا قدموا إلى بلد أتاهم أهل الشرك فاستعانوا بهم في أعمالهم وكتابتهم لعلمهم بالكتابة والجباية وتدبير المعيشة ولا خيرة ولا تدبير فيما يغضب الله ورسوله وقد كانت مدّة قضاها الله تعالى ولا يعلمنّ أمير المؤمنين أحداً من العمّال أبقى في عمله رجلاً متصرّفاً على غير دين الإسلام إلّا نكّل به فإنّ محو أعمالهم كمحو دينهم وإنزالهم منزلتهم التي خصّهم الله بها من الذلّ والصغار وليكتب إليّ كلّ منكم[1] بما فعله في عمله.

٢،٨،١ وأمر أن يمنع النصارى واليهود من الركوب على السروج ولا يمكّن أحد من الذمّة من دخول الحمّام يوم الجمعة إلّا بعد انقضاء الصلاة ويقدّم إلى الحرس بأن يقفوا على رؤوس النصارى واليهود عند ذبيحة ما يذبحونه وأن يذكر اسم الله واسم محمّد صلّى الله عليه وسلّم عليها. وكتب إلى حيّان عامله على مصر باعتماد ذلك فكتب إليه أمّا بعد يا أمير المؤمنين فإنّه إن دام هذا الأمر في مصر أسلمت الذمّة وبطل ما يؤخذ منهم. فأرسل إليه رسولاً جلداً وقال له ائت مصر فاضرب حيّان على رأسه ثلاثين سوطاً أدباً على قوله وقل له ويلك يا حيّان من دخل دين الإسلام ضع عنه الجزية فوددت لو أسلموا كافّةً إنّ الله بعث محمّداً داعياً لا جابياً.

٣،٨،١ وأمر بهدم بيع النصارى المستجدّة فقيل إنّ القبط توصّلوا إلى بعض ملوك الروم وسألوه في مكاتبة عمر بن عبد العزيز فكتب إليه أمّا بعد يا عمر فإنّ هؤلاء الشعب سألوا في مكاتبتك لتجري أمورهم على ما وجدتها عليه وأن تُبقي كنائسهم وتمكّنهم من عمارة ما خرب منها فإنّهم يزعمون أنّ من تقدّمك فعل في أمر كنائسهم ما منعتهم منه فإن يكن المصيب في اجتهاده فاسلك سنّته وإن تكن[2] مخالفاً له فافعل ما أردت. فكتب إليه مثلي ومثل من تقدّمني كمثل ما قال الله عزّ وجلّ

---

١ كذا في ب،د؛ وفي ت: مسلم. ٢ كذا في ت؛ وفي ب،د: يكن.

perished was that they obstructed truth and extended the hand of oppression. I have learnt of certain Muslims in the past who, when they came to a region, would be approached by unbelievers. The Muslims had recourse to these people for their administrative and secretarial needs because of their knowledge of the secretarial art, of taxation, and of how to put in order the means of subsistence.[30] There can be neither good nor order, however, in a thing that angers God and his Messenger. That was a limited span of time, to which God, be He exalted, has now put an end. Therefore if the Commander of the Believers should learn that any of his agents anywhere has kept a man in a position of authority who does not belong to the religion of Islam, he shall chastise him severely. To efface their jobs is to efface their religion. It is to lower them to that station of humiliation and ignominy that God designated for them. Therefore let each one of you write to me concerning what he has done in his district."

'Umar ibn 'Abd al-'Azīz commanded that the Christians and Jews be forbidden to ride using saddles. No dhimmi was to be allowed to enter the public baths on Friday until after the prayer had ended. The authorities were to be informed to supervise the Christians and Jews closely when they slaughtered any animal in order to make sure that the name of God and that of Muḥammad, God bless and keep him, was uttered over it. 1.8.2

'Umar wrote to Ḥayyān, his financial administrator in Egypt, concerning this plan. Ḥayyān wrote to him, "O Commander of the Believers, if this continues in Egypt then all of the dhimmis will convert and we shall lose their tax payments." At this 'Umar dispatched a tough and menacing messenger and instructed him, saying, "Go to Egypt and strike Ḥayyān thirty lashes upon his head to chastise him for what he has said. Say to him, 'Woe to you, Ḥayyān! Lift the poll tax from anyone who enters the religion of Islam. Would that all of them would convert! God sent Muḥammad to call people to Islam, not to collect their taxes.'"[31]

'Umar commanded that the Christians' recently built churches be razed. It is said that the Copts then made contact with the king of the Greeks[32] and asked him to write to 'Umar ibn 'Abd al-'Azīz concerning this matter. The king wrote to him as follows: "O 'Umar, these people have asked that I write to you so that you might permit their affairs to continue in the condition that you found them. They also ask that you let their churches stand and that you allow them to repair those that have fallen into ruin. For they claim that your predecessor treated their churches in just the way that you forbid them to do. If you consider your predecessor to have been correct in his judgment, then follow 1.8.3

﴿وَدَاوُودَ وَسُلَيْمَانَ إِذْ يَحْكُمَانِ فِي الْحَرْثِ إِذْ نَفَشَتْ فِيهِ غَنَمُ الْقَوْمِ وَكُنَّا لِحُكْمِهِمْ شَاهِدِينَ فَفَهَّمْنَاهَا سُلَيْمَانَ ۚ وَكُلًّا آتَيْنَا حُكْمًا وَعِلْمًا﴾.

٤،٨،١ وقال أُسَيد أتانا كتاب عمر بن عبد العزيز إلى محمّد بن المنتشر[١] أمّا بعد فإنّه بلغني أنّ في عملك كاتباً نصرانياً يتصرّف في مصالح المسلمين على غير دين الإسلام والله تعالى يقول ﴿يَا أَيُّهَا الَّذِينَ آمَنُوا لَا تَتَّخِذُوا الَّذِينَ اتَّخَذُوا دِينَكُمْ هُزُوًا وَلَعِبًا مِنَ الَّذِينَ أُوتُوا الْكِتَابَ مِنْ قَبْلِكُمْ وَالْكُفَّارَ أَوْلِيَاءَ ۚ وَاتَّقُوا اللَّهَ إِنْ كُنْتُمْ مُؤْمِنِينَ﴾ فإذا أتاك كتابي هذا فادع حسّان بن يزيد إلى دين الإسلام فإن أسلم وإلّا فلا تستعمله في شيء من مصالح المسلمين. فامتثل وأسلم حسّان بن يزيد وحسن إسلامه.

الفصل التاسع فيما جرى أيّام الخليفة المنصور في ذلك

١،٩،١ قيل انتبه المنصور يوماً مرعوباً من مضجعه فأحضر الربيع وقال اذهب إلى باب الشام فإنّك ترى رجلاً فائتني به قال الربيع فخرجت أعدو حتّى وصلت إلى الموضع الذي ذكر لي فإذا الرجل قائم مستند إلى الباب فقلت أجب أمير المؤمنين قال نعم فأتيت به إلى المنصور وإذا هو جالس ينتظرني فلمّا بصر بي قال هذا هو؟ قلت نعم فقال ما ظلامتك قال يا أمير المؤمنين إنّ بالأنبار كاتباً نصرانياً غصبني ضيعة وسألني بيعها فامتنعت فسعى بي إليك وكتب أنّ الضيعة المذكورة من جملة ضياع بني أميّة المرتجعة لأمير المؤمنين وأقسم بأيمانه الكاذبة لئن رجعت تذكر الضيعة لأسعينّ في دمك كما سعيت في ضيعتك فقلت أيها الرجل أتأخذ ضيعتي على اسم أمير المؤمنين وتأمر

[١] في سائر المخطوطات: المبشر، والمثبت من الأحكام، ١:٢١٤.

his precedent. If, however, you would contradict that judgment, then you may as well simply do whatever you see fit." ʿUmar wrote to him, "I and my predecessor are like the two judges of whom God, mighty and sublime, spoke in his word: «And Dāwūd and Sulaymān, when they gave judgment concerning the tillage, when the sheep of the people strayed there, and We bore witness to their judgment; and We made Sulaymān to understand it, and unto each gave We judgment and knowledge.»"[33]

Usayd said, "A report reached us concerning the letter of ʿUmar ibn ʿAbd al-ʿAzīz to Muḥammad ibn al-Muntashir, as follows: 'I have learnt that you employ a Christian secretary who wields authority in the Muslims' administration in a manner that does not accord with Islam. But God, be He exalted, has said, «O believers, take not as your friends those of them who were given the Book before you, and the unbelievers, who take your religion in mockery and as a sport, and fear God, if you are believers.»[34] When this letter reaches you, summon Ḥassān ibn Yazīd to Islam. He may convert, but if not, then do not employ him in any part of the Muslims' administration.' Muḥammad ibn al-Muntashir obeyed him, and Ḥassān ibn Yazīd made a sincere conversion."[35] 1.8.4

The Ninth Section: The Events That Took Place in the Days of Caliph al-Manṣūr

It is said that one night al-Manṣūr awoke from his bed in a terror. Immediately he summoned al-Rabīʿ and said to him, "Go to the Damascus Gate, where you will see a man whom you must bring to me." 1.9.1

Al-Rabīʿ reported, "I set out running until I reached the place that he had told me. There was the man, leaning up against the gate. Addressing him, I said, 'Obey the summons of the Commander of the Believers!' He consented, so I brought him to al-Manṣūr, who was sitting up waiting for me. When his gaze fell upon me he asked, 'Is this the man?' 'It is,' I said. He turned to the man and said, 'What is the injustice that you wish to report?' The man replied, 'Commander of the Believers, there is a Christian secretary in al-Anbār who deprived me of an estate. He first demanded that I sell it, then when I refused he wrote something false and damaging to you about me. It was a report saying that my estate was one of the ones that had belonged formerly to the Umayyads, and which have since been recovered for the Commander of the Believers. He also swore, with those false oaths of his, and said, "If you mention the estate again,

بحبسي ثمّ تهدّدني بالقتل فقال له المنصور ما الذي قلت وأنت قائم على باب المدينة قال قلت قلت اللّٰهمّ إنّك حليم ذو أناة فلا صبر لي على أناتك فقال المنصور بها والله أقلقتني من مضجعي يا ربيع اكتب بإشخاص هذا النصرانيّ وخذ بضيعة هذا المظلوم منه وسلّمها إليه. وكان المنصور قد أمر بأن يقبض كلّما خلّفه بنو أميّة فصار الكلب النصرانيّ يتعرّض إلى أملاك الناس المطلقة وضياعهم التي ما ملكها أحد من بني أميّة قطّ فمن صانعه تركه وخلّى سبيله ومن لم يصانعه أهانه وضربه على ملكه وماله وقال هذا كلّه لبني أميّة ورفع منه في حسابهم ما أراد.

٢،٩،١ فلمّا حجّ المنصور اجتمع الناس إلى باب شبيب بن شيبة وسألوه أن يسأل المنصور النظر في حالهم ورفع المظالم عنهم وأن لا يمكّن النصارى من ظلمهم. قال شبيب فبينما أنا أطوف بالكعبة وإذا المنصور يطوف خلفي فلمّا رآني شبك أصابعه على أصابعي وطفنا جميعاً فقلت يا أمير المؤمنين أتأذن لي أن أكلّمك بما في نفسي فقال قل ما شئت فقلت له موعظة قلت في آخرها إنّ دون أبوابك نيرانًا تتأجّج من الظلم والجور ولا يُعمل فيها بكتاب الله ولا سنّة رسول الله صلّى الله عليه وسلّم واعلم أنّك سلّطت أهل الذمّة أعداء الدين على المسلمين فظلموهم وعسّفوهم وأخذوا ضياعهم وغصبوهم أموالهم وجاروا عليهم وتوصّلوا بسبب خدمتك إلى أغراضهم من المسلمين لعداوتهم لهم الشاهد بها القرآن وقد جعلوك سلّماً يرقون عليه إلى نيل شهواتهم فإنّهم لن يغنوا عنك من الله شيئاً ﴿يَوْمَ لَا يَنْفَعُ الظَّالِمِينَ مَعْذِرَتُهُمْ ۖ وَلَهُمُ اللَّعْنَةُ وَلَهُمْ سُوءُ الدَّارِ﴾ فقال المنصور يا شبيب خذ خاتمي وابعث به إلى من تعرفه من المسلمين ينادي في الناس كافةً وعامّةً ألا من ظلمه ذمّيّ فليمسك بتلابيبه وليُحضره إليّ لأنصفه منه ثمّ قال يا ربيع اكتب إلى الأعمال كلّها واصرف من بها من

I shall carry out a plan against your life, just as I did against your estate." I said, "Would you, man, really take my estate in the name of the Commander of the Believers and command that I be imprisoned, then threaten me with death?"'

"Then al-Manṣūr said to him, 'What did you say when you were standing at the gate of the city?' He said, 'I said, "O God, indeed You are Forbearing and Patient. But I have not the endurance for your patience."' Al-Manṣūr said, 'In speaking thus you disturbed me from my bed. Rabīʿ, write a command that this Christian be presented before me. Take the estate of this oppressed man from the Christian and give it back to him.'

"Al-Manṣūr had commanded that all the property the Umayyads had left behind them be seized. This Christian dog took this opportunity to meddle with private property and estates that none of the Umayyads had in fact owned. Whoever bribed him would be left alone and allowed to go on his way, but he would revile and beat anyone who refused, so that he might obtain his property and estate, saying, 'All this belonged to the Umayyads.' This is the way he would register to the Umayyads' account the things that he desired."

When al-Manṣūr went on the pilgrimage to Mecca, people gathered at the door of Shabīb ibn Shaybah. They asked him to petition al-Manṣūr to look into their situation and relieve the injustice they had suffered, and to prevent the Christians from oppressing them. Shabīb said, "I was circumambulating the Kaaba, and there behind me was al-Manṣūr. When he saw me, he clasped his fingers in mine and we continued around together. I said, 'Commander of the Believers, will you permit me to tell you what is in my heart?' 'Say what you wish,' he replied. So I delivered an admonition, at the end of which I said, 'Outside your gates, flames are blazing from tyranny and oppression. There the Book of God and the Example of the Messenger of God, God bless and keep him, are not being followed. Know well that you have given power over Muslims to the dhimmis, who are enemies of the true religion. They have oppressed them, overburdened them, taken their estates, illegally seized their property, and tyrannized them. Because they serve you, they have been able to get what they want from the Muslims in their enmity toward them, to which the Qur'an testifies. They have made you into a ladder that they climb to attain their desires. But they will be of no use to you before God «on the day when their excuses shall not profit the evildoers, and theirs shall be the curse, and theirs the evil abode.»'[36] Then al-Manṣūr said, 'Shabīb, take my seal and send to Muslims whom you know, instructing them to proclaim abroad 1.9.2

أهل الذمّة ومن أتاك به شبيب من المسلمين فأعلمنا بمكانه لنوقّع باستخدامه عوضاً عن الذمّة وذلك في سنة ثمانٍ وخمسين ومائة.[1]

الفصل العاشر فيما جرى في ذلك أيّام الخليفة المهديّ

وذلك أنّه اجتمع جماعة كثيرون من المسلمين أيّام المهديّ إلى بعض الزهّاد وسألوه ١،١٠،١
الحديث معه في أمرهم وأنّهم ما بين مظلوم في نفسه ومظلوم في ماله فالمظلوم في نفسه من يصرف ويستبدل عنه في الشغل الذي كان فيه النصرانيّ أو اليهوديّ والمظلوم في ماله من يستضعف فيغصب ماله. وكانت للزاهد عادة أنّه يحضر إلى الخليفة في وقت مخصوص على عادة أصحاب الزوايا فجاءت حجّاب الخليفة خلفه ليحضر على عادته فامتنع فلمّا بلغ المهديّ امتناعه من الحضور مشى إليه وسأله عن سبب تأخّره فقصّ عليه اجتماع طائفة كثيرة من المسلمين إلى بابه شاكين من ظلم الذمّة لهم وقبيح تصرّفهم فيهم وأنشده [الكامل]

بِأَبِي وَأُمِّي ضَاعَتِ ٱلْأَحْلَامُ   أَمْ ضَاعَتِ ٱلْأَذْهَانُ وَٱلْأَفْهَامُ
مَنْ صَدَّ عَنْ دِينِ ٱلنَّبِيِّ مُحَمَّدٍ   أَلَهُ بِأَمْرِ ٱلْمُسْلِمِينَ قِيَامُ
أَلَّا تَكُنْ أَسْيَافُهُمْ مَشْهُورَةً   فِينَا فَإِنَّ سُيُوفَهُمْ أَقْلَامُ

ثمّ قال يا أمير المؤمنين إنّك تحمّلت أمانة هذه الأمّة وقد عرضت ﴿الْأَمَانَةَ عَلَى السَّمَاوَاتِ وَالْأَرْضِ وَالْجِبَالِ فَأَبَيْنَ أَنْ يَحْمِلْنَهَا وَأَشْفَقْنَ مِنْهَا﴾ فتسلّم الأمانة التي خصّك الله بها للذمّة دون المسلمين وماذا يكون جوابك غداً بين يدي ﴿أَسْرَعُ الْحَاسِبِينَ﴾؟ فأمر من حينه بعزل كلّ كاتب نصرانيّ وكتب إلى العمّال

---

١ في سائر المخطوطات: ومائتين؛ وذلك خطأ لا محالة لأنّ المنصور توفّي سنة ١٥٨. وتوجد في ب،د زيادة: والله أعلم؛ و يأتي في هامش ت: صوابه ومائة.

among all the people, saying, "Verily, anyone who has been oppressed by a dhimmi should seize him by the collar and present him before me, that I may give him justice."' Then he said, 'Rabīʿ, write to all of the districts and dismiss the dhimmis there. For every Muslim whom Shabīb brings to you, inform us of his place of origin, that we may issue an edict to employ him there in place of the dhimmis.' That was in the year 158 [774–75]."[37]

The Tenth Section: The Events That Took Place in the Days of Caliph al-Mahdī

On one occasion in the days of al-Mahdī, a great crowd of Muslims gathered **1.10.1**
around a certain ascetic of their own religion, asking him to intervene with the caliph on their behalf. All of them, they said, were oppressed, in respect of either their persons or their property. Those who were oppressed in their persons had been dismissed and replaced in their work by a Christian or a Jew. Those who were oppressed in their property had been exploited and deprived of their possessions.

Now this ascetic, like certain others among the Sufi mystics, had a regular custom of visiting the caliph. One day the caliph's chamberlains came to escort the ascetic for his customary visit, but he declined to accompany them. When al-Mahdī heard of this he went out personally to see him and asked him the reason for his delay. The ascetic told him how the Muslims had thronged to his door, complaining that the dhimmis were oppressing and mistreating them. The ascetic recited the following poetry:

> By my mother and father! Has all discernment been lost,
> or all intellect and understanding?
> Does the one averse to the Prophet's religion
> deserve to rule over Muslims?
> Are not their swords still drawn among us?
> In truth, their swords are now pens.

Then he said, "Commander of the Believers, you have borne the trust of this community. That trust was «offered to the heavens and the earth and the mountains, but they refused to carry it and were afraid of it.».[38] Then you submitted that trust, for which God had singled you out, to dhimmis instead of Muslims. What will be your answer on the morrow before «the Swiftest of Reckoners»?"[39]

بالأقطار ألّا يستكتبوا أحداً من الذمّة وأن ينادى في كلّ عمل أنّ أمير المؤمنين أمر بأنّ كلّ من استكتب ذمّيّاً قطع رزقه وقطعت يده. فاستكتب شاهويه[1] كاتباً نصرانيّاً فقطعت يده في الحال.

٢،١٠،١ وكان للمهديّ قبل ذلك كاتب نصرانيّ على ضياع بعض جهاته بالبصرة فظلم الناس في معاملته لهم فتظلّم المظلومون إلى القاضي سوّار فحضر وكلاء النصرانيّ وحضرت بيّنة تشهد على النصرانيّ بظلم الناس وتعدّيه مناهج الحقّ وسبله فمضى النصرانيّ إلى المهديّ وأخذ كتابه إلى القاضي سوّار بالتثبّت في أمره فجاء النصرانيّ إلى البصرة ومعه الكتاب وجماعة من حمقى النصارى وركب وهم حوله وجاء إلى المسجد الذي فيه القاضي سوّار فوجده جالساً للحكم فدخل المسجد وتجاوز المكان الذي كان ينبغي له الوقوف عنده فمنعه الخدم فلم يعبأ بهم وسبّهم ودنا حتّى جلس عن يمين القاضي سوّار ثمّ دفع له الكتاب فوضعه بين يديه ولم يقرأه وقال له ألست نصرانيّاً فقال بلى أصلح الله القاضي فرفع رأسه وقال للخدم جرّوا برجله فسُحب إلى باب المسجد وعوقب على ذميم فعله تأديباً بليغاً. وحلف القاضي أنّ النصرانيّ[2] لا يبرح واقفاً في موقف الذلّ والهوان[3] حتّى يوفي المسلمين حقوقهم فامتثل. وبلغ ذلك المهديّ فكتب إلى القاضي سوّار يشكره على فعله وأمره أن يستخدم في شغله مسلماً عوضه.

الفصل الحادي عشر فيما جرى أيّام الخليفة هارون الرشيد

١،١١،١ قيل ولمّا ولّى هارون الرشيد الفضل بن يحيى بن خالد أعمال خراسان وولّى جعفر أخاه ديوان الخاتم وأمرهما بالنظر في المصالح المتعلّقة بالمسلمين عمّرا المساجد والجوامع

---

١ كذا في ب، د؛ وفي ت: شاويه. ٢ كذا في ت؛ وفي ب، د: أنّه. ٣ كذا في ت؛ والعبارة من (في) ساقطة في ب، ج، د.

Al-Mahdī immediately commanded that every Christian secretary be removed from his post. To his agents in all the regions he wrote, "Do not take any dhimmi as a secretary." He wrote also that it be proclaimed in every land that the Commander of the Believers had ordered that anyone who took a dhimmi as a secretary would have his hand cut off, as well as his pay. But a certain Shāhawayh took a Christian secretary, so his hand was cut off.[40]

Before all of this took place, al-Mahdī had employed a Christian secretary over some of his estates in Basra. He oppressed the people in his dealings with them, so they brought a protest before Judge Sawwār.[41] The Christian's representatives were brought before the judge, as was evidence testifying to the manner in which the Christian had oppressed the people and strayed from the ways and paths of just conduct. The Christian himself went to al-Mahdī and obtained a letter from him, addressed to Judge Sawwār, stating that the Christian should remain in his position. He then returned to Basra, bringing the letter and a crowd of foolish Christians who escorted him as he rode. When he arrived at the mosque where Judge Sawwār usually heard cases, he found the judge seated for this purpose. Entering the mosque, the Christian passed the place at which he was supposed to stop. The custodians there attempted to prevent him from going further, but, hurling insults at them, he proceeded until he stood at the right hand of Judge Sawwār. He produced the letter and offered it to the judge, who placed it in front of him without reading it. Then the judge asked him, "Are you not a Christian?" He replied, "I am, God prosper the judge." The judge raised his head and said to the custodians, "Drag him out by his leg." Immediately he was dragged to the door of the mosque and punished harshly for the deplorable thing he had done. The judge swore that the Christian would remain in humiliation and disgrace until he restored to the Muslims what they were owed. The Christian was compelled to obey him. 1.10.2

When news of these events reached al-Mahdī he wrote to Judge Sawwār, thanking him for what he had done and commanding him to employ a Muslim to oversee his estates in place of the Christian.[42]

The Eleventh Section: The Events That Took Place in the Days of Caliph Hārūn al-Rashīd

It is said that when Hārūn al-Rashīd appointed al-Faḍl ibn Yaḥyā ibn Khālid over the districts of Khurasan, and his brother Jaʿfar over the Office of the Seal, 1.11.1

والمرافق والصهاريج للسبيل وعملا المكاتب لأيتام المسلمين وأجريا لهم الأرزاق وصرف كلّ منهما الذمّة عن أشغال المسلمين ودواوينهم وخرّب الفضل معابدهم بخراسان وأمر ألّا يمكّنوا من بياض شيء ممّا بقي منها في البلاد كيلا يتشبّهوا بمساجد المسلمين.

الفصل الثاني عشر فيما جرى في ذلك أيّام الخليفة المأمون

قال عمر بن عبد الله الشيبانيّ استحضرني المأمون ولد الرشيد أيّام خلافته في ١،١٢،١
بعض الليالي ونحن بمصر وقد كثرت سعايات[١] النصارى وتظلّم منهم المسلمون فأمر بالكشف عنهم فوجد النصارى قد خانوا السلطان في المال وفاز به بعضهم دون بعض فقال لي المأمون يا عمر أتعرف من أين أصل هؤلاء القبط قلت هم بقيّة الفراعنة الذين كانوا بمصر وقد نهى أمير المؤمنين عمر بن الخطّاب عن استخدامهم في أمر من أمور المسلمين فقال صف لي كيف كان تناسلهم بمصر فقلت يا أمير المؤمنين لمّا أخذ الفرس الملك من أيدي الفراعنة قتلوا القبط فلم يبق منهم إلّا من اصطنعته يد الهرب واختفى بأَنْصِنا والأقصرين فتعلّموا أطبّاءً وكتّاباً فلمّا ملك الروم مُلك الفرس كان القبط سبب إخراج الفرس من ملكهم بسعيهم والمكاتبة عليهم ولم يزالوا في مملكة الفرس إلى أن ظهرت كلمة المسيح عيسى بن مريم عليه السلام. وفيهم يقول خالد بن صفوان [الكامل]

يا عَمْرُو[٢] قَد مَلَكَتْ يَمِينُكَ مِصْرَنَا ... وَمَلَكْتَ فِيهَا ٱلْعَدْلَ وَٱلْإِقْسَاطَا
فَاقْبُضْ[٣] بِسَيْفِكَ مَن تَعَدَّى طَوْرَهُ ... وَاجْعَلْ قُوتَ سُيُوفِكَ ٱلْأَقْبَاطَا

١ ت: شكايات؛ ب،د: شعابات؛ والمثبت يقتضيه السياق. ٢ كذا في ب، ج،د؛ وفي ت: عمر. ٣ كذا في ت؛ وفي ب، ج،د: فاقتل.

he commanded them to oversee all administrative matters pertaining to the Muslims. They built local and congregational mosques, structures for public benefit, and cisterns on the roads. They also established schools for Muslim orphans and provided them with stipends. Both of them dismissed dhimmis from the official posts and offices of the Muslims. Al-Faḍl pulled down their places of worship in Khurasan and commanded that they not be allowed to whitewash any of those that remained, so that these would not resemble the Muslims' mosques.[43]

The Twelfth Section: The Events That Took Place in the Days of Caliph al-Maʾmūn

ʿUmar[44] ibn ʿAbdallāh al-Shaybānī said, "One night when al-Maʾmūn the son of **1.12.1**
al-Rashīd was caliph, he called me into his presence. This was during our stay in Egypt. In those days, the Christians' schemes were multiplying and many Muslims were protesting their oppressive ways. Al-Maʾmūn had ordered an investigation, which found that the Christians had been unscrupulous with the authorities in their financial dealings. Some of them had amassed great wealth in this way. Al-Maʾmūn asked me, "Umar, what do you know about the origins of these Copts?' I said, 'They are the surviving descendants of the pharaohs who once ruled Egypt. The Commander of the Believers ʿUmar ibn al-Khaṭṭāb forbad their employment in any of the Muslims' affairs.' Al-Maʾmūn then said, 'Tell me the story of their progeny in Egypt.' I replied, 'O Commander of the Believers, when the Persians wrested the kingship from the hands of the pharaohs, they slaughtered the Copts. The only ones who survived were those who managed to flee. These disappeared into the regions of Ansinah and Luxor, where they studied to become doctors and secretaries.[45] When the Greeks conquered the Persian empire, the Persians were driven from their kingdom by reason of the Copts' scheming and covert conspiracies. The Copts remained under Persian rule until the appearance of Jesus, son of Mary, peace be upon him. Concerning them Khālid ibn Ṣafwān has said:

O ʿAmr,[46] your right hand possessed this Egypt of ours;
　there you have grasped justice and equity,
So stop with your sword whoever transgresses his limits,
　and make your sword to win its triumphs among the Copts.

فَهِمْ أُقِيمَ ٱلْجَوْرُ فِي جَنَبَاتِهَا وَرَأَى ٱلْأَنَامُ ٱلْبَغْيَ وَٱلْإِفْرَاطَا
لَا تَرْكَنَنَّ إِلَى ٱلنَّصَارَى إِنَّهُمْ شَعَبٌ عَلَى دِينِ ٱلْإِلٰهِ تَعَاطَا[1]
وَٱذْكُرْ أَمِيرَ ٱلْمُؤْمِنِينَ وَقَوْلَهُ إِنْ كُنْتَ فِي طَاعَاتِهِ مُحْتَاطَا
لَا تَحْفَظَنَّ لِمُشْرِكٍ عَهْدًا وَلَا تَرْعَى لَهُ ذِمَمًا وَلَا إِخْلَاطَا

٢،١٢،١ فبقي في نفس المأمون منهم حزازات فلمّا عاد إلى مقرّ ملكه ومحلّ خلافته أساؤوا على الكسائيّ الاعتماد وجاهروه بالظلم والبغي والفساد فاتّفق أن قرأ عليه المأمون قوله تعالى ﴿يَا أَيُّهَا الَّذِينَ آمَنُوا لَا تَتَّخِذُوا الْيَهُودَ وَالنَّصَارَىٰ أَوْلِيَاءَ ۘ بَعْضُهُمْ أَوْلِيَاءُ بَعْضٍ ۚ وَمَن يَتَوَلَّهُم مِّنكُمْ فَإِنَّهُ مِنْهُمْ ۗ إِنَّ اللَّهَ لَا يَهْدِي الْقَوْمَ الظَّالِمِينَ﴾ وقال الكسائيّ أيقرأ أمير المؤمنين كتاب الله ولا يعمل بما فيه قال ولِمَ فقصّ عليه قصّته فأمر المأمون بإحصائهم فكان عدّة من صرف منهم وسجن ألفين وثلاثمائة كاتب.

٣،١٢،١ وبقي جماعة من اليهود متخازين إلى حماية بعض جهاته فخرج توقيعه بما نسخته أخبث الأمم اليهود وأخبث اليهود السمرة وأخبث السمرة بنو حبيب فليقطع ما بأسمائهم من ديوان الجيش والخراج إن شاء الله تعالى.[2] ودخل بعض الشعراء على المأمون وفي مجلسه يهوديّ جالس فأنشده[3] [السريع]

يَا ٱبْنَ ٱلَّذِي طَاعَتُهُ فِي ٱلْوَرَى وَحُكْمُهُ[4] مُفْتَرَضٌ وَاجِبُ
إِنَّ ٱلَّذِي شُرِّفْتَ مِنْ أَجْلِهِ يَزْعُمُ هٰذَا أَنَّهُ كَاذِبُ

فقال المأمون لليهوديّ أصحيح ما يقول هذا قال نعم فعظم على المأمون ذلك وأمر بقتل اليهوديّ فأسلم من ساعته. فانظر إلى هذا التجرّؤ ومجاهرة هذا الكلب

---

١ ويزيد هنا في هامش ت: تواطى. ٢ كذا في ت؛ والقصّة ساقطة في ب، ج،د، ويأتي مكانها: وكان بعض اليهود قد استولى على المأمون وبلغ منه محلاً عظيماً. ٣ كذا في ت؛ والعبارة من (وفي) ساقطة في ب، ج،د، ويأتي مكانها: واليهوديّ عنده فلمّا رآه جالسًا بالقرب منه أنشده. ٤ كذا في ت: وفي ب، ج،د: حبّه.

It is thanks to them that tyranny stands proud throughout our land,
while men behold outrage and abuses.
Rely not upon the Christians, for they are a people who
conspire against the religion of God.
Remember the Commander of the Believers and his words,
if you are prudent and obedient to him.
Keep no covenant with an unbeliever, observe no pact made with him,
and maintain no relations with him.'[47]

"After this, rancor toward the Christian secretaries remained etched in the heart of al-Ma'mūn. Around the time when he returned to the center of his realm and the seat of his caliphate, certain Christian secretaries conspired to mistreat the grammarian al-Kisā'ī, for at that time they openly flaunted their oppression, outrages, and corruption.[48] It happened, however, that al-Ma'mūn was reciting to al-Kisā'ī the word of God, be He exalted: «O believers, take not Jews and Christians as friends; they are friends of each other. Whoso of you makes them his friends is one of them. God guides not the people of the evildoers.»[49] Al-Kisā'ī said, 'Does the Commander of the Believers recite the Book of God and not act according to what is in it?' 'What do you mean?' the caliph asked. So al-Kisā'ī told him his own story. Al-Ma'mūn promptly commanded that the Christians be counted. The number of secretaries dismissed and imprisoned was twenty-three hundred."[50] 1.12.2

There was a group of Jews, however, who retained a role in the defense of one of his districts. Then his edict issued forth, containing the following words: "The vilest of peoples are the Jews, the vilest of Jews are the Samaritans, and the vilest of Samaritans are the Banū Ḥabīb. Therefore let their names be struck from the register of the army and the land tax, if God, be He exalted, so wills it." 1.12.3

A poet came in to al-Ma'mūn, who was sitting with a certain Jew, and recited to him:

O scion of him whom all men must obey,
and whose judgment is a holy obligation,
This man would claim that the one for whose sake
you are honored is a liar.

Al-Ma'mūn asked the Jew, "Is it true what this man says?" "Yes," he replied. Al-Ma'mūn was greatly troubled by this. He commanded that the Jew be

اليهوديّ للمسلمين بين يدي خليفة الله في أرضه وإقدامه بحضرة خلفاء الإسلام وسادات الأنام على مثل ذلك.

وأنشد بعض المتأخّرين في بعض النصارى وكان يدعى بابن الفأر [الرمل] ٤،١٢،١

سَلَّطَ ٱللهُ عَلَى ٱبْنِ ٱلْـ ـفَأْرِ قِطًّا مِن نِعَالِ
مُحْكَمُ ٱلدَّبْغِ بَدِيعُ ٱلْـ ـخَرْزِ مِنْ جِلْدِ ٱلْجِمَالِ
شَعَبُ ٱلشَّهْوَةِ لَا يُصْـ ـطَادُ إِلَّا فِي ٱلْقَذَالِ

وقال آخر [الطويل]

بَرَى جَسَدِي حُمْقُ ٱلنَّصَارَى وَجَهْلُهُمْ وَأَنْفُهُمُ ٱلْعَالِي عَلَى كُلِّ مُسْلِمِ
وَشَنُّهُمُ ٱلْغَارَاتِ فِي ٱلْمَالِ ظَاهِرًا وَلَا يَتَّقُونَ ٱلصَّفْعَ فِي رُبْعِ دِرْهَمِ
تَرَى كُلَّ قِبْطِيٍّ لَدَى ٱللَّفِّ عَنْتَرًا وَأَقْلَامُهُ تُرْبِي عَلَى كُلِّ لَهْذَمِ
إِذَا لَاحَ فِي ٱلْعَيُّوقِ فَلْسٌ يَلُفُّهُ تَرَقَّى إِلَيْهِ ٱلنَّذْلُ مِنْ غَيْرِ سُلَّمِ
وَيَجْمَعُ فِي تِلْكَ ٱلْأَنَامِلِ بُتْكَتْ حِسَابًا لَهُ مِن ذَاكَ تِسْعَةُ أَسْهُمِ
فَفَازُوا مِنَ ٱلدُّنْيَا بِمَا يَطْلُبُونَهُ وَمَأْوَاهُمُ فِي ٱلْحَشْرِ نَارُ جَهَنَّمِ

الفصل الثالث عشر فيما جرى أيّام المتوكّل في ذلك

قيل في أيّام المتوكّل استحوذ النصارى الكتّاب على الولايات في الدواوين شرقًا وغربًا يتوصّل بعضهم لبعض حتّى خدموا الجهات الكبار كجهات أمّ المتوكّل وحرمه وجهات أستادّاره ومماليكه ملوك الأطراف وغيرهم. وسبب ذلك أنّه تكرّر طعنهم في الكتّاب المسلمين ورفعوا حسابات من جهات متعدّدة تشهد بتأخّر جمل أموال في جهات الكتّاب المسلمين زورًا وبهتانًا وكذبًا وافتراءً محضًا وكرّروا ذلك في سمع ١،١٣،١

killed, but instead the Jew converted that very hour. Behold the audacity of this Jewish dog in his open hostility to Muslims, even before God's caliph, his deputy on earth! How shameless he was to speak thus in the presence of one of the caliphs of Islam, the lords of men.[51]

A more recent poet has declaimed, concerning a Christian who was called "Son of the Mouse": **1.12.4**

> May God give over the Son of the Mouse to, as it were, a cat of shoes,
> Marvelously sewn of well-tanned camels' hide,
> The greedy one can only be caught by the back of the head.[52]

Another composed these lines:

> My very body is worn down by the Christians' folly,
>   their ignorance, and their noses upturned at every Muslim,
> And by their open attacks upon property;
>   they fear no blow when a quarter silver coin is at stake.
> You will see each Copt, when battle is joined, an equal to
>   the hero ʿAntar, his pens rising above all sharpened blades.
> When a copper coin glimmers around the star Capella,
>   the vile man scrambles to it without a ladder.
> In those fingers—may they be cut off!—he grasps an account,
>   of which nine shares belong to him.
> What they seek of this world they have won, but on the
>   Day of Resurrection their dwelling shall be the fire of Gehenna.[53]

The Thirteenth Section: The Events That Took Place in the Days of al-Mutawakkil

It is said that in the days of al-Mutawakkil the Christian secretaries gained control over the administrative posts from the East to the West. They contrived ways to serve powerful people, such as al-Mutawakkil's mother, his majordomo, his slaves, the rulers of the border regions, and others. The tactic they employed to accomplish this was to launch relentless attacks on the Muslim secretaries. They submitted financial records from various districts that showed these Muslim secretaries to be withholding the payment of funds they had collected. Although this was in every way false, untrue, dishonest, and fabricated, they repeated it **1.13.1**

المتوكّل وجعلوا في الحساب بٱسم بعض النصارى متأخّرًا يسيرًا حقيرًا كيلا يُنسبوا إلى الغرض في المسلمين فكره المتوكّل كتّاب المسلمين لأجل ما قرّروه في سمعه. وكان من كتّاب النصارى سلمة بن سعيد وكان المتوكّل يأنس به ويحاضره ويسامره فقال يومًا ويلك يا سلمة تترك مجلسنا وتمضي إلى من دوننا[1] إنّك لأحمق فقال يا مولانا أتركك لأنّك تلازم الصحارى والصيد وأنا أمضي إلى معادن الذهب والفضّة تلقى والله بين يديّ الأموال فأشرب عليها وأتفكّه فيها ولقد جئت الآن وتركت ورائي من ذلك ما لا أقدر على وصفه فقال له المتوكّل ويلك وهذا كلّه[2] عند من فقال عند الحسن بن مخلد وأحمد بن اسرائيل وموسى بن عبد الملك وميمون ابن هارون ومحمّد بن موسى يشير إلى كتّاب المسلمين الذين أسماؤهم في الحساب الذي رفعوه يشهد بتأخّر الأموال الكثيرة في الجهات التي هم متولّوها حسب ما كذب النصارى عليهم. فقال المتوكّل ما تقول في عبد الله بن يحيى فسكت عنه فقال له المتوكّل بحياتي عليك قل ما عندك فقال قد حلّفتني بحياتك ولا بدّ من صدقي لك على كلّ حال لوالله يا أمير المؤمنين لقد صاغ له صوالج وأكرًا من ثلاثين ألف دينار فقلت له أمير المؤمنين يضرب كرة جلد بصولجان خشب وأنت تضرب كرة فضّة بصولجان ذهب فتغيّر وجه المتوكّل وقال للفتح بن خاقان أحضر هؤلاء وضيق عليهم فأحضر جماعة كتّاب المسلمين وعلموا ما وقعوا فيه مع الكافر الملعون فاجتمعوا إلى عبد الله بن يحيى فأنفذ رسولاً إلى سلمة بن سعيد النصرانيّ وعاتبه على ما جرى منه فاعتذر إليه إنّي ما قلت ذلك إلّا لأنّ السكر غلب عليّ حتّى كذبت واخترعت ما لم يكن من الأكر والصوالج. فبقي خطّه عند عبد الله بن يحيى بذلك فدخل على المتوكّل وعرّفه بما تمّمه كتّاب النصارى في الحساب المرفوع من جهة كتّاب المسلمين وأوقفه على رقعة سلمة بن سعيد النصرانيّ يشهد عليه خطّه

---

[1] كذا في ت؛ وفي ب، ج، د: إلى سرّ من رأى. [2] كذا في ب، د؛ والعبارة من (ويلك) ساقطة في ت.

often in the hearing of al-Mutawakkil. They even edited the records to ascribe some insignificant delay to one of the Christians, so as not to be suspected of having designs against the Muslims. Al-Mutawakkil grew to dislike the Muslim secretaries because of these accusations lodged against them in his presence.

One of the Christians, Salamah ibn Saʿīd, a favorite of al-Mutawakkil, often engaged in conversation with him late into the night. On one such occasion the caliph said to him, "What possesses you, Salamah, that instead of sitting with us you go off and spend time with less important people? Truly you are a fool." He replied, "Master, I take my leave of you because you are forever in the desert after the hunt. I, however, make my way to veritable mines of gold and silver. I swear to God that in the place of which I speak, money is simply doled out to me. I drink from it and eat delicacies upon it. But here I am, I have come now, and left behind me so much that I cannot begin to describe it to you." Al-Mutawakkil said to him, "Confound you! With whom is all of this to be found?" He replied, "With al-Ḥasan ibn Makhlad, Aḥmad ibn Isrāʾīl, Mūsā ibn ʿAbd al-Malik, Maymūn ibn Hārūn, and Muḥammad ibn Mūsā." In naming these individuals he was referring to the Muslim secretaries whose names were on the falsified account that the Christians had submitted, testifying to the withholding of great sums from their districts. Al-Mutawakkil said, "What do you have to say about ʿAbdallāh ibn Yaḥyā?"[54] At this Salamah fell silent. "By my life!" al-Mutawakkil said, "Say what you know!" Salamah said, "You have adjured me by your life. I have no choice but to tell you the truth, come what may. By God, Commander of the Believers, he has had balls and polo mallets made for himself from thirty thousand gold coins. I even said to him, 'The Commander of the Believers strikes a leathern ball with a wooden mallet, but you strike a silver ball with a mallet of gold?'"

At this al-Mutawakkil's face darkened and he said to his official al-Fatḥ ibn Khāqān, "Bring these people in and take action against them." The Muslim secretaries were brought in together as had been commanded. Discovering the predicament into which they had fallen thanks to the machinations of the accursed infidel, they repaired together to ʿAbdallāh ibn Yaḥyā. He dispatched a messenger to Salamah ibn Saʿīd the Christian, rebuking him for what he had done. Salamah sent back with his apologies, saying, "The only reason I said those false things was that I was so overcome by drink! That story about the balls and mallets was of my own invention." ʿAbdallāh ibn Yaḥyā carefully kept this note in its author's handwriting. He went to al-Mutawakkil and informed

فيها أنّه كذب وقال هذا قصده أن تخلو الدولة من الكتّاب المسلمين ليتمكّن هو ورهطه الكفرة الملاعين منها.

٢،١٣،١ وكان المتوكّل قد رتّب من يحضر المتظلّمين إليه على خلوة فأُحضر بين يديه شيخ كبير ذكر أنّه من أهل دمشق وابن سعيد بن عمرو[١] النصرانيّ غصبه داره. فلمّا وقف المتوكّل على قصّة الشيخ اشتدّ غضبه إلى أن ظهر ذلك عليه وأمر أن يكتب إلى صالح عامله بردّ داره. قال الفتح بن خاقان فقمت ناحيةً لأكتب ما أمرني به فبعث إليّ رسولاً يستحثّني فنجزت الكتاب وبادرت به إليه فلمّا وقف عليه زاد فيه بخطّه نُفيتُ عن ظهر العبّاس لئن تأخّر ما أمرتك به لآتينّ برأسك. ووصل الشيخ بألف دينار وأرسل معه حاجباً فسلّم إليه داره وكتبها.

٣،١٣،١ فتظلّم الناس من الكتّاب النصارى وتتابعت الاستغاثات عليهم. ثمّ حجّ المتوكّل على الله في تلك السنة فرأى الحرس رجلاً يطوف بالبيت حاسر الرأس وهو يدعو على المتوكّل فأمسكوه وجاؤوا به إليه فأمر بعقوبته على ما صدر منه. فقال والله يا أمير المؤمنين ما قلت ذلك إلّا وقد أيقنت بالقتل فاسمع كلامي ومرْ بقتلي فقال قل فقال يا أمير المؤمنين قد اكتنف دولتك كتّاب الذمّة فأحسنوا الاختيار لأنفسهم وابتاعوا دنياهم بفساد آخرتك وأنت مسؤول عمّا اجترحوه وليسوا مسؤولين عمّا اجترحت فلا تُصلح دنياهم بفساد آخرتك فإنّ أخسر الناس صفقةً يوم القيامة من أصلح دنيا غيره بفساد آخرته. فبكى المتوكّل حتّى سُمع صوت بكائه وطلب الرجل فلم يوجد.

١ كذا في ت؛ وفي ب، ج،د: عون.

him of the plot that the Christian secretaries had carried out by falsifying the Muslim secretaries' financial records. He also showed him the note from Salamah ibn Saʿīd the Christian, whose handwriting bore witness to his own lie. ʿAbdallāh said, "This is his purpose: to rid the state of Muslim secretaries so that he and his cabal of accursed infidels can gain power over it."[55]

Now al-Mutawakkil had arranged for someone to bring to him, in private, 1.13.2
those of his subjects who wished to protest injustices done to them. One day this official brought an old man to see him. The man said he was from Damascus, and that Ibn Saʿīd ibn ʿAmr the Christian had deprived him of his house. When al-Mutawakkil heard the old man's story, he grew visibly angry and commanded his officials to write to Ṣāliḥ, the caliph's agent, that the man's house should be returned to him. Al-Fatḥ ibn Khāqān said, "I rose and went away to write what he had commanded me. He sent a messenger after me to hurry me along, so I finished the letter and rushed back to him with it. When it was brought before him, he added to it, in his own handwriting, 'May I be struck from among the Abbasids if I do not have your head, should you delay the least bit in carrying out my command.' Al-Mutawakkil granted the old man a thousand gold coins and sent a chamberlain to accompany him who returned his house to him and registered the deed in his name."[56]

The people continued to protest the Christian secretaries' oppressiveness, 1.13.3
supplicating ceaselessly against them. Around this same time al-Mutawakkil made the pilgrimage to Mecca. His guards spotted a man circumambulating the House bareheaded, cursing al-Mutawakkil. They seized him and brought him before the caliph, who ordered that he be punished for his deed. The man said, "By God, Commander of the Believers, I said what I did in full certainty that I would be killed for it. So listen to what I have to say, then command my execution." "Speak," al-Mutawakkil said, and the man said, "Commander of the Believers, the dhimmi secretaries have beset your state on every side. They have chosen the best for themselves, purchasing this world for themselves at the cost of your lot in the next. It is you who will be called to account for the wrongs they commit, and not the reverse. I pray you, do not improve their lot in this world by ruining your lot in the next. For there is no one who will be a greater loser on the Day of Resurrection than the person who improves someone else's lot in this world at the expense of his own lot in the next one." At this al-Mutawakkil wept audibly and called for the man who had told him these things, but he was not to be found.[57]

فخرج أمره من ساعته إلى الأعمال بأن لا يُستخدم أحد من الذمّة في أمر من أمور المسلمين ولا يُستكفى من نسلهم ولا يُستصلح منهم أحد لعمل من أعمال المسلمين حتّى يكون له سبعة أجداد مسلمين ولا تقبل شهادة أحد منهم حتّى يعدّ له سبعة أجداد مسلمين ولا يمكّنوا من لبس الثياب البيض كيلا يكثر تشبّههم بالمسلمين وأن يلبسوا العسليّ من الثياب ويكون ركب سروجهم خشباً وتهدم بيعهم المستجدّة بعد بعثة رسول الله صلّى الله عليه وسلّم ولا يبقى منها إلّا ما كان قبل البعثة ولا يمكّنوا من بياض كنائسهم وتضاعف عليهم الجزية ولا يفسح لهم في دخول حمّامات المسلمين ويُفرد لهم حمّامات خدمها ذمّة ولا يستخدموا مسلماً في حوائجهم ويعيّن لهم في كلّ عمل رجل عريق في الإسلام يحتسب عليهم. ١،١٣،٤

وأمر بكتب كتاب نسخته أمّا بعد فإنّ الله اصطفى الإسلام ديناً فشرّفه وكرّمه وأناره ونصره وأظهره وفضّله وأكمله وجعله الدين الذي لا يقبل غيره فقال سبحانه وتعالى ﴿وَمَنْ يَبْتَغِ غَيْرَ الْإِسْلَامِ دِيناً فَلَنْ يُقْبَلَ مِنْهُ وَهُوَ فِي الْآخِرَةِ مِنَ الْخَاسِرِينَ﴾. وبعث نبيّه ورسوله وحبيبه وصفيّه وخيرته من خلقه محمّداً صلّى الله عليه وسلّم خاتم النبيّين وإمام المتّقين وسيّد المرسلين ﴿لِيُنذِرَ مَن كَانَ حَيًّا وَيَحِقَّ الْقَوْلُ عَلَى الْكَافِرِينَ﴾. وأنزل كتاباً عزيزاً عربيّاً مبيناً ﴿لَا يَأْتِيهِ الْبَاطِلُ مِنْ بَيْنِ يَدَيْهِ وَلَا مِنْ خَلْفِهِ ۖ تَنْزِيلٌ مِنْ حَكِيمٍ حَمِيدٍ﴾ أسعد به أمّته وجعلهم ﴿خَيْرَ أُمَّةٍ أُخْرِجَتْ لِلنَّاسِ تَأْمُرُونَ بِالْمَعْرُوفِ وَتَنْهَوْنَ عَنِ الْمُنْكَرِ وَتُؤْمِنُونَ بِاللَّهِ ۗ وَلَوْ آمَنَ أَهْلُ الْكِتَابِ لَكَانَ خَيْرًا لَهُمْ ۚ مِنْهُمُ الْمُؤْمِنُونَ وَأَكْثَرُهُمُ الْفَاسِقُونَ﴾ وأهان الشرك وأهله ووضعهم ومقتهم وأصغرهم وأخملهم وأذلّهم وخذلهم وتبرّأ منهم وضرب عليهم الذلّة والمسكنة وقال تعالى ﴿قَاتِلُوا الَّذِينَ لَا يُؤْمِنُونَ بِاللَّهِ وَلَا بِالْيَوْمِ الْآخِرِ وَلَا يُحَرِّمُونَ مَا حَرَّمَ اللَّهُ وَرَسُولُهُ وَلَا يَدِينُونَ دِينَ الْحَقِّ مِنَ الَّذِينَ أُوتُوا الْكِتَابَ حَتَّىٰ يُعْطُوا الْجِزْيَةَ عَنْ يَدٍ وَهُمْ صَاغِرُونَ﴾ فطبع على قلوبهم ونغّل صدورهم وخبّث سرائرهم ١،١٣،٥

At once the caliph's command issued forth that not a single dhimmi was to be employed in any of the Muslims' affairs. None of their progeny was to be declared competent or qualified for any of the Muslims' official posts or to give legal testimony until he could count seven Muslim ancestors. They were not to be allowed to wear white, lest they resemble Muslims too strongly. Instead they were to wear honey-colored clothing. Their saddles were to be made of wood. Those of their churches that had been built or repaired after the mission of the Messenger of God, God bless and keep him, were to be torn down; only those that had existed before his mission might remain. They were not allowed to color their churches white, their poll tax was doubled, and they were not allowed to enter the Muslims' baths. Instead they were to have their own baths, staffed by dhimmis. They were not to employ any Muslim for their own needs. In every district, a man of long standing in Islam was appointed over them to serve as inspector of their affairs.[58] 1.13.4

Al-Mutawakkil also commanded that the following document be written: 1.13.5

God has chosen Islam among the religions, and ennobled it, honored it, illumined it, championed it, made it victorious, favored it, perfected it, and designated it the only religion that shall be accepted. For He has said, be He glorified and exalted, «Whoso desires another religion than Islam, it shall not be accepted of him; in the next world he shall be among the losers.»[59] And He has sent his Prophet, his Messenger and Beloved, his Chosen and the best of his creation, Muḥammad, God bless and keep him, the Seal of the Prophets, Spiritual Leader of the Pious, Lord of the Emissaries, «that he may warn whosoever is living, and that the Word may be realized against the unbelievers.»[60] He also has sent down an illustrious, clear, Arabic Book—«falsehood comes not to it from before it nor from behind it; a sending down from One Wise, Laudable»[61]—by which He has gladdened his community. He made them «the best nation ever brought forth to men, bidding to right, and forbidding wrong, and believing in God. Had the People of the Book believed, it were better for them; some of them are believers, but the most of them are ungodly.»[62] He reviled unbelief and its adherents, lowering them, abhorring them, reducing them, effacing them, humiliating them, afflicting them, abasing them, declaring himself rid of them; and «abasement . . . and poverty shall be pitched on them.»[63] He said, be He exalted, «Fight those who believe not in God and the Last Day, and who do not forbid what God and his Messenger have forbidden—such men as practice not the religion of truth, being of those who have been given the Book—until they pay the tribute out of hand and have been humbled.»[64] Therefore He sealed their hearts, causing their

وضمائرهم ونهى عن ائتمانهم والثقة بهم لعداوتهم للمسلمين وغشّهم وبغضائهم فقال تعالى ﴿يَا أَيُّهَا الَّذِينَ آمَنُوا لَا تَتَّخِذُوا بِطَانَةً مِنْ دُونِكُمْ لَا يَأْلُونَكُمْ خَبَالًا وَدُّوا مَا عَنِتُّمْ قَدْ بَدَتِ الْبَغْضَاءُ مِنْ أَفْوَاهِهِمْ وَمَا تُخْفِي صُدُورُهُمْ أَكْبَرُ ۚ قَدْ بَيَّنَّا لَكُمُ الْآيَاتِ ۖ إِنْ كُنْتُمْ تَعْقِلُونَ﴾ . وقد انتهى إلى أمير المؤمنين أنّ أناساً لا رأي لهم ولا رؤية من العمّال يستعينون بأهل الذمّة في أعمالهم ويتّخذونهم بطانةً من دون المسلمين ويسلّطونهم على الرعيّة فيعسفونهم ويبسطون أيديهم في ظلمهم وقهرهم وغشّهم والعدوان عليهم فأعظم أمير المؤمنين ذلك وأكبره وتبرّأ إلى الله منه وأحبّ التقرّب إلى الله ورسوله بحسمه والنهي عنه. ورأى أن يكتب إلى عمّاله بالكور والأمصار وولاة الثغور والأمراء والأجناد في ترك استعمالهم الذمّة في شيء من أعمالهم وأمورهم والإشراك لهم في أماناتهم وما قلّدهم أمير المؤمنين واستحفظهم إيّاه إذ جعل في المسلمين الثقة والدين والأمانة على إخوانهم المؤمنين وحسن الرعاية لما استرعوا والكفاية لما استكفوا والقيام بما حملوا ما أغنى عن الاستعانة بأحد من المشركين بالله المكذّبين لرسله الجاحدين لآياته الجاعلين معه إلهاً آخر لا إله إلّا هو وحده لا شريك له. ورجاء أمير المؤمنين بما ألهمه الله من ذلك وقذف في قلبه أن يكون له جزيل الثواب وكريم المآب وبالله يستعين أمير المؤمنين على نيّته في تعزيز الإسلام وأهله وتذليل الشرك وحزبه فليعلم هذا من رأي أمير المؤمنين فلا يستعان في دولته ولا أيّامه في طرف من أطراف البلاد بأحد من المشركين وتنزل أهل الذمّة منازلهم التي خصّهم الله بها. وليقرأ كتاب أمير المؤمنين هذا على أهل كلّ عمل ويشاع فيهم ولا يعلمنّ أمير المؤمنين أنّ أحداً من عمّال أعماله ولا من عمّالهم وأعوانهم استعان بأحد من أهل الذمّة في عمل من الأعمال.

breasts to fester and their inner selves and consciences to grow wicked. God made it forbidden to trust them or place confidence in them, because of their animosity to the Muslims and their deception and hatred. Thus has He said, be He exalted, «O believers, take not for your intimates outside yourselves; such men spare nothing to ruin you; they yearn for you to suffer. Hatred has already shown itself of their mouths, and what their breasts conceal is yet greater. Now we have made clear to you the signs, if you understand.»[65]

The Commander of the Believers has discovered that certain officials who lack judgment and discernment have sought the assistance of dhimmis in their tasks. They take them for their intimates outside the Muslims, empowering them over the state's subjects. These last the dhimmis treat injuriously, reaching out to oppress them, subjugate them, deceive them, and assail them. The Commander of the Believers is immensely troubled by this. He considers it a great wrong from which he has dissociated himself before God. It has been his good pleasure to seek the favor of God and his Messenger by decisively ending this practice and forbidding it. He deems it fitting to write to his agents in the villages and the cities, as well as the governors of the marches, the emirs, and the military districts, that they desist from employing dhimmis in their tasks and affairs and from including them in their confidence and in any of that which the Commander of the Believers has conferred upon them and committed to their care. For since Muslims possess the qualities of confidence, religion, trustworthiness toward fellow believers, solicitude for what they are asked to guard, competence in what they are asked to do, and concern for what is entrusted to them, they have no need to seek assistance from people who ascribe partners to God, give the lie to his messengers, reject his signs, and place another god alongside Him, when «there is no god but He»;[66] «no associate has He.»[67]

It is the hope of the Commander of the Believers that he will receive abundant reward and an honored abode because of this act to which God has inspired him and which He has cast into his heart. The Commander of the Believers seeks God's aid in his intention to uphold Islam and its adherents while humiliating unbelief and its partisans. Let this be known of the judgment of the Commander of the Believers. Therefore let not the aid of any unbeliever be sought in his state or in his times, in any corner of the land. May the dhimmis be lowered to their stations that God designated for them. And may this letter of the Commander of the Believers be read out in every district and spread among them. Let not the Commander of the Believers learn that any of his agents, or their own agents and helpers, have sought assistance from a dhimmi in any task.[68]

فلمّا قُرِئ الكتاب أسلم جماعة من أعيان[1] النصارى المشهورين كأبي نوح عيسى ابن ابراهيم وقدامة بن زيادة والهيثم بن خالد وعبد الله بن الأبرش وسهلان وعبدان الواسطيّ وغيرهم من الكتّاب وتظاهروا بالإسلام خوفاً ممّا أمرهم به وأمّا أمر بواطنهم وسرائرهم فإلى الله الذي ﴿ يَعۡلَمُ خَآئِنَةَ ٱلۡأَعۡيُنِ وَمَا تُخۡفِي ٱلصُّدُورُ ﴾ . ٦،١٣،١

الفصل الرابع عشر فيما جرى في ذلك أيّام المقتدر بالله

قيل خرج أمر المقتدر بالله بأن لا يُستعمل الذمّة في أمر من أمور المسلمين وقبض على أبي ياسر النصرانيّ الكاتب عامل مؤنس[2] الحاجب وأخذ جميع ما يملكه من ذهب وفضّة وحليّ وحلل ولآلئ وجواهر وأثاث فاخر. ١،١٤،١

وكتب ابن الفرات بما نسخته عوائد الله عند أمير المؤمنين أطال الله بقاه توفي على غاية رضاه ونهاية أمانيه. وليس يظهر أحد عصيانه إلّا جعله الله موعظة للأنام ومثلة في الأيّام[3] والله ﴿عَزِيزٞ ذُو ٱنتِقَامٍ﴾ فمن نكث ومرق وغدر وفسق وعصى وطغى وبغى وخالف أمير المؤمنين وخالف محمّداً صلّى الله عليه وسلّم وسعى في فساد دولة أمير المؤمنين ومملكته وقصد أذيّة قوّاده وخواصّه ورعيّته عاجله أمير المؤمنين بسطوته وطهّر من رجسه أيّام دولته ﴿وَٱلۡعَٰقِبَةُ لِلۡمُتَّقِينَ﴾ . وقد أمر أمير المؤمنين بترك الاستعانة بأحد من الذمّة في عمل من أعمال المسلمين فليحذر العمّال تجاوز أوامر أمير المؤمنين ونواهيه والسلام. ٢،١٤،١

---

١ كذا في ت؛ وفي ب، د: أعوان. ٢ ت: شوس؛ ب، د: سوس. والمثبت من الأحكام، ١:٢٢٤. ٣ كذا في ت؛ وفي ب، ج، د: وبادره بعاجل الاصطلام.

When the letter was read out, a number of eminent and renowned Christians converted to Islam, including Abū Nūḥ ʿĪsā ibn Ibrāhīm, Qudāmah ibn Ziyādah, al-Haytham ibn Khālid, ʿAbdallāh ibn al-Abrash, Sahlān, and ʿAbdān al-Wāsiṭī, along with other secretaries. They made an outward show of converting, being fearful of what he had commanded concerning them. But the state of their inner souls and selves is known only to God, who «knows the treachery of the eyes and what the breasts conceal».[69] 1.13.6

The Fourteenth Section: The Events That Took Place in the Days of Caliph al-Muqtadir Bi-llāh

It is said: The command of al-Muqtadir issued forth that no dhimmi was to be employed in any of the Muslims' affairs. Abū Yāsir, the Christian secretary of Mu'nis the chamberlain, was arrested. All that he owned was confiscated: gold, silver, finery, clothing, pearls, gems, and rich furnishings.[70] 1.14.1

Ibn al-Furāt wrote the following: "The benefits of God rest upon the Commander of the Believers, God prolong his life. They are fulfilled to the extent of his favor, and to the very limit of his aspiration. God makes those who manifest rebellion against him an example for men and an admonition for the ages, for God «is Almighty, Avenging.»[71] Whosoever should violate, deviate, defraud, stray, rebel, terrorize, wrong, infringe against the Commander of the Believers, infringe against Muḥammad, God bless and keep him, scheme against the government and realm of the Commander of the Believers, or contrive to harm his commanders, intimates, or subjects, the Commander of the Believers shall overtake him with his power and cleanse of his filth the days of his own reign, for «the issue ultimate is to the godfearing.»[72] The Commander of the Believers has commanded that no assistance of the dhimmis be sought in any task of the Muslims. Therefore, let all officials be warned against contravening the Commander of the Believers' commands and prohibitions. Farewell."[73] 1.14.2

الفصل الخامس عشر في ذكر لمعة من خزي اليهود وخبثهم وغشّهم

١،١٥،١ قيل إنّ المقداد بن الأسود الكنديّ جمعته الطريق في بعض أسفاره مع يهوديّ فوقعت دابّة اليهوديّ فساعده عليها ثمّ تعب وعجز عن المشي فركّبه فلمّا وصلا إلى باب المدينة أمسك المقداد اليهوديّ وقال سمعت رسول الله صلّى الله عليه وسلّم يقول ما صحب مسلم يهوديًّا ولا عامله إلّا غشّه وأنت فمسائري إلى المدينة ففي أيّ شيء غششتني؟ فقال اليهوديّ الغشّ يكون في معاملة وأنا فما عاملتك أو في أكل وشرب ولم يجرِ بيننا ذلك فشدّد المقداد عليه القول وخوّفه وهدّده فقال اليهوديّ أتأمنني على نفسي فأصدقك قال نعم قال صدق والله نبيّك لمّا أعياني الأمر ولم أقدر على مكروه أوصله إليك كنت أمشي بنعلي على ظلّك الممتدّ وأدوس ظلّ رأسك بقوّة وتثاقل فيحصل لي اشتفاء في الجملة وتصوّر قدرة على إهانتك وأذاك.

٢،١٥،١ وكان رجل يُعرف بابن الهارونيّ اليهوديّ عند بعض الملوك بمنزلة رفيعة زائدة على رتب اليهود فلعب معه الشطرنج في مجلس شرابه على تمنّي حاجة في نفسه ووعده أنّه متى اقترح عليه أمرًا عظيم القدر قضاه له فلمّا فرغ من لعبه وغلبه سأل الملك وفاء ما وعده من إبلاغه ما تمنّاه فقال له الملك سل فقال تضع من آي القرآن قوله ﴿إِنَّ الدِّينَ عِندَ اللَّهِ الْإِسْلَامُ﴾ فانظر إلى قصد هذا الكافر فإنّه لم يتمنّ إلّا هدم قاعدة من دين الإسلام.

٣،١٥،١ وأخبرني بعض الظرفاء قال كان لي صديق يهوديّ يجبي لبعض المغفّلين فكان يحضر له في الجباية النحاس فيردّها عليه ويدفعها له. فإذا أخذها قال لعن الله من

The Fifteenth Section: Examples of the Jews' Ignominy, Wickedness, and Trickery

It is said that on one of his journeys, al-Miqdād ibn al-Aswad al-Kindī fell in with a certain Jew upon the road. When the Jew's beast stumbled, al-Miqdād assisted him with it. The Jew tired of walking and was unable to go on, so al-Miqdād placed him upon an animal of his own. When they reached the gate of the city,[74] al-Miqdād seized the Jew, saying, "I heard the Messenger of God, God bless and keep him, say, 'No Muslim ever accompanied a Jew, or had dealings with him, but that the Jew tricked him.' Now you have traveled beside me all the way to the city; in what matter, then, have you tricked me?" The Jew answered him, saying, "Trickery takes place only in business dealings, and I have had none with you. Or, it can take place in eating and drinking, but we did not do that together, either." But al-Miqdād spoke sternly to him, intimidated him, and threatened him, so the Jew said, "Will you give me security for my life, so that I may tell you the truth?" "Yes," he replied. The Jew said, "Your prophet spoke truly, by God. But when I saw that the act was beyond my power, and that I would be unable to do you harm, I walked with my sandal upon your outstretched shadow, treading firmly and heavily on the shadow of your head. In this way I satisfied my urge, imagining myself able to insult you and harm you."[75] 1.15.1

A man known as Ibn al-Hārūnī the Jew enjoyed high standing with a certain king, higher than the station proper to Jews. He played chess with the king during his drinking session, wagering with him for what he wanted. The king promised him that even if he demanded some great and momentous thing, he would have it done. When the game ended, the Jew had bested the king, so he asked the king to make good on his promise regarding the Jew's wish, which he would now declare. "Ask," said the king. So he said, "Remove from among the verses of the Qur'an God's word: «The true religion with God is Islam.»"[76] Just look at the plan of this infidel! There was nothing he wanted more than to destroy a fundament of Islam.[77] 1.15.2

A raconteur told me this story: "I had a Jewish friend who collected taxes on behalf of an associate of his, who was rather simple and naive. In the course of his collecting, the Jew would be given copper money. This he would bring to the other man, who however would simply return it to him. When he took it back, the Jew would say, 'God curse the person who gave me these coins, and curse his parents too.' His simpleminded associate imagined that he was 1.15.3

دفعها إليّ ولعن والديه. فيتوهّم المغفّل أنّه لعن الذي قبضها منه أوّلاً وما قصده باللعنة إلّا هو لردّه عليه النحاس. فلو شرعت في وصف مخازي اليهود لطال الشرح ولكنّهم أحقر وأقلّ وأذلّ.

cursing the person from whom he had first received the coins. But in fact he meant to curse the man himself, for handing back the copper."[78]

If I began describing all the disgraceful things about Jews, the account of them would be lengthy indeed. But the Jews are more insignificant, fewer, and more lowly.[79]

الباب الثاني في وصف الأقباط وخياناتهم ويشتمل على خمسة عشر فصلاً

الفصل الأوّل في وصفهم من حيث الجملة

يكفي في ذلك ما روي عن رسول الله صلّى الله عليه وسلّم أنّه قال اليهود والنصارى خونة لعن الله من ألبسهم ثوب عزّ.[١] وقال ذو النون المصريّ رحمه الله وجدت في بِرّبَى إِخميم مكتوباً احذروا العبيد المعتقين والأقباط المتعرّبين فإنّ الأقباط ألأم جيل وأخسّ قبيل إن أكرمتهم أهانوك وإن أهنتهم أكرموك وإن ائتمنتهم خانوك يلقاك أحدهم والمنيّة[٢] في كمّه والتحيّة في فمه فإن رهبك حيّاك وإن لم يخفك[٣] وجاك. ٢،١،١

وما عسى أن تعدّ مخازي قوم محاسنهم مساوئ السفل ومساوئهم فضائح سالف الأُمم؟ ألسنتهم معقولة بالعيّ واللكن وأيديهم مبسوطة بالخيانة في السرّ والعلن وأعراضهم أغراض لسهام الذمّ وأشخاصهم مجلبة الهمّ والغمّ قد لبّس بهم الدهر شرّ ثيابه وأوقفهم ذلّ الطمع ببابه. ٢،١،٢

الفصل الثاني في سبب اشتغال الأقباط بالكتابة دون بقيّة الحرف

قلت قد ورد في التاريخ أنّ قبط مصر لمّا نُزعت من أيديهم مملكة مصر ودخلوا تحت ذمّة الإسلام أجمعوا على رأي يفعلونه لتبقى أقوالهم بين المسلمين مسموعة ٢،٢،١

---

١ كذا في ب، د؛ والجملة ساقطة في ت. ٢ في سائر المخطوطات: المذية؛ والمثبت يقتضيه السياق. ٣ كذا في ب، ت؛ وفي د: يخف.

The Second Chapter, A Description of the Copts and Their Perfidies, in Fifteen Sections

The First Section: A General Description of Them

Here it would be sufficient to refer to what is narrated from the Messenger of God, God bless and keep him, namely, "The Jews and Christians are treacherous. Therefore may God curse him who dresses them in the raiment of power."[80] **2.1.1**

Dhū l-Nūn al-Miṣrī said, "I found the following inscription in the ancient temple of Ikhmīm: 'Be on your guard against manumitted slaves and Arabized Copts. For the Copts are the most despicable race and the lowliest tribe. Honor them and they revile you; revile them and they honor you; trust them and they cheat you. The Copt comes to meet you with a dagger[81] in his sleeve and a greeting in his mouth. If he reveres you, he will greet you, but if he does not fear you he will stab you.'"

Yet how could anyone possibly enumerate the disgraces of a people whose merits would be counted as faults in the basest commoner, and whose faults are the worst infamies that have been known among all the nations past? Their tongues are tied by stammering and speech impediment, but their hands are outstretched in corruption, both open and concealed. The noblest parts of their reputations are easy targets for the arrows of blame; their very selves are formed from affliction and distress. In them, Fate dons her worst; they gather at greed's shameful gate. **2.1.2**

The Second Section: Why the Copts Specialize as Secretaries and Neglect Other Professions

It is important that I note here how it is passed down in the annals of history that when the rule of Egypt was wrested from the Copts and they entered into the pact with Islam, they devised a strategy to ensure that their voices would be heard by the Muslims and that their new overlords would be compelled to **2.2.1**

ومصالحهم عليهم مجموعة فقال عقلاؤهم وأكابرهم أنتم قوم كانت البلاد لكم وقد نُزع منكم مجد السيف فاجتهدوا في تحصيل مجد القلم قالوا فماذا نفعل قال عقلاؤهم تعلّمون أولادكم الكتابة ليشاركوا المسلمين في أموالهم ومصالحهم وآرائهم. فأجمعوا على ذلك فكان منهم ما يُرى وتمكّنوا من دواوين المسلمين وتحكّموا في دولتهم. وما أحسن ما نظمه الشاعر في وصف اليهود والنصارى إذ علّم اليهود أولادهم الطبّ وعلّم النصارى أولادهم الكتابة فقال [الكامل]

لَعَنَ ٱللهُ ٱلنَّصَارَى وَٱلْيَهُودَ فَإِنَّهُم بَلَغُوا بِنَا مِن دَهْرِهِم آمَالَا
خَرَجُوا أَطِبَّاءً وَكُتَّابًا لِأَنْ يَتَنَاهَبُوا ٱلْأَرْوَاحَ وَٱلْأَمْوَالَا[١]

الفصل الثالث في عموم تصرّفهم في الديار المصريّة من حيث لا يُشعر بهم

وذلك أنّ هؤلاء النصارى أصناف إمّا مستوفي ديوان فيحكم في البلاد والعباد بكلمه ١،٣،٢
وقلمه ويصل إلى أغراضه ومقاصده لأنّه في صورة من يذكر مستحقًّا للسلطان أو حقًّا لبيت مال المسلمين فله من عزّ السلطنة بهذا السبب سيف مشهور يضرب به من شاء كيف شاء. وإمّا كاتب والٍ فهو يحكم في جميع ولايته بما يختار ومعه سيف الولاية يعتزّ به وسيف النيابة عن السلطنة يصول به ويحكم فلا يردّ أمره ولا يرتكب نهيه فيصل بذلك إلى سائر أغراضه فإن صدر منه أمر يجاهر الشريعة المطهّرة بالمخالفة حتّى يقوم فيه أحد من العلماء أو المسلمين أهل الدين خلا بصاحبه وأظهر نوع مصلحة فيما قصده فلا يفيد قيام من قام في ذلك. ومتى أعيته الحيل كذب على الذي يقوم في ذلك الأمر وأخبر مخدومه أنّه شتمه أو أساء أدبه أو ذمّ

١ كذا في ب،د؛ والفقرة من (وما أحسن) ساقطة من ت.

look after their interests. The wisest and greatest Copts said to their people, "You were once masters of this land. But the glory of the sword has been wrested from you. Strive, therefore, to attain the glory of the pen." "How shall we do this?" they asked. Their wise men said to them, "By teaching your children the secretarial art, that they may share with the Muslims in their property, their interests, and their decisions." They all agreed upon this plan, and the result is plain to see. They gained power in the Muslims' administration and did as they pleased in the government. How apposite are the lines a poet composed to describe the Jews and Christians, observing that the former train their children in medicine, the latter theirs in the secretarial art, as follows:

God curse the Christians and Jews!
They have attained what they wanted to get from us:
They have emerged as doctors and secretaries
that they might seize both souls and property.[82]

The Third Section: Concerning Their Pervasive yet Imperceptible Influence in the Land of Egypt

These Christians are of several types. The first is the accountant of an adminis- 2.3.1
trative office, who rules over the land and the people by means of his word and his pen. He attains his goals and his aims because he is in a position to nominate candidates for office to the sultan, and to pass judgment concerning what is owed the central treasury of the Muslims. He thus wields the power of the sultanate as a naked sword, striking whomever he wishes, however he wishes.

The second type of Christian is the governor's secretary. He rules without restriction in all matters over which he has power. He carries two swords: of his appointment, in which he exults, and of the authority he wields on behalf of the sultanate. With the latter sword he leaps to the attack and wins mastery. No command of his is defied, no act committed that he has forbidden. Thus is he able to achieve anything he purposes. When he issues a command that so flagrantly contravenes the Pure Law that some learned man or other pious Muslim is moved to oppose it, the Christian secretary takes his master aside and explains to him how he actually plans to bring about some benefit by that command. The Muslim's opposition avails nothing. If the Christian's usual tricks fail him, however, he concocts lies about the Muslim who has risen up to oppose him, informing the one he serves that this Muslim has slighted the master,

أيّام ولايته أو شكر الوالي الذي كان قبله أو أنّه عزم على الوقوف للسلطان فيه ويُنهي جملاً من أحواله ناشئة عن كذب وزور وبهتان فتأخذ ذلك الوالي العزّة بالإثم فيردّه أقبح ردّ ويصدّه أعظم صدّ. هذا إذا كان الوالي يقظاً خبيراً مطّلعاً بارزاً للناس يدخل عليه وجوه أهل ولايته ويسمع بالأذن الواعية المقالة من أرباب نصيحته فأمّا إن كان على غير هذه الصفة لا يسمع ولا يعي انقطع الحديث. ولا ينثني كاتب الوالي الموصوف بهذه الصفة عن قطع المصانعات[1] وارتكاب المنهيات إلى أن يحصّل الجمل الكثيرة من الأموال وأكثرهم لا يخرج عن زيّه ولا يظهر غناه إلّا في بيته وخلوته في ليله. وإمّا كاتب هو عامل بلاد فهو الحاكم يتصرّف فيها كيف شاء ولا تخلو بلد في مصر أن يجري حكمهم فيها وقلمهم عليها حتّى تواثبوا على الخدم الشرعيّة وصار لهم أحاديث في الوظائف الدينيّة يسترفعون حسبانات الأحباس[2] والأوقاف والجوامع والمدارس وغيرها[3] ويتحدّثون فيها.

الفصل الرابع فيما اطّلع عليه أحمد بن طولون من خيانتهم المشهورة وما اعتمده فيهم

ولمّا دخل أحمد بن طولون مصر نهار الأربعاء لسبع بقين من شهر رمضان سنة ١،٤،٢
أربع وخمسين ومائتين ورُدّ إليه أمر الخراج والنظر في المصالح وجد الذي أخذته القبط بأرض مصر والشام جملةً مستكثرة. ووجد ممّا اعتمدوه وأقدموا عليه أنّ النطرون كان مباحاً كالكلاء والماء والحطب والملح من أخذ منه شيئاً وحمله إلى البلاد باعه للناس واتّسع[4] بثمنه. فضمّنوه بجملة مستكثرة وسرقوه ولم يرفعوه في حسابهم وكذلك المصائد فضمّنوا ما أطلقه الله سبحانه من صيد البحر لمن انتصب لذلك

١ كذا في ت؛ وفي ب، ج،د زيادة: وبيع المصالح. ٢ كذا في ت؛ وفي ب،د: حسابات الأجناس. ٣ كذا في ت؛ والعبارة من (والأوقاف) ساقطة في ب،د. ٤ كذا في ب،د؛ وفي ت: وتوسّع؛ ج: وانتفع.

or spoken ill of his comportment, or found fault with his rule, or professed some attachment to the previous governor, or resolved to denounce him to the sultan. In short, he tells his master anything about him that lies, untruth, and slander suggest to his mind. The Muslim's righteous pride, therefore, appears to the governor as a sin, so he rejects and rebuffs him in the harshest way.

What's worse, this is the best-case scenario—when the governor is alert, experienced, and informed, and when he makes himself available to the people and allows their prominent representatives to see him, lending an attentive ear to solicitous advisors. If, however, the governor is not like this, being neither alert nor attentive, then no remonstrance with him is possible. The secretary of such a governor does not shrink from blocking any outside attempt to influence his master, all the while committing forbidden acts until he has amassed enormous wealth. Most of them never allow this wealth to show. Such a secretary displays his wealth only when he is alone in his own house at night.

The third kind is the Christian government official in the towns. He acts as the true ruler in his territory, exercising authority according to his whim. Not a town in Egypt is free of the rule of such pens. Together they set upon even the offices of the Law. They gain for themselves a say in the administration of religious posts, whereupon they work to deprive charitable endowments, congregational mosques, law colleges, and other such institutions of their income and to dispose of it as they wish.

The Fourth Section: How Aḥmad ibn Ṭūlūn Discovered Their Notorious Malfeasance, and How He Resolved to Act toward Them

Aḥmad ibn Ṭūlūn entered Egypt on a Wednesday, seven days before the end 2.4.1
of the month of Ramadan, in the year 254 [September 15, 868].[83] When control of the tax collection and administration was handed over to him, he found that the Copts had commandeered vast resources in Egypt and Syria. Among those things which they had shamelessly plotted to control was the supply of natron. The natron found in Egypt had long been a free resource, like pasture, water, firewood, and salt. Whoever took some of it into town and sold it was free to profit from his activity. The Copts, however, took control of it by paying a huge sum to the government. In this way they effectively stole it, without reporting the income that they derived from it. They did likewise with the fisheries, giving control over what God, be He glorified, had declared absolutely free to

واسترزق به بجملة مستكثرة وسرقوها ولم يعرّجوا[1] في الحساب لها على ذكر وكذلك المراعي وهو ضمان الكلاء المباح الذي جاء في الحديث عن رسول الله صلّى الله عليه وسلّم أنّه قال الناس شركاء في ثلاث وذكر الكلاء. فضمّنوا المراعي بجملة كثيرة ولم يذكروها في حسابهم بل كانوا يستخرجون ذلك لنفوسهم فاستخرجه ابن طولون منهم لبيت مال المسلمين واستمرّ استخراج ضمان هذه الجهات لبيت مال المسلمين إلى الآن. فلينظر الإنسان إلى إقدام هؤلاء الخونة على أموال المسلمين وخيانتهم لبيت المال الذي هو ذخيرة السلاطين.

الفصل الخامس فيما جرى لهم مع محمّد بن سليمان

١،٥،٢ ولمّا وصل محمّد بن سليمان إلى مصر وبلغه خيانة أقباطها واطّلع على القبائح من مخازيهم ووثوب من أسلم من أولادهم على العظائم الهائلة ومناطاتهم[2] كبار المسلمين العريقين في الإسلام ونهبهم الأموال من كلّ عمل يتولّونه وظهور الأموال الكثيرة لهم من غير سبب يقتضيه ولا كنز وجدوه كشف عن مبادئ أحوالهم وما كان لهم ثمّ صادرهم وأخذ جميع ما استجدّوه وأظهروه. ثمّ اتّفق أنّ بعض النصارى منهم صالحه على خمسين بدرة والبدرة عشرة آلاف وكان النصرانيّ عنده في الاعتقال فبعث رقعة إلى أخيه بحمل المال الذي صالح عليه فحمله فلمّا اعتبره زاد بدرة فقال محمّد بن سليمان مال يُغلط فيه ببدرة إنّه لمال كبير فأخذ منه تتمّة مائة بدرة.

٢،٥،٢ قال الجاحظ وأعجبني قوله الخيانة عشرة أجزاء تسعة منها في القبط وجزء في الناس كلّهم.

١ كذا في ت؛ وفي ب، ج،د: يرفعوا. ٢ كذا في ب، ت،د؛ وفي ج: ومضاهاتهم.

whomever had sufficient means to pay for it, and who by paying a large sum made it a source of his livelihood. They simply stole it, again without making any mention of this among the income that they reported in the tax registers. And they did the same with grazing lands, regulating the freely available pasture that was mentioned in the hadith transmitted from the Prophet, God bless and keep him, in which he said, "People share freely in three things," and proceeded to name pasture as one of them.[84] They took control of the grazing lands by paying a large sum, but they did not record this in their registers, extracting profit for themselves instead. Ibn Ṭūlūn, however, wrested it from them and gave it to the central treasury of the Muslims. The Muslims' treasury has maintained control over these things down to the present day.[85] Just look at the shamelessness of these corrupt people, who act against the Muslims' property, and at the malfeasance they have perpetrated against the treasury, the storehouse of sultans!

The Fifth Section: What Befell Them at the Hands of Muḥammad ibn Sulaymān

When Muḥammad ibn Sulaymān came to Egypt, he learnt of the Copts' perfidy and was informed of their disgraceful and heinous acts, and of the propensity of converts to Islam from their ranks to commit enormities. He was informed, too, that they would vie for superiority with Muslim grandees of long standing in the faith, that they would plunder property whenever they were appointed to a post, and that great sums of money would, for no apparent reason, appear in their possession, and without their having discovered some lost treasure. Upon learning all of this, he conducted an investigation into how much they originally possessed. Then he ordered a general confiscation, taking everything that they had subsequently acquired and flaunted openly. A certain wealthy Christian came to an agreement with him whereby he would pay fifty "purses," a purse being the sum of ten thousand silver coins. From detention, the Christian dispatched a note to his brother, instructing that he should bring him the agreed-upon sum. When the money had been counted, it was found to contain an extra purse. Muḥammad ibn Sulaymān said, "Wealth that is miscounted by a whole purse is wealth indeed!" To supplement the original sum, therefore, he took from him another hundred purses. 2.5.1

Al-Jāḥiẓ has a saying that I like very much: "Perfidy has ten parts, nine of which are found in the Copts and one of which is found in all of mankind."[86] 2.5.2

الفصل السادس فيما جرى أيّام الحاكم بأمر الله في ذلك

قيل إنّ الحاكم رأى في منامه أنّ البارئ سبحانه وتعالى في صورة إنسان حيّ محمول ١،٦،٢
على الأيدي وقد حُمل حتّى أتي به باب القصر فمات.[١] ففسّره لنفسه وقال الحقّ يكون في الدنيا كلّها حقّاً حتّى إذا وصل إلينا بطل. واحتسب على نفسه وأهله ثمّ التفت إلى اليهود والنصارى فاحتسب عليهم في أفعالهم وأنفسهم وكنائسهم وبنى على كلّ كنسية في مملكته مأذنة وهدم ما استجدّوه فيها وأمر أن تلبس الذمّة الثياب السود والعسليّ والسمائيّ. وضاعف عليهم الجزية وأفرد حمّاماتهم عن حمّامات المسلمين وجعل من يخدم فيها ذمّةً وجعل في أعناقهم صلباناً من الجمّيز كلّ صليب منها وزنه ثلاثة أرطال والصلبان المذكورة عند النصارى إلى الآن وفي كنيسة العدويّة منها شيء. وأخذ على أيديهم أن لا يستخدموا في حوائجهم ولا في تصرّفاتهم مسلماً وهدم الكنيسة التي لهم بالقدس الشريف المعروفة بقمامة. وكتب في ذلك بما نسخته أمرتْ حضرة الإمامة بهدم قمامة فلتُجعل سماؤها أرضاً وطولها عرضاً. وهدم الدير المعروف بالقُصَير وأطلق لتمام هدمه وتعفية آثاره ثلاثمائة دينار وأمر بهدم الكنيسة المعروفة بالعجوز[٢] بثغر دمياط وذلك في السابع عشر من شعبان سنة إحدى وتسعين وثلثمائة. وبنى رجل يُعرف بٱبن التمّار وزرعة بن نسطورس كنيسةً في الموضع المعروف براشدة خارج مصر فوجد فيها رجل نصرانيّ يُعرف بٱبن الزنانيريّة مع مسلمة فأمر بهدم الكنيسة المذكورة وبنى موضعها مسجداً وهو الجامع المعروف الآن بجامع راشدة الحاكميّ وأمر أن يُقبض على الرباع المحبّسة على كنائس النصارى واليهود وأحصاها وجبى أموالها مع رباع بيت المال وهدمت منازلهم التي عُلّيت على مساكن المسلمين وأمر ألّا يمكّنوا من تحبيس شيء على كنائسهم ولا من ابتياع عبد مسلم ولا[٣] مجهول

١ كذا في ت؛ والكلمة ساقطة في ب،د. ٢ في سائر المخطوطات: العمرى، وهو تحريف. ٣ كذا في ت،د؛ وفي ب زيادة: من.

The Sixth Section: The Events That Took Place in the Days of al-Ḥākim bi-Amr Allāh

It is said that al-Ḥākim saw a vision of the Creator, be He glorified and exalted, in a dream. The Creator was in the form of a living man who was being carried by human hands. He was borne in this manner to the gate of the palace, whereupon he died. Interpreting the dream for himself, al-Ḥākim said, "The Truth remains true in all the world. Yet when it reaches us it becomes falsehood." He first called himself and his family to account, then turned to the Jews and Christians, calling them to account, too, in respect of their deeds, their persons, and their places of worship. He built a minaret on every church or synagogue in his realm. All those that were of recent construction he tore down. He also commanded that the dhimmis wear black, honey-colored, and sky-blue clothing. He doubled the poll tax and set their baths apart from those of the Muslims, ordering that those who served there also be dhimmis. He commanded that crosses of sycamore wood be placed upon their necks. Each of these crosses weighed about three pounds. The Christians still have these crosses even today; some of them are preserved in the Church of al-ʿAdawiyyah. **2.6.1**

Al-Ḥākim compelled them to swear that they would not employ any Muslim in any task or dealing of theirs. He also tore down their church in Noble Jerusalem known as "Rubbish."[87] Concerning this he wrote, "The Presence of the Imam commands the destruction of Rubbish. Therefore let its loftiness be razed to earth and its great expanse laid low." He tore down the monastery known as al-Quṣayr, too, spending three hundred gold coins to completely raze it and efface its ruins. He also commanded that a church in the border region of Damietta, known as "The Old Woman," be torn down, on the seventeenth of Shaʿban in the year 391 [ca. July 12, 1001].[88] One Ibn al-Tammār joined with ʿĪsā ibn Nasṭūrus to build a church in the place known as Rāshidah, outside of Cairo. A Christian man known as Ibn al-Zanānīriyyah was found in this church with a Muslim woman. Al-Ḥākim commanded that the church be destroyed and built a mosque in its place. This is the congregational mosque known today as the Ḥākimī Congregational Mosque of Rāshidah.[89] He also commanded that rental incomes dedicated to the churches and synagogues be seized and counted, and their fees collected along with the rental incomes of the central treasury. Christians' houses that were taller than Muslims' were torn down. Al-Ḥākim commanded that they not be permitted to endow any

النصرانيّة أو اليهوديّة ولا من ابتياع عُدّة من آلات الحرب ولا استرهانها. ونودي مَن فعل ذلك منهم فقد برئت منه الذمّة، معناه صاروا مثل أهل الحرب يسبى حريمهم وتستباح أموالهم ودماؤهم.

وخرج أمره ألّا يكتب أحد في الدواوين بالقبطيّ بل بالعربيّ وكتب على الكتّاب التداريك[١] بذلك ومن خالف وفعل تقطع يده فأقدم على المخالفة في ذلك جماعة من النصارى استغفالاً لولاة الأمر من قبله فقطعت أيديهم بأسرهم حين علموا بهم وأُخذ جميع أموالهم لأجل ذلك. ٢،٦،٢

ومن جملة إقدام الأقباط النصارى أنّهم اجتمعوا وقرّروا لكنائسهم فُدُنًا من أراضي بيت المال فلمّا انتهى ذلك إلى الحاكم أنكره وأكبره وأعظمه وضرب على الجميع ثمّ أمر بعمل شونة قبالة مسجد تبرٍ المقابل لأرض المطريّة وملأها حلفاءً وحطباً ولم يعلم مراده بذلك فأشاع الناس أنّه عزم على إحراق الكتّاب من النصارى واليهود فيها فاجتمع شيوخهم وأطفالهم وعجائزهم وحريمهم وتمسّكوا بأبواب القصر وضجّوا ضجيج الخائف من النار فبلغ ذلك جهات القصر فرقّوا لهم عند ملاذهم من النار بأبواب الحاكم فشفعوا إليه فيهم فعفا عنهم بعد أن لم يُبقِ لذي مال منهم مالاً. ثمّ صار أيّ من بلغه عنه من النصارى أو أولادهم الذين أسلموا أنّه جمع مالاً أو عمّر ملكاً ضرب عليه وأخذه منه وجعله لبيت المال وإنّما فعل ذلك لعلمه بهم وبإقدامهم فخشي أن تجتمع إقدام ومال وعُدد وأصالة[٢] في البلاد فلا تؤمن غائلتهم وأن يكاتبوا العدوّ ويجعلوا له طريقاً إلى البلاد وطمعاً[٣] فيها أو يسلكوا بالمال أنواعاً من الفساد.[٤] ٣،٦،٢

---

١ كذا في ت؛ وفي ب، د: مكاتيب. ٢ كذا في ت؛ وفي ب، ج، د: وتمكّن. ٣ كذا في ت؛ وفي ب، د: إطماعًا.
٤ تأتي هنا في ج زيادة: والذي خاف منه الحاكم جرى أيّام يلبغا وأبيعت لهم الاسكندريّة حتّى ملكوها وأخذوا أموالها وقتلوا أهلها فلا حول ولا قوّة إلّا بالله العليّ العظيم.

property for the benefit of their places of worship, or to purchase Muslim slaves, or those of whom it was unknown whether they might be Christians or Jews. They were also not permitted to buy or take as security any weapon or materiel of war. It was decreed, "Whosoever of them does this shall lose the Pact of Security."[90] The meaning of this declaration was that they would become tantamount to the People of the Non-Muslim Lands; their women might be taken prisoner and their property and blood declared licit.

His command issued forth that no one in the offices of the state was to write in Coptic; all officials were to write in Arabic instead. To this writ he appended an additional charge: "Whosoever disobeys shall have his hand cut off." A group of Christians dared to disobey, believing those in authority to be unmindful of them. When their deed was discovered, every one of them lost his hand, and all of their property was taken from them. 2.6.2

An example of how brazen the Copts were in this period was that they met together and assigned countless acres of land to their own churches that belonged properly to the central treasury. When al-Ḥākim learnt of this, he condemned it as an enormity and arrested them all. He then commanded that a silo be constructed opposite the Mosque of Tibr, hard by the area of al-Maṭariyyah. This silo he filled with grass and dry wood. Although no one knew what he intended to do, a rumor spread among the people that he had resolved to burn the Christian and Jewish secretaries in the silo he had built. All the Christians and Jews congregated at the gates of the palace—elders and children, old women and young—and raised an uproar such as only those gripped by fear of Hellfire can produce. News of this reached certain persons within the palace, who pitied these people who had taken refuge from the fire at the gates of al-Ḥākim. These persons interceded successfully with al-Ḥākim to forgive the Christians and Jews, but only after they had been stripped of all their wealth. After that, if al-Ḥākim heard that one of the Christians or their progeny who converted to Islam had amassed wealth or invested in some property, he would arrest him, take his property from him, and make it over to the central treasury. The reason for this policy of his was that he knew how audacious the Copts were. He feared lest that audacity be amplified by wealth, materiel, and deep roots in the lands of Egypt, to the point that the Copts might come to pose a real danger. They might correspond with the enemy and furnish him with a way into the land and a desire to conquer it. In truth, there was no limit to the wicked things they might do with their wealth. 2.6.3

الفصل السابع فيما جرى في ذلك أيّام[1] الآمر وما وقع للملعون الراهب من المصادرة

وذلك أنّ النصارى امتدّت أيديهم في أيّام الآمر إلى الأموال ونفق سوقهم بالنفاق ١،٧،٢ وبسطوا أيديهم بالخيانة وتعدّت أفعالهم إلى أذيّة المسلمين حتّى وصلوا بالمضرّة إلى أصحاب الزوايا والمنقطعين من الصالحين. وكان فيهم كاتب يُعرف بالراهب لقّب بالأب القدّيس الروحانيّ النفيس أبي الآباء وسيّد الرؤساء مقدّم دين النصرانيّة وسيّد البطريركيّة[2] ثالث عشر الحواريّين فجلس الملعون وصادر الوارد والصادر وجميع من حوته الديار المصريّة حتّى الشهود والحكّام والأجناد والتجّار وغيرهم وامتدّت يده إلى العوامّ أرباب المعايش والناس على اختلاف طبقاتهم. فمن أغرب ما جرى لهذا الملعون الكلب الكافر أنّه رُفعت إليه ورقة في قاضي القضاة فكشف عنها وأهان القاضي بالكشف ثمّ كشف عن حواصل الجامع العتيق بمصر وأهان بذلك متصدّريه وقرّاءه وإمامه وخطيبه ومؤذّنيه وقومته والناظر فيه فجاء إليه بعض الناس وخوّفه من العاقبة في معارضته ومصادمته للأمور الشرعيّة وإهانته لخدّام الشرع الشريف ومقاومته لهم فقال نحن كنّا أصحاب هذه البلاد فأُخرجنا منها وأُهنّا وسُبينا وضُربت علينا الجزية فإذا أمكنتنا الفرصة من المسلمين الذين فعلوا بنا ذلك بواسطة خدمة صاحب السيف وتمكّنّا بحيلتنا من إظهار النصائح وجمع المال له توصّلنا بذلك إلى إهانة المسلمين كان ببعض ما جرى علينا منهم فنحن نصل بخدمة من يملك البلاد إلى أغراضنا في أموال المسلمين وأنفسهم ورعيّتهم وإهانة أهل دينهم ويكون ذلك منّا استيفاءً لبعض ما لنا عليهم. وأنشد لعنه الله متمثّلاً [الرمل]

---

١ كذا في ت؛ وفي ب،د زيادة: الخليفة. ٢ كذا في ت؛ وفي ب،د: البطريكيّة.

The Seventh Section: The Events That Took Place in the Days of al-Āmir, and the Confiscations Carried Out by the Accursed Monk

In the days of al-Ḥākim, the Christians stretched out their hands to lay hold 2.7.1
of property. They did a brisk trade in dissimulation and outdid themselves in perfidy. So far did they transgress that they did great damage to the Muslims, harming even the Sufi ascetics, the people who dedicate their lives to pious devotion. One of these Christians was a secretary known as the Monk. He was addressed by the titles Saintly Father, Excellent Divine, Father of Fathers, Lord of Superiors, Foremost in the Christian Faith, Lord of the Patriarchate, and Thirteenth Disciple. This cursed man sat in authority over the land of Egypt, confiscating the property of everyone within reach, all that the land contained. His confiscations touched the professional witnesses and the judges, military men, traders, and others. His hand even reached the common working people and the sundry classes of the whole population.

One of the more disturbing deeds of this accursed infidel dog occurred when a report was brought to him of misconduct involving the Chief Judge. The Monk opened an investigation into this report, thereby insulting the judge. Then he opened another into the financial affairs of the ancient mosque in Fusṭāṭ,[91] thereby insulting its professors, its Qur'an reciters, its imam, its preacher, its muezzins, its custodians, and its overseer. Some notables came to him and attempted to impress upon him the consequences of his antagonism, his hostile interference in religious affairs, and his insults and opposition to the servants of the Noble Law of the Muslims. This was his response: "It is we who were masters of these lands. We were expelled from them, we were insulted, we were taken prisoner, we were subjected to the poll tax. Thus whenever we find an opportunity to get back at the Muslims who did this to us by serving a man of the sword, feigning goodwill, and collecting money on his behalf, it allows us to insult the Muslims. We consider this a reparation for just a fraction of what they did to us. By serving the one who controls these lands we obtain what we want from the Muslims' property, their persons, and their subjects, and are able to insult their coreligionists. Thus are we compensated for a little bit of what they owe us." He recited these verses, God curse him, to make his point:

بِنْتُ كَرْمٍ غَصَبُوهَا أُمَّهَا   وَأَهَانُوهَا بِوَطْءٍ بِالْقَدَمْ
ثُمَّ عَادُوا حَكَّمُوهَا فِيهِمِ   وَلَنَاهِيكَ بِخَصْمٍ يُحْتَكَمْ

فاستحسن من حوله من السفلة النصارى هذا القول منه.

٢،٧،٢ وكان الملعون لمّا تفاقم أمره في سوء تدبيره وشاع ذكره واطّلع الآمر على العورات التي سُطرت في صحيفة سيرته وعلم أنّ الناس منه ومن فعله فيهم في أمرٍ مريج قبض عليه وأهانه غاية الإهانة وفعل فيه أنواعاً من العذاب أنزّه هذا المختصر عن ذكرها لفحشها وضرب على جميع ماله من الأموال والرباع.[١] ولقد اعتبر ما اغتصبه الراهب المذكور من أملاك المسلمين في الديار المصريّة بين حانوت ودار ومعصرة وفندق وطاحون وربع ومسقّف وساحة فكان عدّته مائة ألف وسبعين ألف ملك. ولمّا[٢] أن ولي أبو عليّ ابن الأفضل بن شاهن شاه بن أمير الجيوش أعاد ذلك جميعه على أصحابه وقيل إنّ الراهب الملعون[٣] سُمّر على لوحٍ وألقي في البحر وكان الناس يحصبونه بالحجر والقاذورات[٤] وكان لإلقائه فيه يوم مشهود.

الفصل الثامن فيما جرى من خيانتهم في أمر عريب المغنّية

١،٨،٢ وممّا جرى من خيانة النصارى العظيمة ما حكاه الهشاميّ ورواه أبو الفرج الإصبهانيّ وهو أنّ عريب المأمونيّة وهي المغنّية المشهورة بالغناء وما يناسبه هي ابنة جعفر بن يحيى بن خالد بن برمك وذلك أنّه رأى في بعض آدُر أهله يتيمةً ربّتها أمّ عبد الله بن يحيى بن خالد يقال لها فاطمة فأعجبته فتزوّجها سرّاً من أبيه فولدت له عريب وماتت فدفعها لامرأةٍ نصرانيّة كانت هي وزوجها من جملة خدمه اللابسين حلل نعمه وأمرها بتربيتها فلمّا أصيب جعفر في نفسه باعتها النصرانيّة برأي النصرانيّ واتّفاق

١ تأتي الفقرة من (وكان الملعون) في شطرين بعد عدة أسطر في ب،د؛ انظر الحاشيتين رقم ٢ ورقم ٣ بالأسفل. ٢ يأتي هنا في ب،د الشطر الأوّل من الفقرة المشار إليها فوق؛ انظر الحاشية رقم ١. ٣ يأتي هنا في ب و د الشطر الثاني من الفقرة المشار إليها فوق؛ انظر الحاشية رقم ١. ٤ كذا في ت؛ والعبارة من (وكان الناس) ساقطة في ب، ج،د.

A grape—a daughter of the vine—whom
they stripped from her mother and insulted under their feet,
Yet they then turned and made her ruler over them;
what, pray, shall happen when the foe has her way?

The degenerate Christians who were around him praised what he said.[92]

As the problem of this accursed man and his evil plans went from bad to worse, word about him spread among all the people. Caliph al-Āmir was informed of the shameful deeds that filled the pages of the Monk's life, and learnt that the people were in a state of great disturbance and confusion because of him and his deeds. Thereupon al-Āmir arrested the Monk and humiliated him to the utmost degree. He tortured him in ways too horrific to describe here. He confiscated all of his property, both cash and real estate. The amount this Monk had seized from the Muslims of Egypt—including shops, houses, presses, hostels, mills, living quarters, and structures, both canopied and open—was reckoned at one hundred seventy thousand properties. When Abū ʿAlī ibn al-Afḍal ibn Shāhān Shāh ibn Amīr al-Juyūsh took command in Egypt, he returned all this property to its rightful owners. It is said that the accursed Monk was crucified on a plank and cast into the Nile as the people pelted him with stones and garbage. Everyone in the city came out on that day. 2.7.2

The Eighth Section: Their Perfidy in the Story of ʿArīb the Singer[93]

One instance of the Christians' boundless perfidy was recounted by al-Hishāmī and narrated by Abū l-Faraj al-Iṣbahānī, as follows. ʿArīb al-Maʾmūniyyah, Caliph al-Maʾmūn's famously talented singer, was actually the daughter of Jaʿfar ibn Yaḥyā ibn Khālid ibn Barmak.[94] Jaʿfar had taken an interest in an orphan girl named Fāṭimah, who had been raised in his extended family by Umm ʿAbdallāh ibn Yaḥyā ibn Khālid. He liked her, and married her, but kept the matter secret from his father. She bore him ʿArīb but died soon thereafter. Jaʿfar gave ʿArīb to a Christian woman, who with her husband was one of those servants who enjoyed his special favor. He charged this woman with the task of raising the girl. After Jaʿfar's fall from favor, however, the Christian woman sold her to a slave trader at the behest of her husband. The slave trader in his turn sold her to al-Marākibī, who carried her to Basra and there taught her Arabic grammar. From that point her story is well known from the history 2.8.1

منه لرجل نخّاس فباعها النخّاس للمراكبيّ فحملها إلى البصرة وعلّمها النحو وكان من أمرها ما كان ممّا هو مشهور في التواريخ ولم تزل في المملكة حتّى ماتت فهذا من أعجب ما جرى من إقدامهم وخيانتهم.

الفصل التاسع فيما جرى من تميمهم أيّام[1] الحافظ وخيانتهم في دولته وإفسادهم ما صلح من سيرته

وذلك أنّ الموفّق بن الخلّال رحمه الله كان متولّياً ديوان الإنشاء ومتصرّفاً فيه كيف ١،٩،٢
شاء وكان الحافظ قد ولّاه ديوان المجلس وردّ إليه النظر على الدواوين كلّها وذلك
في سنة ثلاث وثلاثين وخمسمائة فأجرى أمور الدولة على الصراط المستقيم وفكّ
المعتقلين وأنصف المظلومين من الظالمين وٱستخدم الكتّاب المسلمين وجمع بين
حسن السمعة[2] وطيّب قلوب الرعيّة وحبّب أجناد الدولة لها وأفاض عليهم من نيلها
وٱستخرج الأموال من جهاتها وحمل إلى الخزائن في ميقاتها وفصّل بنور اجتهاده
بين خير الأمور وشرّها ونفعها وضرّها فلم يُسمع بمعتقل في مدّة ولايته ولا متظلّم
من ناحيته ولا أهان مسلماً بسبب استخراج مالٍ ولا غيره ولا أستأدى[3] جعلاً
على حالةٍ من الأحوال فبقيت الدولة به رافلة في حلّة الكمال متلفّعة أثواب[4] الجمال
وأعلن الناس بالدعاء للدولة بالبقاء لما نالهم من خيرها وخصّهم من جلالة قدرها.

فعظم ذلك على النصارى وفقدوا ما كان يصل إليهم من المصانعات وعسر
عليهم جريان الأمور على السداد وولاية المسلمين للأشغال. فٱجتمعوا إلى رجل ٢،٩،٢
يقال له الأخرم المعروف بٱبن أبي[5] زكريّاء الكاتب وسألوه أن يشير عليهم بما

١ كذا في ت؛ وفي ب،د زيادة: الخليفة. ٢ يحتمل سقوط بعض الكلمات هنا في سائر المخطوطات. ٣ كذا في ت؛ وفي ب،د: غرم مستخدمًا. ٤ كذا في ت؛ وفي ب،د: متلفّفة بثياب. ٥ ت: بابن؛ وفي بقيّة المخطوطات: بأبي، ولعلّ الصواب ما أثبتناه من المواعظ، ٣٣١-٢:٣٢، ح ٣.

books; she remained prominent at the highest levels of the realm until her death. This is among the more noteworthy instances of their shamelessness and perfidy.

The Ninth Section: Their Scheming in the Days of al-Ḥāfiẓ, Their Perfidy during His Regime, and the Way in Which They Corrupted Aspects of His Life Which Had Otherwise Been Righteous

At that time al-Muwaffaq ibn al-Khallāl, God have mercy on him, had charge of the Office of the Chancery, which he directed as he wished. Al-Ḥāfiẓ had also appointed him over the Office of the Council and made him overseer of all the offices of the state; this was in the year 533 [1138–39]. Al-Muwaffaq ensured that the affairs of government were on the straight path; he released those imprisoned for financial reasons, gave the oppressed justice vis-à-vis their oppressors, employed Muslim secretaries, and joined a good reputation to goodwill in the hearts of all the subjects. Because of him, the armies were well disposed toward the government, for he granted them a generous share in the state's income. He collected taxes from those who really owed them, bore them to the treasuries in their proper seasons, and by the light of his judgment distinguished between matters good and evil, beneficial and harmful. During his appointment, it was unheard of for anyone to be imprisoned for financial reasons or to protest a wrong. Nor did he injure anyone, Muslim or otherwise, by extracting wealth from him, or demand the wages of anyone under any circumstance. Thus by his good management the government strode forth proudly in the flowing garments of perfection, enfolding itself in the robes of beauty. The people, because of the good benefit and glorious pride that they derived from his rule, prayed openly that it might continue forever in this manner. 2.9.1

To the Christians, however, all of this was intolerable. They lost the bribes they were accustomed to receiving and were vexed that the government's affairs ran so well, and that Muslims were employed to carry out its functions. The Christian secretaries gathered together and went to a man referred to as al-Akhram, the Cut-Nosed, and known as Ibn Abī Zakariyyā the Secretary.[95] Complaining of the income they had lost when Muslims were employed in the government service, they asked Ibn Abī Zakariyyā to advise them about what they should do given their situation. They informed him that they had agreed 2.9.2

يعتمدونه في أمرهم وشكوا إليه ما نالهم من انقطاع رزقهم بآستخدام المسلمين في الخدم وأخبروه أنّهم أجمعوا على حيلة يصنعونها ومكيدة يبتدعونها إلى أن يصلوا إلى أغراضهم ويتحكّموا في الدولة بأقلامهم فضربوا في ذلك أراء متعدّدة انتهى آخرها إلى رأي أجمعوا عليه وهو أن يقرّروا مع منجّم الحافظ ما يقوله له وكان للحافظ منجّم يسيّر مولده في كلّ سنة ويحكم له بما يتجدّد في دولته حسب ما اقتضاه فنّه وما يدّعيه في عمله وكان الحافظ محبّاً للنجامة قائلاً بها عاملاً بما يخيّل إليه من أحكامها معتقداً بغلبة ظنّه أنّها حقّ فاتّفق رأيهم على مصالحة المنجّم بمالٍ له جسد وهان عليهم بذل ذلك في بلوغ غرضهم. وسألوه أنّه إذا سيّر المولد الحافظيّ أن يشرح في فصل منه أنّه متى نظر في أمر الدواوين وأبواب المال من كانت صفته كذا وكذا وحليته كذا وكذا زكا فيه الارتفاع ونما واستمرّت زيادة النيل في كلّ سنة وبلغ الحدّ الذي يعمّ نفعه وأمن نقصه وانقطاعه وتوالت المسرّات إلى الحافظ وعمرت البلاد وصلح ما فسد من الأحوال. فوافقهم المنجّم على ذلك وأجابهم إلى ما التمسوه منه لأجل ما أخذه منهم من المال[١] والتحف. ورفع المولد المسيّر وقد ضمّنه ما رتّبوه من الحيلة فتصفّح الحافظ المولد جميعه ولم يشتغل بغيره فعند وقوفه على فصل الحيلة المتضمّن ذكر الحلية أمر في الحال أن يُكشف له في أرباب الدولة عمّن حليته كذا وصفته كذا فكشفوا فوجدوا المطلوب فقيل له هذه حلية ابن أبي زكريّاء[٢] الكاتب فأحضره وقابل بحليته ما في المولد فلمّا صحّ عنده بالمقابلة أنّه هو سلّم إليه الديوان وعزل القاضي الموفّق فأقام ابن أبي زكريّاء[٣] المذكور يستخرج الأموال ويصرف منها في بلوغ أغراضه ونيل أمانيه ويصانع من حول الحافظ وكنز لنفسه الأموال وأغنى

---

١ كذا في ت؛ وفي ب، ج،د زيادة: والقماش. ٢ في سائر المخطوطات: أبي زكريا. ٣ في سائر المخطوطات: فأقام أبو زكريا.

to devise a stratagem, a ploy that would allow them to get what they wanted, namely to reign supreme in the government by means of their pens. After reviewing the opinions of their fellows, they agreed together on a plan. They would conspire with a certain astrologer of al-Ḥāfiẓ and entrust to him a message to convey to the caliph. Al-Ḥāfiẓ had an astrologer who each year would predict the future by recasting the caliph's horoscope,[96] adjudging for him what new events would occur in his state, as the astrologer's art required and his practice dubiously asserted. The caliph loved astrology; he pronounced according to its dictates, acted according to what he imagined to be its rules, and believed strongly that it was the truth. The plan that the Christians agreed upon was to suborn the astrologer with an amount of money that, though quite substantial, was nothing to them compared to what they stood to gain. They asked this astrologer, when he would write out the prediction from the caliph's horoscope, to explain in one section that when the caliph would espy a man of a certain description in the government financial offices, whose face would have such-and-such an aspect, it would portend every kind of good thing. The tax receipts would increase and grow, and the level of the Nile flood would swell and rise in each successive year until it reached the point at which general prosperity was assured and security obtained against shortfall and failure.[97] The resultant happiness would swell uninterrupted to benefit al-Ḥāfiẓ himself; the lands would prosper and all that had been subject to corruption would be restored.

The astrologer agreed, assenting to what they requested in exchange for money and gifts he would receive. He submitted the horoscope, within which was secreted the stratagem they had devised. Al-Ḥāfiẓ read the entire horoscope, concerning himself with nothing else until he had finished it. When he came to the section that contained the stratagem, and its description of the man's appearance, he commanded straight away that a search be made among the grandees for a man of that appearance and those qualities. The search was made, and the man was found. Al-Ḥāfiẓ was told, "That is the description of Ibn Abī Zakariyyā the Secretary!" They summoned Ibn Abī Zakariyyā at once, and indeed his looks matched the description found in the horoscope. After establishing that he was the man, al-Ḥāfiẓ ceded to him command of the administration and removed Judge al-Muwaffaq. Ibn Abī Zakariyyā promptly set about confiscating property, spending from what he collected to achieve his own purposes and reach his aims. He bribed people close to al-Ḥāfiẓ, piled up wealth for himself, enriched his relations, and appointed them over

أقاربه وولّاهم معالي الأمور والجهات التي فيها الأموال المجهولة وما لا يضطرّ إلى الأمانة.

٣،٩،٢ فلم يكن إلّا برهة من الزمان حتّى ظهر للحافظ ما تمّمه النصرانيّ وما دسّ عليه المنجّم وكشف أمر الأموال فوجدها من النقص على أسوأ حال فأمر بقتل الكلب النصرانيّ ابن أبي زكريّا[١] وقتل المنجّم فقتلا شرّ قتلة ومُثّل بهما أعظم مُثلة ورسم بإعادة القاضي الموفّق بن الخلّال فلم يفعل.[٢]

٤،٩،٢ فلينظر الإنسان إلى دقيق هذه الحيلة والتوصّل بهذه الأفعال الشيطانيّة والإقدام على الأمور السلطانيّة العظيمة الخطر والتتيم على جلال الخلافة بالزور والكذب واستغفال عقول قد أسرتها الشهوات وغيّبتها عن المصالح حجب اللذّات.[٣] وفي هذا النصرانيّ يقول الشاعر [الوافر]

إِذَا حَكَمَ ٱلنَّصَارَى فِي ٱلْفُرُوجِ　　وَغَالَوْا بِٱلْبِغَالِ وَبِٱلسُّرُوجِ
وَذَلَّتْ دَوْلَةُ ٱلْإِسْلَامِ طُرًّا　　وَصَارَ ٱلْأَمْرُ فِي أَيْدِي ٱلْعُلُوجِ
فَقُلْ لِلْأَعْوَرِ ٱلدَّجَّالِ هٰذَا　　زَمَانُكَ إِنْ عَزَمْتَ عَلَى ٱلْخُرُوجِ

الفصل العاشر فيما جرى من إقدامهم على الشهادة في حجج المسلمين

١،١٠،٢ وذلك أنّ رجلاً دخل سوق البزّازين ومعه حجّة شرعيّة يلتمس شهوداً عدولاً يشهدون له فيها على خصمه فوجد قوماً من النصارى عليهم لباس المسلمين وزيّهم ولم يعرفهم حقّ المعرفة لكونه غريباً فقدّم الحجّة إليهم فشهدوا فيها وجسروا على هذا الأمر الخطر وراح صاحب الحجّة مدحوض الحجّة وبقي في أمانة غريمه.

١ في سائر المخطوطات: أبي زكريا. ٢ كذا في ت؛ وتأتي هذه الفقرة كلّها من (فأقام ابن أبي زكريّاء) بالأسفل في ب ،د؛ انظر الحاشية رقم ٣. ٣ كذا في ت؛ وتأتي هنا الفقرة المشار إليها فوق؛ انظر الحاشية رقم ٢. وتأتي هنا أيضا زيادة في ج: كما في زماننا هذا.

important matters and to positions in which uncounted sums of money were handled without any oversight to compel honesty.

Hardly any time passed before the Christians' plot became apparent to al-Ḥāfiẓ and he saw how the astrologer had intrigued against him. He investigated the finances and found them badly deficient. Upon discovering this, he commanded that the Christian Ibn Abī Zakariyyā and the astrologer both be executed. The command was carried out promptly; they were executed in a most gruesome manner that set a grisly example for others. Al-Ḥāfiẓ commanded that Judge al-Muwaffaq ibn al-Khallāl be restored to his post, but it was not done.[98] **2.9.3**

See how carefully this stratagem was planned! We must not fail to mark how they were able to proceed by means of these demonic deeds, shamelessly aspiring to control the great and solemn affairs of state. They plotted even against the splendor of the caliphate using falsehood and lies, thinking to take advantage of minds that were bound fast by passions and blinded by veils of desire to the best interests of the state. Concerning this Christian, the poet said: **2.9.4**

When the Christians rule in the far reaches of the land,
raining down destruction from their mules and their saddles,
While all the state of Islam is humiliation,
and authority passes to uncouth infidels,
Say to the One-Eyed Antichrist,
"This is your time, if you would come forth."[99]

The Tenth Section: Their Shameless Testimony in Court Cases Involving Muslims

One day a certain man came to the Market of the Textile Merchants with a legal document. He was looking for upright, approved legal witnesses to testify for him against his opponent. In the market he found a group of Christians who were dressed just like Muslims. Since he was a stranger there, he did not know who they really were. He presented them the document and they appended their signatures to it, daring to involve themselves in an affair of considerable gravity! As a result, the man lost his case and found himself at the mercy of his rival.[100] **2.10.1**

قلتُ ولمّا سُمعت هذه القضية كانت سبباً لتجديد التأكيد في لبس الذمّة الغيار ٢،١٠،٢ والتحريج[١] عليهم في التزامهم لبسه وإقامة محتسب يحتسب عليهم في أحوالهم ليس له شغل سواهم وصارت ولاية من جملة الولايات وذلك في زمن الآمر.

ثمّ أنشئ في دولته كتاب بليغ ذو خطبة صادعة قرئ على المنابر وصار زاداً للمسافر ٣،١٠،٢ وحديثاً للمسامر ورواية للبادي والحاضر وهو كتاب طويل ذو خطبة طويلة. تركت ذكره قصداً للاختصار وتجنّباً للإكثار فإنّ في الآيات الشريفات التي تقدّم ذكرها في مبدأ هذا الكتاب كفاية لكنّي أذكر لُمعاً من الخطبة فمنها ومعلوم أنّ اليهود والنصارى موسومون بغضب الله ولعنته وبالشرك بالله والجحد لوحدانيّته وقد أمر الله سبحانه عباده المسلمين في أمّ الكتاب المختوم إحرازاً لثوابها عند تلاوتها وهي السورة التي لا يتمّ فريضة ولا نافلة إلّا بها بأن يدعوا ويرغبوا إليه أن يهديهم سبيل المؤمنين ويعيذهم من هذين الفريقين الكافرين المجرمين فقال ﴿اهْدِنَا الصِّرَاطَ الْمُسْتَقِيمَ صِرَاطَ الَّذِينَ أَنْعَمْتَ عَلَيْهِمْ غَيْرِ الْمَغْضُوبِ عَلَيْهِمْ وَلَا الضَّالِّينَ﴾ فالمغضوب عليهم اليهود بالإجماع وبإقرارهم والضالّون النصارى الذين آذن بخزيهم ومصيرهم إلى دار البوار قال سبحانه في اليهود ﴿وَضُرِبَتْ عَلَيْهِمُ الذِّلَّةُ وَالْمَسْكَنَةُ﴾ ﴿ذَٰلِكَ بِأَنَّهُمْ كَانُوا يَكْفُرُونَ بِآيَاتِ اللَّهِ وَيَقْتُلُونَ النَّبِيِّينَ بِغَيْرِ الْحَقِّ ۗ ذَٰلِكَ بِمَا عَصَوْا وَكَانُوا يَعْتَدُونَ﴾ وقد قال رسول الله صلّى الله عليه وسلّم شرّ الناس من قتل نبيّاً أو قتله نبيّ. فمن جملة[٢] ما[٣] في الكتاب المذكور ولا تمكّن الذمّة بأن يتسمّوا بأسماء المسلمين فينادى ذمّيّ يا أبا الحسن، يا أبا الحسين، يا أبا عليّ، يا أبا الطاهر وكذلك المنع من إطلاق اسم المشيخة فإنّ ذلك ممّا تأباه النخوة الإسلاميّة والعزّة الإيمانيّة وأن يلزموا بلبس الزنانير وشدّها في أوساطهم ظاهرةً وليحذر الراكب من إخفاء زنّاره بالجلوس عليه ولا يمكّنوا من ركوب شيء من الخيل ولا من البغال[٤] ولا يسلكوا مقابر المسلمين في نهار ولا ليل ولا يمكّنوا من المراكيب

---

١ كذا في ت؛ وفي ب: جرج؛ د: خرج. ٢ كذا في ج؛ وفي ب، د: عمل. ٣ كذا في ب، ج، د؛ والفقرة من (وهي السورة التي) ساقطة في ت. ٤ كذا في ت؛ وفي ب، د زيادة: ولا يمكّنوا من الركب الحديد ولا من السروج الحديد.

I would add that when the news of this incident spread, it led to renewed demands that the dhimmis be pressured to observe the requirement to wear the outward markers that distinguish them from Muslims. This requirement, duly observed, effectively disqualified them as potential witnesses. An official inspector was also appointed whose sole responsibility was to oversee their affairs. Thereafter it became a regular office; this was in the time of al-Āmir. **2.10.2**

In that same time a most eloquent document was indited, abounding in frank admonition, that was read aloud from the pulpits. For the wayfarer it became a veritable store of provisions, and for the conversationalist the very substance of his speech. It was discussed among the people near and far. It is a long document, full of long discourses; I have chosen not to reproduce it here, in order to achieve concision and to eschew excess. Indeed, the Noble Verses which were produced at the beginning of this book are sufficient for the purpose, but I shall present a very small selection as follows: **2.10.3**

> It is well known that the Jews and Christians are marked by the anger of God and his curse, by unbelief toward God and denial of his unity. Indeed God, be He exalted, has commanded his servants the Muslims in the first surah of the Sealed Book[101]—this being the surah without which no prayer, obligatory or supererogatory, is complete—to pray and beseech Him to guide them in the way of the believers and to save them from these two wrongdoing infidel bands, so that by reciting these words they may obtain a reward. For He said: «Guide us in the straight path, the path of those whom Thou hast blessed, not of those against whom Thou art wrathful, nor of those who are astray.»[102] Those against whom He is wrathful are the Jews, by universal agreement and by their own admission. Those who are astray are of course the Christians, whose disgrace and destiny in the House of Perdition He announced. Concerning the Jews, God, be He exalted, has said, «And abasement and poverty were pitched upon them»; «that, because they had disbelieved the signs of God and slain the Prophets unrightfully; that, because they disobeyed, and were transgressors.»[103] The Messenger of God, God bless and keep him, said, "The worst person is the one who kills a prophet, or is killed by one."[104]

Also contained in the above-mentioned document were the following lines: "The dhimmis must not be permitted to call themselves by Muslim names, being addressed as 'Abū l-Ḥasan,' 'Abū l-Ḥusayn,' 'Abū 'Alī,' 'Abū Ṭāhir,' and the like. Likewise, we must bar them from using the honorific title of Shaykh, for the dignity of Islam and the pride of the faith flatly forbid that they should

المحلّاة ولتكن توابيت موتاهم مشدودة بحبال الليف مكشوفة غير مغشّاة[1] وليمنعوا من حمل توابيتهم على الأكتاف فلتجرّ على التراب جرًّا. وآخر الكتاب وأن يمنعوا من تبييض قبورهم مع وصايا كثيرة شُرطت عليهم أقاموا تحتها مدّة طويلة والله أعلم.[2]

الفصل الحادي عشر في ما جرى من تميمهم في المساحة وإقدامهم على الأذى من غير مراقبة الله تعالى ولا خوف فضيحة من الوقوف على خزيهم ولا نظر في عاقبة

وذلك أنّ بعض النصارى العمّال توجّه لمساحة بعض الأعمال فعدّى في بعض المعادي ١،١١،٢
قاصدًا موضع مساحته فلمّا وصل إلى البرّ التمس منه صاحب المعدية أجرة تعديته فمنعه ولم يعطه شيئًا وعسر عليه أن يستمهله إلى أن يرجع بل أغلظ عليه في الكلام وتحامق وتراقع. فأخذ صاحبُ المعدية لجام دابّته رهنًا على حقّه فترك النصرانيّ اللجام ومضى فلمّا مسح الأراضي ثبت في قنداق المساحة أرض اللجام بٱسم ضامن المعدية عشرين فدّانًا ثمّ نقل ذلك من القنداق إلى المكلّفة وخلّد الكلّ في الديوان. فلمّا توجّه المندوبون لٱستخراج مال الأراضي والخراج ومعهم التذاكير بأسماء أربابها طولب ضامن المعدية بما كُتب في جهته فأقسم أنّه ما زرع قطّ وسأل أن يكشف من المزارعين هل ثَمّ أرض تُعرف باللجام وحكى القصّة التي جرت له مع العامل النصرانيّ في أخذ لجامه رهنًا على أجرة التعدية فلم يُقبل منه ذلك وضُرب وسُجن حتّى قام بما كان في التذكرة منسوبًا إليه وشهدت أعمال المستخرج ومياومته[3] بٱستخراجه منه بجملته.

---

١ كذا في ت؛ وفي ب، د زيادة: ولا مغطاة. ٢ كذا في ب، د؛ والفقرة من (مع وصايا) ساقطة في ت. ٣ كذا في ت؛ وفي ب،د: ساومته.

do this. They must be compelled to wear their distinguishing belts and clasp them about their waists in plain view. Let the rider take care not to hide his distinguishing belt by sitting on it. They must not be permitted to ride any kind of horse or mule. Let them not pass by the tombs of Muslims by day or by night. They must not be permitted caparisoned mounts. Let the caskets of their dead—open, not closed—be pulled along the ground by ropes of palm fiber. They must be forbidden to carry their caskets on their shoulders. Let them instead be dragged through the dust." The last part of the document reads: "Let them be forbidden to make their tombs white." There were also many other instructions that were imposed upon them, under which they lived for a long time. God knows best.[105]

The Eleventh Section: Concerning Their Scheming in Carrying Out the Cadastral Survey, and Their Shamelessness in Causing Harm, with No Concern for God, Be He Exalted, No Fear of Scandal from the Discovery of Their Disgrace, and No Regard for Consequences

A Christian official set out to survey a certain district. He crossed the river on a **2.11.1** ferry in the direction of the land he was to survey. When he reached the shore, the ferryman requested the fare, but the official refused, and gave him nothing. Instead he pressured the ferryman to defer the payment until his return, speaking harshly to him and affecting foolishness and stupidity. As surety for what he was owed, the ferryman seized the bridle of the official's mount. Leaving the bridle behind him, the Christian continued on his way.

When the lands had been surveyed, there in the survey log, under the name of the ferry owner, was "the Land of the Bridle, twenty acres." This information was copied from the log into the notice of the land tax that was to be given to the landowner.[106] All of these records were filed at the central office. When in due course the land-tax collectors went out, carrying with them the demand-slips on which were written the names of those who owed taxes, they commanded that the ferry owner pay what the record showed him to owe. Swearing that he had never cultivated any land, the ferry owner requested that the local farmers be asked whether there existed any "Land of the Bridle" in that region. He also told them the story of how he had taken the Christian official's bridle as surety for the fare. The tax collectors, however, did not accept his story, but beat him and threw him into prison until he paid what he owed

واستمرّ على القيام به في كلّ سنة ظلماً وعدواناً إلى أن تولّى على ذلك العمل رجل[1] له دين فكشف عن الأمور واتّبع الحقّ وأنف من الباطل وعلم حال الرجل وما أقدم عليه الكلب في أمره فحطّ ذلك عنه وألزم العامل بغرامة جميع ما قام به بعد أن اعترف بما اعتمده معه فعاقبه على ذلك بأشدّ العقوبة.[2]

ومن جملة سوء اعتمادهم وسرقاتهم أنّ بعض النصارى تولّى مدينة تنّيس وديوان المستخرج بها على البحر فوقعت له سكّين في البحر فقرّر على المراكب كلّ مركب يصل ربع دينار وضمن هذا المقرّر بجملة كثيرة. ثمّ لم يزل مستمرّاً إلى أن ولي السلطان السعيد الشهيد وحطّ المكوس فحطّ ضمان ذلك مع ما حطّه رحمه الله. ٢،١١،٢

الفصل الثاني عشر فيما جرى من تمّيمهم على مرافقيهم من العدول وأنّه لا يمكن ضبطهم عن الخيانة

وذلك أنّ بعض كتّاب القبط ممّن يسم نفسه بالثقة والأمانة وليس بثقة ولا أمين[3] كان معه عدل يضبط عليه المعاملة التي هو متولّيها فأعمل الحيلة كيف يسرق ولا يفطن به ويكون مأمون العاقبة لعدم ظهور سرقته فسرق تعليق الشاهد العدل فلمّا عدم الشاهد تعليقه خاف من الفضيحة ودعته الضرورة إلى النقل من تعليق الكاتب فكان الكاتب لمّا أن سرق تعليق رفيقه عمل الشغل في تعليقه ونقص فيه وزاد وعمل ما أراد فطلب الشاهد من الكاتب التعليق الذي له فأعطاه إيّاه وقد عمل فيه غرضه ومصلحته من حيث لا يشعر رفيقه فنقل منه ونال غرضه وأوقع الشاهد المسكين في الكذب. ١،١٢،٢

---

١ كذا في ت؛ وفي ب، ج،د زيادة: مسلم. ٢ كذا في ت؛ والعبارة الأخيرة ساقطة في ب، ج،د. ٣ كذا في ت؛ والعبارة من (وليس) ساقطة في ب، ج،د.

according to the demand-slip—until, that is, the registers and daily records of the collection showed that it had been paid in full. He was forced to continue paying it every year, all because of the Christian's oppressiveness and animosity. This continued until a devout man, one who followed truth and avoided falsehood, was appointed over that district and investigated its affairs. Upon learning the man's situation and what that dog had dared to do to him, he removed the tax obligation from him. The Christian official, after confessing what he had done, was compelled to compensate him for everything he had paid. He was then punished most severely.[107]

Another example of their ill will and thievery is that of a certain Christian who was appointed over the city of Tinnis, where the office of the tax collector is located right on the water. When he lost a knife, dropping it in the river, he promptly imposed a tax of a quarter gold coin upon every ship. He paid a huge sum to the government in order to gain control over this revenue. This levy of his remained in place until the blessed, martyred sultan[108] ascended to power and cancelled the unlawful taxes. As part of this measure of his, God have mercy on him, the collector of this tax was also dispossessed. 2.11.2

The Twelfth Section: Their Scheming against a Certain Judicial Witness Who Was in Their Company, and How They Cannot Be Restrained from Malfeasance

A certain Coptic secretary—one of those self-proclaimed trustworthy and faithful ones who are in fact nothing of the sort—was working with a judicial witness who would check the work the Copt had been assigned. After considering how he might embezzle money without the witness noticing and without leaving a trace or risking any consequence, this secretary decided to steal the witness's record book. When the witness noticed that the record book was missing, he was seized with fear of the scandal that its loss would cause. Under the circumstances, he had no choice but to copy the records from the secretary. But the secretary, when he had stolen his associate's record book, had made alterations to his own, removing here, adding there, and generally adjusting the figures as it suited his purpose. When the witness asked the secretary for his record book, he gave it to him, having already accomplished his self-serving purpose without his associate's knowledge. The latter copied from it and the secretary obtained his aim and caused the poor witness to fall into a lie. 2.12.1

الفصل الثالث عشر في ما جرى من تدقيق الحيلة من نصرانيّ على رفيق له يهوديّ وهو من العجائب التي لا يُقدِم عليها إلّا هذه الطائفة الخبيثة

٢،١٣،١ وذلك أنّ بعض النصارى الكتّاب في زمن ابن ولخشي[١] سأل رئيس اليهود مساعدته في خدمة فآستخدمه وأشرك معه يهوديّاً فثقل على النصرانيّ شركته فأكثر معه الحديث والسؤال عن العبرانيّ وتفسيره بالعربيّ وهو يفسّر له ما يسأله عنه إلى أن سأله يوماً عن اسم الخليفة بالعبرانيّ فقال له اليهوديّ المالخ. وسأله عن اسم الوزير فقال اليهوديّ القوصيم فصبر عنه أيّاماً ثمّ سأله عن اسم القتل فقال الشفر يقال شفرته إذا قتلته.

٢،١٣،٢ وكان الأمر في زمن رضوان شديداً لا يجسر أحد أن يذكر الخليفة ولا شيئاً من أحواله ولا ما يتعلّق به ولا يذكر الدولة ولا شيئاً يتعلّق بها فلمّا أصبح النصرانيّ رتّب لليهوديّ من أوجعه ضرباً فخرج وهو مستغيث إلى القصر فأحضره رئيس اليهود من ساعته بين يدي حاجب الحافظ فبعث من أحضر النصرانيّ ليعاقب على افتياته[٢] على اليهوديّ فقال النصرانيّ أنا ما ضربته وإنّما ضربه المسلمون لكونه تكلّم بفضول لم يلزمه ولا كان يسوغ له الحديث فيه فقيل له ماذا قال حتّى ضربه المسلمون قال تكلّم بالعبرانيّ شيئاً ما أعرفه ففسّره من عرفه من المسلمين فضربوه وما علمت أنا معناه إلّا بعد ضربه.[٣] فقيل له إن كنت صادقاً فقل اللفظ الذي سمعته منه فقال سمعته يقول المالخ يشفر القوصيم الليلة ومفهوم ذلك الخليفة يقتل الوزير في هذه الليلة فأنكر اليهوديّ ذلك وحلف وأخذ يحكي قصّته مع النصرانيّ وسؤاله عن الكلام العبرانيّ وما اعتمده معه فلم يُمهل عند سماع ذلك بل صُفع وحُمل إلى السجن حتّى يُكشف عنه.

---

١ في سائر المخطوطات: وحشي، وهو خطأ. ٢ كذا في ت؛ وفي ب،د: افتانه؛ ج: اقترائه. ٣ كذا في ب،د؛ و(إلّا بعد ضربه) ساقطة في ت.

The Thirteenth Section: Concerning a Calculated Stratagem Carried Out by a Christian against His Jewish Associate, a Shocking Act That Only Someone of That Accursed Community Would Dare to Commit

In the time of Ibn Walakhshī, there was a Christian secretary who enlisted the Head of the Jewish community to help him in a certain task of administration. The request was granted, and a Jew was appointed to work alongside the Christian. This partnership, however, proved to be onerous for the Christian. He began asking his Jewish associate all kinds of questions, particularly about Hebrew and its translation into Arabic. The Jew would explain whatever he asked. One day, he asked him the word for "caliph" in Hebrew. The Jew explained that the word was *mālikh*. Next he asked him the word for "vizier"; the Jew told him that it was *qūṣīm*. After this the Christian waited for a time, then asked him how to say "kill" in Hebrew. The Jew told him that the word was *shafar*, and that to say "*shafartah*" means "You killed him."[109] **2.13.1**

Now the government's rule in the time of Ibn Walakhshī was exceedingly harsh. No one dared to discuss the caliph or anything pertaining to him, or indeed anything about the government at all. When the Christian rose the next morning, he sent men to waylay and attack the Jew. The Jew, calling out for assistance, went straight to the palace. The Head of the Jewish community brought him immediately to an audience with the chamberlain of Caliph al-Ḥāfiẓ. The chamberlain also sent an agent to bring the Christian, in order to punish him for his offense against the Jew. But when he appeared, the Christian said, "It was not I who beat him up! It was the Muslims, because he had been talking too much about things that were no business of his." The person questioning him asked, "What did he say, that the Muslims beat him up?" The Christian said, "He said something in Hebrew that I didn't understand. But one of the Muslims was able to understand it, so they beat him up. I didn't know what it meant until afterwards." "If you are telling the truth," the questioner said, "then tell us exactly what you heard him say." He said, "I heard him say, 'The *mālikh yashfar* the *qūṣīm allaylah*.' Apparently this means, 'The caliph will kill the vizier this very night.'" The Jew denied this strongly, swearing many oaths. He told the story of his conversations with the Christian, and of all the questions that he had asked about Hebrew, and how he had plotted against him. Relating these things did not buy him any time, however. Instead he was treated roughly and taken to the prison until an investigation could be undertaken. **2.13.2**

فانظر إلى هذه الحيلة التي لا يهتدي لها ﴿ٱلشَّيْطَٰنُ ٱلرَّجِيمُ﴾ ولا يأتي بمثلها فنعوذ بالله من هذه الطائفة الخبيثة التي لا ترقب في أغراضها حقًّا ولا تعتمد في كلامها صدقًا[1] ولا ترعى إلًّا ولا ذمّةً فكيف يتولّى هؤلاء شيئًا من الأعمال أو يؤمّنون على بلد أو مال؟ ٣،١٣،٢

الفصل الرابع عشر فيما جرى من مخازيهم في أيّام العاضد حين كان السلطان الملك الصالح طلائع بن رزّيك

وذلك أنّه لم يكن في الدولة أمكن من كلب نصرانيّ يقال له خاصّ الدولة أبو الفضل ابن دخان وكانت مخازيه في صحائف الأيّام مسطورة ومثالبه في التواريخ مخلّدة مذكورة فممّا أقدم عليه أنّه حمله جهله وتقدّمه في الدولة على أن وقّع في قصّة رجل نصرانيّ أسلم أن يردّ إلى دين النصرانيّة ويؤمر بالخروج عن دين الإسلام ولم يزل توقيعه لعنه الله محفوظًا عند بعض الكتّاب[2] إلى أن ملك الشهيد صلاح الدين ووقف عليه فأمر من ساعته بأن لا يولّى نصرانيّ ديوانًا ولا عملًا وغضب لذلك غضبًا شديدًا حتّى أنّه قال وددت والله لو أدركت هذا الكلب الكافر حتّى أجعله عبرةً لكلّ نصرانيّ فرضي الله عنه. ١،١٤،٢

وممّا جرى لهذا النصرانيّ ابن دخان أنّه لمّا وصل الشيخ العالم زين الدين عليّ بن ابراهيم بن نجا الأنصاريّ جدّي لأمّي رحمه الله إلى الديار المصريّة[3] قرّر له أوّل قدومه راتب يسير دون ما يستحقّ إذ لم يكن المصريّون يعلمون حاله إذ ذاك من الدين والعلم. وتقدّم إلى خاصّ الدولة المذكور بتسهيل المبلغ المقرّر وصرفه وتعجيله والحذر من تأخيره فلمّا رجع الأمر إليه وعوّل فيه عليه خلّد توقيعه في ديوان الإهمال ونزّله في جرائد الإغفال ورسل الشيخ زين الدين يتردّدون إليه فلا يؤهّلهم للكلام ويحيّونه فلا ينصفهم في السلام هذا وداره معمورة برسل الفرنج لا يخلو مجلسه منهم ولا ٢،١٤،٢

[1] كذا في ت؛ و(ولا تعتمد في كلامها صدقًا) ساقطة في ب، ج،د. [2] كذا في ت؛ وفي ب، ج،د زيادة: المسلمين.
[3] كذا في ت؛ وفي ب، ج،د زيادة: في أيّام المصريّين.

Mark well this deception, such as not even «the accursed Satan»[110] would lead people to commit, or even commit himself. We ask God's protection from this wicked community, which respects the rights of no one in its quest to get what it wants. It practices no honesty in its speech and cares for no agreement or covenant. How is it that such people are appointed over any district, or are entrusted with the oversight of any town or any financial matter? 2.13.3

The Fourteenth Section: Their Disgraceful Deeds in the Days of al-ʿĀḍid, When al-Malik al-Ṣāliḥ Ṭalāʾiʿ ibn Ruzzīk Was Sultan

There was no one more powerful in the government at that time than a Christian dog called Khāṣṣ al-Dawlah Abū l-Faḍl Ibn Dukhān. His shameless acts are set down in writing for the ages, his vices forever fixed on history's pages. One of his audacious deeds involved a Christian man who had converted to Islam. Ibn Dukhān's folly and his high standing in the government allowed him to decree that this man should return to Christianity; in effect he was commanded to leave Islam. This order of his, God curse him, was retained by a certain secretary until the martyred sultan Ṣalāḥ al-Dīn ascended the throne and became aware of it. He ordered at once that no Christian was to be appointed over any office or district. Indeed, he was greatly angered at this, and said, "I wish, by God, that I had met that infidel dog so that I could have made an example of him for every Christian." God have mercy on him.[111] 2.14.1

Another incident involving the Christian Ibn Dukhān occurred after my maternal grandfather, the learned Shaykh Zayn al-Dīn ʿAlī ibn Ibrāhīm ibn Najā al-Anṣārī, God have mercy on him, arrived in Egypt. At first my grandfather was allocated a rather measly stipend—much less than he deserved—as the Fatimid rulers were unaware of his great piety and learning. He approached this Khāṣṣ al-Dawlah Ibn Dukhān to expedite the payment of the stipend, urging that it be released speedily and not delayed in any way. When the matter was referred to Ibn Dukhān for a decision, however, he filed away his official writ in the Office of Neglect and recorded it in the Registers of Disregard, though the messengers of the Shaykh Zayn al-Dīn were constantly at his door. These he treated as unworthy to converse with him; whereas they greeted him with respect, he responded with none. Meanwhile, the messengers of the Franks, by contrast, frequented his house. They were never absent from his council and he saw 2.14.2

يفتر عن قضاء حوائجهم ويأمر بتيسير مطالبهم[1] وحمل الإضافة إليهم[2] من جهتهم أضعاف ما قُرِّر لهم على الديوان. فعوتب على ذلك وقيل له لِمَ لا تُجري الشيخ زين الدين على أجمل عوائده فإنّك لا تأمن أن يصف أفعالك المشهورة ومخازيك المسطورة وقبائحك التي يستحيي من فعلها الأوغاد من السفهاء فضلاً عمّن ينتظم في سلك الرؤساء. فبان لعاتبه أنّه طاغٍ متمرّد مبالغ في عداوته للإسلام وأهله متجرّد منقبض عن فعل الخير متحقّر متحقّد منهمك على الفساد.

٣،١٤،٢ فبقي الشيخ زين الدين رحمه الله ينتظر له الفرصة فلم يمض إلّا أيّام يسيرة حتّى جلس الملك الصالح مجلساً عامّاً جمع فيه وجوه الدولة وأهل العلم والدين والدواوين والكتّاب المسلمين. وسأل الشيخ زين الدين أن يتكلّم فنُصب له كرسي فجلس واتّفق أن قرأ أحد قرّاء الحضرة ﴿يَوْمَ تَأْتِي السَّمَاءُ بِدُخَانٍ مُبِينٍ﴾ فتكلّم الشيخ زين الدين على تفسير الآية والسورة وبالغ وأطنب ثمّ خرج إلى ذكر الدخان ومضرّته للعين وهي أشرف الأعضاء وإلى آلات التنفيس وبها قوام الحياة بجولان الروح فيها وتسويد الدخان للبياض وتوليده للسعال وتكلّم من باب الحكمة على ما يولّده الدخان من المضرّة للروح والبدن إلى غير ذلك ثمّ أخذ في ذكر النصارى ومخازيهم والنهي عن استخدامهم وذكر جملاً ممّا ورد في ذلك من الكتاب والسنّة. ثمّ التفت إلى الملك الصالح وقال أيّها الملك طهّر هذه الدولة الشريفة من النصارى بحيث لا يتولّى أحد منهم عملاً من أعمال المسلمين وإن قيل للسلطان إنّهم حسبة فقد كذب القائل. كيف يوصفون بالحسّاب وقد جعلوا الواحد الفرد ثلاثاً؟ وذلك أنّهم يجعلون الله ثالث ثلاثة ديناً ويعتقدون أنّ الثلاثة واحد يقيناً لا[3] يخرجون عن هذه المقالة أبداً والله سبحانه وتعالى يقول ﴿لَقَدْ كَفَرَ الَّذِينَ قَالُوا إِنَّ اللَّهَ ثَالِثُ ثَلَاثَةٍ ۘ وَمَا مِنْ إِلَٰهٍ إِلَّا إِلَٰهٌ وَاحِدٌ﴾ وأنشد [الخفيف]

كَيْفَ يَدْرِي ٱلْحِسَابَ مَنْ جَعَلَ ٱللّٰـ ـهَ بِزَعْمٍ ثَلَاثَةً وَهْوَ وَاحِدْ

[1] كذا في ت؛ وفي ب،د زيادة: وتسهيل مآربهم. [2] كذا في ت؛ وفي ب، ج،د: الضيافة إليه (ج: إليهم). [3] كذا في ب،د؛ والكلمة ساقطة في ت.

tirelessly to their needs, commanding that their demands be granted and that support be given them that far exceeded what had been officially earmarked for the purpose. He was censured for this and was told, "Why have you not treated the Shaykh Zayn al-Dīn as he full well deserves? You know, you cannot be sure that he will not report your infamous deeds, your indelible disgraces, your acts so wicked that the meanest rascal would shrink from performing them, let alone someone counted among the leading lights of the state!" It was obvious to the man who censured him that he was an overweening tyrant, extreme in his animosity to Islam and its people, completely bereft and devoid of any good deed, vilely and hatefully engrossed in corruption.

The Shaykh Zayn al-Dīn, God have mercy on him, watched for an opportunity to act against him. Just a few days later, al-Malik al-Ṣāliḥ held a general council in which were gathered the most important men of state, along with persons distinguished for their learning and piety, prominent administrators, and Muslim secretaries. When the Shaykh Zayn al-Dīn asked to speak, a seat was set up for him. Now it happened that just before this, one of the ruler's Qur'an reciters had recited «a day when heaven shall bring a manifest smoke.»[112] The Shaykh Zayn al-Dīn explained the surah and the ayah, speaking at length on every detail. He then proceeded to the subject of smoke, for Ibn Dukhān's name means "son of smoke." He spoke of how noxious it is to the eye—the most noble of organs—and to respiration, by which life is sustained in its support of the spirit, and how it makes white things black and causes coughing. He spoke thus in general terms about the damage done by smoke to body and soul, and about related topics. Then he turned to the topic of the Christians, of their disgraceful deeds and how it is forbidden to employ them, citing copious evidence from the Book and the Example of the Prophet. Finally he addressed al-Malik al-Ṣāliḥ directly, saying, "O King, cleanse this noble state of Christians, so that none holds any position among Muslims. If it should be said to the sultan that they are clever at accounting, know that he who says so has lied. How can they be so described when they have made the Unitary One into three? In their religion they make God «the Third of Three,» being convinced that three is one. They stubbornly refuse to budge from this position. God, be He glorified and exalted, has said, «They are unbelievers who say, 'God is the Third of Three.' No god is there but One God.»"[113] He quoted a line of poetry: 2.14.3

How can he know arithmetic who asserts that God the One is three?[114]

ثمّ قال الشيخ زين الدين يا مولانا فعلى هذا الاعتقاد إذا استخرج النصرانيّ من مال السلطان ثلاثة جعلها واحداً يدين الله بذلك. فانتقل المجلس إلى الخليفة[1] العاضد في وقته وجرى ذكر ما ورد فيه من خزي ابن دخان النصرانيّ.

٤،١٤،٢ فتواثبت عليه الأعداء وآنهتك ستره وظهر أنه كان يكاتب الفرنج ويحملهم على غزو البلاد وأنّه كتب لهم أوراقاً بآرتفاع الديار المصريّة[2] فقتل أقبح قتلة لعنه الله وفيه يقول عُمارة [السريع]

قُلْ لِٱبْنِ دُخَّانٍ إِذَا جِئْتَهُ ... وَوَجْهُهُ يَنْدَى مِنَ ٱلْقَرْقَفِ
حِرْمٌ[3] جَارِيَّ وَلَوْ أَنَّهُ ... أَضْعَافُ مَا فِي سُورَةِ ٱلزُّخْرُفِ
وَٱصْفَعْ قَفَا ٱلذُّلِّ وَلَوْ أَنَّهُ ... بَيْنَ قَفَا ٱلْقِسِّيسِ وَٱلْأُسْقُفِ
مَلَّكَكَ ٱلدَّهْرُ[4] سِبَالَ ٱلْوَرَى ... فَٱحْلِقْ لِحَاهُمْ آمِنًا وَٱنْتِفِ
خَلَّى لَكَ ٱلدِّيوَانُ مِنْ نَاظِرٍ ... مُسْتَيْقِظِ ٱلْعَزْمِ وَمِنْ مُشْرِفِ
فَٱكْسِبْ وَحَصِّلْ وَٱدَّخِرْ وَٱكْتَنِزْ ... وَٱسْرِقْ وَخُنْ وَٱبْطِشْ وَخُذْ وَٱخْطَفِ
وَٱبْكِ وَقُلْ مَا صَحَّ لِي دِرْهَمٌ ... فَرُدَّ وَصَلِّبْ وَٱبْتَهِلْ وَٱحْلِفِ
وَٱغْتَنِمِ ٱلْفَتْرَةَ مِنْ قَبْلِ أَنْ ... يَرْتَفِعَ ٱلْإِنْجِيلُ بِٱلْمُصْحَفِ

٥،١٤،٢ وممّا جرى من قلّة حياء النصارى وخزيهم ورضاهم بالفضيحة لأنفسهم في بلوغ أغراضهم أنّه جرى في أيّام شاور وزير العاضد غريبة مشهورة لم يحدّث بمثلها وذلك أنّه لمّا هلك بطريرك النصارى اجتمع كبارهم وسألوا إقامة غيره عوضاً عنه فأجمعت آراء الكتّاب الخاصّة على أبي الفرج بن زرعة البطريرك وأجمعت فرقة أخرى على رجل يعرف بآبن زين الدار فآفترق النصارى فرقتين. ومن شرائط البطريرك عندهم أنّه لا ينكح ولا يذبح ولا يُعرف له ذنب عندهم على زعمهم وكانت شوكة أبي

١ كذا في ت؛ والكلمة ساقطة في ب، ج،د. ٢ كذا في ت؛ وفي ب، ج،د زيادة: وعدّة جيشه. ٣ كذا في ت؛ وفي ب،د: حِرامُ. ٤ كذا في ب، ت؛ وفي د: الله.

Then Shaykh Zayn al-Dīn said, "Master, according to this belief, when the Christian takes three from the sultan's property, he considers them one, and in the process passes judgment on God." At this point the whole council repaired to Caliph al-ʿĀḍid, and news spread of how the disgraces of the Christian Ibn Dukhān had been discussed in that assembly.[115]

Ibn Dukhān's enemies lost no time in pouncing on him. His veil, as it **2.14.4**
were, was rent, and it was discovered that he had been corresponding with the Franks and encouraging them to invade the land. He had sent them documents revealing the tax receipts of Egypt's territories. His punishment, God curse him, was a most gruesome execution. The poet ʿUmārah composed the following lines about him:

Say to Ibn Dukhān when you see his wine-wetted face,
"To hell with my stipend, though it be
many times the wealth described in Sūrat al-Zukhruf!"[116]
And slap the nape of his shameful neck,
though you find it twixt those of priest and bishop.
"Fate has made you master of men's beards,
so shave and pluck them without fear.
Look! The office is empty of any stern and wakeful watcher,
or overseer severe,
So earn, amass, hoard, and hide away!
Steal, embezzle, seize, take, grab!
Then weep, and say, 'Not a coin of it mine.'
Give back, cross yourself, implore, and swear.
Seize the day, ere the Gospel is supplanted by the Qur'an."[117]

The Christians' shamelessness, disgracefulness, and willingness to coun- **2.14.5**
tenance scandal to achieve their aims are all demonstrated by a singular and well-known event that occurred in the time of Shāwar, the vizier of al-ʿĀḍid. Nothing quite like it had ever been told of. It began with the death of the Patriarch of the Christians. Their elders met soon thereafter and requested that someone be appointed to replace him.[118] The high secretaries of the state agreed together on the eventual Patriarch Abū l-Faraj ibn Zurʿah; another faction, however, came out in support of a man called Ibn Zayn al-Dār. Thus the Christians were divided one against another. Now among the conditions they set for the patriarch are that he not marry, not slaughter any animal, and not

الفرج المذكور أقوى وكلمته بمن اجتمع إليه من الرؤساء على من دونهم أعلى وكان في جملتهم كاتب نصرانيّ يعدّ من الكتّاب المشهورين وتؤخذ بقلمه الحقوق فنودي على ابن زين الدار من يعلم من حاله شيئاً فليذكره فقام الكاتب المذكور ووقف بين الجماعة الحاضرين وقال هذا رجل فسق بي وفسقت به فضحك الحاضرون وبطلت تقدمة المذكور ولم يعبأ القائل بما ذكر عن نفسه من الفضيحة المخزية في الملأ العامّ.[١]

الفصل الخامس عشر في ذكر السبب الذي لأجله صار إذا أسلم أحد منهم بكائنة أو جائحة جاء أنحس ممّا كان وأكثر خيانةً[٢] وأشدّ قِحة

وذلك بدليل واضح كالشمس الطالعة والأنوار الساطعة[٣] لأنّه ثبت بما تقدّم في هذا الكتاب ما هم مجبولون عليه من المخازي والخيانة والكذب والإقدام على العظائم وما ظهر من ذلك في كلّ زمان وما قمعوا به من الخلفاء والملوك في كلّ أوان ومع ذلك فلا ينكر أنّ خمول النصرانيّة وذلّ أداء الجزية وقهر دخولهم تحت سطوة سيف الإسلام يمنعهم من الإفراط في دِبْرهم[٤] وإظهار مخازيهم فلا بدّ أن يتوقّوا بعض التوقّي ويتخفوا ما أمكنهم فإذا جرت لأحدهم كائنة يخاف منها على نفسه أو ماله واحتاج إلى التخلّص منها بالتلفّظ بكلمتَي الإسلام تكلّم بها وخلص من عقوبة ما ارتكبه وزال بذلك العُذر من تخفية مخازيه وتوقّيه بقبائحه ومعائبه وأقدم بحسب طبعه وجبلته على المخازي والخيانة والفساد على كلّ أمر كان يتوقّاه غير خائف ولا مراقب للعواقب بل يذلّ بما تلفّظ به من كلمتَي الإسلام فيكون مسلماً بين المسلمين في الظاهر وإذا خلا في بيته كان بين أبيه النصرانيّ وأمّه النصرانيّة وأخيه وأخته ١،١٥،٢

---

١ كذا في ت؛ والجملة الأخيرة ساقطة في ب، ج،د. ٢ كذا في ت؛ وفي ب، ج،د زيادة: وأقلّ أمانة. ٣ كذا في ت؛ والفقرة من (واضح) ساقطة في ب، ج،د. ٤ كذا في ب، ت؛ وفي د: تدبّرهم.

be known to have committed any sin, as they claim. This Abū l-Faraj was in much the stronger position, thanks in large part to the support of the lay elites who rallied behind him. One of these was a Christian secretary whom they considered eminent; debts that were owed would be taken at the stroke of his pen. During the selection process, the following announcement was made concerning Ibn Zayn al-Dār: "If anyone knows something that might affect his candidacy, let him come forward now." This secretary duly came forward. He stood before the assembled crowd and said, "This is a man who fornicated with me, and I with him!" Everyone there began laughing, and the candidacy of Ibn Zayn al-Dār collapsed. But the man who had spoken was untroubled by the disgraceful scandal that he had brought upon himself in the public assembly.

The Fifteenth Section: Why It Is That When One of Them Converts to Islam Due to Some Predicament or Calamity, He Becomes Even More Miserable and Dishonest than He Had Been Formerly, and Even More Insolent

The evidence for this is as clear as the midday sun and the most radiant light. **2.15.1** Everything recorded in this book so far confirms the nature of these Christians, their disgraces, their perfidy, their mendacity, and their effrontery in committing heinous deeds. We have reviewed these things historically, showing how they were restrained by successive caliphs and kings in every age. Nevertheless it cannot be denied that the feeble nature of Christianity, the humiliation of paying the poll tax, and their forced subjugation to the power of Islam's sword prevents them from being too grossly excessive in their wealth and from flaunting their disgraceful deeds. They are compelled to take certain precautions and to keep as low a profile as they can. Yet if one of them falls prey to some sudden predicament, causing him to fear for his life or his property and forcing him to save himself by professing his conversion to Islam,[119] he does so readily and is thereby spared the punishment for his deed. At this point, and because of his conversion, he abandons his former caution and ceases to hide his disgraces, turning instead to heinous and shameful deeds. In accordance with his nature and innate character, he boldly brings new disgraces, perfidy, and corruption into every affair in which he had formerly shown caution, now neither fearing nor considering the consequences. In fact, the profession of faith he has made leaves him even more depraved. Among Muslims he is a Muslim, outwardly.

وأولاده وزوجته وأصهاره وأقاربه نصرانياً على الحقيقة معتذراً إليهم ممّا صدر منه قائلاً لهم والله ما دخل في قلبي من دين هؤلاء المسلمين شيء وإنّما الضرورة ألجأتني إلى موافقتهم في التلفّظ بذي الكلمتين لسلامة النفس بسبب تلك الكائنة التي جرت ووالله إنّي إذا عبرت على الكنيسة الفلانيّة أو الدير الفلانيّ ما يبقى فيّ جارحة ولا عرق إلّا وٱشتاق إلى تلك المواضع وتلك الصور وتلك الهياكل[1] وإنّما كما قال الشاعر [المنسرح]

تُلْجِي ٱلضَّرُورَاتُ فِي ٱلْأُمُورِ إِلَى   سُلُوكِ مَا لَا يَلِيقُ بِٱلْأَدَبِ

يا فلان عندك خبر؟ إنّي أعبر على الكنيسة الفلانيّة ما أقدر من شرّ المسلمين أن أتطلّع إليها ولا أملأ عيني منها لكن أردّ وجهي عنها خوفاً أن ينتقد عليّ أحد من المسلمين في نظري إليها. وهو الكلب الملعون ينشد بلسان حاله لا بلكنة مقاله قول البحتريّ [الكامل]

أَحْنُو[2] عَلَيْكِ وَفِي فُؤَادِي لَوْعَةٌ   وَأَصُدُّ عَنْكِ وَوَجْهُ وِدِّي مُقْبِلُ
وَإِذَا هَمَمْتُ بِوَصْلِ غَيْرِكِ رَدَّنِي   وَلَهٌ عَلَيْكِ وَشَافِعٌ لَكِ أَوَّلُ

وإذا عوتب على خروجه عن دين النصرانيّة أنشد لسان حاله [الكامل]

نَقِّلْ فُؤَادَكَ حَيْثُ شِئْتَ مِنَ ٱلْهَوَى   مَا ٱلْحُبُّ إِلَّا لِلْحَبِيبِ ٱلْأَوَّلِ
كَمْ مَنْزِلٍ فِي ٱلْأَرْضِ يَأْلَفُهُ ٱلْفَتَى   وَحَنِينُهُ أَبَدًا لِأَوَّلِ مَنْزِلِ

ولقد أخبرني رجل حضر في خلوة لبعض النصارى الذين أسلموا بسبب كائنة وقد ٢،١٥،٢
طالت مدّته في الإسلام حتّى صار يقف الوقوف مثل المسلمين على سبيل الخيرات[3]

١ كذا في ت؛ وفي ب، د زيادة (وفي ج مثلها): وذلك التقديس وذلك القربان. ٢ كذا في ب، د؛ وفي ت: اجفو.
٣ كذا في ت؛ وفي ب، ج، د: يعمل الأوقاف على سبيل الخيرات ويتصدّق ويصوم بعض أيّام الشهور.

But when he returns home, he is a Christian in truth, alongside his Christian father, his Christian mother, brother, sister, children, wife, brother-in-law, and all his relations.[120] He excuses himself to them for what he has done by saying, "I swear to God that nothing of the Muslims' religion has entered into my heart. It is only that necessity compelled me to placate them by speaking those words, in order to preserve myself after what happened. Whenever I pass by a certain church or monastery, by God, my every limb and vein longs for those places, those icons, those sanctuaries! As the poet put it,

> Necessity compels recourse to what proper conduct would renounce.[121]

"You! Can you tell me what I want to know? I go by that church, but I dare not gaze at it nor allow my eye to linger upon it because of the Muslims' malice. Instead I turn my face away, fearing that a Muslim will disparage me for looking at it." Were that accursed dog not so stammering of speech, then in his condition he might well recite the lines of al-Buḥturī:

> With heart tormented I show you my affection;
> then turn away, though my love's face draws nearer still,
> If I would go to another, passion for you turns me back,
> first intercessor on your behalf.[122]

If he is castigated for leaving Christianity, then were he not so tongue-tied, he might then recite the lines:

> In idle fancy fling your heart where you wish;
> true love is hers whom you loved first,
> How many dwellings a youth may know,
> yearning ever for that of his birth.[123]

I was told the following account by a man who attended a private party with **2.15.2**
one of these Christians who convert under duress. He had been a Muslim for some time, so much time, in fact, that he made charitable endowments after the Muslim fashion, and did other such things as well. If he observed that a Christian was colluding with other Christians against a Muslim, he would say to him, "If this man were a Christian, you would not be taking sides against him." In saying this he intended to distance himself from any accusation, and to show that he had entered entirely into Islam. The man who told me the story said, "Now this fellow was drinking, as were the others in attendance. One of

إلى غير ذلك وصار إذا تعاون النصارى على مسلم يقول لوكان هذا نصرانيًا ما تحاملتم عليه يقصد بذلك البعد عن التهمة وأنّه دخل في دين الإسلام دخولًا تامًّا. قال المخبر بهذه الحكاية فشرب المذكور وشرب الحاضرون فقال أحدهم للمغنّي بالله غنّني في حجازيّ، فغنّى أبياتًا منها [الطويل]

كَأَنْ لَمْ يَكُنْ بَيْنَ ٱلْحُجُونِ إِلَى ٱلصَّفَا أَنِيسٌ وَلَمْ يَسْمُرْ بِمَكَّةَ سَامِرُ

فرفع الكلب أنفه وقال وقد تمكّنت منه النشوة بالله يا فلان دعني من الحجون والصفا ومكّة وهذه الأسماء المزعجة وغنّ لنا يا ديرسمعان وأيّامنا بالدير وذاك الشعر الذي فيه ذكر القسوس والرهبان. ثمّ التفت وقد زادت به النشوة وقال أقول لكم الصحيح ما دين النصرانيّة إلّا مليح ومعابدهم وكنائسهم وتلك الصور وذاك الحفر الذي عليها والله كأنّها إلّا تنطق وتلك الهياكل وتلك المواضع وذاك التقديس فسبحان من قدّر ما قدّر ما للإنسان في نفسه حيلة. ثمّ قال يا فلان سمعت أنّ هؤلاء الذين يروحون إلى مكّة يقبّلون حجرًا أسود قال، ويأخذون معهم حجارة من موضع ويرمونها في موضع آخر قال، ويجرون جريًا شديدًا شيء ما يشبه شيء يابني ايش ما هذا كلّه؟ يترك الناس دينهم ويدخلون معهم بدون ذا.[1] قال المخبر فوالله لقد ترقّبت فرصة الخلوة به لأقتله لله تعالى فحال بيني وبين ذلك كثرة الحاضرين.

٣،١٥،٢ قلت[2] وهذا لا ينكر من هؤلاء السفلة الجهّال النصارى فإنّه لو جرى لبعض المسلمين العريقين في الإسلام كائنة في دار الحرب أو في موضع للكفّار فيه شوكة حتّى لا ينجيه منها إلّا التلفّظ بالكفر فتلفّظ به لم يأثم ولم يخرج عن دين الإسلام ومتى لم يمكنه أن يظهر دين الإسلام الذي هو يعتقده أبقاه في قلبه وتلفّظ به سرًّا في خلوته ومع نفسه وتعبّد مهما أمكنه خفية وإذا رأى جامعًا أو مسجدًا أو محرابًا حنّ بجبلته إليه وأنّ آسفًا عليه واشتاقه بقلبه وتوسّل في إظهار دينه إلى ربّه.

---

١ كذا في ت؛ والجملة الأخيرة ساقطة في ب،د. ٢ كذا في ت؛ وفي ب،د: قال المصنّف؛ ج: قال مؤلّف هذا الكتاب.

them said to the singer, 'Sing me something in Ḥijāzī!' So he sang several lines, one of which was:

> It is as though no close friend had ever dwelt between al-Ḥajūn and Ṣafā,
> as though there were no one in Mecca to make pleasant talk by night.[124]

"At this point the dog of whom I have been speaking turned up his nose and, overcome with drink, said, 'By God, man, spare me this Ḥajūn and Ṣafā and Mecca and these obnoxious names. Sing to us, "O Monastery of Simon! O our days in the monastery!" And sing that poetry about priests and monks!' Then he turned, even more drunk, and said, 'To tell you the truth, Christianity is really quite nice. Their shrines, their temples, those icons, that painting upon them that makes them look—by God—as though they were about to speak, those sanctuaries, all those sacred places, and the service . . . Praise be to the One who decrees what He decrees; there is nothing for a man to do but to obey!' Then he said to someone there, 'I heard that these people who go to Mecca kiss a black stone, and that they take pebbles from one place and fling them in another, and go racing around. What's all this about, my boy? People can leave their own religion and follow those people's without going that far.'" The man telling this story said to me, "I watched for my chance to be alone with him, by God, so that I might kill him for God's sake, be He exalted. But the presence of the crowd interfered with my plan."

My own view is that one can hardly blame these base and ignorant Chris- 2.15.3
tians for acting this way. Consider the parallel case of what might happen to a tried-and-true Muslim in a foreign land or in some seat of infidel power. If the situation is such that his only hope is to pronounce words of unbelief, he pronounces them. In doing so he commits no sin and does not leave Islam. Though he may be prevented from openly practicing the religion of Islam in which he believes, he keeps it in his heart, speaking its words in secret in his soul when he is alone. He worships as much as possible in hiding. If he sees a congregational mosque, or a smaller neighborhood one, or a mihrab, he longs for it in his inmost nature. He groans wistfully, craves it in his heart, and pleads with his Lord for the chance to practice his religion openly.[125]

وقد جرى مثل ذلك لعمّار بن ياسر رحمه الله فإنّ الكفّار عذّبوه بالنار لكي يتلفّظ بالكفر فلم يجبهم وصبر على العذاب ظنّاً منه أنّه لا يجوز له التلفّظ بحال فمرّ به رسول الله صلّى الله عليه وسلّم وهو يعذّب فأذن له أن يرضيهم بالتلفّظ حتّى يخلص من العذاب ففعل ونزل قوله تعالى ﴿ إِلَّا مَنْ أُكْرِهَ وَقَلْبُهُ مُطْمَئِنٌّ بِالْإِيمَانِ ﴾ .

٤،١٥،٢ فثبت إذاً أنّ النصرانيّ إذا أسلم لكائنة صار أنحس ممّا كان وأخزى بل حكمه عندي إذا كان كما وصفت حكم المرتدّ مباح الدم[١] مستوجب القتل بل حكم المستهزئين بالشريعة والطاعة لا يحلّ إبقاءه في الحياة ساعة اللّهم إلّا من أسلم منهم بالدليل القائم عنده على نسخ شريعته وصدّق نبوّة سيّدنا محمّد صلّى الله عليه وسلّم ودخل في الإسلام طائعاً مختاراً راغباً لا لكائنة ولا لمصيبة فذلك هو المسلم الذي يرجى صحّة إسلامه.[٢]

١ كذا في ت؛ وفي ب، ج،د زيادة: والمال. ٢ كذا في ب،د؛ والفقرة من (اللهمّ) ساقطة في ت.

This is just what happened to ʿAmmār ibn Yāsir, God show him mercy. The infidels tortured him with fire so that he would profess unbelief. Yet he did not do as they wished, but bore the torment, believing that he might not lawfully say such a thing, no matter what. The Messenger of God, God bless and keep him, passed by while he was being tortured. He gave ʿAmmār permission to appease his tormentors by saying what they wanted him to say, so as to save himself from the agony. ʿAmmār did so, and the words of God, be He exalted, were promptly revealed: «. . . excepting him who has been compelled, and his heart is still at rest in his belief.»[126]

It is established, then, that in converting to Islam due to some predicament, the Christian becomes even more of a miserable disgrace. In my view, in fact, a person of this description is to be considered an apostate, whose blood is licit and who must be killed. More than this, he is equivalent to someone who mocks the Holy Law and obedience to God. It is unlawful for him to be left alive for a single moment, unless (I beseech God!) he is one of those who converts because he is convinced that his own Law has been abrogated, who affirms the prophethood of our master Muḥammad—God bless and keep him—and who enters Islam obediently, freely, and willingly, not due to some predicament or calamity. That is the Muslim whose conversion one may hope is authentic.[127] **2.15.4**

الباب الثالث في وصف الكتابة والكتّاب وفيه فصول ثلاثة

الفصل الأوّل في وصف الكتابة

وإذ جرى ذكر الكتابة وذكر من تزيّا بها من غير أهلها وباشر متعدّيًا جليل شغلها ناسَبَ ١،١،٣
أن أصفها وأصف المتحلّين بها وأذكر لمعًا من محاسن الكتّاب وأطرّز بها طرف هذا الكتاب. فأقول الكتابة صناعة شريفة ورتبة جليلة منيفة من جهل فضلها فما عرف أهلها والكتّاب الموصوفون بها على الحقيقة هم معنى لفظ الوجود ولبّ قشر هذا العالم الموجود وروح جسم هذا التكوين وصقال مرآته التي يظهر فيها الفضل ويبين.[١]

الفصل الثاني في ذكر من يجوز أن يوصف بالكتابة ويقال له كاتب وذكر شيء من محاسنهم في النثر ولو كلمة واحدة لكلّ واحد منهم ليعرف بها فضله

فأقول لا يوصف بالكتابة إلّا من حوى فنونًا من العلوم وأحاط بطرف حسن من كلّ ١،٢،٣
معلوم فيكون قد قرأ القرآن العزيز وتفقّه في الدين برهةً من الزمان وروى الحديث بعد سماعه وعرف مبانيه وفهم معانيه وعلم الفرائض وتضلّع من العربيّة ورقي إلى ذروتَي النظم والنثر وتصرّف في الإنشاء كيف شاء وروى الأشعار والأمثال وطالع السير

١ كذا في ت؛ وفي ب،د زيادة (وفي ج ما يشابهها): وبها تمّ شرفًا قوله تعالى في وصف ملائكته ﴿كرامًا كاتبين﴾.

The Third Chapter, A Description of Secretaries and Their Art, in Three Sections

The First Section: A Description of the Secretarial Art

3.1.1 Since the subject of the secretarial art has been broached, and since we have had occasion to mention those who unworthily don its robes and thereby encroach upon its sublime offices, it is fitting that I describe what it is. Indeed, it is appropriate that I bedeck the end of this book with a description of those men whom the secretarial art has adorned and that I offer a sample of their merits.

Therefore I would state clearly that the secretarial art is a noble craft, a splendid and lofty rank for those who master it. He who is ignorant of its excellence has surely never known one of its true practitioners. As for those secretaries worthy of the name, they are in truth the very meaning of existence; they are the kernel within the shell of this present world, the spirit in the body of this creation and the sheen upon its mirror, which reveals all excellence in its perfect clarity.

The Second Section: An Account of Those Men Who May Properly Be Called Secretaries, along with Some of Their Achievements in Prose, Though It Be but a Single Phrase to Demonstrate the Excellence of Each One

3.2.1 I am of the view that the only men who may properly be called secretaries are those who combine knowledge of divers sciences and who comprehend every branch of knowledge. The true secretary will have recited the Illustrious Qur'an, spent time in the study of religious law, heard and narrated hadith and understood its principles and fine points, studied inheritance law, mastered Arabic, scaled the twin summits of poetry and prose, gained complete command of epistolary style, recounted poems and aphorisms, read the epic tales of old, and understood the nuances of poetry and its varieties and forms. He will have committed to memory a great many poems, by Arabs and non-Arabs

وعرف[1] معاني الشعر وأنواعه وأوصافه وأكثر من أشعار العرب والعجم وعرف أيّامهم وأحاديثهم وسيرهم وتواريخهم ووقائعهم وأخذ بطرف جيّد من الحساب ودخل إلى كلّ علم من أوسع باب وتحلّى بالأدب الذي هو أجمل ما التحفته الهمّة وعرفته هذه الأمّة لأنّه يطلق اللسان من عقال وينطق الإنسان بفصيح المقال بل لا يطلق إلّا على من ظهر نوره وإشراقه وبهر فضله وكرمت أخلاقه حتّى صار راحة الروح وأنس النفس فلا يتقلّص في الفضل برده الضافي ولا يتكدّر في العلم وِردُه الصافي. يهزّ الزمان بهم عطفه ويظهر بهم لطفه. زند المنى بهم وارٍ[2] وكوكب السعد عنهم غير متوارٍ وقد وصف الله سبحانه الملائكة الكاتبين بالكرم والعلم فقال تعالى ﴿وَإِنَّ عَلَيْكُمْ لَحَافِظِينَ كِرَامًا كَاتِبِينَ﴾.

ومن الكتّاب المشهورين والفضلاء المذكورين عبد الحميد بن يحيى كاتب مروان آخر خلفاء بني أميّة المقتول ببوصير سدر من أعمال الجيزيّة وهو أوّل مَن أوضح منهاج الكتابة والبراعة وحرّر موازين الصياغة[3] والبلاغة وله الرسائل المعروفة والفضائل الموصوفة وقد قيل في حقّه بدأت الكتابة بعبد الحميد وختمت بابن العميد. ومن محاسن كلامه قوله القلم شجرة ثمرها المعاني والقلب بحر لؤلؤه الحكمة. ومن محاسنه قوله استدم نعمة القدرة بالعفو. ولا تنسَ مع نصيبك من الدنيا نصيبك من رحمة الله. ومن وفائه الذي سُطّر في التواريخ[4] ليستحيي منه من لا مروّة له ويقتدي به من فيه مروّة أنّ مروان مخدومه قال له لمّا أحسّ بانقراض دولته بخروج السفّاح[5] إنّ هذا الأمر لا بدّ أن يخرج من أيدينا ويرجع إلى هؤلاء القوم، يعني السادة[6] الخلفاء بني العبّاس وإنّي أشيرُ عليك بالمصير إليهم فهم يقدّمونك لفضيلتك فلعلّك تنفعني ٢،٢،٣

١ كذا في ت؛ وفي ب: النثر وعرف؛ د: النثر وعلم. ٢ ب،د: زيد المجد بهم ولد؛ ت: زند الميّ بهم واري؛ ج: زند المجد لمحاسنهم وارٍ؛ والمثبت يقتضيه السياق. ٣ كذا في ت؛ وفي ب، ج،د: الفصاحة. ٤ كذا في ت؛ وفي ب، د زيادة (وفي ج مثلها): نذكر هنا. ٥ كذا في ب،د؛ وفي ت: المنصور. ٦ كذا في ت؛ والكلمة ساقطة في ب، ج،د.

alike, and studied their battles, their speeches, their biographies, their historical chronicles, and the record of all events concerning them. He will have learnt a goodly amount of arithmetic. Indeed, he will have entered into every arena of learning by the widest gate. Refined literature holds a singular place in his preparation; it is his special adornment, for the Muslim community knows nothing more lovely, nor is there any garment more comely for ambition to wear. It frees the tongue of any hobble and allows men to speak with supreme eloquence. Only he may be associated with its refinement whose brilliant light shines forth, whose excellence glitters, and whose character is ennobled to such a degree that he gives rest to souls and joy to spirits. Neither does his flowing stream of excellence dry up, nor does any impurity cloud the clear pool of his learning. Fate is moved to rejoice by such men, and in them she displays her kindness. By them the spark of Destiny is kindled; from them the star of Fortune is never concealed. God, glorified be He, has said concerning those angels who in all nobility and knowledge play the part of secretaries: «Yet there are over you watchers noble, scribes who know whatever you do.»[128]

One of the most renowned secretaries and noted men of culture was ʿAbd 3.2.2
al-Ḥamīd ibn Yaḥyā, the secretary of the last Umayyad caliph, Marwān, who was killed at Būṣīr Sidr in the vicinity of Giza.[129] ʿAbd al-Ḥamīd was the first to elucidate the proper methods that guide the secretarial art and the use of the pen, and to formulate the conventions of composition and rhetoric. He has many well-known epistles and many praiseworthy virtues as well.

It has been said concerning him, "The secretarial art began with ʿAbd al-Ḥamīd and ended with Ibn al-ʿAmīd."

Among his excellent sayings are, "The pen is a tree the fruit of which is meaning, and the heart a sea the pearl of which is wisdom." And also, "Practice forgiveness, that the grace of your power may endure." And, "Do not let your share in this world cause you to forget your share in God's mercy."

Here follows an instance of ʿAbd al-Ḥamīd's loyalty that history has preserved for us so that the ignoble might feel shame and the honorable might follow in his steps. When his master Marwān realized that his rule was coming to an end with the rebellion of al-Saffāḥ, he said to ʿAbd al-Ḥamīd, "This authority shall surely pass from us and revert to those people," meaning the Abbasid caliphs, who are of the Prophet's family. "I advise you to transfer your allegiance to them, for they shall advance you in their service because of your estimable qualities. It may even be that you shall still do me some good

في مخلفيّ[١] فقال له وما الذي يُعلم الناس أنّك أمرتني بذلك ولو أنّي فعلت ذلك لعنفني الناس وأنشد [الطويل]

أُسِـرُّ وَفَـاءً ثُـمَّ أُظْـهِرُ غَـدْرَةً   فَمَنْ لِي بِعُذْرٍ يُوسِعُ ٱلنَّاسَ ظَاهِرُهْ

ولم يزل معه حتّى قُتل قتله صالح بن عليّ.[٢]

ومن الكتّاب الأجلاء الوزراء خالد بن برمك وزير المهديّ وهو الذي سمّى السوّال الذين يقصدون الأكابر للرزق المستميحين. وما أحتاجُ أن أصفه لأنّ قول الشاعر فيه يكفي [الطويل] ٣،٢،٣

حَذَا خَالِدٌ فِي جُودِهِ حَذْوَ جِدِّهِ   فَجُودٌ لَهُ مُسْـتَطْـرَفٌ وَأَثِيـلُ
وَكَانَ بَنُو ٱلْإِعْدَامِ[٣] يُدْعَوْنَ قَبْلَهُ   بِاسْمٍ عَلَى ٱلْإِعْدَامِ فِيهِ دَلِيـلُ
يُسَمَّوْنَ بِٱلسُّوَّالِ فِي كُلِّ مَوْطِنٍ   وَإِنْ كَانَ فِيهِمْ نَابِهٌ وَجَلِيـلُ
فَسَمَّاهُمُ ٱلزُّوَّارَ سَتْرًا لِإِسْمِهِمْ   فَأَسْتَارُهُ فِي ٱلْمُجْتَدِينَ سُدُولُ

ومن الكتّاب الكبار الأجلاء يعقوب بن داود وزير المهديّ الذي يقول فيه سَلْمٌ[٤] الخاسر شعر [البسيط] ٤،٢،٣

قُلْ لِلْإِمَامِ ٱلَّذِي جَاءَتْ خِلَافَتُهُ   تُهْدَى إِلَيْهِ بِحَقٍّ غَيْرِ مَرْدُودِ
نِعْمَ ٱلْمُعِينُ عَلَى ٱلتَّقْوَى أُعِنْتَ بِهِ   أَخُوكَ فِي ٱللهِ يَعْقُوبُ بْنُ دَاوُدِ

وفيه يقول أبو الشيص [البسيط]

---

١ كذا في ت؛ وفي ب، ج،د زيادة: وأهلي من بعدي. ٢ كذا في ب، ت، إلّا أنّه يأتي فيهما (صالح بن عبد الرحمن)، وهو خطأ؛ والجملة ساقطة في د. ٣ كذا في ت؛ وفي ب، ج،د: الاعلام. ٤ في ت: سالم؛ وفي ب، ج،د: مسلم؛ واسم هذا الشاعر معروف مشهور.

by serving those whom I leave behind." But ʿAbd al-Ḥamīd replied, "How shall the people know that this is your command? If I obey you, the people will curse me!" Then he recited these verses:

> Am I to be loyal in secret and flaunt perfidy?
> what excuse could I give to convince people?[130]

Thereafter ʿAbd al-Ḥamīd stayed at Marwān's side until he was slain by Ṣāliḥ ibn ʿAlī.[131]

Among the great secretaries who were also viziers was Khālid ibn Barmak, 3.2.3
vizier to the Abbasid caliph al-Mahdī. It was he who coined a euphemism for people who made their living by approaching prominent men for gifts. He requires no more description from me, however, for a poet composed the following lines about him:

> Khālid gave freely, like his ancestor;[132]
> his was generosity deeply rooted and yet new.
> Before him, those who had nothing were called
> by a name that pointed to their poverty.
> They were everywhere called Beggars,
> though among them were men high-born and eminent.
> To veil that name, he called them Visitors,
> thus did his veils upon the alms-seekers become a string of pearls for him.[133]

Another great and distinguished secretary was Yaʿqūb ibn Dāwūd, also 3.2.4
vizier to al-Mahdī. The following lines by the poet Salm al-Khāsir are in praise of him:

> Tell the Deputy of God, when Guidance irresistible
> grants to him the rightful rule,
> "In piety you have ever had a helper true:
> your brother in God, Yaʿqūb ibn Dāwūd"[134]

Abū l-Shīṣ also composed poetry about Yaʿqūb:

أَبْلِغْ إِمَامَ ٱلْهُدَى أَنْ لَسْتَ مُصْطَنِعاً   لِلنَّائِبَاتِ كَيَعْقُوبَ بْنِ دَاوُدِ
أَمْسَى يَقِيكَ بِنَفْسٍ قَدْ حَبَاكَ بِهَا   وَٱلْجُودُ بِٱلنَّفْسِ أَقْصَى غَايَةِ ٱلْجُودِ
إِنْ تَبْتَغِي مِثْلَهُ فِي ٱلنَّاسِ كُلِّهِمِ   طَلَبْتَ مَا لَيْسَ فِي ٱلدُّنْيَا بِمَوْجُودِ

ومن الكتّاب الكبار الأجلّاء يحيى بن خالد بن برمك الذي يقول فيه مروان ابن ٥،٢،٣
أبي حفصة [الطويل]

إِذَا بَلَّغَتْنَا ٱلْعِيسُ يَحْيَى بْنَ خَالِدٍ   أَخَذْنَا بِحَبْلِ ٱلْيُسْرِ وَٱنْقَطَعَ ٱلْعُسْرُ

ومن قوله السكر[١] كفر للنعمة. وفاعل الشرّ خادم الجهل. ومن قوله الدنيا ذلّ والمال عارية ولنا بمن قبلنا أسوة وفينا لمن بعدنا عبرة. ومن تواقيعه الخراج عمود الملك فما استغزر بمثل العدل ولا استنزر بمثل الجور.

ومن قوله ما رأيت باكيًا أحسن من القلم. وفيه يقول الشاعر [الكامل]

عِنْدَ ٱلْمُلُوكِ مَضَرَّةٌ وَمَنَافِعُ   وَأَرَى ٱلبَرَامِكَ لَا تَضُرُّ وَتَنْفَعُ
إِنَّ ٱلْعُرُوقَ إِذَا ٱسْتَسَرَّ بِهَا ٱلثَّرَى   أَثْرَى ٱلنَّبَاتُ بِهَا وَطَابَ ٱلْمَزْرَعُ
فَإِذَا جَهِلْتَ مِنِ ٱمْرِئٍ أَعْرَاقَهُ   وَقَدِيمَهُ فَٱنْظُرْ إِلَى مَا يَصْنَعُ

ومنهم جعفر ولده قال ثمامة بن أشرس كان جعفر بن يحيى أحسن الناس لفظاً ٦،٢،٣
وأدومهم عند الحديث لحظاً لا يتوقّف ولا يتلجلج ولا رآه أحد ملتمساً للتخلّص في معنى أعياه فهو كما قال الشاعر [الوافر]

بَدِيهَتُهُ وَفِكْرَتُهُ سَوَاءٌ   إِذَا ٱلْتَبَسَتْ عَلَى ٱلنَّاسِ ٱلْأُمُورُ

---

[١] كذا في د؛ وفي ب، ت، ج: الشكر.

Inform the Imam of Guidance[135] that none of his servants
bears troubles like Yaʿqūb ibn Dāwūd.
Through the night he guards you, risking his very life;
in self-giving lies the highest form of generosity.
Search out his equal among all mankind
and seek what the world does not contain.[136]

Also among the great and distinguished secretaries was Yaḥyā ibn Khālid ibn Barmak. A noteworthy line of poetry was composed about him by Marwān ibn Abī Ḥafṣah: 3.2.5

When fine camels bore us to Yaḥyā ibn Khālid
life became easy and our hardship ceased.[137]

It was also Yaḥyā who said, "Drunkenness is ingratitude."[138] And, "The evildoer is a servant to ignorance." And also, "This world around us is ignominy, and wealth is but borrowed money. We have in our predecessors a model, but in us posterity finds a lesson." In one particularly noteworthy document he wrote, "Tax revenues are the pillar of a king's rule; nothing makes them abound like justice or diminish like tyranny."

Another saying of Yaḥyā's is, "I have seen nothing weep so well as the pen." Concerning him, a poet declared,

With kings one finds both harm and benefit,
yet from the Barmakids I see benefits alone.
When roots conceal within them moisture
plants are gladdened and the fields delight.
If you do not know a man's roots—
and if he lacks a storied heritage—then look to his deeds.[139]

Yaḥyā's son Jaʿfar was another iconic secretary. Thumāmah ibn Ashras had this to say about him: "Jaʿfar ibn Yaḥyā was exceptionally articulate and unfailingly perceptive in conversation. He never paused, never stumbled over words, never seemed at a loss for the best way to express a complex thought. As the poet has said, 3.2.6

No more surely did he ponder than intuit
where others amid matters murky founder."[140]

وكذا يكون من يتصدّى لِخَدَم الملوك موسوماً بالعلم والفتوّة معروفاً بالفضل والمروّة واسع الصدر رحب الفناء حاضر البديهة في الخير.

ووقّع على رقعة لأهل فارس ضمنت لكم إن لم تعقني عوائق بأنّ سماء الجور عنكم ستُقلع. ووقّع على ظهر رقعة لعليّ بن عيسى حُبّب إليك الوفاء الذي أبغضته وبُغّض إليك الغدر الذي أحببته. فما جزاء الأيّام أن تحسن ظنّك بها وقد رأيت غدرها عياناً وإخباراً.

وكان الأصمعيّ يحبّه وينتاب مجلسه ويمدحه فمن قوله فيه [المتقارب]

يُحِبُّ ٱلْمُلُوكُ نَدَى[1] جَعْفَرٍ وَلَا يَصْنَعُونَ كَمَا يَصْنَعُ
وَلَيْسَ بِأَوْسَعِهِمْ فِي ٱلْغِنَى وَلٰكِنَّ مَعْرُوفَهُ أَوْسَعُ

٧،٢،٣ ومن الكتّاب الفضل أخوه كان بين يدي الرشيد وقد رأى مع بعض الخدم قبضة خيزران فقال يا فضل ما هذه قال هذه عروق الرماح يا أمير المؤمنين ولم يذكر الخيزران لأنّ اسم أمّ الرشيد خيزران.

وكان العتابيّ الشاعر قد رُمي عند الرشيد بالاعتزال فهدر دمه فعظم ذلك على الفضل وهرّب العتابيّ عن بغداد فأحضر الفضل الكسائيّ وأمره أن يقرئ المأمون والأمين ولدي الرشيد شعر العتابيّ ورسائله ففعل فسمعها الرشيد منهما فسأل الفضل لمن هي فقال هي كلام العتابيّ فقال الرشيد لو روياها عنه كان أبلغ في إتقانها. فتلطّف الفضل حتّى أخذ للعتابيّ أماناً من الرشيد وسيّره إليه فجاء وأنشده [البسيط]

مَا زِلْتُ فِي سَكَرَاتِ ٱلْمَوْتِ مُطَّرَحًا قَدْ غَابَ عَنِّي وُجُوهُ ٱلْأَمْنِ مِنْ حِيَلِ
فَلَمْ تَزَلْ دَائِبًا تَسْعَى لِتُنْقِذَنِي حَتَّى ٱخْتَلَسْتَ حَيَاتِي مِنْ يَدَيْ أَجَلِي

---

١ كذا في ت؛ وفي ب،د: يدا.

Indeed, so must anyone be who aspires to serve kings: marked by learning and magnanimity, renowned for excellence and manliness, broad of mind, generous of spirit, always prepared to act for the good.

Ja'far wrote the following line on a document issued to the people of Fars: "You have my assurance that, barring obstacles unforeseen, the tyrannical sky above you shall be lifted away." He also wrote this on the back of a petition submitted by 'Alī ibn 'Īsā: "May you come to love the loyalty you detest, and to detest the perfidy you love. For it is not the reward of Fate for you to think well of her when you have heard of her perfidy and seen it with your own eyes."

Al-Aṣma'ī loved him dearly and would frequently attend his assembly and praise him. Concerning him he recited,

> Kings admire Ja'far's generosity,
>   yet they fail to bestow favors as he does.
> He is far from the richest among them,
>   but his gifts are richer.[141]

Ja'far's brother al-Faḍl was also a secretary. He was once in attendance with al-Rashīd when the caliph saw one of the servants holding a bundle of bamboo. Turning to him, al-Rashīd asked, "Faḍl, what is that?" and al-Faḍl replied, "Those are what spears are made of, Commander of the Believers." He avoided mentioning the bamboo, since the name of al-Rashīd's mother was Bamboo.[142] 3.2.7

The poet al-'Attābī found himself in grave danger, having been accused of being a Mu'tazilite in the presence of al-Rashīd and condemned to death. Al-Faḍl, much troubled at this, helped him to flee Baghdad. He also summoned al-Kisā'ī[143] and told him to teach al-'Attābī's poetry and treatises to al-Ma'mūn and al-Amīn, the sons of al-Rashīd, which he did. Soon thereafter al-Rashīd happened to hear the boys reciting some of it, and asked al-Faḍl whose work it was. "That is the work of al-'Attābī," al-Faḍl said. "It would be better for their mastery of it," the caliph replied, "if they learnt it from him directly." Al-Faḍl eventually managed to secure a writ of safe conduct for al-'Attābī from al-Rashīd, and to convey it to him. Al-'Attābī returned and dedicated these lines to al-Faḍl:

> Fast in the throes of death I lay,
>   no scheme had I with which to save myself.
> Yet you worked tirelessly to rescue me,
>   until you snatched my life from its appointed hour.[144]

ومنهم الفضل بن الربيع وزير الرشيد والأمين الذي قال فيه أبو نواس [الطويل] ٨،٢،٣

لَعَمْرُكَ مَا غَابَ ٱلْأَمِينُ مُحَمَّدٌ عَنِ ٱلْأَمْرِ يَعْنِيهِ إِذَا شَهِدَ ٱلْفَضْلُ
وَلَوْلَا مَوَارِيثُ ٱلنُّبُوَّةِ إِنَّهَا لَهُ[1] دُونَهُ مَا كَانَ بَيْنَهُمَا فَضْلُ
فَإِنْ يَكُنِ ٱلْأَيَّامُ فِيهَا تَبَايُنٌ فَقَوْلُهُمَا قَوْلٌ وَفِعْلُهُمَا فِعْلُ

وقال له المهديّ يوماً كذبت فقال وجه الكذّاب لا يقابلك ولسانه لا يخاطبك.

٩،٢،٣ ومنهم أحمد بن أبي خالد من قوله بالأقلام تُساس الأقاليم. ومنهم اسماعيل بن صبيح من قوله في شكر ما تقدّم من إحسانك شاغل عمّا تأخّر. ومنهم عمر بن مسعدة من مكاتباته قوله كاتبي ومَن قبلي من أجناد[2] أمير المؤمنين أطال الله بقاءه وقوّاده في الطاعة والانقياد على أحسن ما تكون عليه طاعة جند تأخّرت أرزاقهم عنهم واختلّت أحوالهم.

١٠،٢،٣ ومن الكتّاب المشهورين الفضل بن سهل الذي يقول فيه ابراهيم بن العبّاس [مجزوء المتقارب]

لِفَضْلِ بْنِ سَهْلٍ يَدٌ تَقَاصَرَ عَنْهَا ٱلْمَثَلْ
فَبَاطِنُهَا لِلنَّدَى وَظَاهِرُهَا لِلْقُبَلْ
وَبَسْطُهَا لِلرَّجَا وَقَبْضَتُهَا لِلْأَجَلْ
مِنَ ٱلْفَضْلِ أَمْوَالُهُ وَمِنْ سَائِلِيهِ ٱلْأَمَلْ

ومن قوله كشفت الخبرة قناع الشكّ لحمد السابق وذمّ الساقط. ومن كلامه الشرف في السرف فقيل له لا خير في السرف فقال لا سرف في الخير، فقلّب اللفظ واستوفى المعنى.

---

١ في سائر المخطوطات: لها؛ والمثبت يقتضيه السياق. ٢ كذا في ج؛ وفي ب، د: قلب من أجناد؛ ت: قبلي من أجنادي.

Al-Faḍl ibn al-Rabīʿ, vizier to al-Rashīd and al-Amīn, was another famous secretary. Abū Nuwās composed the following lines in praise of him: 3.2.8

By your life! Muḥammad al-Amīn overlooks no affair
 that concerns him, when al-Faḍl is there.
If not for the Prophetic heritage, which belongs to one of them
 but not the other, neither would have precedence.
Though the passage of days bring contrast and change
 their words and their deeds remain as one.[145]

Al-Mahdī once accused al-Faḍl of lying. "The face of a liar could not confront you," he replied, "nor could a liar's tongue address you."

There are a few other notable secretaries whose *bons mots* we ought to mention here. 3.2.9

Aḥmad ibn Abī Khālid: "It is by reed pens that climes are governed."[146]

Ismāʿīl ibn Ṣubayḥ: "My gratitude for your past gifts distracts me from your more recent ones."

ʿUmar ibn Masʿadah wrote, "My letter, along with those of the forces and officers of the Commander of the Believers, may God prolong his life, who are with me, is as obedient and submissive as one could wish an army whose pay is late and whose condition is abysmal to be."[147]

Yet another famous secretary was al-Faḍl ibn Sahl, about whom the poet Ibrāhīm ibn al-ʿAbbās declaimed, 3.2.10

Al-Faḍl ibn Sahl has a hand that no saying can describe;
 Its palm for gifts, its back for kisses.
Its opening brings anticipation, its closing signals death.
 From God's favor comes his wealth; from his supplicants comes
  hope.[148]

This is a saying of al-Faḍl's: "Only through long proving is the mask of uncertainty lifted away. Then the one who holds the course receives praise, but the one who falls away is rebuked."[149]

He also said, "The secret of true nobility lies in excess." Someone responded, "It is impossible that there should be good in excess!" "It is impossible that there should be excess in good," he replied, thus reversing the words while giving the meaning its full due.

وهو الذي قال فيه أبو العيناء وقد سئل عنه فقال خلّفه آدم في ولده فهو ينفع غلّتهم ويسدّ خلّتهم ولقد رفع الله للدنيا من شأنها إذ جعله من سكّانها.

١١،٢،٣ ومنهم أخوه الحسن بن سهل وهو الذي كتب إلى المأمون يستعطفه للناس ويحثّه على أفعال البرّ وإيصال الأرزاق إلى المجتمعين ببابه إنّ داعي نداك ومنادي جدواك جمعا ببابك الوفود يرجون نائلك فمنهم من يمتّ بحرمة ومنهم من يدلّ بخدمة وقد أجحف بهم المقام وطالت عليهم الأيّام فإن رأى أمير المؤمنين أن ينعشهم بسَيبه ويحقّق ظنّهم بطوله فعل. فوقّع على ظهر رقعته الخير متّسع وأبواب الملوك مواطن لذوي المروّات فأحص أسماءهم وأجلل مراتبهم ليصل إلى كلّ منهم قدر استحقاقه ولا تكدّر معروفنا بالمطل والحجاب فإنّ الأوّل يقول [الوافر]

فَإِنَّكَ لَنْ تَرَى طَرْدًا لِحُرٍّ   كَإِلْصَاقٍ بِهِ بَعْضَ ٱلْهَوَانِ
وَلَنْ تَجْلِبْ مَوَدَّةَ ذِي وَفَاءٍ   بِمِثْلِ ٱلْبَذْلِ أَوْ لُطْفِ ٱللِّسَانِ

١٢،٢،٣ ومنهم الحسن بن وهب كتب يصف خطًّا حسنًا فقال لله ما ضمّنته من وشي ألفاظك وأودعته من نسج أقلامك وتمعّنته من بدائع حروفك وطرائف خطوطك التي هي أحسن من الخيلان في خدود الحِسان وأبهج من العقائص في فروع الأوانس وأبهى من الخضاب في أطراف الغانية الكعاب وأزهر من اللؤلؤ والمرجان في سموط سلكات القيان وأنور من القلائد في لبّات الخرائد وأبلج من منتظم العقود في جيد المِغناج الرُود وأزين من الدُرّ والزبرجد في صدور النواعم الخُرَّد.

١٣،٢،٣ ومنهم محمّد بن عبد الملك الزيّات من كلامه في الحزم لا تخدعنّك نفسك عن الحزم فتميل إلى التواني في صورة التوكّل ويسلّبك الحذر ويورّثك[١] الهوينا بإحالتك على الأقدار فإنّ الله سبحانه إنّما أمرنا بالتوكّل عند انقطاع الحيل وبالتسليم بعد الإعذار

١ ب،د: وتسليك وتوريك؛ ت: فيسلبك الحذر ويوثرك؛ والمثبت يقتضيه السياق.

When asked about al-Faḍl ibn Sahl, Abū l-ʿAynāʾ said, "Adam himself has appointed him as a successor among his descendants. He brings them benefit and keeps them from want. God elevated the status of this world when He placed al-Faḍl ibn Sahl among its inhabitants."

Al-Faḍl's brother, al-Ḥasan ibn Sahl, was also a renowned secretary. He once wrote the following lines to al-Maʾmūn, entreating him on behalf of deserving people and urging him to perform righteous deeds, specifically to distribute stipends to those gathered at his gate: "One man speaks out to summon your generosity, another calls on you for benefit; together they convene delegations at your gate, all hoping for your favor. Some seek advancement by appealing to their inviolable bond with you; others are humiliated by servile employment. They have suffered while standing there these days long. If the Commander of the Believers sees fit to restore them with gifts and to confirm thereby their belief in his power, he should do so!" 3.2.11

Upon the back of the petition the caliph wrote this response: "Our wealth is vast and ample, and the gates of kings are where men of virtue belong. Register their names, therefore, and elevate their stations, that each one of them may be rewarded as he deserves. Do not obscure our generosity with any manner of delay or obstruction. As one of the ancient poets said,

You shall find nothing more repugnant to a free man
  than a near brush with disgrace.
Nor shall you win the affection of one loyal
  with anything so well as a gift or kind word."[150]

Another great secretary, al-Ḥasan ibn Wahb, described some particularly fine handwriting in the following terms: "How wonderfully and subtly do you embellish your words, impart the weaving of your pens, and intently craft your letters and exquisite lines! They are more comely than moles upon the cheeks of rare beauties, more resplendent than the plaited tresses of young ladies, more lovely than henna on the fingers of a shapely lass, more radiant than pearls and coral strung upon singing girls, brighter than necklaces at the throats of virgins, fairer than fine ornaments upon the tender necks of coquettes, more graceful than pearls and chrysolite on the bosoms of soft maidens." 3.2.12

Another of the great secretaries, Muḥammad ibn ʿAbd al-Malik al-Zayyāt, composed the following lines about firm action: "Do not deceive yourself and stray from firmness, slipping into laxity in the guise of trust in God. It will strip 3.2.13

والاجتهاد وبذلك أنزل كتابه وأمضى سنّته فقال تعالى ذكره ﴿خُذُوا حِذْرَكُمْ﴾ وقال تعالى ﴿وَلَا تُلْقُوا بِأَيْدِيكُمْ إِلَى التَّهْلُكَةِ﴾ وقال نبيّنا صلّى الله عليه وسلّم اعقلها وتوكّل.

ومنهم سليمان بن وهب من كلامه قوله رسوم الكرم ديون. وقوله النعمة عروس مهرها الشكر وأثواب صونها البشر. وقوله لا ضمان على الزمان ولا مضاعة بين الصناعة والقناعة. ١٤،٢،٣

ومن الكتّاب المشهورين أبو بكر الخوارزميّ من كلامه أراحني الشيخ أطال الله بقاءه ببرّه لكن أتعبني بشكره وخفّف ظهري من ثقل المحن لا بل أثقله بأعباء المنن وأحياني بتحقيق الرجا لا بل أماتني بفرط الحيا. ١٥،٢،٣

ومنهم أحمد بن محمّد المعروف ببديع الزمان من قوله لو رأيت يا سيّدي صدري وقد انبسط بالولاء واتّسع ولساني وقد انبعث بالثناء واندفع لقلت أقلادة هذه الجانحة أم صدر ولسان هذه الجارحة أم بحر؟ ومن كلامه هو سيف إلّا أنّه إنسان وعالم إلّا أنّه فرد ونجم إلّا أنّه سعد. ومن كلامه كيف صدئتَ يا سيدي وأنت ذهب وأظلمت وأنت لهب وضللت وأنت نجم وأبطأت وأنت سهم وكيف كدّرتك قذاة وأنت بحر وكسفتك نقطة وأنت بدر؟ ١٦،٢،٣

ومن الكتّاب المشهورين أبو الفضل بن العميد من كلامه يصف يوم حرٍّ وجدتُ حرًّا يشبه قلب الصبّ ويذيب دماغ الضبّ. ١٧،٢،٣

ومنهم سعيد بن حُميد من قوله معروفك معروف سبقت عائدته واتّصل به ما بعده فصار نسباً اعتزي إليه وركناً اعتمد عليه. وله يستدعي صديقاً لزيارته طلعت ١٨،٢،٣

away your caution and leave you passive, making you ascribe all things to Fate. God, be He exalted, has in fact commanded us to trust in Him when all else fails, resigning ourselves only after vigorous exertion. It was in this spirit that He sent down his Book and caused the Example of his Prophet to be set forth. For He of exalted mention has said, «Take your precautions»[151] and «Cast not yourselves by your own hands into destruction.»[152] Our Prophet, God bless and keep him, said, 'Trust in God but tether your camel.'"[153]

The secretary Sulaymān ibn Wahb said, "The dues of generosity are debts that must be paid." And also, "Benefaction is a bride whose dowry is gratitude; the garments in which she is bedecked are delight." And also, "There is no guarantee against the deeds of Time." And, "Where industry and contentment are, there want cannot go."[154] 3.2.14

It is recorded that the famous secretary Abū Bakr al-Khwārizmī said, "The good sir, may God prolong his life, sets me at ease by his good favor toward me but wearies me by the gratitude that it imposes. No sooner does he lighten my burden of trials than he freights me with the obligation of thanks. He revives me by fulfilling my hopes, then slays me with my own immense chagrin." 3.2.15

The secretary Aḥmad ibn Muḥammad, the one known as Badīʿ al-Zamān—"the Marvel of His Age"—has in like fashion a number of noteworthy sayings.[155] For instance: "Were you to see my chest, my lord, filled with feelings of loyalty, and my tongue breaking forth with praise unbidden, then you would say, 'Is it a mere chest that these ribs form, or a precious necklace? And can this organ be a tongue, or is it rather an ocean?'" He also said, "A sword he is, though human; an entire world, though but a single man; a star, though he is Saʿd."[156] And also, "How could you rust, my lord, when you are gold, or cast a shadow, being pure flame? How could you, a guiding star, lead anyone astray, or, as a speeding arrow, ever tarry? How could you, an ocean, be tainted by a fleck, or, full moon, be in any way eclipsed?"[157] 3.2.16

The famous secretary Abū l-Faḍl ibn al-ʿAmīd described a hot day in this manner: "It is as hot as the heart of a great serpent, hot enough to dissolve the brain of a lizard."[158] 3.2.17

Another great secretary was Saʿīd ibn Ḥumayd, who said, "The benefit of your gift extends outward in time, touching what is past and reaching unto what is yet to come. It is a noble lineage to which men trace their descent, a support on which they depend." 3.2.18

نجوم تنتظر بدراً لها فرأيك[1] في الطلوع قبل غروبها؟ وكتب إليه بعض أصحابه رقعة يعتذر فيها عن حضور مجلسه فوقّع على ظهرها أنت في أوسع العذر عند ثقتي بك وفي أضيقه عند شوقي إليك. وكتب في عهد لبعض الولاة البس من ثوب عفافك ما يشمل كافّة أطرافك. وكتب إلى بعض أوليائه وصل كتابك بما يستعبد الحرّ وإن كان قديم العبوديّة ويستغرق الشكر وإن كان سابق فضلك لم يبق منه بقيّة.

ومنهم أبو الحسن بن الفرات كتب إلى بعض الوزراء في صباه حرس الله لي ودّك ولا فطن الدهر بحسن حالي عندك ومنحني الإمتاع بك. وكتب إلى بعض أصدقائه أنا أسرّ بموعدك وأكون جذلاناً[2] بانتظارك فإن عاق عائق عن إنجاز وعدك كنت قد ربحت السرور بالتوقّع لما أحبّه وأصبت أجراً عند الحسرة بما حرمته من رفدك. ٣،٢،١٩

ومنهم أبو الفتح البستيّ من قوله القلم مطيّة يمشي راكبها رهواً وتكسو الأنامل زهواً. ومن قوله من أطاع غضبه أضاع أدبه. ومن قوله عادات السادات سادات العادات. ومن قوله الرشوة رشا الحاجة والحلم مطيّة وطيّة وإفراط الدماثة غثاثة والإنصاف من أحسن الأوصاف. ٣،٢،٢٠

ومنهم أبو[3] عليّ بن مقله من كلامه ما أحبّ الوزارة إلّا لوليّ أنفعه أو عدوّ أقمعه. ومن قوله الأصاغر يهفون والأكابر يعفون. ومن قوله إذا رضيت آثرت وإذا غضبت أثّرت. واعتذر إليه رجل فقال حسبك يا هذا فإنّ الوليّ لا يحاسَب والعدوّ لا يحسب له. ٣،٢،٢١

---

١ كذا في ت؛ وفي ب: بدرها فرأيك؛ د، ج: بدرها فرأيك. ٢ ب: حذلانا؛ ت، ج: جدلانا؛ د: خذلانا؛ و لعلّ المثبت هو الصواب. ٣ الكلمة ساقطة في جميع المخطوطات وكنية ابن مقله مشهورة.

He invited a friend to visit with the following words: "The stars are out! They await their moon. Will you rise before they are inclined to set?"

One day a friend wrote him a note to apologize for being unable to join his company. Saʿīd wrote upon the back of the note, "My absolute trust in you has accepted the apology completely. My desire to see you, however, is hardly willing to receive it at all."

Upon a document of appointment issued to a governor he wrote, "May you wear your integrity in such a way that it envelops your limbs entirely."

To a close friend he wrote, "The contents of your letter enslave a free man, even one long since in your service. They lay wholesale claim to his gratitude, and even though they precede the full proof of your favor, not a shred of thanks is withheld."

When the secretary Abū l-Ḥasan ibn al-Furāt was still a boy, he wrote the **3.2.19**
following words to a certain vizier: "May God preserve your affection for me, and may Fate not get wind of my good standing with you. Instead, may He grant that I benefit from my closeness to you."

To one of his friends he wrote, "I am elated at what you have promised and shall await it in high spirits. If anything should obstruct the fulfillment of your commitment, then I shall have derived joy by looking forward to something I love, and shall thereby be compensated for my distress at being deprived of your gift."

The secretary Abū l-Fatḥ al-Bustī said, "The pen is a mount whose rider **3.2.20**
goes forth in tranquility and which clothes the fingertips in adornment."

He also said, "He who obeys his anger ruins his comportment." And also, "The habits of lords are the lords of habits." And, "A bribe is a rope in the hour of need." And, "Forbearance is an easy mount to ride." And, "Excessive mildness amounts to weakness." And, "Fairness is among the most seemly of attributes."[159]

Some sayings of the secretary Abū ʿAlī ibn Muqlah[160] are also worth recall- **3.2.21**
ing here. It was he who said, "I love the vizierate only on account of the friends I benefit and the enemies I subdue." And, "Little people err, great ones forgive."[161] And also, "Show good favor and you give honor; show anger and you leave scars."[162]

A man who apologized to him received the following reply: "That is accounted sufficient for you, for a friend is not called to account and an enemy's account is not on that account credited."

٢٢،٢،٣ ووصف بعض الكتّاب رجلاً فقال هو أملس ليس فيه مستقرّ لخير ولا لشرّ. وقال بعض الكتّاب الشكر وإن قلّ ثمر لكلّ نوال وإن جلّ. وخرج كاتب من دار الخلافة فقيل له كيف رأيت الناس فقال الداخل راجٍ والخارجُ راضٍ. ومن كلام العبّاس بن محمّد الكاتب للرشيد يا أمير المؤمنين إنّما هو مالُك وسيفك فازرع بهذا مَن شكرك وأحصد بهذا مَن كفرك. وكتب بعض الكتّاب إلى جليل ما رجائي عدلك زائداً على مأملي فضلك.[1]

٢٣،٢،٣ قلت فهؤلاء هم الذين يُطلق عليهم الكتّاب ولقد كان الأوائل يتخيّرون الناس للكتابة لا سيّما إن كانت في ولاية على أعمال يحصل بها رئاسة ويحتاج فيها إلى سياسة فيسألون عن منشأ الشخص ومرباه وصبوّته وأصله وبيتوته حتّى يسألوا عن طالعه وولادته ووقت مسقط رأسه من بطن أمّه فإذا قيل لهم في ذلك قالوا ألا يحسن لخدم الملوك إلّا من له سعد في الطالع وأصل المولد وفضيلة تميّزه فإنّ من لا سعد في طالعه ولا فضيلة فيه لا تكون به سعادة ولا عليه طلاوة. ثمّ ترك هذا الاستقصاء وصار يبحث عن وصف الإنسان فمَن كان فيه شين أعرضوا عنه وجنّبوه مناصبهم وطهّروا منه مراتبهم فيشتغل بالنسخ أو الوراقة أو ما يشتغل به الكتّاب الذين لا يصلحون لخدم الملوك، حتّى أنّه ذُكر لبعض الوزراء كاتب احتاج إليه لجهة شغرت من كاتبها فذكر بين يديه وشكر فقال بعض الحاضرين للذي شكره بحضرة الوزير: هو محمّد بن راشد بن اسحٰق النظيف الثياب المتصرّف في الآداب؟ قال نعم قال هو الذي قال فيه أبو[2] عمران الشاعر السلميّ [الخفيف]

١ كذا في ب،د؛ والجملة ساقطة في ت. ٢ في سائر المخطوطات: ابن، وهو خطأ.

A secretary described someone in the following way: "He is perfectly smooth; there is nothing about him to which either good or evil might stick." 3.2.22

Another secretary said, "Gratitude, however little, is the yield of every gift, however great."[163]

Someone asked a secretary who had just left the caliph, "What did you notice about people there?" "They enter hopeful and emerge satisfied," he replied.[164]

Al-ʿAbbās ibn Muḥammad, secretary to al-Rashīd, said, "Commander of the Believers, wealth and the sword indeed are yours to command. Sow therefore with the first among those who show you gratitude, and reap with the second among those who do not."[165]

A certain secretary wrote to a great man, "My expectation of your justice is no greater than my hope for your favor."

These, in my view, are the people who truly deserve to be called secretaries. 3.2.23
The ancients were very selective in choosing individuals for this role, especially when the choice involved the conferral of authority in positions of prominence that required political acumen. They would ask about a person's birthplace, upbringing, youth, roots, childhood—even his ascendant,[166] his birth omens, and the precise time he descended from his mother's womb. If anyone raised an objection to this procedure, they would say, "Kings should only be served by men whose ascendant contains an auspicious star and who have an excellent birth hour and virtues that set them apart. For no happiness will be obtained through someone who possesses neither auspicious ascendant nor virtue; neither will he be seen to possess any particular grace."

Next after these inquiries would come close study of a person's character. The authorities would reject anyone in whom any blemish was found; they would keep him far from their posts and cleanse their ranks of his kind. Such a person could find work as a copyist or bookseller, or in one of the other occupations that are suitable for secretaries who are unfit for the service of kings.

Thus, for example, a certain secretary was recommended to a vizier to fill a vacant position, by being mentioned and praised in his presence. One of the people there, however, asked the attendant who had praised him before the vizier, "Is that Muḥammad ibn Rāshid ibn Isḥāq, that cultured fellow with the spotless clothes?"

"Indeed it is," the attendant replied.

"So is he the man about whom the Sulamī poet Abū ʿImrān[167] recited these lines:

بِأَبِي يَا ٱبْنَ رَاشِدٍ يَا كَرِيمَ ٱلْمَشَاهِدِ
أَنْتَ أَشْهَى إِلَيَّ مِنْ كُلِّ عَذْرَاءَ نَاهِدِ

قال نعم فقال الوزير من كان فيه شين لا يُذكر لأعمال السلطان لأنّ كاتب العمل نائب عن السلطان في كلامه وكتابته وأمره ونهيه فليكن بأحسن الأوصاف حتّى يصلح أن يلي أمور الناس. ووصف آخر فقال أحد الحاضرين هذا كان يبيع الزيت في صباه فأنكره الواصف وقال ما باع الزيت قطّ فقال أليس لابن أبي العلاء فيه وقد خدم مرةً [الطويل]

يُمَاكِسُنِي ٱلزَّيَّاتُ حَتَّى لَوَ ٱنَّهُ مِنَ ٱلرِّزْقِ يُعْطِينِي ٱلْعَطِيَّةَ مَا عَدَا

فقال الوزير لا يصلح هذا لعملنا.

وذُكر شخص عنده بخير فقال واصفه ما أحسنه لولا إفراط عُجبه وكبره وأنشد

مَا أَقْبَحَ ٱلْعُجْبَ وَأَرْدَأَهُ وَأَسْمَجَ ٱلْكِبْرَ وَأَدْنَأَهُ

والله ما يصلح لتلك الحماقة ولاية إلّا نقل أخبار المسجونين[١] بأن يكون منصبه الحبس مع المحابيس.

ولقد كان الخلفاء والملوك والرؤساء ينهون عن استعمال أهل الريف وأهل السواد في شغل من أشغال الملوك أو أن يكون لهم في الدول حديث[٢] حتّى أنّ بعض أهل الريف رفع قصّة إلى أحد وزراء كسرى أنوشروان يتضمّن التزامه بمال كبير في عمل من الأعمال بشرط أن يتولّى العمل من يرضاه السلطان ويكون هذا الريفيّ بين يديه ينهي إليه وجوه المال فعرض الوزير القصّة على كسرى فأنكر عليه غاية الإنكار وقال لو كان فيك صلاحيّة لتدبير الملك والرعيّة لما عرضت قصّة ٢٤،٢،٣

---

١ كذا في ت؛ وفي ب، ج،د زيادة: يعرض. ٢ كذا في ت؛ وفي ب، ج،د زيادة: من قديم الزمان.

By my father! O Ibn Rāshid, liberal with your looks,
You are more desirable to me than any buxom virgin?"[168]

"Indeed it is," replied the attendant.

At this the vizier interjected, "Anyone thus disgraced should not be recommended for government work. For the secretary at his post represents the ruler in his speech and his writing, in what he commands and what he forbids. He must possess only the best qualities if he is to be considered worthy to take charge of the people's affairs."

Another candidate was once brought up for discussion in a similar situation. In the course of this, someone mentioned that as a boy he had been an oil seller. The man who had recommended him denied this, claiming that he had never sold oil. But the other replied, "Doesn't Ibn Abī l-ʿAlāʾ have that line about him, when he once held some official post . . . ?

The oil seller never fails to haggle with me
even if he purports to pour me a gift from his skin."[169]

The vizier said, "This person is not fit for our work."

Another person was described in the vizier's presence as a good man. The one who described him added, "What a fine man, if it were not for his excessive vanity and pride!" He then recited:

How disagreeable is vanity, and how vile!
How loathsome pride, and how base![170]

On the whole, then, people exhibiting such deficiency deserve no authority, unless it be to relay messages sent by prisoners, so that they are in effect assigned to confinement alongside the inmates.

Caliphs, kings, and leaders of all kinds have steadfastly forbidden the **3.2.24**
employment of country-bred rural folk for any royal task. Such people are not to have any say in matters of state. One such rustic once petitioned a vizier of Chosroes Anūshirwān. He proposed that he be made the tax farmer for a certain district in exchange for a large advance payment. The state, he said, would still be able to appoint whomever it wished to carry out the work, but the rustic himself would accompany this official and supply him with detailed information about the local taxpayers.

ريفيّ رُبّي بين الأبقار والمعز وأجهده كلّ الزروع يزخرف لك بما يؤذي به الناس حتّى يرتفع من ذلّ السواديّة وخساسة الأصل والريفيّة[١] أن يصير له في الحكم على الرعايا نسب[٢] يتوصّل به إلى إهانة ذوي البيوت العريقة والحطّ من مراتبهم إنّ هذا لِمن أسوأ الأحوال المفسدة للمُلك المضرّة بقوانين تدبيره. ثمّ نهى أن يشتغل أولاد الأرياف بالكتابة والعلم.

٢٥،٢،٣ وقد ورد أنّ رجلاً كان يبيع الفول نشأ له ولد بعد هذه الكائنة فبذل لخزانة الكسرى مائة ألف درهم على أن يؤذن لولده في الاشتغال بالعلم والكتابة فوقّع على قصّته لا حاجة لنا بما بذله ولا يمكّن من الاشتغال بالعلم والكتابة فإنّ أولاد الأطراف متى اشتغلوا بالعلم مع اشتغال أولاد الرؤساء بالنعم والملاذّ وإهمالهم أسباب التقدّم واللحوق بآبائهم تقدّم الأطراف وولوا الأمور وأهانوا أولاد الأشراف وأضاعوهم ولا حاجة لنا إلى استعمال طرف البتّة.

٢٦،٢،٣ واشتغل رجل يقال له حُميد بن بشر بالكتابة فذُكر عند بعض الوزراء لشغل فقال رجل في المجلس هذا من أهل السواد أي الريف فقال الوزير لو غسلت عاميّة السواديّ بألف بحر من الأدب ما طهرت وقال تصدُّر الأرياف في المجالس عار يذكر إلى آخر الزمان فقال بعض الحاضرين للوزير يا مولانا أنت تنظر بنور الله فإنّ بعض الشعراء قد أنشد في حميد بن بشر هذا المذكور [المتقارب]

حُمَيْدُ بْنُ بِشْرٍ لَهُ هِمَّةٌ وَلٰكِنَّهُ قَدْ نَشَا فِي ٱلسَّوَادِ
يُطَلِّبُ مَا لَيْسَ مِن شَأْنِهِ فَفِي تَعَبٍ دَهْرَهُ وَٱرْتِيَادِ

١ كذا في ت؛ وفي ب، ج،د زيادة: إلى عند (ج: عزّ) الكتّابة و. ٢ كذا في ج؛ وفي ب: الرعية نشب؛ ت: الرعايا نشب؛د: الرعية كسب. وما بعد هذه الكلمة إلى (ثمّ) ساقط في ب، ج،د.

The vizier relayed this proposal to Chosroes, but the king rebuked him harshly, saying, “If you were fit to administer the affairs of this state and its people, you would not have troubled me with the proposal of a rustic who was brought up among cows and goats and worn down by raising crops, who bewitches you with an elaborate scheme that can only harm the people. He merely hopes to raise himself up from the humiliation of his roots in the Sawad, from lowly origins and rusticity, and to gain newfound status to rule over the subjects, through which he plans to lord it over the well-born and to abase their ranks. This is one of the worst and most insidious scenarios that our rule could possibly envisage; it threatens serious harm to the steady function of our administration.” He then forbad the offspring of any country folk to work in the secretarial or learned professions.

Some time after this, it is told, a son was born to a certain bean seller. The **3.2.25**
man offered one hundred thousand silver coins to Chosroes’s treasury so that his son might be permitted to work in the learned and secretarial arts. Chosroes wrote upon his petition the following reply: “We have no need of the money that this man has offered. Moreover, his son cannot be permitted to occupy himself with learning and the secretarial arts. For when the sons of the low-born busy themselves with learning, while those of the leading men are distracted with luxuries and pleasures, neglecting the means of advancement to their fathers’ accomplishments, the low-born themselves advance and take control of affairs. Thereupon they treat the well-bred sons with scorn and bring them to ruin. There is no need whatsoever for us to employ any low-born person.”

A man called Ḥumayd ibn Bishr was working as a secretary when he was **3.2.26**
recommended to a certain vizier to fill a position. However, someone who happened to be present in the council pointed out that his origins were in the Sawad, meaning the countryside. At this the vizier said, “Even if you were to wash the vulgarity of a man from the Sawad in a thousand seas of refined comportment, it would not be cleansed.” He also said, “For a rustic to occupy the seat of honor is a disgrace to be recounted throughout the ages.”

Someone present said to the vizier, “Master, you must be able to see by God’s own light! For concerning this same Ḥumayd ibn Bishr a certain poet has said,

> Though Ḥumayd ibn Bishr has ambition, he hails from the Sawad,
> Demands what is not his to ask, in toil and wandering all his life.”[171]

فقال الوزير لهذا نهينا عن تقديم الأرياف السواديّة الأطراف.

وعرض على بعض ولاة الأمر جماعة ليتولّوا مراتب فسأل عن مرباهم فقيل له الريف فأنكر عليهم وقال نحن طلبنا أناساً أو طلبنا أبقاراً للحرث فقال له أحد الحاضرين وفّق الله مولانا الوزير في قوله وفعله هؤلاء المذكورون لمولانا من أهل الريف ولهم اجتماع بشهرة وخلطة وقد قال فيهم الشاعر [الطويل] ٣،٢،٢٧

أُولٰئِكَ قَوْمٌ بِٱلفَدَانِ[١] كَأَنَّهُـم   إِذَا مَا عَدَوا يَا قَوْمُ فِي بَقَرِ ٱلْحَرْثِ

ولمّا تولّى أبو يعلى الكاتب الديوان بالعراق أنشد فيه [البسيط] ٣،٢،٢٨

سَاوَى ٱلْوَزِيرُ أَبَا يَعْلَى وَسَائِرَهُ   بَعْدَ ٱلْمَحَاجِمِ وَٱلْمِقْرَاضِ وَٱلْجَلَمِ
فَقَالَ قَوْمٌ وَشَانَتْـهُ كِتَابَتُهُ[٢]   يَا رَبِّ حُكْمَكَ[٣] إِذْ عَلَّمْتَ بِٱلْقَلَمِ

وتقرّب[٤] بعض أهل الريف بمال لمن كان يرتفق في خدمته حتّى خدم فلمّا خدم انكشف جهله وفسد عليه شغله فصُرف وغرم عوض ما أتلفه بسوء تدبيره فعمل فيه الشاعر [البسيط]

مَنْ كَانَ مَا يَطْلُبُ فَوْقَ قَدْرِهِ   لَمْ يَعْدَمِ ٱلدَّهْرُ فَسَادَ أَمْرِهِ

وأنشد فيه آخر [الطويل]

لَقَدْ كَانَ مَسْتُورًا عَنِ ٱلنَّاسِ عَجْزُهُ   إِلَى أَنْ وَلِي أَمْرًا فَضَاقَ بِهِ صَدْرَا

وصُرف بعض الفضلاء بجاهل من أهل الريف كان قديماً يبيع الرمّان والتمر يُعرف بأبي الهرطمان فأنشد فيه [السريع]

---

١ كذا في ت؛ وفي ب، ج،د: للفدان. ٢ كذا في ت؛ و في ج،د: وسامتهم كتّابتهم (ج: كتّابته). ٣ كذا في ج، د؛ والكلمة غير مقروءة في ب؛ وفي ت: ما ربّ حلمك. ٤ كذا في ب،د؛ وفي ت: وتقرّر.

"For this very reason," said the vizier, "have we forbidden the promotion of low-born rustics from the Sawad."

Several men were presented to a certain governor as candidates for official positions. When he asked about their origins, he was told that they were from the countryside. Upon hearing this he denounced the men's candidacy, saying, "Did we ask for men, or for cattle with which to plow?" Someone said, "God grant success to our lord the vizier in his word and deed! These men who were presented to our lord are country folk. They have an understanding amongst themselves to collude in notorious deeds. Concerning them, the poet has said, 3.2.27

Those indeed are plow people, so that hardly do they go out
except (oh people!) among plow-oxen"[172]

When Abū Yaʿlā the Secretary was appointed over the administrative offices in Iraq, someone composed these lines about him: 3.2.28

The vizier has made Abū Yaʿlā the equal of any other man,
after the cupping glasses and scissors and shears;
When his scribing put him to shame, people cried,
"Pass judgment, Lord, for it was You who taught by the pen!"[173]

Another one of these rustics used bribes to insinuate himself into the graces of an official whom he accompanied in his work, until he himself won an appointment. Hardly had any time passed, however, before his ignorance was discovered and his incompetence became obvious. He was dismissed and fined for the damage that his mismanagement had done. His example did, however, inspire the poet to compose a line:

Fate shall not fail to mar his affairs,
whose aspirations overreach his worth.[174]

Another poet added this line:

His incapacity was hidden from all until
he gained command and forthwith shrank from it.[175]

A man of learning was dismissed in favor of an ignorant rustic, who had once sold pomegranates and dates and who was known as Abū l-Hurṭumān. The man responded with the following poetry:

يُصْرَفُ مِثْلِي بِأَبِي ٱلْهُرْطُمَانْ   بِبَائِعِ ٱلرُّمَّانِ فِي ٱلنَّهْرَوَانْ
وَبَائِعِ ٱلتَّمْرِ عَلَى رَأْسِهِ   أَلَيْسَ هٰذَا مِنْ عَجِيبِ ٱلزَّمَانْ

وأنشد غيره [الطويل]

أَلَا رُبَّ خَطٍّ جَازَ بِٱلْمَرْءِ قَدْرَهُ   فَبَلَّغَهُ مَا لَمْ يَكُنْ قَطُّ يَأْمُلُهُ

وأنشدوا في ابن التعاويذيّ [الطويل] ٢٩،٢،٣

لَقَدْ نَفَقَ ٱلْمَجْنُونُ فِي كُلِّ دَوْلَةٍ   وَظَنُّوا بِهِ ظَنًّا وَلَيْسَ كَمَا ظَنُّوا

واستُخدم ريفيّ ساقط كان إذا خلا يسخر منه جلساؤه ويشيلوا رجله وإذا جلس ٣٠،٢،٣
في الديوان يتحامق ويتراقع ويتجانن فقيل فيه شعر [مجزوء الكامل]

لَوْ قَدْ تَرَاهُ إِذَا خَلَا   فِي ٱلْبَيْتِ قَدْ شَالُوا كِعَابَهْ
لَرَأَيْتَ أَقْبَحَ مَنْظَرٍ   وَتَكَشَّفَتْ تِلْكَ ٱلْمَهَابَهْ

وبذل بعض أهل الريف مالاً لمن توسّط له في خدمة وكان يعرف بٱبن منارة فلمّا ٣١،٢،٣
خدم في الديوان تحامق وطاش عقله وكاد يفتضح فقال يوماً أنا أكلّم الناس بربع عقلي
فقال فيه الشاعر [الطويل]

لَقَدْ نَالَ يَحْيَى إِذْ وَلِيَ فَوْقَ قَدْرِهِ   وَأَظْهَرَ كِبْرًا مُفْسِدًا كُلَّ أَمْرِهِ
يُخَاطِبُنَا بِٱلرُّبْعِ مِنْ كُنْهِ عَقْلِهِ   وَيُسْرِفُ فِيمَا يَدَّعِيهِ بِكِبْرِهِ
فَلَا بَارَكَ ٱلرَّحْمٰنُ فِي ٱبْنِ مَنَارَةٍ   وَأَفْقَدَهُ مِنْ عَيْشِهِ شَطْرَ عُمْرِهِ

قال بعض الحكماء موت ألف من الأكابر الأصلاء العريقين أخفّ في الدول من ٣٢،٢،٣
ارتفاع واحد من السفل. وقال بعض الحكماء إيّاكم وتقديم الأطراف فإنّ من ربّاه

Shall such as I be dismissed for Abū l-Hurṭumān,
a pomegranate peddler from al-Nahrawān,
Who sells dates from atop his head?
Is this not a wonder for the ages?[176]

Another proclaimed these lines:

Does not many a writ elevate a man beyond his limits
bringing him whither he had never hoped to go?[177]

Concerning Ibn al-Taʿāwīdhī the poets recited, 3.2.29

The madman is in high demand in every government;
though they think well of him at first, he is not as they suppose.[178]

Once, a disreputable rustic, whose associates would mock and deride him 3.2.30
behind his back, was employed in an official post. When he arrived for work at the office, he would act in the most stupid, foolish, and senseless manner. He, too, inspired poetry:

If you spy him alone in the house, his honors
stripped away by their mockery,
Then you shall see something awful:
that dread reverence full exposed.[179]

A rustic known as Ibn Manārah paid someone to procure him official 3.2.31
employment. When he arrived at the office to take up his position, however, he acted foolish and distracted, nearly bringing scandal upon himself. One day he said, "I speak to people using only a quarter of my brain." At this, a poet was moved to compose,

Yaḥyā overreached by his appointment,
the pride he showed corrupted all he did.
He speaks to us with a quarter of his mind,
passing all moderation by what he claims in pride.
May the Merciful not bless Ibn Manārah,
but take from him instead half his life.[180]

A certain sage said, "The death of a thousand of the most senior, steadfast, 3.2.32
and noble men is more easily borne by regimes than the elevation of a single

الهوان أبطرته الكرامة. وقال بعض الحكماء مَن عظّم لئيماً شاركه في لؤمه. وقال بعض الحكماء من كان الإكرام داءه كان الهوان دواءه والمرء متى ألف الهوان فلا يقبل الإكرام.

٣٣،٢،٣ ومن أعجب ما جرى في زمن المعتصم أنّ ريفياً كثر ماله فتوسّل به إلى أن ذُكر عند وزير المعتصم واستأذن له بعضُ من قبل رشوته أن يركب في موكب الوزير فأذن له فصار يركب الخيل الجياد وٱزدادت حماقته وكان يقال له مُقران فعمل فيه أبو تمّام

[المتقارب]

أَمُقْرَانُ يَا ٱبْنَ بَنَاتِ ٱلْعُلُوجِ وَنَسْلَ ٱلْيَهُودِ شِرَارِ ٱلْبَشَرْ
لَقَدْ صِرْتَ بَيْنَ ٱلْوَرَى عِبْرَةً رَكِبْتَ ٱلْهَمَالِيجَ بَعْدَ ٱلْبَقَرْ
وَبَدَّلْتَ بِٱلْمَرِّ ذَا مَيْعَةٍ[1] وَمَا إِنْ لِسَوطِكَ فِيهِ أَثَرْ
فَقُولَا لِمُقْرَانَ فِيمَ ٱلْمَقَامُ وَهٰذَا حِصَادُكُمُ قَدْ حَضَرْ
بِعِ[2] ٱلسَّيْفَ ثُمَّ ٱسْتَجِدْ مِنْجَلاً وَدَعْ عَنْكَ حَمْلَ ٱلْحُسَامِ ٱلذَّكَرْ

فلمّا بلغ الوزير الشعر قال لا يليق أن يكون في موكبنا من للشعراء في عرضه هذا المجال فقبّح الله من غشّنا بذكره في مجلسنا واستأذن في ركوبه معنا. وأمره بالرجوع إلى أشغاله بالريف وسقط مَن ذكره من عين الوزير وتغيّر عليه وتقهقرت أحواله.

٣٤،٢،٣ ومن غرائب ما جرى من الاتّفاق الغريب العجيب ما أنهيته للسلطان السعيد الشهيد الملك الكامل قدّس الله روحه فتعجّب منه وهو أنّي كنت مشتغلاً بالعلم منذ نشأتُ ولم يكن لي تعلّق بالديوان فبينا أنا راكب في بعض الأيّام إذ لقيني رجل مصريّ أسمر اللون قد خطّه الشيب وهو راكب بغلة فسلّم عليّ فرددتُ عليه السلام فقال

---

١ الكلمة غير منقوطة في ب،د؛ وفي ت: منعة؛ والمثبت يقتضيه السياق. ٢ كذا في ت؛ وفي ب،د: دع.

man of lowly birth." To another are ascribed the words, "Beware lest you promote the lower sorts. For he whom disgrace has nurtured, generosity shall make insolently haughty." And another has said, "He who empowers a baseborn man shares in his baseness." And still another, "If being honored ails a man, being disgraced shall cure him. For one accustomed to disgrace cannot receive honor."

In the days of Caliph al-Muʿtaṣim, an astonishing thing of the same sort took place. A rustic had gained great wealth and won such favor by means of it that he managed to have his name mentioned in the presence of al-Muʿtaṣim's vizier. A man he had bribed asked that he be permitted to ride in the vizier's entourage. The request was granted, so the rustic began riding fine horses and generally outdoing himself in folly. This man was called Muqrān and the poet Abū Tammām composed the following verses about him: 3.2.33

> Ho, Muqrān! Of rough infidels' daughters born,
> scion of the Jews, the worst of mankind.
> You have become an example for all,
> you ride horses now; cows no longer!
> You have exchanged the spade for a docile mount,
> your whip leaves no marks upon it.
> Ask Muqrān, "Why do you still stand there,
> now that your harvest season is at hand?
> Sell the sword and take up a scythe,
> leave off carrying that keen and noble blade."[181]

When the vizier heard this poetry, he said, "It is inappropriate for our entourage to include someone with whose honor the poets take such liberties. God curse the man who tricked us by mentioning him in our council, and asked that he be permitted to ride with us!" He then ordered Muqrān to return to his work in the countryside, and the man who had recommended him fell from the vizier's favor and saw his career disintegrate.

Among the strangest and most wondrous incidents I can recall is one I related to the blessed, martyred sultan, al-Malik al-Kāmil, God sanctify his spirit, and which truly amazed him. 3.2.34

In my youth I busied myself with the study of religious subjects and had no involvement with government administration. One day when I was riding along I met a dark-skinned man, a native Egyptian with silvering hair who was

يا مولاي لا تسمع فيّ كلام أصحاب الأغراض فأنا مملوك والدك القاضي[١] علم الدين ولي عليه خدمة فقلت يا أخي من أنت فوالله ما أعرفك ومن أنا حتّى أسمع فيك كلام المتعرّضين؟ هذا الحديث إنّما يسوغ قوله لولاة الأمور ولستُ منهم فقال أمّا أنا فابن الصخر الذي بإيار وقد بلغني من ابن صاحب ترتيب[٢] أنّك قلت لا بدّ أن أغرّم ابن الصخر سبعة آلاف دينار وآخذ خطّه بها للسلطان فقلت يا شيخ أمّا أنت فسمعتُ بك وأمّا مَن ذكرته فوالله ما أعرفه وليس لي إلمام بخدمة السلطان ولا الوزير وإنّي رجل منقطع في مدرسة أشتغل بالعلم ولا أعرف شيئًا من حالك ولا غيرك ولا أنا من ذلك القبيل فعلّك غالط فيّ وتعجّبت من حديثه.[٣]

ثمّ اتّفق لي الحضور بين يدي السلطان الشهيد في مباحثة فسمع كلامي ورسم ٣٥،٢،٣
بانتظامي في سلك المماليك. وخرج أمره إليّ في مباشرة الدواوين بالديار المصريّة كلّها ما خلا مواضع يسيرة فكتبت أنهي إلى السلطان أنّي لم أحضر ديوانًا قطّ ولا عرفتُ شيئًا من عُرف الدواوين ولا أوضاعها ومتى علم المستخدمون[٤] بالبلاد أنّه قد وُلّي عليهم جاهل بالديوان اتّفقوا مع المستوفين بالباب ونهبوا الأموال.

فلمّا وقف السلطان قدّس الله روحه على ورقتي رسم بإعفائي وشكرني وقال كم بين من يتوسّل حتّى يخدم في فرع من الفروع وبين من نولّيه من مكّة حرسها الله تعالى إلى دمياط فيستعفي ويقول ما رأيت ديوانًا قطّ؟ فقال من كان حاضرًا يا مولاي إن كان كما قال فيولّيه السلطان الشرقيّة والغربيّة يتعلّم فيهما عُرف الديوان فإذا عَرف ذلك ينقله السلطان إلى هذه الأشغال فقال ما نكثر عليه بل نولّيه الشرقيّة يتعلّم فيها عُرف الديوان فإنّها خفيفة الحال.

١ كذا في ت؛ والكلمة ساقطة في ب،د. ٢ كذا في ت؛ وفي ب، ج،د: بلغني من صاحب أنّك. ٣ كذا في ت؛ وفي ب، ج،د زيادة: ومضى على ذلك مدّة طويلة. ٤ كذا في ت؛ وفي ب: المستحدثون؛د: المتحدثون.

riding on a mule. He greeted me and I returned the greeting. Then he said, "My master, don't listen to what conniving people say about me! For I am a servant of your father, Judge ʿAlam al-Dīn, and he owes me a favor."

"Brother," I replied, "who are you? I don't recognize you, by God. Who am I that I should be privy to what your adversaries say about you? That's the kind of thing one says to powerful people. I am certainly not one of them."

"I am Ibn al-Ṣakhr, from Ibyār," he said. "The son of a certain official[182] told me that you said, 'I shall have to fine Ibn al-Ṣakhr seven thousand gold coins and obtain a signed document from him agreeing to the payment.'"

"Listen, old fellow," I said, "I've heard of you, but this other person you mention, I swear I don't know him. I know nothing about serving any sultan or vizier. In reality I'm one of those people who spends all his time in the law college, doing nothing but studying. I know absolutely nothing about your situation, or anyone else's for that matter. I'm not that type at all. Perhaps you've made some mistake about me." I was quite astonished at what he had said.

A long time after this, it so happened that I took part in a debate in the 3.2.35
presence of the martyred sultan. After hearing me, the sultan directed that I be enrolled among the servants of the state and issued a command that I take charge of the administrative offices in all of Egypt, except for a few places. I replied in writing, informing the sultan that I had never worked in an office of any kind, and that I did not know anything about the customs of the offices or their current condition. I added that when the officials in the various towns found out that someone entirely ignorant of administration had been appointed over them, they would conspire with the supervising accountants and embezzle the funds.

When the sultan, God sanctify his spirit, received my letter, he directed that I be excused from what he had commanded. He also thanked me, saying, "Do any of the men who beg to serve in some branch office, or whom we in fact appoint, from Mecca (God protect it) to Damietta, ever ask to be excused and say, 'I have never so much as seen an administrative office?'"

Then one of the attendants said, "Master, if this is the case, let the sultan appoint him over al-Sharqiyyah and al-Gharbiyyah. He will learn the customs of administration in those places, then the sultan can transfer him to these central offices."

فأحضرني قدّس الله روحه بين يديه وقال أنا أولّيك الديار المصريّة تأبى وتقول ما أُحسِن وأوراق القاضي[١] صفيّ الدين بن شكر عندي بأنّك أهل لتدبير الدولة كلّها فقلت يا مولانا القاضي صفيّ الدين أحسن الظنّ بي وأنا أعرف بنفسي فقال لا تراددني فوالله لي فيك أمل أن أعظّم قدرك وأجعل هؤلاء كلّهم يتردّدون إلى بابك، يعني قوماً كانوا خواصّ في خدمته. فدعوت له وخرجت إلى الشرقيّة كما أمر.

فلمّا عاد ركابه العزيز[٢] من الشرق[٣] طلبني وأحضرني بين يديه وأمرني أن ألازم ٣٦،٢،٣ خدمته فكنت أحضر في كلّ يوم مبكّراً فإذا علم أنّي بالباب خرج أمره بإحضار مستوفي الخزانة وهو سعيد الدولة الإبياريّ وإحضار الصنيعة وكان إذ ذاك مستوفي النظر فيخلوا بين يديه فيقرؤون الأموال وجهاتها والبواقي وأربابها فلا يتقضّى نهار إلّا بتقرير مصالح واستخراج أموال وترتيب دواوين ونظّار وولاة.

وصرت أجلس أنا وفخر الدين عثمان رحمه الله وكان قد فوّض إليه أمر الدواوين في اجتماعهم وٱستخراج الأموال بكتبه ورسله فرسم السلطان قدّس الله روحه بالكشف عن جهات من جملتها دمياط وعيّن لها ابن مفشين[٤] وابن هبلان[٥] وعيّن فخر الدين عثمان ابنَ الصخر يكون مع ابن مفشين وابن هبلان في الكشف على ابن حسّون والي دمياط فرأى ابن الصخر التذكرة فيها ثمانية وعشرون ألف دينار فحمله سخف عقل أهل الريف على الخوف من هذه الجملة وتوهّم أنّها لازمة له فٱستعفى من الكشف وقال من في قدرته ثمانية وعشرون ألف دينار؟

فقال له فخر الدين عثمان يا شيخ أنت تريد ألف كاشف يكشفون عليك؟ فإنّ عند السلطان في حقّك من الأوراق[٦] بما اعتمدته في إبيار[٧] ما يوجب أخذ روحك.

١ كذا في ت؛ وفي ب، ج،د: الصاحب. ٢ كذا في ت؛ والكلمتان ساقطتان في ب، ج،د. ٣ كذا في ب، ت؛ وفي د: الشرقيّة. ٤ كذا في ت؛ وفي ب، ج،د: هفسين. ٥ كذا في ت؛ وفي ب، ج،د: هيلان. ٦ كذا في ت؛ وفي ب، ج،د زيادة: والمرافعات. ٧ كذا في ت؛ وفي ب،د: إتيان.

"Let us not overburden him," the sultan replied. "We shall appoint him over al-Sharqiyyah alone to learn the customs of administration, since it is a relatively minor district."

Then the sultan, God sanctify his spirit, summoned me into his presence and said, "I appoint you over the lands of Egypt and you refuse, saying, 'I am not suitable'? I have here a recommendation from Judge Ṣafī l-Dīn ibn Shukr that says you are qualified to manage the whole state."

"Master," I said, "Judge Ṣafī l-Dīn thinks too highly of me. I know myself better."

"Do not try to dissuade me," he said, "for I have high hopes for you. I want to make you great, so great that all these people"—he meant all his private servants—"go running back and forth to your door."

So I blessed him and departed for al-Sharqiyyah as he had commanded.

When his mighty cavalcade made its return from the East he asked for me 3.2.36
and, summoning me into his presence, commanded that I serve him personally.[183] So each day I would arrive early. When he heard that I had come, he would summon the accountant of the treasury, Saʿīd al-Dawlah al-Ibyārī, as well as al-Ṣanīʿah, who at that time was the accountant of the audit. They would meet with him in private and read out the receipts and their origins, as well as what was still owed and by whom. Not a day went by without some affair being decided, funds being withdrawn, or offices, auditors, or governors being assigned.

I would sit with Fakhr al-Dīn ʿUthmān, God show him mercy, to whom had been delegated command of all the offices together, as well as the extraction of tax payments by means of his writs and emissaries. At this time the sultan, God sanctify his spirit, ordered an audit of several districts, including Damietta. Ibn Mufshīn and Ibn Hablān were appointed to carry out the audit of Damietta.[184] Fakhr al-Dīn ʿUthmān appointed Ibn al-Ṣakhr to go along with Ibn Mufshīn and Ibn Hablān to audit Ibn Ḥassūn, the governor of the town. When Ibn al-Ṣakhr saw the ticket for twenty-eight thousand gold coins, his idiotic rural mind was filled with fear at such a sum. He imagined it would be demanded of him. Begging to be excused from the audit, he said, "Who in the world can answer for twenty-eight thousand gold coins?"

Fakhr al-Dīn ʿUthmān said to him, "Look old fellow, do you want a thousand auditors breathing down your neck? The sultan could take your very life on the evidence of records in his possession that document the things you authorized

وما قصدنا أن تروح كاشفاً إلّا ليزول ما في خاطر السلطان منك وأنت توقّف ولو كان في التذكرة مائة ألف دينار ما لزم الكاشف منها شيء فلم يدخل في عقله هذا الكلام وسألني أن أطالع السلطان بأنّه استعفى.

فلمّا حضرت بين يديه قال دبّرنا فيمن[1] يكشف لنا جهة أخرى فدمياط قد راح لها كاشف قلت يا مولانا فلم ينبتّ في دمياط أمر إلى الآن قال كيف ذلك قلت ابن الصخر كأنّه حمله عقل أهل الريف على الخوف من جملة التذكرة فٱستعفى فقال هذه حركات فخر الدين عثمان ما زال بي حتّى جعله كاشفاً وهو يريد ألف كاشف يكشفون عليه. ثمّ طلب فخر الدين وقال له أنت لصداقتك مع ابن الصخر جعلته كاشفاً وعندي عليه أوراق بثلاثين ألف دينار يريد من يكشفها عليه فقال وكذا قلت له فأمر بإحضاره وقال له أبعثك للكشف تأبى وأنت أحقّ بالكشف عليك؟ فٱعتذر فقال أمسكوه فسحبه أمير جاندار[2] بطيلسانه وأخرجه.

ثمّ قال لي السلطان رحمه الله يا فلان هؤلاء الأرياف متى طال ذيلهم طغوا وبغوا وعصوا وصادقوا مقدّمي العربان وتحدّثوا معهم في الفساد وأضمروه لوقته وهم ذخائر رديئة. ٣٧،٢،٣

ثمّ قال والله ما كان للسلطان[3] رحمه الله عند ابن الصخر شيء وانّما لمّا سمع بطول ذيله وكثرة ماله علم أنّ ذلك يحمله على الفساد فغرمه جملة. وأنا ساعدته فيها بألفين وخمسمائة دينار لأنّه كان يخدمني إذا جئت إلى إبيار وكنت أتفرّج في بستانه ثمّ سامحته فيها بألف دينار.

---

١ كذا في ت؛ وفي ب، ج،د زيادة: يروح. ٢ كذا في ب،د؛ وفي ت: جمدار. ٣ كذا في ت؛ وفي ب، ج،د: الملك العادل.

previously, in Ibyār. Our entire plan in having you go out as an auditor is for the sultan to change his mind about what to do with you. Just hold steady, even if the ticket says a hundred thousand gold coins. The auditor is not held responsible for any of it." Ibn al-Ṣakhr, however, unable to absorb this, asked me to explain to the sultan that he requested to be excused.

When I came before the sultan he said to me, "Advise us about who should audit another district for us, now that an auditor for Damietta has gone out."

"Master," I said, "the matter of Damietta is actually not quite settled yet."

"How can that be?" he asked.

"It's Ibn al-Ṣakhr. . . . It's as though his rural mind is afraid at the sum on the sheet. He asks to be excused."

"This is all the work of Fakhr al-Dīn ʿUthmān," the sultan said. "He kept at me until I let him make Ibn al-Ṣakhr an auditor. In reality, there should be a thousand auditors auditing him."

He then called for Fakhr al-Dīn ʿUthmān and said to him, "You made Ibn al-Ṣakhr an auditor because you're friendly with him. I have records that say he owes me thirty thousand gold coins. For that, someone should be auditing him."

"That's exactly what I told him," Fakhr al-Dīn replied.

So the sultan summoned Ibn al-Ṣakhr and said to him, "Do you refuse when I send you out to audit, when what you really deserve is to be audited yourself?" Ibn al-Ṣakhr apologized, but the sultan ordered that he be seized, and the Emir Jāndār dragged him out by his cowl.

After this the sultan, God show him mercy, said to me, "You know, as soon 3.2.37
as these rustics get too much influence they start oppressing everyone in sight. They get restless and cut deals with the Arab chieftains to wreak some havoc or other, then they watch for their opportunity. Beneath the surface they're a bad lot."

Then al-Malik al-Kāmil said, "My predecessor the sultan[185] did not actually have any evidence against Ibn al-Ṣakhr. But when he heard about his growing influence and the increase of his wealth he knew that it would eventually corrupt him, so he fined him a hefty sum. I actually assisted Ibn al-Ṣakhr by lending him two thousand five hundred gold coins, because he had served me well when I came to Ibyār. I enjoyed myself in his garden there. Then I even forgave the debt of a thousand of those gold coins."

قلت يا مولانا الذي نظره السلطان يعضده فيه القرآن قال الله تعالى ﴿ كَلَّآ إِنَّ ٱلْإِنسَٰنَ لَيَطْغَىٰٓ أَن رَّءَاهُ ٱسْتَغْنَىٰٓ ﴾ قال فكيف بمن هو غير إنسان ثمّ قال لي قدّس الله روحه كم تقرّر عليه قلت لا إله إلّا الله يا مولانا لقد جرى لي مع هذا الرجل قضيّة عجيبة وهي من غرائب ما يقع في الوجود وذلك أنّه لقيني في سنة إحدى عشرة وستّمائة وأنا لا أعرفه وقال لي أنا مملوكك ولي على والدك خدمة وقد بلغني أنّك تريد أن تثبت في جهتي سبعة آلاف دينار وذكرت للسلطان حديثي معه إلى آخره.

ثمّ قلت يا مولانا ها نحن في سنة سبع وعشرين[١] وقد قال مولانا بكم تأخذ خطّه وتقرّر عليه وبين حديثه معي وخوفه منّي وبين حضوري بين يدي السلطان ستّ عشرة سنة. فتعجّب السلطان قدّس الله روحه من ذلك ثمّ قال والله ما نخرج عنها ثمّ قال يا فخر الدين خذ خطّه بالسبعة آلاف دينار التي خاف من فلان أن يأخذ خطّه بها من ستّ عشرة سنة فأخذ خطّه بذلك.

ثمّ قال السلطان إنّ هؤلاء النصارى الأقباط متى كثر مالهم هاجوا وكاتبوا الفرنج القريبين والبعيدين وأطلعوهم على ارتفاع الدولة وأحوال العساكر وعدّتهم ورغّبوهم في قصد البلاد بكلّ طريق وآووا جواسيسهم وعملوا كلّ نحس وكذلك أهل الريف ينبغي قصّ أجنحتهم وما يبالون بذلك فإنّهم يزرعون ويفعلون كما فعلوا أوّلاً وأموالهم تزداد على عادتهم وضروعهم تدرّ ودوابّهم تنتج وبساتينهم تثمر وما ثمّ إلّا أخذ المال الذي يطغون به والسلام فالله تعالى يتغمّده برحمته ويسكنه فسيح جنّته إنّه غفور رحيم.[٢]

١ كذا في ب،د؛ وفي ت زيادة: وسبعمائة، وهو خطأ. ٢ كذا في ت؛ والجملة ساقطة في ب،د.

"Master," I said, "the thinking of the sultan is supported by the Qurʾan. God, be He exalted, said, «No indeed; surely Man waxes insolent, for he thinks himself self-sufficient.»"[186]

"How much more so for one who is not a man!" he replied.

Then he asked me, God sanctify his spirit, "How much would you oblige him to pay?"

"There is no god but God!" I exclaimed. "Master, a truly marvelous thing happened between me and this man, one of the strangest you could imagine. Back in the year 611 [1214–15] we fell in together on the road. I didn't know him at the time, but he said to me, 'I'm your servant, and your father owes me a favor. I've heard that you want to put me on the hook for seven thousand gold coins. . . .'" And I told the sultan the rest of our conversation.

Then I said, "Now here we are in the year 627 [1230], and our Master asks how much he owes. It's been sixteen years from the time he spoke to me in fear to this moment as I stand in the sultan's presence."

The sultan, God sanctify his spirit, marveled at this. "Then by God," he said, "that's what we'll do. Fakhr al-Dīn, compel him to agree to pay the seven thousand gold coins that he was afraid this fellow would make him pay sixteen years ago." And in the end this is what happened.

Then the sultan said, "When these Copts get too rich they go and write to the Franks near and far. They inform them about the tax income of the government and the shape of the troops and their state of readiness, trying in every possible way to lure them to Egypt. They give shelter to their spies and do every kind of evil thing you can imagine. Rural people are the same; their wings must be clipped. Of course, they will pay no attention to this. They just go on sowing as they did before. They keep getting richer, their udders flow copiously, their beasts bear young, their gardens produce fruit. The only thing to do is to confiscate the property by means of which they act wrongfully."

May God shower him with his mercy and make him dwell blissfully in Paradise, for He is Forgiving and Merciful.

الفصل الثالث في ذكر شيء من أشعار الكتّاب الفضلاء ولو بيت واحد

خالد بن برمك الكاتب [المتقارب] ١،٣،٣

رَقَدْتَ وَلَمْ تَرْثِ لِلسَّاهِرِ ... وَلَيْلُ ٱلْمُحِبِّ بِلَا آخِرِ
وَلَمْ تَدْرِ بَعْدَ ذَهَابِ ٱلرُّقَا ... دِ مَا فَعَلَ ٱلدَّمْعُ بِٱلنَّاظِرِ

وله من أبيات [الكامل]

فَجَعَلْتُ أَطْلُبُ وَصْلَهَا بِتَذَلُّلٍ ... وَٱلشَّيْبُ يَغْمِزُهَا بِأَنْ لَا تَفْعَلِي

يعقوب بن داود وزير المهديّ [الكامل] ٢،٣،٣

نَزَعَ ٱلْمَشِيبُ شَرَاسَتِي وَغَرَامِي ... وَمَرَى ٱلْجُفُونَ بِمُسْبَلٍ سِجَامِ
وَلَقَدْ حَرَصْتُ بِأَنْ أُوَارِيَ شَخْصَهُ ... عَنْ مُقْلَتَيَّ فَرُمْتُ غَيْرَ مَرَامِ
وَصَبَغْتُ مَا صَبَغَ ٱلْمَشِيبُ فَلَمْ يَدُمْ ... صِبْغِي وَدَامَتْ صِبْغَةُ ٱلْأَيَّامِ
لَا تَبْعُدَنَّ شَبِيبَةٌ ذَيَّالَةٌ ... فَارَقْتُهَا مِنْ سَالِفِ ٱلْأَعْوَامِ
مَا كَانَ مَا ٱسْتَصْحَبْتُ مِنْ أَيَّامِهَا ... إِلَّا كَمِثْلِ طَوَارِقِ ٱلْأَحْلَامِ

الفضل بن الربيع [البسيط] ٣،٣،٣

أَمَا تَرَى ٱلْيَوْمَ مَا أَحْلَى شَمَائِلَهُ ... صَحْوٌ وَغَيْمٌ وَإِبْرَاقٌ وَإِرْعَادُ
كَأَنَّهُ أَنْتَ يَا مَنْ لَا شَبِيهَ لَهُ ... وَصْلٌ وَهَجْرٌ وَتَقْرِيبٌ وَإِبْعَادُ

محمّد بن عبد الملك الزيّات [الخفيف] ٤،٣،٣

The Third Section: Examples of the Poetry Produced by the Most Excellent Secretaries, Though It Be but a Single Line Each

By Khālid ibn Barmak the Secretary: 3.3.1

Down to sleep you went, not pitying the wakeful one;
how endless the lover's night!
After sleep had gone you did not know
what tears had done to the eye.[187]

He also composed the following lines:

I sought union with her, pitifully humble,
as my silvering head signaled her, "Don't!"[188]

By Yaʿqūb ibn Dāwūd, vizier to al-Mahdī: 3.3.2

Gray hair has stolen my vehemence and my passion
and loosed from my eyelids a flowing torrent.
Much as I strove to conceal its form
from my sight, my wish was unattainable;
What grayness had colored, I colored too,
though my color did not last, Time's did.
May the strutting time of youth that I quitted
many long years past not draw far off.
Those days I had of it were as nothing
but a fleeting dream in the night.[189]

By al-Faḍl ibn al-Rabīʿ: 3.3.3

Can you not see the day's lovely qualities:
sun and clouds, flashing lightning, peals of thunder?
It is much like you, my peerless one—
sweet union and desertion, bringing me near and pushing me away.[190]

By Muḥammad ibn ʿAbd al-Malik al-Zayyāt: 3.3.4

رُبَّ لَيْلٍ أَمَدَّ مِنْ نَفَسِ ٱلعَا   شِقِ طُولًا قَطَعْتُهُ بِٱنْتِحَابِ
وَنَسِيمٍ أَلَذَّ مِنْ وَصْلِ مَعْشُو   قٍ تَبَدَّلْتُهُ بِسُوءِ ٱلعِتَابِ

وله أيضاً [الكامل]

وَهِيَ ٱلَّتِي[1] قَالَتْ وَقَدْ جَعَلَتْ   تَنْسَلُّ مِنْ وَجَنَاتِهَا ٱلْخَمْرُ
بَدْرًا يَلُوحُ بِخَدِّهِ ٱلْبَدْرُ[3]   أَكْمَدْ[2] بِدَائِكَ هَلْ رَأَيْتَ كَذَا

إبراهيم بن العبّاس الصوليّ [الخفيف] ٥،٣،٣

صَدَّ عَنِّي وَصَدَّقَ ٱلْأَقْوَالَا   وَأَطَاعَ ٱلْوُشَاةَ وَٱلْعُذَّالَا
أَتُرَاهُ يَكُونُ شَهْرَ صُدُودٍ   وَعَلَى وَجْهِهِ رَأَيْتُ ٱلْهِلَالَا

وله أيضاً [الطويل]

بِنَفْسِي وَأَهْلِي سَاحِرُ ٱلطَّرْفِ فَاتِرُهْ   مُحَكَّمَةٌ أَجْفَانُهُ وَمَحَاجِرُهْ
يُبَاشِرُ خَدِّي خَدَّهُ فَكَأَنَّنِي   بِبَاطِنِ أَحْشَائِي وَقَلْبِي أُبَاشِرُهْ

وله إلى ابن الزيّات في يوم مطرٍ [الخفيف]

يُوضِحُ ٱلعُذْرَ فِي تَرَاخِي ٱللِّقَاءِ   مَا تَوَالَى مِن هٰذِهِ ٱلأَنْوَاءِ
فَسَلَامُ ٱلْإِلٰهِ أُهْدِيهِ مِنِّي   كُلَّ يَوْمٍ لِسَيِّدِ ٱلْوُزَرَاءِ
لَسْتُ أَدْرِي مَاذَا أَذُمُّ وَأَشْكُو   مِنْ سَمَاءٍ تَعُوقُنِي عَنْ سَمَاءِ
غَيْرَ أَنِّي أَدْعُو عَلَى تِلْكَ بِٱلصَّحْوِ   وَأَدْعُو لِهٰذِهِ بِٱلْبَقَاءِ

أبو العبّاس أحمد بن الروميّ الكاتب [الخفيف] ٦،٣،٣

---

١ كذا في ب، ت،د؛ وفي ج: ومليحة. ٢ كذا في ب، ت،د؛ وفي ج: اذهب. ٣ كذا في ب، ت،د؛ وفي ج: الجمر.

So many nights, drawn longer than the sigh of a lover,
have I rent with sobbing.
So many breezes, more delicious than union with the beloved,
have I exchanged for a sore reproach.[191]

The following lines are by him, too:[192]

She it is who said, as the wine
had begun to escape from her cheeks,
"Eat your heart out! Have you seen such a moon
at the sides of which there twinkles another?"[193]

By Ibrāhīm ibn al-ʿAbbās al-Ṣūlī: 3.3.5

He shunned me, trusting in rumor,
following those who slander and reproach.
Can it still be a month for shunning lovers
when I spy the gleaming crescent upon his face?[194]

He also said,

By my soul and my kin, the most enchanting glance is the most languid,
the eyelids and the hollow 'round them held just so.
With my cheek touching his, it is as though
I were touching him in my heart and in the depths of my body.[195]

He once sent the following poem to Ibn al-Zayyāt on a rainy day:

These ceaseless storms make clear
the excuse for my delay attending you.
Yet the wonted greeting do I give: God's peace,
on this as on all days, be upon the lord of all viziers!
I know not what to blame, or how to protest
the sky that keeps me from that other generous sky.
I only know to pray that one grow bright and clear
and the other's rain clouds not depart.[196]

By Abū l-ʿAbbās Aḥmad ibn al-Rūmī the Secretary: 3.3.6

رَوْضُ وَرْدٍ خِلَالَهُ نَرْجِسٌ غَضٌّ   يَحُفَّانِ أُقْحُوَانَا نَضِيرَا

ذَا يُبَاهِي لَنَا خُدُودًا وَذَا يَحْـ   ـكِي عُيُونًا وَذَا يُضَاهِي ثُغُورَا

٧.٣.٣   أبو جعفر محمد بن العباس [السريع]

قَدْ بَرَّحَ ٱلْحُبُّ بِمُشْتَاقِكَ   فَأَوْلِهِ أَحْسَنَ أَخْلَاقِكَ

لَا تَجْفُهُ وَٱرْعَ لَهُ حَقَّهُ   فَإِنَّهُ آخِرُ عُشَّاقِكَ

٨.٣.٣   أبو بكر محمد بن العباس [الوافر]

وَشَمْسٍ مَا دَنَتْ إِلَّا أَرَتْنَا   بِأَنَّ ٱلشَّمْسَ مَطْلَعُهَا فُضُولُ

تَزِيدُ عَلَى ٱلسِّنِينَ سَنًا وَحُسْنًا   كَمَا رَقَّتْ عَلَى ٱلْعِتْقِ ٱلشَّمُولُ

٩.٣.٣   أحمد بن الحسين المعروف ببديع الزمان [البسيط]

وَكَادَ يَحْكِيكَ صَوْبُ ٱلْغَيْثِ[1] مُنْسَكِبًا   لَوْكَانَ طَلْقُ ٱلْمُحَيَّا يَمْطُرُ ٱلذَّهَبَا

وَٱلدَّهْرُ لَوْ لَمْ يَخُنْ وَٱلشَّمْسُ لَوْ نَطَقَتْ   وَٱللَّيْثُ لَوْ لَمْ يَجُرْ وَٱلْبَحْرُ لَوْ عَذُبَا

١٠.٣.٣   أبو الفتح علي بن محمد البُستي [البسيط]

لَمَّا أَتَانِي كِتَابٌ مِنْكَ مُبْتَسِمٌ   عَنْ كُلِّ فَضْلٍ وَبِرٍّ غَيْرِ مَحْدُودِ

جَلَّتْ[2] مَعَانِيهِ فِي أَثْنَاءِ أَسْطُرِهِ   آثَارُكَ ٱلْبِيضَ فِي أَحْوَالِي ٱلسُّودِ

وله أيضًا [الوافر]

―――――――――

١ كذا في د؛ وفي ب: الغيب؛ ت: الغيث.   ٢ كذا في ت؛ وفي ب، ج، د: حكت.

A garden of roses, all entwined in lush narcissus
that surround the blooming chamomile.
The one seems to us like cheeks, the other
eyes resembles, the last a row of teeth.[197]

By Abū Jaʿfar Muḥammad ibn al-ʿAbbās: **3.3.7**

Love has afflicted the one who desires you
so treat him with utmost kindness;
Do not be rough, give him his due,
for none will ever love you so.[198]

By Abū Bakr Muḥammad ibn al-ʿAbbās: **3.3.8**

A sun, whose approach makes plain
that the sun itself need not trouble to rise,
You grow, despite your years, in brightness and in beauty
as wine grows more delicate in its old age.[199]

By Aḥmad ibn al-Ḥusayn, known as Badīʿ al-Zamān, "The Marvel of His Age": **3.3.9**

The heavy downpour would nearly be your like
if the calm and smiling sky rained gold.
As would Fortune be, if it did no treason; the sun, if it spoke words;
the lion, were it no tyrant; the sea, were its waters sweet.[200]

By Abū l-Fatḥ ʿAlī ibn Muḥammad al-Bustī: **3.3.10**

When a letter came to me, from you, smiling forth,
revealing every excellence, kindness without limit,
The messages among its lines illumined
through my darkened condition, your luminous traces.[201]

He also composed,

أَرَانِي ٱللهُ وَجْهَكَ كُلَّ يَوْمٍ لِأَسْعَدَ بِٱلْأَمَانِ وَبِٱلْأَمَانِي
فَوَجْهُكَ حِينَ أَنْظُرُهُ عِيَانًا يُرِينِي ٱلْبِشْرَ[1] فِي وَجْهِ ٱلزَّمَانِ

وله أيضاً [الكامل]

وَمُهَفْهَفٍ غَنِجِ ٱلشَّمَائِلِ أَزْعَجَتْ قَلْبِي مَحَاسِنُ وَجْهِهِ إِزْعَاجَا
دَرَتِ ٱلطَّبِيعَةُ أَنَّ فَاحِمَ شَعْرِهِ لَيْلٌ فَأَذْكَتْ وَجْنَتَيْهِ سِرَاجَا

أبو منصور محمّد بن أحمد الكاتب[2] [مجزوء الخفيف] ١١،٣،٣

يَوْمُ دَجْنٍ سَمَاؤُهُ فَاخِتِيٌّ رِدَاؤُهُ
دَاوِ بِٱلْقَهْوَةِ ٱلْخُمَا رَ فَفِيهَا دَوَاؤُهُ
أَشْبَهَ ٱلْمَاءَ رَاحُهُ وَحَكَى ٱلرَّاحَ مَاؤُهُ
مَطَرَتْنَا مَسَرَّةٌ حِينَ صَابَتْ سَمَاؤُهُ
لَا تُعَاتِبْ زَمَانَنَا إِنْ عَرَانَا جَفَاؤُهُ
شِدَّةُ ٱلدَّهْرِ تَنْقَضِي ثُمَّ يَأْتِي رَخَاؤُهُ

صالح بن عبد القدّوس الكاتب [الطويل] ١٢،٣،٣

وَمَا زُرْتُكُمْ عَمْدًا وَلٰكِنَّ ذَا ٱلْهَوَى إِلَى حَيْثُ تَهْوِي ٱلنَّفْسُ تَهْوِي بِهِ ٱلرِّجْلُ

أبو محمّد بن المهلّبيّ [الوافر] ١٣،٣،٣

أَرَانِي ٱللهُ وَجْهَكَ كُلَّ يَوْمٍ صَبَاحًا لِلتَّيَمُّنِ وَٱلسُّرُورِ
فَأُمْتِعَ نَاظِرَيَّ بِصَفْحَتَيْهِ وَأَقْرَا ٱلْحُسْنَ فِي تِلْكَ ٱلسُّطُورِ

---

١ كذا في المخطوطات، ولعلّ الصواب هو: البشّ. ٢ في سائر المخطوطات: أبو أحمد محمّد بن منصور؛ والمثبت من اليتيمة، ج ٤، ص ٣٩٩.

May God show me your face each day
that I might rest easy in assurance and high hopes.
For when I behold your face directly
it shows me joy in the face of Time itself.[202]

And he also composed,

Many a slender youth, of coquettish qualities,
has troubled my heart sore by his fine features.
Nature knew his coal-black hair
to be night—so it lit his two cheeks as a lamp.[203]

By Abū Manṣūr Muḥammad ibn Aḥmad the Secretary:[204] 3.3.11

On a gloom-skied day, garbed in gray[205]
Treat your hangover with wine; that is its cure.
The wine clear as water, the water, streaming down, like wine.
When its sky poured, it showered us with delight.
Do not reprove this age, should it roughly afflict us;
Fortune's severity shall cease anon, and her prosperity follow.[206]

By Ṣāliḥ ibn ʿAbd al-Quddūs the Secretary: 3.3.12

Unwitting I visited you; the footfalls of the lovelorn
incline to where his soul desires.[207]

By Abū Muḥammad al-Muhallabī: 3.3.13

May God show me your face each day
by morning, for auspice and for gladness.
My eyes gain pleasure in its pages unfurled
as I read loveliness in those lines.[208]

١٤،٣،٣ يزيد بن محمّد المهلّبيّ [الطويل]

وَمَنْ ذَا ٱلَّذِي تُرْضَى سَجَايَاهُ كُلُّهَا كَفَى ٱلْمَرْءَ فَخْرًا أَنْ تُعَدَّ مَعَايِبُهْ

وله في خادم مطرب [الخفيف]

يَا هِلَالًا يَبْدُو فَيَزْدَادُ شَوْقِي وَغَزَالًا يَشْدُو فَيَزْدَادُ عِشْقِي
زَعَمَ ٱلنَّاسُ أَنَّ رِقَّكَ مِلْكِي كَذَبَ ٱلنَّاسُ أَنْتَ مَالِكُ رِقِّي

١٥،٣،٣ أبو الفضل بن العميد [المتقارب]

دَعَوْتُ ٱلْمُنَى وَدَعَوْتُ[١] ٱلنَّدَى فَلَمَّا أَجَابَا دَعَوْتُ ٱلْقَدَحْ
وَقُلْتُ لِأَيَّامِ شَرْخِ ٱلشَّبَابِ أَلِمِّي فَهٰذَا أَوَانُ ٱلْفَرَحْ
إِذَا بَلَغَ ٱلْمَرْءُ آمَالَهُ فَلَيْسَ لَهُ بَعْدَهَا مُقْتَرَحْ

١٦،٣،٣ أبو القاسم[٢] محمّد بن محمّد بن جبير[٣] الكاتب [المتقارب]

أَرَى ٱلدَّهْرَ يَنْسَى ذُنُوبَ ٱلرِّجَالِ وَيَذْكُرُ ذَنْبِي وَذَنْبِي كَمَالِي
يَرُومُونَ شَأْوِي وَمَا إِنْ لَهُمْ مِنَ ٱلْفَضْلِ قَوْلٌ وَفِعْلٌ كَمَا لِي
فَمَا لَهُمُ مِثْلَ عِرْضِي مَصُونٌ وَعِرْضُهُمُ مُسْتَبَاحٌ كَمَالِي

١٧،٣،٣ أبو العبّاس أحمد بن اسحٰق الكاتب [الكامل]

يَا وَيْحَ قَلْبِي لَا يَزَالُ يَرُوعُهُ مِمَّنْ يَعِزُّ عَلَيْهِ وَشْكُ فِرَاقِ
تَتَقَاذَفُ ٱلْبُلْدَانُ بِي فَكَأَنَّنِي وُلِّيتُ أَمْرَ مِسَاحَةِ ٱلْآفَاقِ

---

١ كذا في ب، د؛ وفي ت: وصنوف. ٢ كذا في ت؛ وفي ب، ج، د: الفتح. ٣ ت: الحسين؛ ب، د: الحسن؛ والمثبت من اليتيمة، ٤:٣٩٠.

By Yazīd ibn Muḥammad al-Muhallabī: 3.3.14

Who is the man whose every trait deserves approval?
It is sufficient merit that his faults can be counted.[209]

Concerning a singing servant, he composed these lines:

O crescent moon, my longing waxes when you appear!
O gazelle, my passion waxes when you sing!
People say I own you; they lie,
in truth, you are my owner.[210]

By Abū l-Faḍl Ibn al-ʿAmīd: 3.3.15

I called upon desires, and upon generosity;
when they replied, I called upon the goblet.
I said to the prime of youth,
"Take what you will, for these are the times of joy."
When a man attains his hopes
nothing else remains for him to do.[211]

Abū l-Qāsim Muḥammad ibn Muḥammad ibn Jubayr[212] the Secretary: 3.3.16

I see Fate forget the faults of men,
yet remember mine; my fault is my perfection.
They covet my high status, yet have not
excellence in word or deed as I have.
Their wealth is well guarded, as my honor is,
their honor, available to all, is like unto my wealth.[213]

By Abū l-ʿAbbās Aḥmad ibn Isḥāq the Secretary: 3.3.17

Woe to my heart! It is constantly alarmed
that the one dear to it may suddenly part from me.
I am tossed from land to land as if
I had been appointed to survey the horizons.[214]

أبو منصور أحمد بن محمّد البلخيّ [الطويل] ١٨،٣،٣

إِذَا أَفْكَرَ ٱلإِنْسَانُ فِكْرَةَ عَاقِلٍ   رَأَى عَيْشَهُ مَعْنًى لِمَعْنَى مَمَاتِهِ
إِذَا نَالَ يَوْمًا زَائِدًا فِي مَعَاشِهِ   فَذٰلِكَ يَوْمٌ نَاقِصٌ مِنْ حَيَاتِهِ

أبو القاسم الصاحب بن عبّاد [المتقارب] ١٩،٣،٣

وَقَائِلَةٍ لِمَ عَرَتْكَ[١] ٱلْهُمُومُ   وَأَمْرُكَ مُمْتَثَلٌ فِي ٱلأُمَمْ
فَقُلْتُ دَعِينِي عَلَى غُصَّتِي   بِقَدْرِ ٱلْهُمُومِ تَكُونُ ٱلْهِمَمْ

أبو عبد الله الحسين بن حجّاج الكاتب [الكامل] ٢٠،٣،٣

يَا صَاحِبَيَّ ٱسْتَيْقِظَا مِنْ رَقْدَةٍ   تَزْرِي عَلَى عَقْلِ ٱللَّبِيبِ ٱلأَكْيَسِ
هٰذِي ٱلْمَجَرَّةُ فِي ٱلسَّمَاءِ كَأَنَّهَا   نَهْرٌ تَدَفَّقَ فِي حَدِيقَةِ نَرْجِسِ
وَأَرَى ٱلصَّبَا قَدْ غَلَّسَتْ[٢] بِنَسِيمِهَا   فَعَلَامَ شُرْبِي[٣] ٱلرَّاحَ غَيْرَ مُغَلِّسِ

وله أيضاً [مجزوء الكامل]

وَنَبَتْ بِنَا أَرْضُ ٱلْعِرَاقِ   فَمَا ٱمْتَحَنَّاهَا بِمِحْنَهْ
غَيْرَ ٱلرَّحِيلِ كَفَى ٱلْبِلَادَ   بِرِحْلَةِ ٱلْعُلَمَاءِ هُجْنَهْ

وله أيضاً [المتقارب]

وَأَسْكَرَنِي بَدْرُ تِمٍّ غَدَتْ   مِنَ ٱلْوَرْدِ وَجْنَتُهُ فِي نِقَابِ
بِخَمْرِ ٱلدِّنَانِ وَخَمْرِ ٱلْجُفُونِ   وَخَمْرِ ٱلْمُحَيَّا وَخَمْرِ ٱلرُّضَابِ

---

١ كذا في ب، د؛ وفي ت: عرفت. ٢ كذا في ب؛ وفي ت: غلفت؛ د: علست. ٣ في سائر المخطوطات: شرب؛ والمثبت من اليتيمة، ٣:٧٦.

By Abū Manṣūr Aḥmad ibn Muḥammad al-Balkhī: 3.3.18

When a man considers as the wiser sort would do
he sees his life's meaning in his death;
Were he to add a single day to his life's span
that would be one less day he'd lived.[215]

By Abū l-Qāsim al-Ṣāḥib ibn ʿAbbād: 3.3.19

Many a woman has said to me, "Why do cares
afflict you, when your command is obeyed in every nation?"
"Leave me to my agony," I said,
"careers are measured in cares."[216]

By Abū ʿAbdallāh al-Ḥusayn ibn Ḥajjāj the Secretary: 3.3.20

Awake, my companions two, from such slumber
as might call rebuke upon a bright and clever mind!
Behold the far-flung galaxy aloft, a river
gushing forth in a garden of narcissus.
I see the east wind's breeze travel by the gloom at dawn,
why then should I drink wine at any other time?[217]

He also composed,

The land of Iraq mistreated us,
yet with no hardship did we afflict it
Save to depart; for it is sufficient fault
in a land that learned men should quit it.[218]

The following lines are also by him:

A full moon of perfection—whose cheek became,
beneath its veil, a very rose—made me drunk,
With wine of the jug, wine of the eyelids,
wine of the face, wine of the mouth.[219]

أبو منصور عليّ بن الفضل [الطويل] ٢١،٣،٣

تَخَاوَصَتِ ٱلْحَسْنَاءُ عَنْ شَيْبِ لِمَّتِي وَلَمْ تَلْتَفِتْ إِلَى[١] سِنِّي ٱلْقَلَائِلِ
وَلَيْسَ شُعَاعًا مَا رَأَتْ مِنْ بَيَاضِهِ وَلٰكِنَّهُ نُورُ ٱلنُّهَى وَٱلْفَضَائِلِ

وله [الخفيف]

لَا تَظُنَّنَّ بِي سُلُوًّا وَإِنْ كُنْـ ـتُ عَزِيزَ[٢] ٱلدُّمُوعِ بَيْنَ ٱلْجُفُونِ
إِنَّمَا يَصْعُبُ ٱلدَّفِينُ مِنَ ٱلدَّا ءِ وَسَهْلٌ مَا كَانَ غَيْرَ دَفِينِ
وَبُكَاءُ ٱلْقُلُوبِ أَسْرَفُ فِي حُكْـ ـمِ ٱلْمُحِبِّينَ مِنْ بُكَاءِ ٱلْعُيُونِ[٣]

أبو منصور بن عبدون الكاتب [الطويل] ٢٢،٣،٣

أَكُتَّابُ دِيوَانِ ٱلرَّسَائِلِ مَا لَكُمْ تَجَمَّلْتُمُ بَلْ زِدْتُمُ فِي ٱلتَّجَمُّلِ
وَأَرْزَاقُكُمْ لَا تَسْتَبِينُ رُسُومُهَا لِمَا نَسَجَتْهَا[٤] مِنْ جَنُوبٍ وَشَمْأَلِ
إِذَا مَا شَكَا ٱلْإِفْلَاسَ وَٱلضُّرَّ بَعْضُكُمْ تَقُولُونَ[٥] لَا تَهْلِكْ أَسًى وَتَجَمَّلِ
وَقَفْتُمْ عَلَى بَابِ ٱلْأَمِيرِ كَأَنَّكُمْ قِفَا نَبْكِ مِنْ ذِكْرَى حَبِيبٍ وَمَنْزِلِ

وله في غلام أعجميّ مليح [الخفيف]

بِأَبِي مَنْ لِسَانُهُ أَعْجَمِيٌّ وَأَرَى وَجْهَهُ فَصِيحَ ٱلْكَلَامِ[٦]

أبو عليّ بن عبد الله الساجيّ الكاتب [السريع] ٢٣،٣،٣

---

١ في سائر المخطوطات: تلفّت نحو؛ والمثبت من صرّدرّ، الديوان، ٢٣٨. ٢ كذا في د؛ وفي ب: غزير. ٣ كذا في ب، د؛ والأبيات ساقطة في ت. ٤ ب، د: لما منحتها؛ ت: بما نسجتها؛ ج: لما نسخته؛ والمثبت تصويب يقتضيه السياق. ٥ كذا في ت؛ وفي ب، ج: يقولون؛ د: نقولون؛ وهو في معلّقة امرئ القيس: يقولون. ٦ كذا في ب، د؛ والبيت ساقط في ت.

By Abū Manṣūr ʿAlī ibn al-Faḍl: 3.3.21

The lovely one blinked just so, not to spy my graying temples,
nor did she mark my few remaining years;
It was not streaks she perceived in the whiteness
but the light of intelligence and virtues.[220]

He also composed,

Do not think me content without the departed, though tears
seldom pass my eyelids.
The most difficult malady is the buried one;
that which is left unburied is easy.
The heart's weeping is more immoderate
in lovers than the eyes'.[221]

By Abū Manṣūr Ibn ʿAbdūn the Secretary: 3.3.22

Secretaries of the chancery! What affects you?
You adorn yourselves altogether too much.
Your stipends leave no trace at all,
their tracks effaced by the south wind, then the north.
When one of you laments his ruin and his harm
you all say, "Perish not from grief; bear up!"
You tarry at the emir's gate, as though you would recite:
"Wait, companions two! Let us weep for the memory of a beloved
and an abode."[222]

Concerning a handsome Persian boy he composed,

There stands at my door a lad of foreign tongue,
yet whose face is to me more eloquent of speech.[223]

By Abū ʿAlī ibn ʿAbdallāh al-Sājī the Secretary: 3.3.23

لَا تَأْسَ فِي ٱلدُّنْيَا عَلَى فَائِتٍ　وَعِنْدَكَ ٱلْإِسْلَامُ وَٱلْعَافِيَهْ
فَإِنْ فَاتَ شَيْءٌ كُنْتَ تَشْتَاقُهُ　فَفِيهِمَا مِن فَائِتٍ كَافِيَهْ[1]

محمّد بن منصور البلخيّ [الكامل] ٢٤،٣،٣

كَمْ فِيكَ مِنْ رَشَإٍ أَغَنَّ كَأَنَّمَا　خُلِقَتْ مَفَاصِلُهُ بِغَيْرِ عِظَامِ
كَمْ قَدْ غَلَلْتَ يَدَ ٱلنَّدِيمِ بِقَهْوَةٍ　شَهِدَتْ بِأَنَّ ٱلْغَلَّ مِنْ إِكْرَامِ

وله أيضاً [الكامل]

دَانَتْ عَلَى قَوْمٍ سَمَاؤُكَ بِٱلنَّدَى　وَنَدًى تَرَدَّدُ[2] تَحْتَ غَيْمٍ جَامِدِ
وَأَنَا ٱلَّذِي إِنْ جُدْتَ لِي أَوْ لَمْ تَجُدْ　لَكَ فِي ٱلثَّنَاءِ عَلَى طَرِيقٍ وَاحِدِ

وله يخاطب بعض الأجلّاء [الكامل]

حَمْلُ ٱلرِّئَاسَةِ مَا عَلِمْتَ ثَقِيلُ　وَٱلدَّهْرُ يَعْدِلُ مَرَّةً وَيَمِيلُ
مَا زَالَتِ ٱلْأَيَّامُ فِي سُلْطَانِهِ　ٱنْظُرْ إِلَى ٱلْأَيَّامِ كَيْفَ تَحُولُ
هِيَ مَا سَمِعْتَ وَمَا رَأَيْتَ سَبِيلُهَا　ٱلتَّنْقِيلُ وَٱلتَّحْوِيلُ وَٱلتَّبْدِيلُ
لَا تَعْتَلِلْ بِٱلشُّغْلِ إِنَّكَ إِنَّمَا　تُرْجَى لِأَنَّكَ دَائِمًا مَشْغُولُ
وَإِذَا فَرَغْتَ وَلَا فَرَغْتَ فَغَيْرُكَ ٱلْـ　ـمَرْجُوُّ لِلْحَاجَاتِ وَٱلْمَأْمُولُ[3]

وله يهجو بخيلاً [مجزوء الكامل]

اللّٰهُ صَوَّرَ كَفَّهُ　لَمَّا بَرَاهُ فَأَبْدَعَهْ
مِنْ تِسْعَةٍ فِي تِسْعَةٍ　وَثَلَاثَةٍ فِي أَرْبَعَهْ

١ كذا في ب، د؛ والبيت ساقط في ت. ٢ كذا في ب، د؛ وفي ت: تتردّد. ٣ كذا في ب، د؛ والأبيات الأربعة الأخيرة ساقطة في ت.

Do not grieve, in this world, over that which passes
when you have your faith and your good health.
Should something slip away which you desired,
you shall find in them a world to recompense you.[224]

By Muḥammad ibn Manṣūr al-Balkhī: 3.3.24

You have many fawns, melodious and plaintive, who look as though
their joints were formed without bones.
How often have you shackled the boon companion's hand with wine,
testifying that shackling is hospitality indeed?[225]

He also composed,

Your sky draws near a people with its moisture
yet some moisture hesitates beneath frozen clouds.
But from me, whether you give freely, or not at all,
you shall have high praise all the same.[226]

Addressing a person of high standing, he recited the following:

To bear leadership, you well know, is a heavy thing
when Fortune is now just and now askew.
All our days are in her power;[227]
behold how they change apace.
She—as you have heard and seen—has a way of
transporting, transforming, transmuting.
Plead not the excuse that you are busy, for indeed
you are sought for your constant activity.
Yet should you find leisure—may it never come to pass—then another
shall be sought out for needs and hopes.[228]

To ridicule a miser he composed these lines:

God molded his hand, when He created it, most wonderfully,
from nine by nine, and three by four.[229]

وأشعار هؤلاء الفضلاء كثيرة وفضائلهم غزيرة والاختصار يحسن في الباب ٢٥،٣،٣
لأنّ المقصود به غير ذلك.

The poems of such worthies are many, and their virtues plentiful. However, it is fitting that we curtail the discussion here, for our true purpose lies elsewhere. 3.3.25

الباب الرابع في ذكر الجهّال الذين تزيّوا بزيّ الكتّاب وليسوا منهم وفيه فصول ثلاثة

الفصل الأوّل في الأشعار التي قيلت فيهم قديماً وحديثاً

قال بعض الشعراء [الوافر] ١،١،٤

بَلِيدٌ فِي ٱلْكِتَابَةِ يَدَّعِيهَا   كَدَعْوَى آلِ حَرْبٍ فِي زِيَادِ
فَدَعْ عَنْكَ ٱلْكِتَابَةَ لَسْتَ مِنْهَا   وَلَوْ سَوَّدْتَ وَجْهَكَ بِٱلْمِدَادِ
فَدِيوَانُ ٱلْخَرَاجِ بِحَذْفِ جِيمٍ   وَدِيوَانُ ٱلضِّيَاعِ بِفَتْحِ ضَادِ

وقال آخر [الكامل] ٢،١،٤

تَعِسَ ٱلزَّمَانُ فَقَدْ أَتَى بِعُجَابِ   وَمَحَا رُسُومَ ٱلظَّرْفِ وَٱلْآدَابِ
وَأَتَى بِكُتَّابٍ لَوِ ٱنْبَسَطَتْ يَدِي   فِيهِمْ رَدَدْتُهُمُ إِلَى ٱلْكُتَّابِ
جِيلٌ مِنَ ٱلْأَنْعَامِ إِلَّا أَنَّهُمْ   مِنْ بَيْنِهَا خُلِقُوا بِلَا أَذْنَابِ
صُوَرٌ تُرَى لَكِنْ إِذَا فَتَّشْتَهُمْ   ظَفِرَتْ يَمِينُكَ مِنْهُمُ بِسَرَابِ
لَا تَغْتَرِرْ بِرُوَائِهِمْ وَجُسُومِهِمْ   فَهُمُ ٱلْفَضَائِحُ غُطِّيَتْ بِثِيَابِ

وقال آخر [المتقارب] ٣،١،٤

يَدُلُّ عَلَى أَنَّهُ كَاتِبٌ   سَوَادٌ بِأَظْفَارِهِ لَازِبُ
فَإِنْ كَانَ هٰذَا دَلِيلًا لَهُ   فَإِسْكَافُنَا كَاتِبٌ حَاسِبُ

The Fourth Chapter, An Account of the Ignorant Men Who Have Unworthily Donned the Garments of the Secretaries, in Three Sections

The First Section: Poetry Composed about Such Men in Former and More Recent Times

A poet said, 4.1.1

The idiot's claim to the secretarial art
  is like that of Ziyād to Ḥarb's clan.[230]
So abandon it, you have nothing of it,
  though you blacken your face with ink,
The Office of Land Tax is "shit,"
  the Office of Estates is "in ruin."[231]

Another poet said, 4.1.2

May old Time stumble and fall! He brings the astonishing
  but blots out all trace of charm and culture.
He brings "secretaries" who, had I authority
  over them, I would return forthwith to the "primary school."[232]
They are a race of beasts, but they alone
  among the beasts were created without tails.
They have visible forms, but if you search them out
  your right hand grasps nothing but a mirage.
Do not be deceived by their fine appearance and their bodies;
  they are infamies draped in clothes.[233]

Another poet said, 4.1.3

There is a blackness that clings upon his fingernails
  and gives proof he is a secretary.
If this be his proof,
  then our cobbler is a clever secretary indeed.[234]

وقال آخر [المتقارب] ٤،١،٤

تَوَلَّى ٱلرِّئَاسَةَ مِنْ بَيْنِنَا كَأَنَّا جَمِيعًا لَهُ حَاشِيَهْ
يَتِيهُ عَلَيْنَا بِأَثْوَابِهِ وَيُزْهِي بِبَغْلَتِهِ ٱلْمَاشِيَهْ
وَيُوهِمُنَا أَنَّهُ كَاتِبٌ كَأَنَّا قَدِمْنَا مِنَ ٱلْبَادِيَهْ

وقال آخر [الوافر] ٥،١،٤

إِذَا وَلِيَ ٱبْنُ عَبَّاسٍ وَمُوسَى[1] فَأَمْرُ ٱلنَّاسِ لَيْسَ بِمُسْتَقِيمِ
فَدِيوَانُ ٱلضِّيَاعِ بِفَتْحِ ضَادٍ وَدِيوَانُ ٱلْخَرَاجِ بِحَذْفِ جِيمِ

وقال آخر في كاتب أبخر [الرمل] ٦،١،٤

قُلْ لِمَنْ أَصْبَحَ فِي ٱلدِّيـ وَانِ يَسْتَوْفِي ٱلْخَرَاجَا
سُدَّ عَنَّا فَمَكَ ٱلْأَبْـ خَرَ وَٱسْكُتْ فَٱلْخَرَا جَا

وقال آخر في ريفيّ تولّى في خدمة [الوافر] ٧،١،٤

تَغَيَّرَتِ ٱلْبِلَادُ وَمَنْ عَلَيْهَا وَزَادَ ٱلنَّاسُ فِي ٱلشِّطْرَنْجِ بَغْلَا
وَوَلَّتْ عَنْكُمُ ٱلْآدَابُ طُرًّا وَزَادَ ٱلدَّهْرُ فِي ٱلْكُتَّابِ نَغْلَا

وقال آخر في جاهل [البسيط] ٨،١،٤

يَا كَاتِبًا يَقْرَأُ ٱلْعُنْوَانَ فِي سَنَةٍ وَٱلْفَصْلَ مِنْ بَعْدِ أَمَّا بَعْدُ فِي حِينِ
لَا يَعْرِفُ ٱلْفَرْقَ مِنْ عَمْرٍو إِلَى عُمَرَ جَهْلًا وَلَا ٱلْفَرْقَ بَيْنَ ٱلسِّينِ وَٱلشِّينِ

---

١ في سائر المخطوطات: ابن عباس بن موسى؛ والمثبت من الوافي، ١١:١٥٧.

Another poet declared, 4.1.4

He assumed authority among us,
as though we were all his retinue.
In garments fine, his bearing toward us haughty
on his mule, showing off to the cattle.
He tries to persuade us that he is a secretary
ss though we had just arrived from the hinterlands.[235]

Another poet recited, 4.1.5

When Ibn ʿAbbās and Mūsā took charge,[236]
all governance over people went awry.
The Office of Estates was "in ruin,"
the Office of the Land Tax was "shit."[237]

Another poet recited the following concerning a secretary whose breath reeked: 4.1.6

Say to the one lately become accountant
of the "land tax" in the government office,
"Shut your stinking mouth and keep it away from us!
be silent and close it fast—the 'shit is out.'"[238]

Another poet said of a rustic appointed to an administrative position, 4.1.7

Have the lands changed for the worse, and their overseers too,
of whom the people have many more than they require?
All decorous custom has abandoned you,
and Fate increased the secretaries by one bastard.[239]

Another poet declared, concerning a fool, 4.1.8

O secretary, who reads the title in a year's time
and the opening paragraph . . . by and by;
Who, the fool, can't tell between ʿAmr and ʿUmar,
nor between *s* and *sh*.[240]

وقال آخر [البسيط] ٩،١،٤

هُوَ ٱلْغَنِيُّ وَلَا يُغْنِي لِسَائِلِهِ ... مَا ٱلْفَرْقُ بَيْنَ ٱسْمِ مَوْجُودٍ وَمَعْنَاهُ
فَٱلتَّاءُ وَٱلثَّاءُ جَهْلًا عِنْدَهُ شَرَعٌ ... وَٱلْهَمَ إِنْ خَطَّ حَرْفًا أَوْ تَهَجَّاهُ[١]

وقال آخر في جاهل [المتقارب] ١٠،١،٤

أَطَالَ فَأَتْعَبَ أَقْلَامَهُ ... وَلَمْ يَأْتِ فِي ٱلْقَوْلِ مُسْتَمْتَعَا
وَجَدَّ لِمَا يَقَعْ بِٱلصَّوَابِ ... فَقَدْ أَخْطَأَ ٱلْخُطَطَ ٱلْأَرْبَعَا
سَخِيفُ ٱلْمَعَانِي ثَقِيلُ ٱلْكَلَامِ ... لَا يَعْرِفُ ٱلْبَدْءَ وَلَا ٱلْمَقْطَعَا

وقال آخر في كاتب جيش [الطويل] ١١،١،٤

وَكَاتِبِ جَيْشٍ لَيْسَ يَدْرِي مَنِ ٱلَّذِي ... يُبَنْدِقُ هٰذَا ٱلْبَعْرَ فِي ٱسْتِ ٱلْأَبَاعِرِ
فَلَيْسَ بِذِي عَقْلٍ وَلَيْسَ بِكَاتِبٍ ... وَلَيْسَ بِذِي فَضْلٍ وَلَيْسَ بِشَاعِرِ

وقال آخر في جاهل صاغ حلى دواته ذهباً [البسيط] ١٢،١،٤

يَا كَاتِبًا كَاسِيًا مِنْ كُلِّ مَنْقَصَةٍ ... وَعَارِيًا مِنْ جَمِيعِ ٱلْفَضْلِ وَٱلْأَدَبِ[٢]
هَلْ تَنْفَعَنْكَ دَوَاةٌ حَلْيُهَا ذَهَبٌ ... وَلَيْسَ طَبْعُكَ فِي ٱلتَّمْيِيزِ مِنْ ذَهَبِ

---

١ كذا في ب،د؛ والبيتان ساقطتان في ت. ٢ في سائر المخطوطات: والآداب.

Another poet declared, 4.1.9

Though rich, he is unable to enrich his questioner
with knowledge of the difference between a word and its meaning.
The *t* and *th* are alike to him,
he writes a proper letter only if inspired from on high.[241]

Concerning a fool, another poet said, 4.1.10

He rambled on, wearing out his pens;
no pleasing idea did his words convey.
When he stumbled upon a proper expression
he strove, but missed the mark by missing the limits of the page.[242]
His words lightwitted, his speech heavy,
he knows neither how to begin, nor how to conclude.

Concerning a secretary of the army, another spoke these lines: 4.1.11

How many an army secretary does not know who
forms the dungball in the camel's anus.
No reasoner he, no secretary either,
neither a man of learning nor a poet.[243]

Another, speaking of a fool who encrusted his inkwell with golden ornament, declared, 4.1.12

O secretary, who garbs himself in every defect
yet is stripped of any learning or refinement,
Can an inkwell ornamented with gold possibly avail you
when your powers of discernment are hardly gilded?

الفصل الثاني وهو المضحك في عاميّة ألفاظهم وجهلهم

ولو أخذت أستقصي وصفهم وما يبدو من عوراتهم وفضائحهم في مكاتباتهم ١،٢،٤
ورسائلهم لخرجت عن قصد الاختصار ونُسبت إلى الإسهاب والإكثار ولكنّني أذكر ممّا رأيته لمعة لطيفة يظهر بها الفرق بين الهمم الخسيسة والهمم النفيسة.[١]

فممّن رأيته من أولاد الأقباط الذين تنقّلوا في درجات الرذائل وخدموا[٢] في مزابل ٢،٢،٤
الخدم بل في خدم المزابل صبيّ[٣] وقعت له كائنة حصل بها تحت يده مال جزيل صانع ببعضه وأسلم استبقاءً لبقيّته ثمّ بذل منه جملةً لمن كان يلي أمر الديوان[٤] حتّى خدم في ديوان يخدم فيه أماثل الناس.

فمدّ يده ونهب وصانع ووهب وتَطَيْلَسَ وصار يشابه المسلمين في الزيّ وظهور كلمة الإسلام ويتواجد عند سماع القرآن ويخضع ويتذلّل عند ذكر الرسول صلّى الله عليه وسلّم[٥] ويعلن[٦] بأنّه كاتب على الحقيقة وسالك في الكتابة أحسن طريقة ويناطي السعداء في البناء ويميل إلى مماثلة الأماثل[٧] والأفاضل ويعاني شراء المماليك الترك ويسأل عن أجناسهم فلم يحفظ سوى القفجاق إلّا أنّه إذا تلفّظ به لا يقول إلّا الشفشاق فاتّفق اجتماعي به يوماً وتجارينا الحديث وخرجنا إلى ذكر الرقيق وأجناسه وذكرنا الترك فقال ليس فيهم أحسن من جنس الشفشاق فعجبت من كلامه وقصدت تنبيهه على صحّة اللفظ فقلت له صدقت إنّ القفجاق جنس حسن لكنّ غيره أحسن منه وثنّيت له الكلمة ليعلم أنّه غلط فيها فقال لا يقول سيّدنا هذا ما ثمّ مثل الشفشاق، وأعادها بعينها مراراً فعلمت أنّ جهله طبيعيّ لا يقبل التغيير ولا ينتقل عمّا طُبع عليه من طباع الحمير.

١ كذا في ت؛ وفي ب، ج،د زيادة: يكون على سبيل الظرف عند ذوي الأدب والملح المضحكة لأهل الأرب. ٢ في سائر المخطوطات: خدم. ٣ كذا في ت؛ وفي ب، د: حتّى. ٤ كذا في ت؛ وفي ب، د زيادة: ورضي الاتّفاق به والقبول منه. ٥ كذا في ت؛ والجملة من (ويتواجد) ساقطة في ب، ج،د. ٦ كذا في ت؛ وفي ب، د: وصار بقحة الأقباط يعلن. ٧ كذا في ت؛ وفي ب، د زيادة: ومكاثرة الأكابر.

The Second Section: Concerning Amusing Aspects of Their Vulgar Expression, and Their Foolishness[244]

If I undertook a minute description of the glaring faults and disgraces in their manner of writing letters and compositions, I would veer from my purpose, which is brevity, and expose myself to the charge of gross prolixity. I shall mention, however, just a few cases that I have witnessed, by which to contrast mean and low ambition to its vaulting and priceless opposite. 4.2.1

A certain Copt I knew—one of those who clamber up and down on the rungs of baseness, and serve in the dregs of service, or rather in the service of the dregs—was a boy who came somehow into a substantial fortune. With some of this wealth he bought himself supporters; to keep the rest of his wealth he converted to Islam. Then he handed a goodly sum to the head of the administration, and was promptly appointed to serve in an office in which the very best men were employed. 4.2.2

He stole and plundered, bribed and gifted, and eventually took to wearing the cowl of the learned, the secretaries' uniform.[245] In dress and in outward devotion to Islam he appeared just like a Muslim. When he heard the Qur'an being recited he pretended to be transported; when the Prophet was mentioned, God bless and keep him, he groveled and made a show of reverence. He declared himself a true secretary, a traveler on the loftiest path winding through the secretarial art. He vied with the most fortunate men in commissioning great buildings, and took to imitating the best and most noble of them, going to great lengths, for example, to purchase Turkish slaves.

Although he would inquire earnestly about the various races of slave, he succeeded in remembering only one—the Kipchak—except that when he said the word he unfailingly pronounced it "Shipshak." I met him by chance one day, and we fell into conversation. The topic turned to the races of slaves, and to the Turks in particular. He said, "None of them are better than the Shipshak." This took me by surprise and I resolved to inform him of the correct pronunciation. "You are absolutely right," I said. "The Kipchaks . . . *Kipchaks* . . . are indeed good, but others are better," repeating the word for him so that he would know he had mispronounced it. "May our master not speak thus," he replied. "None of them measure up to the Shipshaks!" pronouncing the word exactly as he had the first time. This incident taught me that his ignorance was an indelible part of his character and that he would never be budged from his ingrained asininity.

٣،٢،٤ وكتب بعض الكتّاب إلى القاضي الفاضل كتاباً يذكر فيه أنّه ملازم على وظيفة الدعاء وكتب الوظيفة بالضاد ولم ينقطها. فقال القاضي الفاضل ما حلّ هذه الوصيفة تكبر فقيل له ما معنى هذا؟ فقال فلان له مدّة ثلاثين سنة يكتب لي أنّه ملازم على وصيفة وفي ثلاثين سنة لا[1] تكبر الوصيفة وتأتي بالأولاد.

٤،٢،٤ وكتب إليّ بعض الكتّاب كتاباً غلط فيه في عدّة مواضع منها أنّه كتب أنّه مواظب بالضاد والصحيح بالظاء وأنّه مصرور بسلامتي بالصاد يعني أنّه مسرور وتعرّض إلى لومي على قلّة السعي في تحصيل الدنيا واشتغالي عن ذلك بالعلم وقال قد قال الله تعالى كونوا وأنا معكم، وما قال الله ذلك.

٥،٢،٤ وتحدّث معي شخص من هؤلاء الجهّال في أمر فسألته عن غرضه فيه فقال قال الله تعالى كل البقل من حيث يؤتى به ولا تسأل عن المبقلة فضحكت وقلت يا رجل اتّق الله ولا تنسب هذا القول إلى الله تعالى فقال لا تأخذ عليّ فإنّي أردت أن أقول قال النبيّ فأنسيت فازددت منه تعجّباً وقلت والله ما هذا قول النبيّ وما هذا إلّا قول بعض الشعراء فلا تعُد إلى مثل هذا فإنّه كفر فقال أنا استغفر الله من هذا.

٦،٢،٤ وكتب شخص من الكتّاب إلى مشدّ الديوان وأمّا فلان فلم يفعل ما فعله باختياره وإنّما أخصب على ذلك، يعني غصب.

٧،٢،٤ لا إله إلّا الله رأيت في كتاب من ابن النوري ناظر دمياط إلى الأمير جمال الدين أيدغدي[2] العزيزيّ رحمه الله في سنة ستّين وستّمائة وقد كتب إليه يستعطفه ويسترضيه كلاماً من جملته ورأى المملوك في كلام مولانا انجعازاً عظيماً يعني انزعاجاً.[3]

٨،٢،٤ وبلغني أنّ بعض الأقباط صار صاحب ديوان بغزّة فكتب كتاباً عنه وعن النائب بها المملوكان يقبّلان الأرض وينهيان أنهمان أقامان يومان ينتظران المرشان فقال

١ (لا) ساقطة في سائر المخطوطات؛ والمثبت زيادة يقتضيها السياق. ٢ في سائر المخطوطات: أيدغري؛ والصواب ما أثبتناه من الذيل، ١:٤٦. ٣ كذا في ب،د؛ والفقرة كلّها ساقطة في ت.

A certain secretary wrote a letter to al-Qāḍī al-Fāḍil in which he mentioned that he had been ceaselessly occupied with a certain task, namely prayer. But he wrote the word *task* with erroneous letters, which he then corrupted further, so that it came out as *lass*.[246] So al-Qāḍī al-Fāḍil said, "Will the lass ever become pregnant?" Someone asked him what he meant and he replied, "This person has been writing to me for thirty years that he is ceaselessly occupied with this lass, and in thirty years she has yet to conceive and give birth." 4.2.3

This secretary sent me a letter in which he committed several errors. He reported, for instance, that he was *ziligent*, using *z* rather than *d*, and that he was *encaptured* at my well-being, a result of using another erroneous letter; he meant *enraptured*.[247] He also blamed me for my "lack of effort in seeking to obtain worldly success, being distracted from it by the pursuit of learning." He wrote, "God, be He exalted, said, 'Be, and I will be with you.'" Of course God has said nothing of the sort. 4.2.4

One of these senseless types was speaking with me on some matter, and I asked him what he was really after. He said, "God, be He exalted, said, 'Eat thou the herbage from whence it is brought, and ask not concerning the land which produced it.'" I laughed and said, "Man, have some fear of God and don't ascribe such things to Him, be He exalted." He said, "Please go easy on me, for I meant to say 'The Prophet said . . . ,' but I forgot." At this I was even more amazed, so I said to him, "By God, this is no saying of the Prophet, either. It's nothing but the saying of some poet. Do not repeat such things as they amount to unbelief," and he said, "I seek God's pardon for this." 4.2.5

A secretary wrote to a high tax official in the administration, "As for so-and-so, he did what he did not by choice, but rather was *pimpled* to do it," by which he meant was *impelled* to do it.[248] 4.2.6

There is no god but God! I saw a letter from Ibn al-Nūrī, overseer of Damietta, seeking the grace and favor of the Emir Jamāl al-Dīn Aydughdī al-ʿAzīzī, God grant him mercy, in the year 660 [1261–62].[249] It contained the following sentence: "This humble slave finds in the words of our master great *quisdietude*," a nonsense word by which he intended *disquietude*. 4.2.7

I heard about a Copt who became the head of an administrative office in Gaza. He issued a letter on behalf of himself and the sultan's viceroy there. He composed the address as follows: "The two slaves kisses the grounds and informs thats theys have awaiteds the maréschal for twos days."[250] A Christian secretary said to him, in praise of this rhetorical display, "May God prosper 4.2.8

له كاتب نصرانيّ زادك الله سعادةً فما وقع للقاضي الفاضل من هذه الكلمات واحدة فقال صدقت هذه الأشياء فتوح.

٩،٢،٤ وأسلم بعض الأقباط وضلّع عمامته وتطيلس فصار يعدّ نفسه من الكتّاب فانقطع يوماً من الديوان فكتب إليه المشدّ يسأل عن سبب انقطاعه فورد جوابه يعتذر أنّه ما انقطع المملوك إلّا لأنّه أصابته حيضة يعني هيضة.

١٠،٢،٤ وكتب قبطيّ آخر وقد أسلم وتطيلس وصار يُدعى بالقاضي إلى ناظر الديوان يعتذر من تأخّره ويقول ما عاقني إلّا خصام الجوزة، يعني الزوجة.

١١،٢،٤ ومرض قبطيّ من الذين أسلموا وتطيلسوا فكتب إليه صديق له يسأل عن حاله فأجابه الحمد لله فإنّي أصبحت اليوم وأنا ناهق، أي ناقه. وقد قال الشاعر في مثله

[السريع]

وَلِي صَدِيقٌ جِئْتُهُ عَائِدًا وَوِدُّهُ لِي أَبَدًا صَادِقُ
قُلْتُ لَهُ أَنْتَ إِذًا نَاقِهٌ فَقَالَ لَا بَلْ إِنَّنِي نَاهِقُ

وكتب هذا الشخص المذكور إلى صديقه المذكور يطلب منه نبيذاً عتيقاً وقال والله لقد طلبته من كلّ أحد فما وجدته لهذا طلبته منك مع أنّي والله ما طلبته إلّا منك فلا تردّ رسولي إلّا به.[1]

١٢،٢،٤ وسافر قبطيّ على حمار فمرض في الطريق وتشوّش حماره وبلغ خبره إلى صاحب له فكتب إليه يسأل عنه وعن حماره فأجابه يا أخي بعد فراقي لك مرضت أنا والحمار إلّا أنّ الحمار أصلح منّي بكثير.

١٣،٢،٤ وأخبرني أحد الأصحاب الفضلاء أنّه مرض أيّاماً وتعافى فجاء إليه صديق له قبطيّ قد أسلم وتطيلس ليهنّئه بالعافية فقال والله لمّا سمعت بعافيتك كأنّي ملكت الدنيا

١ كذا في ب،د؛ والفقرة ساقطة في ت.

your good fortune! Even al-Qāḍī al-Fāḍil never came up with such words as these!" He said, "Truly spoken; these things are gifts of God."

There was another Copt who converted, and took to wearing a ribbed turban, and the cowl of the learned. He thought he was a real secretary. One day he was absent from the office. The high tax official wrote to him to ask the reason for his absence. In reply he apologized, writing as follows: "The slave is absent because he has been *fertile*." He meant *febrile*.[251] 4.2.9

A different Copt, who had also converted, donned the cowl, and come to be addressed honorifically as "Judge," wrote an apology to the overseer of the tax office, saying, "I was held up by a quarrel with the *louse*," when he meant *spouse*.[252] 4.2.10

Another one of these Copts who had converted and donned the cowl fell ill. His friend wrote to ask how he was doing and he replied, "Praise God, this morning I arose *all yell*," by which he meant *all well*. Regarding just such a case, a poet said, 4.2.11

> I have a friend whom I visited when he was sick,
> and whose affection for me is ever sincere,
> "You well then?" I asked.
> "No," he shot back, "I yell."[253]

This same person wrote to his friend, requesting a vintage wine. In the note he wrote, "I swear to God that I have requested it from everyone else, but failed to find it. This is why I am now requesting it from you. I swear to God that I have requested it from no one but you; therefore please do not send my messenger back without it."

A Copt was travelling on a donkey when he fell ill, and his donkey too. News of this reached an associate of his, who wrote to ask how he and the donkey were doing. He replied, "Brother, after I left you I fell ill, the donkey and I, only the donkey is much, much better than I am." 4.2.12

An eminent associate of mine told me how he was once sick for several days. When he had begun to feel better, a friend of his, a Copt who had converted and put on the cowl, came to him to congratulate him on his recovery. The Copt said, "By God, when I heard about your recovery I felt like I owned the world, with *its corn fourers*." The ninny meant to say, *the four corners* of the world. He was trying to allude to the hadith that goes, "For the one who wakes with a healthy body, a faithful heart, and food for the day, it is as though he owned 4.2.13

بأربع حوافيرها، أراد التيس يقول بأربع حذافيرها. أراد ما جاء في الحديث من أصبح معافىً في بدنه آمناً في سِربه عنده قوت يومه فكأنّما ملك الدنيا بحذافيرها. قال الحاكي فضحكت من ذلك وذكرت الحديث لقبطيّ آخر فقال ما هو إلّا أراد أن يقول بحراذيفها فغلط. قال فوجدت الثاني أتيس من الأوّل.

١٤،٢،٤ وأخبرني رجل فقيه أديب عن واحد صار من الرؤساء أنّه جرى في مجلسه ذكر بعض الشعراء فقال لا تطيلوا والله ما هو عندي إلّا سُحبان، بضمّ السين فحكيت القضيّة لرئيس آخر من جنسه فقال ما أظنّه يخفى عنه أنّه سجان وإنّما سها، فغلّط الأوّل الثاني. والمراد سَحبان بفتح السين قلت وبه يضرب المثل في الفصاحة.

١٥،٢،٤ ووقف هذا الرئيس على كتاب فيه صفات الخمر ومن جملة الصفات الخندريس فوقع أنّها بالحاء المهملة وبقيت في ذهنه وكان قد بعث يطلب منجّماً بجواره فرجع الرسول فأخبره سرّاً أنّه في بيته يشرب فأراد الرئيس أن يظهر فصاحته فقال للجماعة الحاضرين طلبنا المنجّم فقيل لنا إنّه في بيته يشرب الحندريس فضحك الجماعة من جهله وهو تيس لا يدري بذلك.

١٦،٢،٤ وعزم بعض الأقباط الذين أسلموا وتطيلسوا على سفر فقال لجماعة عنده ما هذا الشهر؟ فقالوا صفر قال قد عزمت على الصفر في صفر ما هذا مليح؟ فقال التيوس الحاضرون والله مليح هذا مطابق مجالس أي مجانس.

١٧،٢،٤ واجتمع جاهلان من أهل الريف وكانا حرّاثين فتطيلسا ودخلا إلى المدينة وخدما في بعض الخدم فجاءهما في أوّل السنة منجّم ومعه تقويم فنظر فيه أحدهما فرأى في أسماء الشهور بالروميّة نيسان فصحف النون بالتاء فقال للمنجّم من هو تيسان فقال له المولى وأخوه يا حمير هل يخفى على أحد أنّ نيسان اسم شهر من شهور الروم؟

the four corners of the world."[254] My associate continued, saying, "I laughed at this and later on told another Copt about the conversation. He said, 'He must have meant to say the *core fourners*,' thus committing yet another error. So the second proved to be even more of a ninny than the first."[255]

A jurist and man of letters told me about a certain person who had risen to a position of leadership. A poet was being talked about in his presence and he said, "There is no need to go on talking about him, by God, for in my view he is an absolute Suḥbān," pronouncing it with a *u* after the *S*. This was recounted to another person of similar status, who said, "Surely he was aware that it is really *Subḥān*; he must have been distracted," and made bold to speak of the first man's error! The correct pronunciation is of course *Saḥbān*, with an *a* after the *S*. I should add that Saḥbān's name is proverbial for eloquence. 4.2.14

This same important fellow was reading to himself from a book that contained a number of adjectives used to describe wine, one of which was "venerable." In the book, however, a dot had been omitted so that the word appeared incorrectly, and that erroneous word is what stuck in his head. One evening, he sent for an astrologer who lived close by. The messenger whom he had sent soon returned, however, taking him aside and telling him that the astrologer had drunk too much to leave his own house. The man, who wished to make a show of his eloquence, announced to those assembled, "We sought out the astrologer, but it appears that he is in his house drinking fenerable wine!" Everyone laughed at his ignorance, though he, the ninny, failed to notice.[256] 4.2.15

Another Copt who had converted and begun wearing the cowl decided to take a trip. He asked some people who were there, "What month are we in?" "The month of Ṣafar," they replied. "Well then, I have decided to go on ṣafari in Ṣafar," he said, using the wrong kind of *s*. "Now doesn't that have a nice ring?" The ninnies replied, "Very nice, by God! The words go along together; they're downright *honophomous*!" meaning *homophonous*. 4.2.16

Two country bumpkins, plowmen by trade, put on cowls and headed into town, where they succeeded in finding minor clerical jobs. One day near the beginning of the year, an astrologer happened by the place where they were working, carrying a calendar. One of the bumpkins looked at it and saw, among the names of foreign months, Nīsān. He misread the *N* as a *T*, however, and asked the astrologer, "Who's Tīsān?" Since *tīsān* means "the two ninnies," the astrologer replied, "You and your brother, you asses! Who doesn't know that Nīsān is one of the Greek months?"[257] 4.2.17

وحضر بعض الأقباط الذين أسلموا ودعوا بالقضاة دعوة فأمعن في الأكل وأخذ يعتذر ويطالب الجماعة وأراد يقول أنا على الأكل نهم فقال أنا على الأكل نمه[١] فضحك الحاضرون.[٢] ١٨،٢،٤

ونظر قبطيّ في كتاب فوجد فيه حكاية عن فارس أنّه ركب فرسه واستطرد في الميدان فتصحّفت عليه ووقع له أنّها بالشين والباء فقال للحاضرين والله ما اللغة إلّا واسعة فقالوا وكيف قال ما معنى قوله ركب فرسه واشبطرد في الميدان؟ فضحك الحاضرون من غلطه وقالوا قد تصحّف عليك إنّما هو اتسطرد فخجل. ١٩،٢،٤

وودّع بعضهم رجلاً جليل القدر فأراد أن يقول يا من يعزّ علينا أن نفارقه فقال له يا من يهون علينا أن نفارقه فقال له المودّع فآسألني أنا. فشكره ودعا له.[٣] ٢٠،٢،٤

وأراد بعض الجهّال أن يقول لرئيس إذا صحّ منك الودّ فالمال هيّن فقال إذا صحّ منك المال فالودّ هيّن فقال له الرئيس أحسنت. ٢١،٢،٤

وسأل جليل القدر عامّيّاً عن حاله ومن يجتمع عنده وماذا يصنع فقال أمّا أنا فخير وأمّا من يجتمع عندي ففلان وفلان وأمّا الذي نصنع فوالله ما لنا شغل إلّا ذكر مناحس المولى فقال لا جزاكم الله عنّي خيراً فضرب العامّيّ يده على فمه وقال والله ما أردت إلّا محاسن المولى فسبقني لساني فضحك منه. ٢٢،٢،٤

وتحدّث معي إنسان جاهل فأراد أن يقول العادة طبع خامس فقال الخامس طبع العادة. وسألت بعض الجهّال عن انقطاعه عنّي فقال والله ما كنت إلّا منحرف المجاز، يعني المزاج، وشربت خلطاً استفرغت به دواء، أي دواء استفرغت به خلطاً.[٤] ٢٣،٢،٤

وقال جاهل منهم اشتريت جارية تضرب بالموسيقى فاعتقد التيس أنّ الموسيقى آلة تُضرب بها مثل العود وغيره. ٢٤،٢،٤

---

١ في سائر المخطوطات: نه؛ ولعلّ الصواب ما أثبتناه. ٢ كذا في ب، د؛ والفقرة ساقطة في ت. ٣ كذا في ب، د؛ والفقرة ساقطة في ت. ٤ كذا في ب، د؛ والفقرة ساقطة في ت.

One of these Copts who had converted and was addressed as "Judge" accepted a dinner invitation. After becoming completely engrossed in the food, he began apologizing and begging the others' pardon. Meaning to say, "When it comes to food I am rather *devoted*," he blurted out, "When it comes to food I am rather *dumbfounded*," at which everyone laughed.[258] **4.2.18**

A Copt was leafing through a book and found a story about a horseman who "mounted his horse and 'wheeled about' in the square." The text was corrupt, however—the letters had got thoroughly mixed up. He said to some of his companions, "By God, the Arabic language is vast!" "What do you mean?" they asked. He replied, "What can 'He mounted his horse and *bheeled awout* in the square' mean?" Laughing at his error, they said, "You must have read a corrupted text. It should be 'wheeled about.'" He was quite embarrassed at this. **4.2.19**

A Copt was bidding farewell to a great man, and wanted to say, "O thou of whom it is so difficult for us to take leave!" Instead he said, "O thou of whom it is so easy for us to take leave!" The great man said, "Imagine how much more so for me!" For this the Copt thanked him and blessed him. **4.2.20**

An ignorant man wanted to say to a certain leader, "If your affection be sufficient, money is of little account." In the event, however, he said, "If your money be sufficient, affection is of little account." "Well spoken," the leader replied. **4.2.21**

A great man asked one of the common folk how he was, whose company he kept, and what he did. He replied, "As for me, I'm good. As for my company, they are this and that person. As for what we do, by God, we have nothing to do but talk about your vices, my lord." The great man exclaimed, "May you get no reward from God on my account!" The commoner clapped his hand to his mouth and said, "I swear to God that I meant 'your virtues,' but my tongue got away from me!" This made the man laugh at him.[259] **4.2.22**

An ignorant man was conversing with me and meant to say, "Habit is a fifth temperament." But instead he said, "The fifth is the temperament of habit." I asked another foolish fellow why it had been so long since I had seen him. He said, "By God, I was just a bit *interposed*"—meaning *indisposed*[260]—"and I drank a humor by which I expelled the medicine," meaning "drank a medicine by which I expelled the humor." **4.2.23**

Another ignorant fool of this sort said, "I have purchased a slave girl who plays the music." The ninny thought "the music" was an instrument that one plays, like the oud and so forth. **4.2.24**

وقرأ جاهل منهم في ديوان المتنبّي [الوافر] ٤،٢،٢٥

فُؤَادٌ مَا يُسَلِّيهِ ٱلْمُدَامُ

فتصحّف عليه فقال

قَوَّادٌ مَا يُسَلِّيهِ ٱلْمُدَامُ

فضحك الناس منه وقرأ [البسيط]

وَاحَرَّ قَلْبَاهُ مِمَّنْ قَلْبُهُ يَشَمٌّ[١]

وقالوا له تصلح أن تكون راوية للمتنبّي.

وفتح بعض الأقباط الجهّال كتاباً فنظر أسطره قد استغرقت الورق من أوّل الصفحة إلى آخرها فأراد أن يقول ما لهذا الكتاب هامش فقال ما لهذا الكتاب هاشم فضحك الناس من غلطه. والهامش هو البياض المحيط بالسطور.[٢] ٤،٢،٢٦

وسمع ريفيّ قد تعلّم الكتابة وخدم في الديوان قول الشاعر [الطويل] ٤،٢،٢٧

إِذَا لَمْ يَكُنْ إِلَّا ٱلْأَسِنَّةُ مَرْكَبٌ فَلَا رَأْيَ لِلْمُضْطَرِّ إِلَّا رُكُوبُهَا

فتخيّل البيت في ذهنه وصار إذا قعد في الديوان يشتهي أن يتمثّل بالشعر فيقول إذا لم يكن للإنسان في الدنيا مركب إلّا الأسنّة فوالله يا فلان ما للمضطرّ المسكين غير ركوبها. فيُنحس الشعر على قائله ولا يبقى شعراً ولا كلاماً.

وهذا هو الذي لمّا ضمن أبوه جهات الدولة فيما سلف وقعد في الديوان واجتمع الناس حوله أدخل يده في طوقه ومسح إبطه ثمّ شمّ يده وقال أُفُّوه. وصدق والله ٤،٢،٢٨

١ الصواب هو (ممّن قلبه شبم). ٢ كذا في ت؛ والجملة ساقطة في ب،د.

And another ignorant person quoted al-Mutanabbī's line that goes 4.2.25

> A heart that wine cannot console . . .

But, misreading the text, he said,

> A tart whom wine cannot console . . .[261]

The people all laughed. And he recited,

> O heart of mine, inflamed by one whose heart snuffles . . .[262]

The listeners said, "You ought to be a professional reciter of al-Mutanabbī!"

An ignorant Copt opened a book one day and noticed that the lines of text filled its pages completely, from beginning to end. Intending to say, "This book has no margin around its pages," he instead said, "This book has no merging."[263] The people laughed at his error. The margin is the empty area of the page that surrounds the lines of text. 4.2.26

A certain rustic, who had learnt to write and gained employment in a government office, heard the saying of the poet, 4.2.27

> For him who has nothing to ride on but spikes,
> there's nothing to do but mount up.[264]

He took a fancy to this line and turned it over in his mind so that whenever he was sitting in the office and felt the urge to quote poetry to prove some point, he would say, "When someone got nothin' in the world to ride on 'cept spikes, then by God, man, there's nothin' for the poor guy to do but ride 'em." In this way he would botch and muddle what the poet had crafted, so that it could no longer be considered poetry or even proper speech.

This is the same person whose father, when he was tax farmer over certain districts long ago, would sit in the office with people around him. He would slide his hand into his collar and touch his armpit and smell his hand and say, "Faugh!" And by God he was right. Faugh to him and upon him. Then would put his hand into his pocket and draw out his silver coins, all blackened pieces. Placing a coin in his mouth, he would feel it between his teeth to tell its weight, just as low commoners do. Then he would remove it, wet from his mouth, and hand it to one of those present and say, "Take this and go buy me something for body odor." People were astonished that someone who was so uncouth in word and deed could be appointed to oversee the lofty affairs of the lands 4.2.28

أفّ له وعليه. ثمّ أدخل يده في جيبه فأخرج ورقةً قطع فضّة سواد فأخذ منها قطعة ألقاها في فمه وجعل يحسّها بأسنانه ليعلم وزنها على عادة العوامّ الساقطين ثمّ أخرجها مبلولة فدفعها إلى أحد المقدّمين بين يديه وقال اشتر لي بهذه القطعة دواء للصنان فعجب الناس من ولاية من هذا جهله في القول والفعل أمور البلاد والعباد وتدبير الأموال وتمشية الأشغال.

٢٩،٢،٤ وقال ريفيّ من سواد العراق[١] لفقيه يا سيّدنا إذا نزلت إلى النهر أغتسل يكون وجهي إلى القبلة حتّى يصحّ وضوئي أم إلى غيرها فقال يكون وجهك إلى ثيابك التي نزعتها كيلا تُسرق. فتوهّم الجاهل أنّ التوجّه إلى القبلة شرط في صحّة الاغتسال.

٣٠،٢،٤ ولبس بعض الأرياف ثياباً تشبه ثياب الناس ودخل الجامع فرأى شيخاً عالماً وحوله ناس يسألونه ويستفتونه فتقدّم إليه الريفيّ وقال ما يقول سيّدنا في النبيّ عليه السلام وفي هارون الرشيد أيّهم أقدم؟ فضحك الناس منه وقال له الشيخ أنت من أهل الريف؟ قال نعم قال يا هذا لو اشتغلت بحرثك وزرعك كان أصلح لك من الاشتغال بما لا يعنيك فإنّك أضحكت الناس عليك.

٣١،٢،٤ وقال إنسان لريفيّ بلغني أنّ أباك مريض وقد ورمت قدماه فقال أبي والله يا سيّدنا قدمت ورماه قال فله ولد غيرك؟ قال لا قال فإذاً ما أعقب.[٢]

٣٢،٢،٤ ولا عجب من جهل هؤلاء وما يظهر من عوراتهم فلقد أخبرني عدل فقيه أثق بنقله عن قاضي حصن زياد بالشرق أنّه لقيه وقال قد عمل فيّ شاعر بيتين فقد استحسنهما وهما [كلاهما من الطويل]

لِحِصْنِ زِيَادٍ قَاضِياً طُولَ لَيْلِهِ   يُجَامِعُ فِي دَيْرٍ وَيَشْرَبُ فِي دَنِّ
وَمِنْ عَجَبٍ أَنْ يَجْعَلُوهُ بِزَعْمِهِم   لِمَالِ ٱلْيَتَامَى حَافِظاً وَهْوَ شَافِرُ[٣]

---

١ كذا في ت؛ وفي ب،د: العربان.   ٢ كذا في ب،د؛ والفقرة ساقطة في ت.   ٣ كذا في ب؛ وفي د: شافضيّ. ولعلّ الصواب هو (رافضيّ).

and the servants of God, to manage the distribution of funds, and to see to the affairs of the state.

A rustic fellow from the Sawad of Iraq asked a jurist, "Sir, when I go down 4.2.29
to the river to bathe, should I face toward Mecca so that my ablutions are done lawfully, or in some other direction?" The jurist said, "You should face the clothes that you have taken off, lest they be stolen." The ignorant fellow had somehow imagined that facing toward Mecca was necessary for his washing to be lawful.

Another rustic put on clothes resembling those of well-to-do city folk and 4.2.30
went into a congregational mosque. There he saw a learned shaykh, around whom a crowd of people had gathered. They were asking him religious questions and seeking his opinion on legal matters. The rustic presented himself before this man and asked, "Sir, between the Prophet, peace be upon him, and Hārūn al-Rashīd, which one would you say are more ancient?" At this the people laughed, and the shaykh asked him, "Are you one of the country folk?" "Yes," the man replied. "Well my fellow," said the shaykh, "it would be better for you to keep busy with your plowing and sowing than to involve yourself in what does not concern you. For see, you have made people laugh at you."

Someone once said to another rustic, "I heard that your father is ill and that 4.2.31
his feet are swollen." "By God, sir," the rustic replied, "his sweet are all follen." The man said, "Does he have other sons?" "No," the rustic said. "Then he's not left any proper heir, has he?" the man replied.

Indeed, the ignorance of these folk and their embarrassing displays are no 4.2.32
wonder. A certain professional witness, whose word I trust, told me about meeting a judge in Ḥiṣn Ziyād, in the East. This judge said to him, "A poet has composed two lines about me." These two lines, which the judge seemed to think rather nice, were:

> Ḥiṣn Ziyād has a man who judges it proper
> to pass the night copulating in a monastery and drinking from a jug.

And

> A wonder it is, that they entrust the property of orphans
> to a guardian (as they call him!) who ruins his own property.[265]

ثمّ قال بالله عليك ما هو مليح؟ ولا يشعر بما فيه من الهجو ولا القذف.

وحُكي[1] أنّ بعض قضاة الشرع قديماً بلغ الوزير عنه كلام قبيح فعاتبه فأراد أن يقول هذه رقبة المملوك بين يدي مولانا فقال هذه رقبة مولانا بين يدي المملوك إن رسم بالدِرّة فبسم الله فضحك منه وتركه. ٣٣،٢،٤

وحضر بعض القضاة تركة فيها دوابّ ليضبطها بقلمه ومعه جماعة فقالوا يكتب سيّدنا مُهرًا فقال هو ذكر أم أنثى؟ فضحك من جهله الحاضرون. ٣٤،٢،٤

ومن غريب ما جرى أنّ السلطان الشهيد الملك العادل قدّس الله روحه لمّا ولّى صدر الدين شيخ الشيوخ قاضي قضاة الشرع عرض قضاة البلاد فبلغه أنّ قاضي بعض البلاد جاهل إلى الغاية فعزله بمن يصلح للحكم فلمّا جلس السلطان الملك العادل جلوساً عامّاً حضر مجلسه القضاة والفقهاء والشهود وغيرهم فجاء القاضي المصروف بجهله ووقف للسلطان وقال يا خوند أنا قاضٍ في هذا المكان منذ سنين فسل شيخ الشيوخ بأيّ جنحة صرفني فنظر السلطان إلى الشيخ وجعل يسأل عن قضيّته فقال ذُكر لي أنّه قليل الفقه فأردت أن يتخلّى للاشتغال ويتذكّر ما قد نسيه. فأحسن العبارة عن جهله فقال القاضي يا مولانا إنّ أعدائي نقلوا عنّي إلى الشيخ أنّي جاهل وهذا مجلس السلطان وفيه الفقهاء يسألني عمّا أراد فقال السلطان للشيخ اسأله مسألة فقال القاضي من يزوّج المرأة؟ قال ابنها فتبسّم الشيخ والفقهاء وعلم السلطان أنّه أخطأ فقال أستغفر الله إنّما يزوّجها ابنها إذا كانت بكرًا فضحك السلطان وقال إذا كانت بكرًا من أين يكون لها ولد؟ وقام قدّس الله روحه وهو ضاحك من جهله متعجّب من عقله. ٣٥،٢،٤

[1] كذا في ب،د؛ والنصّ من (أثق بنقله) ساقط في ت.

Then he said to my informant, "God! Isn't it witty?" The judge was too ignorant and callous to be affected by the mockery and slander the poem contained.

It is told how long ago a certain vizier heard that a judge of the Holy Law had 4.2.33
been saying unseemly things. Upon being reprimanded, the judge intended to say, "Behold, the slave's neck is in our master's power . . ." But in the event he said, "Behold our master's neck is in the slave's power. If he command flogging, then in the name of God, let it begin!" The vizier laughed at him and set him free.

A judge came with a group of assistants to register a bequest that contained 4.2.34
riding animals. His assistants said, "Sir, please record one colt." "Is he male or female?" he asked. Those present scoffed at his ignorance.

One amazing incident of this kind concerns the martyred Sultan al-Malik 4.2.35
al-ʿĀdil, God sanctify his soul. After he appointed Ṣadr al-Dīn to the offices of Chief Sufi Shaykh and Chief Judge of the Holy Law, the new appointee carried out a review of all the judges in the land. He discovered that the judge in a certain region was a complete fool and summarily dismissed him in favor of someone who was fit to give verdicts. Shortly thereafter, al-Malik al-ʿĀdil held a general audience attended by the judges, the jurists, the professional judicial witnesses, and others. The judge who had been removed from office because of his ignorance also attended. He stood before the sultan and said, "My lord, for many years I have been a judge in this place. Ask the Chief Sufi Shaykh to name the infraction on the pretext of which he removed me." The sultan looked at Ṣadr al-Dīn and began to inquire about the judge's case. Ṣadr al-Dīn replied, "It came to my attention that this man had scant knowledge of jurisprudence. My desire was to give him the free time to focus upon his studies and to recall what he had forgotten." In this way he was diplomatic concerning the man's ignorance.

Then the judge said, "My lord, it is my enemies who told the shaykh that I am ignorant. But this is the audience of the sultan, and here are jurists aplenty. Let him ask me whatever he pleases." The sultan said to the shaykh, "Ask him a question." So he asked, "Who is it, Judge, that gives a woman in marriage?" "Her son," he replied. At this the shaykh and the jurists smiled, and the sultan saw that the man had made a mistake. Then the ignorant judge said, "I beg your pardon! Rather, it is her son who gives her in marriage only if she is a virgin!" The sultan laughed and asked, "If she is a virgin, then where did she get a son?" And he arose, God sanctify his spirit, still laughing at the man's ignorance and marveling at his reasoning.

وسدّ هذا الباب في حقّ القضاة أولى لئلّا ينبسط عذر الأقباط وأهل الريف ٤،٢،٣٦
فالجهل في الناس كثير وهو في هؤلاء أكثر. أخبرني المولى جمال الدين أبو الحسين الجزّار أنّه مدح قاضي ثغر دمياط بقصيدة داليّة وأنّ الحاضرين استجبّوا معانيها وبديعها وألفاظها وطربوا منها فقال القاضي الممدوح والله إنّ فيها لشيء أحسن ممّا قلتم وأعجب فأصغوا إليه وقالوا له علم سيّدنا أوسع وتأمّله وتخيّله أصوب فما هو الذي استحسنه سيّدنا فقال هذه القصيدة كلّها على حرف الدال وآخر كلّ بيت منها دال. وتخيّل الأبله أنّ استعمال القوافي لم يقع إلّا في هذه القصيدة بعينها لا غير.[١]

الفصل الثالث وبمعناه سُمّي الكتّاب فيما ينبغي سلوكه بهم ومعهم من أخذ الأموال التي اختزلوها من أموال المسلمين

فأقول وبالله التوفيق من المعلوم البيّن أنّ أحد هؤلاء[٢] الموصوفين بما تقدّم إذا ٤،٣،١
خدم وليس له مال سوى ما قُرّر له على خدمته وكان المقرّر له على الخدمة لا يقوم بغلامه ودابّته فلم يمض عليه إلّا برهة من الزمان وقد ظهر له من الأموال والأملاك والنعم ما لا يقتضيه المقرّر له على خدمته عُلم بالقطع واليقين لا بالظنّ والتخمين أنّه سرق مال مولاه وخان فيما تولّاه لا سيّما إن كان المخدوم سلطان بلاد وملك عباد وكانت خدمته في الخراج أو في أمرٍ يعمّ كالزكاة والمواريث فإنّها خدم تجمع الحكم على الأحياء والأموات فيكون قد أخذ من هذا شيئاً ومن هذا شيئاً واشترى من معامليه بغير اختيارهم وباع عليهم بغير رضاهم أو ألجأهم إلى بيع موجودهم في أداء ما عليهم في وقت رخصه وكساده وأقام من اشتراه وادّخره إلى حين غلائه ونفاقه

١ كذا في ب،د؛ والنصّ من (أخبرني المولى جمال الدين) ساقط في ت. ٢ كذا في ت؛ وفي ب،د زيادة: النصارى.

It is best that we bring this discussion of judges to a close, lest we make the Copts and the rustics look normal by comparison. For there is a great deal of ignorance among men in general, but far more among them. The master Jamāl al-Dīn Abū l-Ḥusayn al-Jazzār told me how he had once addressed a panegyric poem, each rhyming line of which ended in the letter *d*, to a judge in the port of Damietta. Those present, he told me, were taken with the poem's expression, rhetorical figures, and formulation. All in all they were quite enamored of it. The judge who was being praised said, "By God there is something else about this poem that is even better than everything you have said and even more amazing. Hear it now." They said, "Our master's knowledge is more vast, and his contemplation and imagination more true! Of what has our master thought so highly?" "This entire poem is based on the letter *d*," he replied. "Every single line of it ends in *d*!" The simple fellow thought that rhyme was employed in this poem alone, and no other. 4.2.36

The Third Section, From Which Our Book Gets Its Title: What Should Be Done with Them, Namely, Taking Back the Property They Have Skimmed for Themselves from Public Funds Rightfully Belonging to the Muslims

I would therefore state (though success is God's alone to grant): Consider for a moment a person of the ilk I have described who obtains some administrative appointment, on which he depends exclusively for his income. Suppose that the income does not suffice to pay even the costs of his slave and his mount. Suppose further that after a very short time he begins to exhibit unmistakable signs of wealth, possessions, and benefactions, out of all proportion to the pay he receives. In such a case, it is patently obvious that the man has stolen his master's money and abused the authority granted to him. Indeed it can be known with complete certainty, not merely by conjecture and speculation. This is all the more true when the one whom he serves is sultan of a country and king of its people, and when the man's appointment relates to the land tax, or to some other public function such as supervision of the alms tax or inheritance. For these are appointments that entail authority over both the living and the dead. Here is how the crooked official will have operated. He takes a little here and a little there, buys from those beneath him against their will, and either sells back to them against their will or compels them to sell what they possess when 4.3.1

وتكرّر أخذه وخيانته وطالت مدّته حتّى نسي من أعطاه وٱستمرّ على خطاه فعلى هذه الحالة يجب أن يقطع عليه طريق آماله وأخذ جميع أمواله والدليل على ذلك إجماع المسلمين كافّة على أنّه من أخذ مالاً بغير حقّ من أناس متفرّقين وجهلهم لطول المدّة وكثرة العدّة بحيث تعذّر صرف ما أخذه منهم إليهم وجب حمله إلى بيت مال المسلمين بأسره ولا أعلم أحدًا من العلماء خالف في ذلك وسلك غيره من المسالك.

٢،٣،٤ وقد روى أبو حُميد الساعديّ أنّ رسول الله صلّى الله عليه وسلّم استعمل رجلاً من بني أسد يقال له ابن اللُّتبِيّة على الصدقة فلمّا قدم قال هذا لكم وهذا أُهْدِيَ إليّ. فرَقِي النبيّ صلّى الله عليه وسلّم المنبر وقال ما بال العامل نبعثه إلى بعض الأعمال فيقول هذا لكم وهذا أُهْدِيَ إليّ ألا جلس في بيت أبيه وأمّه ينظر أيُهدى إليه شيء أم لا؟ والذي نفسي بيده لا يأخذ أحد منها شيئًا إلّا جاء يوم القيامة يحمله على رقبته.

٣،٣،٤ وقد روي أنّ عمر بن الخطّاب رضي الله عنه رأى دارًا عالية البناء فقال لمن هذه فقيل لفلان لرجل استعمله فقال لي مع كلّ خائن أمينان الماء والطين أبتّ الدراهم الآن تمدّ أعناقها. وأمر بها لبيت المال وشاطره في ماله. وقوله تمدّ أعناقها يعني أنّ الخائن يحسّن الله له أن يبني ويعمّر فيفتضح بذلك فيطّلع عليه من له الأمر فيأخذه منه لبيت مال المسلمين. وقد روي أنّ عمر رضي الله عنه شاطر عمرو بن العاص ماله حتّى أخذ منه أحد خُفَّيه.

٤،٣،٤ وروي أنّه بعث إلى أبي عبيدة بن الجرّاح وكان مجرّدًا مع خالد بن الوليد في غزاة إنّه بلغني أنّ خالدًا أثرى بهذا العمل فعند وقوفك على كتابي[1] مدّ يدك إلى رأسه

---

١ ينتهي هاهنا نصّ المخطوطة ج.

it is inexpensive and in low demand, in order to pay what they owe. The buyer, of course, holds the goods until they regain value and are back in demand.

His coercion and malfeasance are repeated many times over, and for so long that he even forgets who has begrudgingly given him their possessions, and continues on in his harmful course. In this situation, there is no other option but to bar the way to what he purposes and to confiscate all his property. The reason for this is the universal agreement of all Muslims about the case of a person who unlawfully takes the property of a great many different people, so that he no longer knows their identities due to their great number and the time that has elapsed, making it impossible to return what he has taken. All that ill-gotten property must be conveyed to the central treasury of the Muslims. I know of no religious scholar who has disagreed with this or adopted some other position on the matter.[266]

According to a narration of Abū Ḥumayd al-Sāʿidī, the Messenger of God, God bless and keep him, employed a man of the Banū Asad called Ibn al-Lutbiyyah to take charge of the alms tax. When the man returned, he said to the Prophet, "This much is yours, but this was given me as a gift." 4.3.2

Then the Prophet, God bless and keep him, ascended the minbar and said, "How can it be that I send out my agent and he returns saying, 'This much is yours, but this was given me as a gift?' Why didn't he remain in the house of his father and mother to see whether or not any gifts would be given to him? By the One whose hand holds my soul, anyone who accepts such a gift will arrive carrying it around his neck on the Day of Resurrection."[267]

It is reported that ʿUmar ibn al-Khaṭṭāb, God be pleased with him, once saw a tall house. "Whose is this?" he asked. He was told that it belonged to a man in his employ. Then he said to me, "For every corrupt man I have two faithful witnesses: water and mud. Cut off the silver coins, for now they stick out their necks."[268] He commanded that the money be brought to the treasury and took half the man's property. The phrase "they stick out their necks" meant that God makes it seem a good idea for the corrupt person to build and construct, thereby exposing himself. In this way the ruler may become aware of what he is doing and take his possessions to the treasury of the Muslims. 4.3.3

It was also narrated that ʿUmar, God be pleased with him, took half of everything that ʿAmr ibn al-ʿĀṣ owned; he even took one of his shoes.

It is reported, too, that ʿUmar sent the following message to Abū ʿUbaydah when he was off on a military campaign with Khālid ibn al-Walīd: "I have 4.3.4

فخذ شطر عمامته ثمّ شاطره ماله فورد الكتاب إلى أبي عبيدة ووقف عليه بعض الحاضرين فرأى خالد التغيّر في وجه أبي عبيدة والحاضرين فقال ما شأنكم؟ قالوا ورد كتاب أمير المؤمنين بكذا وكذا فقال السمع والطاعة افعل يا أبا عبيدة ما أمرك به أمير المؤمنين ففعل وشاطره ماله. فهذا فعل عمر بن الخطّاب رضي الله عنه بخالد بن الوليد الذي قال في حقّه رسول الله صلّى الله عليه وسلّم إنّه سيف الله المسلول.[1]

وكتب[2] أبو المختار يزيد بن قيس بن يزيد بن عمرو بن خويلد الصعق النميري الشاعر إلى عمر بن الخطّاب بهذه الأبيات وهي [الطويل] ٥،٣،٤

أَبْلِغْ أَمِيرَ ٱلْمُؤْمِنِينَ رِسَالَةً ... فَأَنْتَ أَمِينُ ٱللهِ فِي ٱلْبَرِّ وَٱلْبَحْرِ
فَأَرْسِلْ إِلَى ٱلنُّعْمَانِ وَٱعْلَمْ حِسَابَهُ ... وَأَرْسِلْ إِلَى جَزْءٍ وَأَرْسِلْ إِلَى بِشْرِ
وَلَا تَدْعَنَّ ٱلنَّافِعَيْنِ كِلَيْهِمَا[3] ... وَذَاكَ ٱلَّذِي فِي ٱلسُّوقِ مَوْلَى بَنِي بَدْرِ
وَمَا عَاصِمٌ مِنْهَا بِصِفْرٍ عِيَابُهُ ... وَلَا ٱبْنُ غَلَابٍ مِنْ سُرَاةِ بَنِي نَصْرِ
نَبِيعُ إِذَا بَاعُوا وَنَغْزُوا إِذَا غَزَوْا ... فَإِنَّا لَهُمْ مَالٌ وَلَسْنَا بِذِي وَفْرِ[4]
تَرَى ٱلْجُرْدَ كَٱلْخِزَّانِ وَٱلْبِيضَ كَٱلدُّمَى ... وَمَا لَيْسَ يُلْفَى مِنْ قِرَامٍ وَمِنْ سِتْرِ
وَمِنْ رَيْطَةٍ مَطْوِيَّةٍ فِي صِيَانِهَا ... وَمِن طَيِّ أَسْتَارٍ مُعَصْفَرَةٍ حُمْرِ[5]
إِذَا ٱلتَّاجِرُ ٱلْهِنْدِيُّ جَاءَ بِفَارَةٍ ... مِنَ ٱلْمِسْكِ رَاحَتْ فِي مَفَارِقِهِمْ تَجْرِي
فَدُونَكَ مَالُ ٱللهِ لَا تَتْرُكَنَّهُ ... سَيَرْضَوْنَ إِنْ قَاسَمْتَهُمْ مِنْكَ بِٱلشَّطْرِ
وَلَا تَدْعُوَنِّي بِٱلشَّهَادَةِ إِنَّنِي ... أَغِيبُ وَلَكِنِّي أَرَى عَجَبَ ٱلدَّهْرِ

[1] يبدأ من هنا نقص كبير في ب،د. [2] ت: ولمّا كتب؛ والمثبت من فتوح مصر، ١٤٨. [3] ت: إليهما؛ والمثبت من فتوح مصر، ١٤٨. [4] ت: وفير؛ والمثبت من فتوح مصر، ١٤٨. [5] ت: أحمر؛ والمثبت من فتوح مصر، ١٤٨.

learnt that Khālid has enriched himself by means of this appointment. Therefore when you read this letter, grab his head and take half of his turban. Then take half his property."

When the letter reached Abū 'Ubaydah, he read it along with some other people there. Khālid noticed the change in their expressions, and asked, "What's the matter?" They replied that the Commander of the Believers had sent a letter, and told him what it contained.

"To hear is to obey," he said. "Abū 'Ubaydah, do as the Commander of the Believers has ordered." So he did and took half of Khālid's property. This, mind you, is what 'Umar ibn al-Khaṭṭāb, God be pleased with him, did with Khālid ibn al-Walīd himself, whom the Messenger of God, God bless and keep him, had called the Drawn Sword of God!

Abū l-Mukhtār Yazīd ibn Qays al-Numayrī the poet[269] wrote the following 4.3.5
to 'Umar ibn al-Khaṭṭāb:[270]

Deliver this letter to the Commander of the Believers:
"You are the trusted agent of God over land and sea,
Therefore, send to al-Nu'mān and examine his accounting.
Send likewise to Jaz', and to Bishr;
Do not neglect either of the Nāfi's,
or the one in the Market, the freedman of the Banū Badr.
Not empty of it are the coffers of 'Āṣim,
or those of Ibn Ghalāb, high in rank among the Banū Naṣr.
We buy when they sell, and raid when they do,
we are their property, though we have little.
You shall see beardless youths, numerous as hares; and fair girls
brightly bedizened,[271]
and such curtains and veils as are scarcely ever found,
And broadcloth, seamless and folded in its chest,
and creased coverlets dyed yellow and red.
When the trader from India comes, bearing a vessel of perfume
it runs down their parted hair.
Before you lies the wealth of God, do not abandon it;
if you demand the half of it they shall agree.
Do not call on me to testify, I only accuse
and yet I behold the wonder of the age."

فلمّا قرأ عمر الأبيات قال إنّا قد أعفيناه[1] من الشهادة ونأخذ منهم نصف أموالهم.

وكان ممّن قاسمه من عمّاله وأخذ منه نصف ماله الحجّاج بن عتيك الثقفيّ وكان على الفرات ومشاجع بن مسعود السلميّ وهو صهر بني غزوان كانت عنده بنت عتبة ابن غزوان وكان على أرض البصرة وصدقاتها وشِبل بن معبد البجَليّ ثمّ الأحمسيّ كان على قبض المغانم وأبو مريم بن محرّش الحنفيّ كان على رام هُرمز وعاصم بن قيس بن الصلت السُلميّ كان على المناذر[2] والصدقة وابن غلاب خالد بن الحارث بن أوس بن دهمان كان على بيت المال بإصبهان وسَمُرة بن جندب كان على سوق الأهواز وجزء ابن معاوية عمّ الأحنف كان على سُرّق وبشر بن المحتفز المُزَنيّ كان يلي جند سابور ونافع بن الحارث وأخوه نفيع أبو بكرة كانا على غنائم الأُبُلّة.

وبعث محمّد بن مَسلَمة رضي الله عنه إلى عمرو بن العاص وكتب إليه أمّا بعد فإنّكم معشر العمّال قد قعدتم على عيون الأموال فجبيتم الحرام وأكلتم الحرام وأورثتم الحرام وقد بعثت إليك محمّد بن مسلمة الأنصاريّ ليقاسمك مالك فأحضره مالك والسلام. ٦،٣،٤

فلمّا قدم محمّد بن مسلمة مصر أهدى له عمرو بن العاص هديّة فردّها عليه فغضب عمرو وقال يا محمّد لِمَ رددت إليّ[3] هديّتي وقد أهديت إلى رسول الله صلّى الله عليه وسلّم مقدّمي من غزوة ذات السلاسل فقبل فقال له محمّد إنّ رسول الله صلّى الله عليه وسلّم كان يقبل بالوحي ما شاء ويمتنع ممّا شاء ولو كانت هديّة الأخ إلى أخيه قبلتها ولكنّها هديّة إمام شرّ خلفها فقال عمرو قبّح الله يوماً صرت فيه لعمر ابن الخطّاب والياً فلقد رأيت العاص بن وائل يلبس الديباج المزرّر بالذهب وإنّ

---

١ ت: أعطيناه؛ والمثبت من فتوح مصر، ١٤٨. ٢ ت: المنابر؛ والمثبت من فتوح البلدان، ٥٤١–٤٢. ٣ ت: إليه؛ والمثبت من فتوح مصر، ١٤٦.

When ʿUmar read these lines, he said, "We excuse him from testifying, and will take from them half their property."

Among his agents whose possessions he divided, taking half their property, were: al-Ḥajjāj ibn ʿAtīk al-Thaqafī, who had charge of the Euphrates province; Mushājiʿ ibn Masʿūd al-Sulamī, who was related by marriage to the Banū Ghazwān, being married to the daughter of ʿUtbah ibn Ghazwān, and who had charge of the land around Basra and the alms tax there; Shibl ibn Maʿbad al-Bajalī—later al-Aḥmasī—who was charged with collecting the spoils of conquest; Abū Maryam ibn al-Muḥarrish al-Ḥanafī, who was appointed over Rāmhurmuz; ʿĀṣim ibn Qays ibn al-Ṣalt al-Sulamī, who was appointed over al-Manādhir and over the alms tax; Ibn Ghalāb, Khālid ibn al-Ḥārith ibn Aws ibn al-Duhmān, who was appointed over the treasury in Isfahan; Samurah ibn Jundab, who supervised the Market of al-Ahwāz; Jazʾ ibn Muʿāwiyah, the uncle of al-Aḥnaf, who had charge of Surraq; Bishr ibn al-Muḥtafiz al-Muzanī, who had authority over Jundishapur; Nāfiʿ ibn al-Ḥārith and his brother Nufayʿ Abū Bakrah, who together administered the spoils of conquest in al-Ubullah.

ʿUmar also sent Muḥammad ibn Maslamah, God be pleased with him, to ʿAmr ibn al-ʿĀṣ, writing, "You appointees have seated yourselves at the sources of wealth, collecting what is forbidden, consuming what is forbidden, and bequeathing what is forbidden. I have sent Muḥammad ibn Maslamah al-Anṣārī to you, in order that he might confiscate half your property. Therefore, present your property to him. Farewell." 4.3.6

When Muḥammad ibn Maslamah arrived in Egypt, ʿAmr ibn al-ʿĀṣ gave him a gift, but he gave it back. ʿAmr grew angry and said, "Muḥammad, why do you return my gift, when the Messenger of God, God bless and keep him, accepted the plunder I presented him from the Dhāt al-Salāsil Expedition?" Muḥammad replied, "The Messenger of God, God bless and keep him, accepted and rejected as he saw fit, according to the guidance of revelation. If this were the gift of one brother to another, then I would accept it. But in fact it is the gift of a leader, which might leave evil in its path."

ʿAmr said, "God curse the day I became a governor for ʿUmar ibn al-Khaṭṭāb! I saw my father al-ʿĀṣ ibn Wāʾil wearing silk brocade with gold buttons, while ʿUmar's father al-Khaṭṭāb ibn Nufayl carried firewood on a donkey in Mecca." Muḥammad ibn Maslamah said to him, "Your father and his are both in hell, and ʿUmar is a better man than you. And if not for what you said today, which you already regret, I would have gone on thinking of you as nothing but a

الخطّاب بن نفيل يحمل الحطب على حمارٍ بمكّة فقال له محمّد بن مسلمة أبوك وأبوه في النار وعمر خير منك ولولا اليوم الذي أصبحت تذمّ لألفيت معتقلاً عنزًا يسرّك غُزرها ويسوؤك بكؤها فقال عمرو هي فلتة الغضب وهي عندك بأمانة. ثمّ أحضره ماله فقاسمه إيّاه ثمّ رجع.

٤،٣،٧ وروي عن جعفر بن ربيعة عن أبيه أنّ جدّه أُوصي أن يدفع إلى عمر بن الخطّاب نصف ماله وكان عمر استعمله على بعض أعماله.

٤،٣،٨ وروي أنّ أبا هريرة رضي الله عنه قال لمّا قدمت من البحرين قال لي عمر يا عدوّ الله وعدوّ الإسلام خُنت مال الله قال قلت لست بعدوّ الله ولا عدوّ الإسلام ولكنّي عدوّ من عاداهما ولم أخن مال الله ولكنّها أثمان خيل لي تناتجت وسهام اجتمعت. قال عدوّ الله وعدوّ الإسلام خنت مال الله قال قلت لست بعدوّ الله ولا عدوّ الإسلام ولكنّي عدوّ من عاداهما ولم أخن مال الله ولكنّها أثمان خيل لي تناتجت وسهام اجتمعت. قال ذلك ثلاث مرّات يقول ذلك عمر ويردّ عليه أبو هريرة هذا القول قال فغرمني إثني عشر ألفًا فقمت في صلاة الغداة فقلت اللّهمّ اغفر لأمير المؤمنين.

فأرادني على العمل بعد فقلت لا قال أوليس يوسف خير منك وقد سأل العمل قلت إنّ يوسف نبيّ ابن نبيّ بن نبيّ بن نبيّ وأنا ابن أُميمة وأنا أخاف ثلاثًا واثنتين قال ألا تقول خمسًا قلت لا قال مه قال قلت إنّي أخاف أن أقول بغير حلم وأقضي بغير علم وأن يُضرب ظهري ويشتم عرضي ويؤخذ مالي.[١]

١ ينتهي هاهنا النقص الكبير في ب،د.

docile little nanny goat that makes me happy when it gives milk and sad when it runs dry."

"It was a slip of anger," ʿAmr replied. "Consider it a secret that you hold in trust." ʿAmr brought his property, and Muḥammad ibn Maslamah confiscated half, and returned to Medina.[272]

It is also narrated, from Jaʿfar ibn Rabīʿah, who heard it from his father, that 4.3.7
his grandfather was charged to pay half his property to ʿUmar ibn al-Khaṭṭāb when he was appointed in a certain district.

It is narrated that Abū Hurayrah, God be pleased with him, said, "When I 4.3.8
returned from al-Baḥrayn, ʿUmar said to me, 'Enemy of God! Enemy of Islam! You have been dishonest with God's property!'" Abū Hurayrah continued, "I said, 'I am no enemy of God, nor am I an enemy of Islam. I am, rather, the enemy of anyone who opposes them. And I have not been dishonest with God's property. In fact what you see is what I have earned from my horses, which have bred and multiplied, and my shares of the spoils of conquest, which have accumulated.' 'Enemy of God! Enemy of Islam!' ʿUmar replied. 'You have been dishonest with God's property!' Again I said, 'I am no enemy of God, nor am I an enemy of Islam. I am rather the enemy of anyone who opposes them. And I have not been dishonest with God's property. In fact what you see is what I have earned from my horses, which have bred and multiplied, and my shares of the spoils of conquest, which have accumulated.'" He said this three times, with ʿUmar beginning and Abū Hurayrah responding in the same way. Abū Hurayrah continued: "Then ʿUmar fined me twelve thousand coins. So when I arose to pray the morning prayer, I said, 'O God, forgive the Commander of the Believers.'

"After this ʿUmar wanted to appoint me as an official again, but I demurred. He said, 'Is not the prophet Joseph, who put himself forward for appointment, a better man than you?' I said, 'Joseph was a prophet, the son of a prophet, who was the son of a prophet, who was the son of a prophet. I, however, am the son of my mother Umaymah,[273] and I am afraid of three and two.'

"'You mean five?' said ʿUmar.

"'No!' I said.

"'What do you mean?' he asked.

"I said, 'I fear lest I speak without understanding and judge without knowledge. And I fear, too, lest my back be flogged, my honor impugned, and my property confiscated.'"[274]

فما ظنّنا بهؤلاء الخونة اللصوص الأقباط الذين بنوا الأملاك والقصور والمناظر على البحر وفي البرّ وظهر من نعمهم ما لا يمكن ستره ولا يخافون عاقبة من له الأمر في أملاكهم؟ وقد سمّاها عمر بن الخطّاب شهود الخيانة فقال لي مع كلّ خائن أمينان الماء والطين، معناه متى خان المتصرّف أظهر الله خيانته ببنيان يبنيه فيكون شاهداً على خيانته. ٩،٣،٤

وليس ذلك ببدع من إقدام هؤلاء وجهلهم وسوء نظرهم في عواقب الأمور ولقد أحسن محمّد بن عبد الملك الزيّات فيما اعتمده مع الخليفة لمّا استوزره لفضيلته وأدبه فإنّه قال اصطنعني أمير المؤمنين صنيعة تفرّد بها إذ نقلني من ذلّ التجارة إلى عزّ الوزارة وأحبّ أن يحدّ لي حدّاً ويكتب لي عهداً فإنّ من أصحّ ما استدلّ به على خيانة الرجل أن يكون لا مال له ويظهر له بعد خدمته مال أو يكون له مقدار معلوم فيظهر له ما هو أكثر وأمير المؤمنين خبير بما شاع من كثرة مال أبي وأنّه خلف لي من المال سبعين ألف دينار ومن الأملاك ما تضمّنه هذا الكتاب وقد أحضرت الشهود وأريتهم المال وأوقفتهم على الكتب وكتبت الجميع في هذا المسطور وأخذت شهادتهم به ليكون في خزانة أمير المؤمنين فإن زاد للعبد شيء فممّا أنعم به أمير المؤمنين عليه أو ممّا خان[1] فيه فحسب[2] ما يحصّل من جاه العمل مع الأمانة انصرف[3] في أرزاق الكتّاب ونفقاتهم يستعينون بها على كلفهم في أكثر الأوقات والسلام.

١ كذا في ب، ت؛ وفي د: خاف. ٢ كذا في ب،د؛ وفي ت: بحسب. ٣ كذا في ت؛ وفي ب،د: أن يصرف.

What, then, are we supposed to think about these thieving, dishonest Copts, who amass estates, palaces, and towers by the sea and on the land, whose luxuries are plainly evident and cannot be hidden away, who have no fear that any consequence from those in authority will affect their estates? These estates ʿUmar ibn al-Khaṭṭāb called "witnesses to corruption," for he said, "For every corrupt man, I have two faithful witnesses: water and mud."[275] He meant that when an official is corrupt, God makes plain his corruption in what he builds, which is then witness to it. 4.3.9

Nor is this some new thing, some innovation of these people's effrontery and ignorance, or of their failure to consider consequences. Muḥammad ibn ʿAbd al-Malik al-Zayyāt, for example, did a very fine thing when the caliph made him vizier because of his excellence and refinement. He said, "The Commander of the Believers has done me a good turn, the like of which no one else has ever performed; he has transported me from the humiliation of commerce to the glory of the vizierate.[276] I desire, therefore, that he clearly delimit my position by writing a covenant for me. One of the truest signs of a man's dishonesty is that he should at first have no wealth, then become manifestly wealthy after his appointment, or that he should possess a known quantity of property and then suddenly appear with more. The Commander of the Believers is acquainted with my father's well-known wealth. He knows that my father left seventy thousand gold coins to me, along with the estates listed in this document. I have therefore brought lawful witnesses, showed them this property, and showed them the documents. I have furthermore written down everything in this register and recorded their witness to its contents, so that it might be kept in the treasury of the Commander of the Believers. If the servant should add anything to his possessions, then whatever its source—whether it be from what the Commander of the Believers has bestowed upon him or by his own dishonesty—it comes from the combination of his lofty rank and the trust placed in him. Let it be spent to maintain the secretaries, and for their outlays, that they may call on it often for their expenses. Farewell."[277]

فصل أختم به هذا الكتاب وأترجم فيه عن سبب وضعي إيّاه[1]

١،٤،٤ فأقول إن وقف واقف على هذا الكتاب وعلم تعبي فيه واستقرائي أحوال هؤلاء الأقباط من عهد رسول الله صلّى الله عليه وسلّم وما جرى لهم وعليهم في زمن خليفة بعد خليفة وملك بعد ملك إلى آخر الدولة الصلاحيّة الناصريّة فيقول ما الذي حمل مؤلّف هذا الكتاب على مطالعة المقام الشريف السلطانيّ سيّد ملوك العصر لعورات هؤلاء القوم وتعريضه بهم وفتواه بأخذ أموالهم وأملاكهم؟

٢،٤،٤ فالجواب وبالله التوفيق قسمي بالله سبحانه أنّه ما حملني على ذلك إلّا أمور ثلاثة أحدها غيرتي على مال الله تعالى الذي هو ذخيرة المسلمين وكنز عصابة هذا الدين. والثاني محبّتي في دولة مولانا السلطان خلّد الله ملكه ما أراه واجباً عليّ وعلى كلّ مسلم من عرض النصائح بين يدي مواقفه الشريفة.[2] والثالث ما رأيت من إفراط غنى هؤلاء الأقباط الذين خدموا في الخدم القليلة وهم لا يقدرون على شيء فأصبح لهم من الأموال الظاهرة والأملاك الباهرة والتجمّل والبذخ ما لا يقتضيه نزارة ما قرّر لهم واتّسعوا في الأموال حتّى جمعوا بين تجارة البرّ والبحر والسواقي والزروع والمواشي والتحف والأملاك والجواهر إلى غير ذلك من أنواع المال.[3]

ولقد وُلّيت النظر في الدواوين الكبار ووُلّيت أكثر الوجهين القبليّ والبحريّ وأكثر معاملات الباب عشرين سنة ووُلّيت نظر الوجه القبليّ والبحريّ بكمالهما ومعاملات أُخر وإنّي في خلال هؤلاء الولايات بعت ما ورثته من أبي من أملاك بالشام وتساوي خمسة آلاف دينار وأنفقت الجميع في ثياب ودوابّ وغلمان وأصبحت في أسر إثنين وخمسين نفرًا من أولاد وأولاد أولاد وعيالي ليس لي ولا لهم في الدنيا

١ كذا في ت؛ والعبارة الأخيرة ساقطة في ب،د. ٢ كذا في ت؛ وفي ب،د: آرائه العالية. ٣ يختلف من هنا النصّ في ب،د إلى آخر الكتاب. ويأتي فيهما: ومن سلك الأمانة وأركب سبلها وجاش خلالها تفيّأ ظلّها أصبح فقيرًا وأمسى لا يملك قطيرًا فقد قام الدليل على أنّ ذلك من بيت المال من مكاسب الأعمال والواجب استرجاع ذلك إلى بيت مال المسلمين ليكون ذخيرة للدين والحمد لله (ثمّ يأتي في ب: ربّ العالمين تمّ وحسبنا الله ونعم الوكيل؛ وفي د: وحده وصلّى الله على سيّدنا محمّد وعلى آله وصحبه وسلّم تسليمًا كثيرًا).

A Section with Which I End This Book, Explaining My Reason for Composing It

I suspect that a certain question will occur to anyone who comes across this book and understands the effort that I invested in it, and how I examined the affairs of these Copts since the age of the Prophet, God bless and keep him, and their rise and fall in the time of caliph after caliph and king after king down to the most recent days of Ṣalāḥ al-Dīn's dynasty.[278] The question is this: What led the author of this book to acquaint his highness—the sultan, lord of the kings of this age—with the defects of these people? Why did he bring them to his attention and advise him to take their property and their estates? 4.4.1

The answer is this (though success is God's alone to grant): I swear to God, be He glorified, that three things alone led me to write this. The first is my zeal for «God's wealth,»[279] which is the Muslims' provision and the treasure of the adherents of their religion. The second is my love for the reign of our lord the sultan, may God make his rule everlasting, for I believe it to be incumbent upon me and upon every Muslim to offer sincere advice to his highness. The third is the excessive wealth of these Copts, which I have beheld with my own eyes. Although they serve in offices of little consequence and have no ability to speak of, they somehow acquire the trappings of wealth, splendid possessions, adornment, haughtiness, and accoutrement entirely out of proportion to their pay. They expand their prosperity to trading on land and sea, to waterwheels and agriculture, to livestock and luxury items, to durable goods, jewels, and various other kinds of possessions. 4.4.2

I, by contrast, have been appointed overseer in major offices. I was appointed over most of the two halves of Egypt, Upper Egypt and the Delta, as well as over the better part of the central administrative affairs for twenty years. I was also appointed supervisor of Upper Egypt and the Delta in their totality, and to other positions as well. In the course of all these appointments I sold the possessions in Syria that I inherited from my father, possessions whose value came to five thousand gold coins. I spent all of it on clothing, riding animals, and servants. I became burdened by a family that grew to include fifty-two persons: children, grandchildren, and wives. Neither they nor I have any stipend in the world, nor any source from which so much as a single silver coin might come to us (or less, let alone more). We scrape by on the income from an endowment that my father made for us, God show him mercy. Most of it is in ruins, since we lack the means to maintain it.

راتب ولا جهة يأتينا منها درهم ولا أقلّ من ذلك ولا أكثر ولا أعيش أنا وهم إلّا من أجرة وقف وقفه علينا والدي رحمه الله وقد خرب أكثره لعجزنا عن عمارته ولم يبقَ لي في الدنيا ملك ولا حصّة في ملك ولا عقار ولا أغنام ولا أبقار ولا ساقية ولا زرع ولا وجه من وجوه المكاسب على اختلافها وتقهقرت في دنياي من عشرة مماليك إلى مملوكين روم ما يساويان ثلاثين ديناراً ومن ستّة عشر رأساً من خيول وبغال خاصّ إلى ثلاثة أرؤس ضعاف وصرت كما قال الشاعر [الكامل]

وَأَعِيْشُ بِٱلرِّزْقِ ٱلَّذِي لَوْ أَنَّهُ   دَمْعٌ لَمَا ٱبْتَلَّتْ بِهِ ٱلآمَاقُ

وبقيت أنا والأولاد نجتهد في ستر ظاهرنا للناس بما نقدر عليه من التجمّل ونكتم باطن أحوالنا بيننا فأنا وهم كما قال الله تعالى ﴿يَحْسَبُهُمُ الْجَاهِلُ أَغْنِيَاءَ مِنَ التَّعَفُّفِ تَعْرِفُهُمْ بِسِيمَاهُمْ لَا يَسْأَلُونَ النَّاسَ إِلْحَافًا﴾.

وعلمت إذاً أنّ سبب ما انتهى إليه حالي من الضائقة ما لزمته من الأمانة وأنّ سبب اتّساع هؤلاء ما اعتمدوه من الخيانة وما أنا والأولاد وأولادهم والعيال راجون من الله تعالى أنْ يتولّانا بنظرة من نظراته وأن يلمّ شعث أحوالنا ببركة من بركاتها إنّه وليّ ذلك والقادر عليه.

والحمد لله وحده وصلاته وسلامه على سيّده محمّد وآله وصحبه الطيّبين الطاهرين والتابعين وتابعيهم إلى يوم الدين وحسبنا الله ونعم الوكيل. ٣،٤،٤

I have no remaining possessions or share of possessions in the world, neither real estate nor cattle nor mill nor field nor any kind of trade. My worldly condition has deteriorated, from ten slaves to just two, Greeks worth scarcely thirty gold coins, and from sixteen fine horses and mules to three weak beasts. I have fallen into that state that a poet describes:

> I live by such provision that, were it tears,
> the corners of the eye would never be damp.[280]

The children and I try to put a good face on things for other people, acting as prosperous as we can while hiding the real state of affairs amongst ourselves. They and I are, as God, be He exalted, said: «The ignorant man supposes them rich because of their abstinence, but thou shalt know them by their mark; they do not beg of men importunately.»[281]

I have concluded that the cause of my straitened circumstance is that I have remained honest in my dealings, and that the cause of the affluence of these Copts is that they have consistently condoned malfeasance. So the children, grandchildren, women, and I all hope that God will take care of us with his compassionate glance, and that He will arrange our disordered affairs through one of his blessings. He attends to such matters and is Most Capable.

Praise be to God alone, and may his blessing and peace be upon his noble Muḥammad, his kin and Companions pure and good, and Followers, and those who follow them, up until the Day of Judgment. God is our sufficiency. How excellent a guardian is He! **4.4.3**

Notes

1 The last phrase refers to the grave error of *shirk*, associating "partners" with God. A person commits *shirk* when he or she, though acknowledging God in some sense, worships Him alongside or through other beings ("partners"). Here the author, somewhat unusually, implicates all non-Muslims, Jews and Christians included, in the commission of *shirk*.

2 Literally, "the red and the black." This phrase, based on a Prophetic hadith, is variously understood in the tradition (e.g., as humans and jinn). For various views, see Goldziher, *Introduction*, 28 n. 34. See further Goldenberg, *The Curse of Ham*, 298 n. 92.

3 This edict was probably the one promulgated in 640/1242 (see Khater and Burmester, *History of the Patriarchs*, 247 [trans.]/120 [ed.]). The edict to which Cahen connected the present work was in fact issued before the reign of al-Malik al-Ṣāliḥ, in 636/1239 (see Cahen, "Histoires coptes d'un cadi médiéval," 134; Khater and Burmester, *History of the Patriarchs*, 189–91 [trans.]/92–93 [ed.]). The requirement that dhimmis "remove the fringes," mentioned for the earlier edict in the *History of the Patriarchs* (which uses the term *dhawāʾib*), probably refers to decorative fringes on turbans or cowls. Earlier edicts of this nature also placed restrictions on fringes, using the same term that our author does here (*ʿadhab*); see Yarbrough, "Origins of the *ghiyār*," 117.

4 Viz., the Qur'an.

5 Q Fuṣṣilat 41:42.

6 Q Mā'idah 5:80–81.

7 Q Mā'idah 5:51.

8 Q Mumtaḥanah 60:1.

9 This passage constitutes the only known reference to this work. For a possible motive for its composition, see the Introduction.

10 This hadith appears in numerous collections. It was disseminated energetically by Mālik ibn Anas (d. 179/796), the famous jurist and eponym of the Mālikī legal rite (*madhhab*). For other versions, see, e.g., Abū Dā'ūd, *Sunan*, 2:280, no. 2732; Ibn Ḥanbal, *Musnad*, 40:450, no. 24386; 42:80–81, no. 25158. On its transmission history and for all known versions, see Yarbrough, "I'll not accept aid from a *mushrik*."

11 I am aware of no other attestations of these aphorisms.

12 The focus on employing polytheists in an otherwise standard account of these wars is unusual.

13 Cf. al-Jahshiyārī, *Kitāb al-wuzarāʾ*, 16–17; al-Balādhurī, *Futūḥ al-buldān*, 630–31 (*The Origins of the Islamic State, Part. II*, 240–41); *Radd*, 29–30. The directive not to employ infidels is not found in the early versions of this account.

14 Cf. *Aḥkām*, 1:211; *Madhammah*, 54. The phrases "to write" and "writing is the glory of" are conjectural emendations, without which the sentence makes little sense.

15 The month of Muharram immediately follows Dhu l-Hijjah in the Islamic calendar. Cf. Ibn Kathīr, *Al-Bidāyah wa-l-nihāyah*, 4:510–16.

16 Cf. *Aḥkām*, 1:211; *Madhammah*, 54.

17 Cf. *Aḥkām*, 1:211; *Madhammah*, 54; *Radd*, 30. This common parable is usually explained as a thought experiment; if the Christian or Jewish official were to die unexpectedly of natural causes, what would the Muslim governor do to replace him?

18 Cf. Ibn Qutaybah, *ʿUyūn al-akhbār*, 1:43: "His secretarial skills are mine, but his religion is his." The phrase echoes Q Kāfirūn 109:6.

19 Q Ḥajj 22:18. For the other surviving versions of this report, see Yarbrough, "Upholding God's Rule."

20 Cf. *Radd*, 30.

21 Not elsewhere attested, except in the *Radd* (38), which is in all likelihood derived from the present work. The exact meaning of the final line is unclear; in general terms, it states that the Umayyad caliphs are conduits of the continuing divine guidance that was brought initially by the Prophet.

22 For a discussion of this and similar accounts, see Noth and Conrad, *The Early Arabic Historical Tradition*, 189.

23 That is, to commit the crime of theft, for which the punishment in Islamic law is fixed as amputation.

24 On these events, see the classic studies of Sprengling in the Bibliography. Gold coins (dinars) tended to carry on East Roman conventions, including Greek and Latin inscriptions in some instances, while early Islamic silver coins (dirhams) continued Sasanian Persian iconography, including Pahlavi inscriptions.

25 I.e., to list their faults would do more harm than good.

26 Q Tawbah 9:28.

27 Q Mujādilah 58:19.

28 Q Kahf 18:103–04.

29 Q Āl ʿImrān 3:87.

30 This is an accurate general description of policy in the immediate aftermath of the conquests, whereby existing administrative structures and personnel were left in place to collect revenues and manage local affairs.

31 For this report and the preceding, cf. *Aḥkām*, 1:212–13; *Madhammah*, 57–58; Ibn ʿAbd al-Ḥakam, *Sīrat ʿUmar b. ʿAbd al-ʿAzīz*, 135–36.

32 In other words, the Byzantine emperor. The trope of ʿUmar ibn ʿAbd al-ʿAzīz corresponding with a Byzantine emperor is a well-established one. See, for example, his putative correspondence with the emperor Leo III, discussed in Hoyland, *Seeing Islam*, 490–501.

33 Q Anbiyāʾ 21:78–79. Cf. *Aḥkām*, 1:213–14; *Madhammah*, 59; *Radd*, 36–37. According to the early exegetes, these verses refer to a legal dispute that was brought before the prophet Dāwūd (David). Some livestock had wandered into a neighbor's field and damaged the crops. Dāwūd judged in favor of the neighbor, but his son Sulaymān (Solomon), guided by God, wisely amended the particulars of his father's ruling. Here ʿUmar ibn ʿAbd al-ʿAzīz, casting himself in the role of Sulaymān, identifies a Qurʾanic precedent for changing earlier caliphs' policy toward churches. For a setting of the same story in which the caliph is al-Walīd I, the emperor Justinian II, and the scriptural riposte delivered by the poet Al-Farazdaq, see Ibn Khallikān, *Wafayāt*, 6:97.

34 Q Māʾidah 5:57.

35 Cf. *Aḥkām*, 1:214; *Madhammah*, 60; al-Ṭurṭūshī, *Sirāj al-mulūk*, 403; above all al-Jahshiyārī, *Kitāb al-wuzarāʾ*, 40.

36 Q Ghāfir 40:52.

37 The manuscripts give the date as 258 AH. However, Caliph al-Manṣūr died in 158. The copyist of manuscript T corrected the error in the margin. Cf. *Aḥkām*, 1:214–15; *Madhammah*, 61–63.

38 Q Aḥzāb 33:72.

39 Q Anʿām 6:62.

40 Cf. *Aḥkām*, 1:215–16; *Madhammah*, 66–67; *Radd*, 44.

41 The judge here is meant to be Sawwār ibn ʿAbdallāh al-Tamīmī, who however is widely held to have died in 156/773, two years before al-Mahdī became caliph. It cannot be his son, ʿAbdallāh ibn Sawwār, as he was not appointed until 192/807–8. This is likely an anachronism introduced by a later historian. For a similar story involving a Kufan judge in the same period, see Yarbrough, "Upholding God's Rule," 71–75.

42 Cf. *Aḥkām*, 1:216–17; *Madhammah*, 67–68.

43 Cf. *Aḥkām*, 1:217; *Madhammah*, 69; *Radd*, 42; al-Jahshiyārī, *Kitāb al-wuzarāʾ*, 34 (a more verisimilar version of the story that takes place in the reign of al-Manṣūr).

44 In the parallel accounts of *Aḥkām*, *Madhammah*, and *Radd*: "'Amr." In any case, this individual is not otherwise attested.

45 These towns are both in upper Egypt. They are not obvious magnets for aspiring doctors and secretaries. The general notion seems to be that the Copts' acquisition of these arts was a strategy used to gain influence. Upper Egypt, where the population remained heavily Christian in the thirteenth century, provides a plausible setting in which to place the origins of this strategy.

46 The poet Khālid ibn Ṣafwān (d. ca. 135/752) could scarcely have addressed ʿAmr ibn al-ʿĀṣ (d. ca. 42/663); ʿAmr's name may be synecdoche for any Muslim ruler of Egypt.

47 *Aḥkām*, 1:218; *Madhammah*, 71–72; *Radd*, 39.

48 This anecdote is anachronistic; the grammarian al-Kisāʾī died in 189/805, long before the accession of al-Maʾmūn, his erstwhile pupil.

49 Q Māʾidah 5:51.

50 Cf. *Radd*, 41.

51 Cf. *Aḥkām*, 1:219; *Madhammah*, 73–74; *Radd*, 48. The poem in this story refers to the Prophet. For other versions of this incident, see Yarbrough, "Upholding God's Rule," 12 n. 1.

52 I have not found this poem attested elsewhere. It draws an analogy between a common means of humiliation, striking an inferior person on the nape of the neck (here performed upon the Christian with a shoe), and a cat catching a mouse.

53 This poem is otherwise attested only in the *Radd* (61).

54 It is highly likely that an earlier version of the story gave the name ʿUbaydallāh ibn Yaḥyā ibn Khāqān here, though this noted official of Caliph al-Mutawakkil apparently did have a brother called ʿAbdallāh (Al-Ṭabarī, *History of al-Ṭabarī, Incipient Decline*, 161).

55 Cf. *Aḥkām*, 1:219–21; *Madhammah*, 75–78.

56 Cf. *Aḥkām*, 1:221; *Madhammah*, 78–79.

57 Cf. *Aḥkām*, 1:221–22; *Madhammah*, 79–80.

58 Cf. *Aḥkām*, 1:222; *Madhammah*, 80.

59 Q Āl ʿImrān 3:85.

60 Q Yā Sīn 36:70.

61 Q Fuṣṣilat 41:42.

62 Q Āl ʿImrān 3:110.

63 Cf. Q Āl ʿImrān 3:112.

64 Q Tawbah 9:29.

65 Q Āl ʿImrān 3:118.

66 Q Baqarah 2:255; Anʿām 6:102; Ḥashr 59:23, etc.

67 Q Anʿām 6:163.

68 Cf. *Aḥkām*, 1:222–24; *Madhammah*, 80–84.

69 Q Ghāfir 40:19.

70 Cf. *Aḥkām*, 1:224; *Madhammah*, 85. In place of the name "Mu'nis," manuscripts of the present work offer *sūs* or *shūsh* an evident corruption. I derive the reading "Mu'nis" from the parallel versions of this story in *Aḥkām* and *Madhammah*.

71 Q Ibrāhīm 14:47.

72 Q Qaṣaṣ 28:83.

73 Cf. *Aḥkām*, 224–25; *Madhammah*, 85–86; al-Qalqashandī, *Ṣubḥ al-aʿshā*, 13:368–69 (Al-Qalqashandī's use of this passage, and of several others that also appear here, derives from the work of Ibn al-Naqqāsh. See Yarbrough, "A Rather Small Genre").

74 Quite possibly the Prophet's city of Medina in the Hijaz. The story does not specify a geographical setting, but al-Miqdād was remembered in connection with the Hijaz.

75 Cf. *Radd*, 48–49; Ibn al-Mawṣilī, *Ḥusn al-sulūk*, 132. The latter passage derives ultimately from the same source as the account here (Yarbrough, "A Rather Small Genre").

76 Q Āl ʿImrān 3:19.

77 Cf. *Radd*, 49.

78 Cf. *Radd*, 50.

79 The author is comparing Jews to the Christians, who are his primary target.

80 For parallel versions of this hadith, which early sources appear to lack, see Ibn Taymiyyah, *Mas'alah fī l-kanā'is*, 137; al-Sakhāwī, *al-Ajwibah al-marḍiyyah*, 2:861; al-Qalqashandī, *Ṣubḥ*, 13:386. Al-Sakhāwī endorses the sentiment expressed in the hadith but evades the question of whether it was really transmitted from the Prophet. In the work of al-Qalqashandī, it is found in a lengthy edict ascribed to the Mamluk sultan al-Malik al-Ṣāliḥ Ṣāliḥ ibn Muḥammad (r. 752–55/1351–54).

81 Literally, "death."

82 Cf. *Radd*, 43. The first line has too many syllables for the meter. This section, like §1.12.1 above, is an unusually hostile narrative of Coptic history. Other Muslim treatments of the subject from medieval Egypt are quite irenic. See, e.g., Antrim, *Routes and Realms*, 135.

83 The Wednesday itself is included in the count of days remaining before the end of Ramadan.

84 The subject of this sentence is more typically "the Muslims." See, e.g., Ibn Mājah, *Sunan*, 2:826–27. For an example with "people" as subject, see Abū ʿUbayd, *Kitāb al-amwāl*, 1:413–14. In most versions, the two remaining free resources are fire and water.

85 Here the author implies a critique of what he sees as an unlawful tax collected by the Ayyubid state in his own day. He traces its origins to the Copts, who, he informs the sultan, are its originators and ultimately to blame for it. However, the historical account closest to these purported events (and probably the ultimate source of this report),

the *Sīrat Aḥmad ibn Ṭūlūn* of al-Balawī, places the blame for the government monopolies squarely on Ibn Ṭūlūn's conniving finance official, the Muslim Ibn al-Mudabbir. The Copts go unmentioned in al-Balawī's account (al-Balawī, *Sīrah*, 43). I am grateful to Matthew Gordon for drawing my attention to this source.

86 This saying, with "theft" in place of "deceit," was part of a longer series of similar sayings attributed to the Prophet. See Abū l-Shaykh, *Kitāb al-ʿAẓamah*, 5:1636–37. Al-Maqrīzī attributes such a saying (with "cunning" for "deceit") to the Companion Ibn ʿAbbās (*al-Mawāʿiẓ*, 1:131), as does Ibn Taghrī Birdī (*al-Nujūm al-zāhirah*, 1:66). I have not succeeded in locating it among the surviving writings of al-Jāḥiẓ. But the misascription is not Ibn al-Nābulusī's; cf. another appropriation of the unidentified source for this passage in al-Saffārīnī, *Ghidhāʾ al-albāb*, 2:15.

87 "Rubbish" in Arabic is *qumāmah*, a common slur on the name of the Church of the Resurrection, *al-qiyāmah* (i.e., the Holy Sepulcher). The slur is produced by the substitution of one Arabic letter (قمامة for قيامة).

88 Cf., e.g., [Abū Ṣāliḥ the Armenian], *The Churches and Monasteries of Egypt*, 150. In the manuscripts of the present work, the name of this church is given as *al-ʿumrā*; multiple independent sources, however, indicate that the correct reading is *al-ʿajūz*, which means "the old woman." See Timm, *Das christlich-koptische Ägypten in arabischer Zeit*, 2:352; Abū l-Makārim, *Tārīkh Abū l-Makārim*, vol. 1, fol. 75A. I thank Alexander Treiger for his advice concerning this matter.

89 On this mosque, see al-Maqrīzī, *al-Mawāʿiẓ*, 4:126–29 and Gil, *A History of Palestine*, 371 n. 24. According al-Musabbiḥī, who is cited by al-Maqrīzī, construction of this mosque began on 17 Rabiʿ al-Thani 393/February 23, 1003.

90 On this term, see the Glossary. Cf. *Radd*, 44–46.

91 The Mosque of ʿAmr ibn al-ʿĀṣ, the first established in Egypt after the Muslim conquests.

92 Cf. *Aḥkām*, 226–27; *Madhammah*, 93; and al-Nuwayrī, *Nihāyat al-arab*, 28:105 for a similar account involving the earlier Christian official ʿĪsā ibn Nasṭūrus. The poem above also features in the last-named account, which is transmitted from al-Athīr ibn Bayān al-Miṣrī, an official of the late Fatimid period.

93 For the life of ʿArīb, including discussion of the anecdote described in this section: Gordon, "ʿArib al-Ma'muniyya." For the original narrative, which differs considerably from the one here, see al-Iṣbahānī, *Kitāb al-Aghānī*, 21:47.

94 Emending the manuscripts' "Jaʿfar ibn Khālid ibn Barmak."

95 The manuscripts differ on this name; T reads Ibn Zakariyyā, the others Abū Zakariyyā. See al-Maqrīzī, *al-Mawāʿiẓ*, 2:331–32 n. 3, which I have followed in establishing his actual name.

96 For the rather intricate set of astrological procedures referred to here, see *EI2*, art. "al-Tasyīr," 10:366–68 (O. Schirmer). See also Abū Maʿshar, *On Historical Astrology*, 1:576–78. I owe this reference to Daniel Stolz.

97 "Gross receipts" translates the Arabic technical term *irtifāʿ*, which is not found in standard lexicons. Frantz-Murphy, *The Agrarian Administration of Egypt*, 101.

98 In al-Maqrīzī's parallel account, the story differs in many details. See next note.

99 Cf. *Radd*, 55–56; al-Maqrīzī, *al-Mawāʿiẓ*, 2:348, where the poem is part of a version of this episode that directly follows the story of the "Land of the Bridle" (§2.11.1). Both stories there are attributed to al-Muwaffaq ibn al-Khallāl himself. Cf. al-Maqrīzī, *Imtāʿ al-asmāʿ*, 13:4 (where attributed to the Andalusī poet Ibn Bassām).

100 Cf. *Radd*, 62. The signatures of witnesses were appended to a document of agreement so that they—if qualified to give testimony—could later testify that the parties to the agreement had indeed signed that document.

101 Viz., the Qurʾan.

102 Q Fātiḥah 1:6–7.

103 Q Baqarah 2:61.

104 A variation of a well-known hadith, a more common form of which is "None shall receive a worse punishment on the Day of Resurrection than the man who kills a prophet or is killed by one, the one who leads others astray, or the maker of likenesses." For this version and additional citations, see al-Ṭaḥāwī, *Sharḥ mushkil al-āthār*, 1:10.

105 For a much longer version of this document, the ascription of which to the Fatimid caliph al-Āmir is open to question, cf. *Aḥkām*, 227–42 (terminus uncertain); *Madhammah*, 94–107.

106 For the technical terms *qindāq/qundāq* (derived from Greek) and *mukallafah*, see Cooper, "The Assessment and Collection of Kharāj Tax"; Frantz-Murphy, *The Agrarian Administration of Egypt*, 62; Rabie, *The Financial System of Egypt*, 73–74. "Acre" renders Arabic *faddān* (see Glossary).

107 For parallel versions of this account, see al-Maqrīzī, *al-Mawāʿiẓ*, 2:346–47; *Radd*, 51–55 (a very detailed version).

108 Viz., Ṣalāḥ al-Dīn (Saladin).

109 *Mālikh* is undoubtedly Hebrew *melekh*. The derivations of the second and third terms, if they are to be taken seriously at all, are uncertain. For the second, Joseph Sadan has suggested Hebrew *qosem*, "wizard, sorcerer, diviner" (cf., Deut. 18:10; Josh. 13:22; see his "Some Literary Problems," 367). Another possibility is a corruption of Hebrew *qazin*, as in Prov. 6:7 ("chief, commander"); the medial consonant is a better fit, but the Hebrew *nun* would have become Arabic *mīm*. For the third term, Sadan suggested a corruption of Hebrew *shafakh* ("to spill, shed [blood]"). But this could hardly function

as a transitive verb meaning "kill." Another possibility, though a rather remote one, is a corruption of Hebrew *sh-m-d*, which in one verbal form (the Hiphil) means "annihilate, exterminate" (e.g., Deut. 1:27).

110 Q Āl ʿImrān 3:36, etc.

111 Cf. *Radd*, 57.

112 Q Dukhān 44:10.

113 Q Māʾidah 5:73.

114 Not elsewhere attested.

115 For a recent discussion of this account, see Catlos, *Infidel Kings*, 213–15.

116 "To hell with": literally "My stipend's mother's vagina," meaning that the poet is prepared to forego his stipend, which Ibn Dukhān controlled (as he did Zayn al-Dīn's), in order publicly to insult his enemy. These are generalized obscenities hurled at an abstract entity (the stipend); no human mothers are involved. The wealth promised in Sūrat al-Zukhruf may be Paradise (Q Zukhruf 43:70–73), that which might have been offered to unbelievers if it would not have effaced distinctions among people (33), or possibly Pharaoh's riches (51).

117 Cf. ʿUmārah, *ʿOumâra du Yémen*, 1:294. This is one of ten poems ʿUmārah wrote against Ibn Dukhān, who obstructed the delivery of his stipend, just as he did that of Ibn al-Nābulusī's grandfather, Zayn al-Dīn (Alwash, *Umara Al-Yamani*, 160–61). According to some accounts, Zayn al-Dīn later brought about ʿUmārah's downfall and execution under Saladin (see the Introduction). For a later use of this account, see *Radd*, 57–61.

118 Requested, that is, from the Muslim authorities, who for centuries had retained the prerogative to appoint leaders in the Christian and Jewish communities. See, e.g., Conrad, "A Nestorian Diploma of Investiture." This prerogative was often used to extract payments from candidates for office (for an example nearly contemporaneous with the present work see Werthmuller, *Coptic Identity*, 57–60).

119 Literally, "pronouncing the two words of Islam," i.e., the double *shahādah* or statement that there is no god but the one God, and that Muḥammad is his Messenger.

120 For what precedes, cf. *Radd*, 68, which is in all likelihood derived from the present work.

121 Cf., for the first hemistich, al-Nawājī, *al-Shifāʾ fī badīʿ al-iktifāʾ*, 80.

122 Cf. Ibn Ḥamdūn, *al-Tadhkirah al-Ḥamdūniyyah*, 6:91.

123 Cf. *Yatīmah*, 3:285.

124 This is an old line. Cf. Ibn Hishām, *Al-Sīrah al-Nabawiyyah*, 1990, 1:133.

125 The author's description of crypto-piety bears comparison to the testimony of the twelfth-century Sicilian crypto-Muslim official ʿAbd al-Masīḥ, as related by Ibn Jubayr (*Travels*, 342).

126 Q Naḥl 16:106.

127 The exception clauses at the end of this section (beginning with "unless") are not found in the most independent and arguably the earliest of the manuscripts (T). In view of their contrast with the foregoing passage, it may be suspected that they were added later, by the author himself or a copyist, to accord with more sedate and orthodox views of conversion to Islam and of apostasy.

128 Q Infiṭār 82:10.

129 Būṣīr is the name of several villages in Egypt (four, according to the geographer Yāqūt). Only a minority of historians held, as Ibn al-Nābulusī does here, that Marwān was killed at Būṣīr al-Sidr, which our manuscripts anomously call "Būṣīr Sidr."

130 Cf. Ibn Khallikān, *Wafayāt al-aʿyān*, 3:229.

131 The manuscripts give the erroneous reading Ṣāliḥ ibn ʿAbd al-Raḥmān.

132 The ancestors of the Barmakids were Buddhist priests at a large temple near Balkh.

133 For a clearer account of what Khālid did in coining the term "Visitor," see Tustarī, *Bahj al-ṣabāghah*, 13:247–48, where this poem is quoted. Cf. al-Jahshiyārī, *Kitāb al-wuzarāʾ*, 151–52.

134 For another attestation of this poetry with explanation of surrounding historical events, see al-Ṣafadī, *Kitāb al-Wāfī bi-l-wafayāt*, 28:72.

135 Both this poem and the preceding develop the lexical meaning of the regnal name al-Mahdī: "the Divinely Guided One."

136 Cf. al-Jahshiyārī, *Kitāb al-wuzarāʾ*, 155–56.

137 Cf. al-Baghdādī, *Khizānat al-adab*, 3:37.

138 A play on words: *sukr* (drunkenness) for *shukr* (gratitude).

139 These lines are attributed to the poet Abū l-Ḥajnāʾ Nuṣayb (and not "al-Jaḥnāʾ" as in this printed edition) in al-Iṣbahānī, *Aghānī*, 23:31. On him (better known as al-Nuṣayb al-Aṣghar), see Yāqūt, *Muʿjam al-udabāʾ*, 6:2752.

140 Cf. a similar line in Waṭwāṭ, *Ghurar al-khaṣāʾiṣ al-wāḍiḥah*, 194.

141 Cf. Tustarī, *Bahj*, 13:271–72, attributed not to al-Aṣmaʿī but to Ashjaʿ al-Sulamī (see *EI3*, s.n. [R. Weipert]).

142 Elite slaves in Islamic societies were sometimes named after inanimate objects, often precious or exotic ones.

143 See above, §1.12.2, where al-Kisāʾī features in an episode that could only have occurred after his death. Here, in the role of tutor to the sons of al-Rashīd, his presence is perfectly plausible.

144 Cf. al-Tanūkhī, *al-Faraj baʿd al-shiddah* (1955), 2:347.

145 Cf. al-Khaṭīb al-Baghdādī, *Taʾrīkh*, 14:304.

146 Here, as frequently in this section of the book, it should be recalled that much of what is thought clever in these phrases is the rhyme in the original Arabic. Reed pens: *aqlām*; climes: *aqālīm*.

147 Cf. al-Thaʿālibī, *al-Iʿjāz*, 112. Ibn al-Nābulusī appears to have borrowed liberally from this work in this section.

148 Cf. Abū Hilāl al-ʿAskarī, *Kitāb al-ṣināʿatayn*, 168–69.

149 Cf. a fuller version in al-Qayrawānī, *Zahr al-ādāb*, 2:356. The phrase comes from a passage the gist of which is that matters are evaluated according to their outcomes: "The racehorse strives for the finish line; only there, after long proving, is the veil of uncertainty lifted away. . . ."

150 Cf. al-Qālī, *Kitāb al-Amālī*, 2:201.

151 Q Nisāʾ 4:71.

152 Q Baqarah 2:195.

153 A widely cited hadith. See, e.g., al-Tirmidhī, *al-Jāmiʿ*, 4:668, no. 2517.

154 "Guarantee": *ḍamān*; "time": *zamān*; "industry": *ṣināʿah*; "contentment": *qanāʿah*; "want": *muḍāʿah*.

155 The name of the famous Badīʿ al-Zamān was Aḥmad ibn al-Ḥusayn, but none of the sayings which follow can presently be traced to an independent source confirming whether they are by him or another.

156 It is likely that the person being praised is named Saʿd, which may mean "a propitious star."

157 "Gold": *dhahab*; "flame": *lahab*. "Star": *najm*; "arrow": *sahm*. "Ocean": *baḥr*; "full moon": *badr*.

158 "Serpent": *al-ṣabb*; "lizard": *al-ḍabb*.

159 "In tranquility": *rahwan*; "in adornment": *zahwan*. "Obeys his anger": *aṭāʿa ghaḍabahu*; "ruins his comportment": *aḍāʿa adabahu*. "Bribe": *rishwah*; "rope": *rishāʾ*. "Easy mount to ride": *maṭiyyatun waṭiyyatun*. "Mildness": *al-damāthah*; "weakness": *al-ghathāthah*. "Fairness": *al-inṣāf*; "attributes": *al-awṣāf*.

160 Emending "ʿAlī ibn Muqlah." Cf. al-Thaʿālibī, *Iʿjāz*, 106.

161 Cf. al-Thaʿālibī, *Iʿjāz*, 105, where the saying is attributed to Abū l-Ḥasan ibn al-Furāt.

162 "Benefit": *anfaʿahu*; "subdue": *aqmaʿahu*. "Err": *yahfūna*; "forgive": *yaʿfūna*. "Give honor": *ātharta*; "leave scars": *aththarta*.

163 "However little": *wa-in qalla*; "however great": *wa-in jalla*.

164 "Hopeful": *rājin*; "satisfied": *rāḍin*.

165 "Show you gratitude": *shakaraka*; "show you ingratitude": *kafaraka*.

166 The degree and sign of the zodiac that was rising above the eastern horizon at the moment of his birth.

167 Correcting the manuscripts' "Ibn 'Imrān."

168 Cf. Ibn al-Jarrāḥ, *al-Waraqah*, 12.

169 Not elsewhere attested.

170 Not otherwise attested. Additionally, it does not match any of the usual Arabic meters.

171 These lines are not elsewhere attested.

172 I have located no separate attestation of this line, the exact meaning of which remains obscure.

173 Cf. Ibn Ḥamdūn, *al-Tadhkirah al-Ḥamdūniyyah*, 5:154, no. 418; Ibn al-Rūmī, *Dīwān*, 3:284, with considerably different wording in both cases. The allusion in the final phrase is to Q 'Alaq 96:4.

174 Not elsewhere attested.

175 Not elsewhere attested.

176 Not elsewhere attested.

177 Not elsewhere attested. Also, I understand the word *khaṭṭ* ("writ") to mean a document of appointment signed by a higher official.

178 Not elsewhere attested.

179 These verses differ considerably from parallel attestations (Yāqūt, *Muʿjam al-udabāʾ*, 1:440; al-Marzubānī, *al-Muwashshaḥ*, 390). Note that the phrase translated "mocked"/"mockery" is a conjectural rendering of an apparent idiom or allusion in the Arabic ("they lifted his leg"), the figurative meaning of which is obscure.

180 Not elsewhere attested, but this Ibn Manārah is satirized at some length by a poet-secretary of Iraq called Abū l-Ṭayyib al-Yūsufī; see al-Ṣūlī, *Kitāb al-awrāq, qism akhbār al-shuʿarāʾ*, 240–42.

181 Cf. al-Khaṭīb al-Tabrīzī, *Sharḥ Dīwān Abī Tammām*, 2:344–45.

182 The precise sense of the phrase *ibn ṣāḥib tartīb* ("son of a certain official") is not clear; it is found only in manuscript T. Later in this account, *tartīb* (which means to arrange or put in order), is used in parallel with *naẓar* (oversight) to describe regularly performed high-level administrative functions.

183 Very probably in Rajab 627/May or June 1230. See al-Maqrīzī, *History of the Ayyubid Sultans*, 213.

184 These two individuals are otherwise unattested and the spelling of their names is uncertain. For a slightly earlier Coptic official of the Ayyubids known as "Ibn Hablān," possibly a relative, see [Abū Ṣāliḥ], *Churches and Monasteries*, 120; Khater and Burmester, *History of the Patriarchs*, 4/2:256.

185 The reference here is to al-Kāmil's predecessor, al-Malik al-ʿĀdil I (r. 596–615/1200–1218).

186 Q 'Alaq 96:6–7.

187 Cf. al-Qālī, *Kitāb al-Amālī*, 1:133.

188 Cf. al-Ibshīhī, *al-Mustaṭraf*, 2:7.

189 Cf. al-Ṭabarī, *History, Victory*, 219–220, where the poem is attributed to Ya'qūb's son, 'Abdallāh.

190 Cf. al-Iṣbahānī, *Kitāb al-Aghānī*, 10:178, attributed to the Abbasid-era poet 'Alī ibn Jahm (d. 249/863). See also, with additional citations, 'Alī ibn Jahm, *Dīwān*, 178–79.

191 Cf. al-Wāḥidī, *Sharḥ Dīwān al-Mutanabbī*, 375; Ibn Qayyim al-Jawziyyah, *Rawḍat al-muḥibbīn*, 396 (traced by the editor to the *dīwān* of al-Wa'wā' al-Dimashqī).

192 Perhaps describing wine pouring from a beautiful vessel.

193 Not elsewhere attested.

194 Cf. al-Azdī, *Badā'i' al-badā'ih*, 231. The month may be Ramadan, when sex is lawful only at night, and the end of which is marked by the sighting of the new crescent moon.

195 More usually attributed to al-Ḥasan ibn Wahb. See, e.g., Yāqūt, *Mu'jam al-udabā'*, 3:1022.

196 The sky is a standard metaphor for the generous patron. These lines are elsewhere attributed to al-Ḥasan ibn Wahb. See Ibn 'Abd Rabbih, *al-'Iqd al-farīd*, 3:143.

197 Cf. an unascribed attestation in al-Sharīf al-Murtaḍā, *Amālī al-Murtaḍā*, 2:128.

198 Usually attributed to others, particularly Abū l-Ḥasan 'Alī ibn 'Abd al-'Azīz al-Jurjānī. See his *tarjamah* (prosopographical entry), which includes this poem, in Ibn Khallikān, *Wafayāt*, 3:279.

199 Cf. *Yatīmah*, 4:239, with slightly different wording.

200 Well-known verses. Cf. Ibn Khallikān, *Wafayāt*, 1:128, where another possible author is mentioned.

201 Cf. *Yatīmah*, 4:353.

202 Cf. al-Tha'ālibī, *al-I'jāz*, 203.

203 Cf. *Yatīmah*, 4:351.

204 Correcting the manuscripts' "Abū Aḥmad Muḥammad ibn Manṣūr."

205 For the color *fākhitī*, probably a ghostly grey (as of moonlight or a pigeon's back), see al-Ṣafadī, *A'yān*, 4:160 (s.n. Kunjashkab).

206 Cf. *Yatīmah*, 4:399 (attributed to Manṣūr ibn al-Ḥākim Abī Manṣūr al-Harawī).

207 Cf. *Yatīmah*, 3:98. This couplet is listed among the "thefts" (*sariqāt*) of Abū 'Abdallāh al-Ḥasan ibn Aḥmad ibn al-Ḥajjāj, borrowed from the poet al-Lajlāj.

208 Cf. *Yatīmah*, 2:281.

209 Cf. *Yatīmah*, 1:181 (attributed to al-Mutanabbī, but described by al-Tha'ālibī as an example of his worst poetry).

210 Cf. *Yatīmah*, 2:282 (attributed to the same al-Muhallabī as the poem in §3.3.13).

211 Cf. *Yatīmah*, 3:218, where the middle line is missing (attributed to Abū l-Fatḥ Ibn al-'Amīd, the son of Abū l-Faḍl); cf. also Ibn Kathīr, *al-Bidāyah wa-l-nihāyah*, 12:337–38 (also attributed to Abū l-Fatḥ).

212 The manuscripts give "al-Ḥasan" and "al-Ḥusayn," an evident corruption.

213 Cf. *Yatīmah*, 4:390 (attributed to Abū l-Qāsim Muḥammad ibn Muḥammad ibn Jubayr al-Sajzī). "My perfection" (*kamālī*), "as I have" (*ka-mā lī*), and "like unto my wealth" (*ka-mālī*) are pronounced alike in Arabic, though composed of different words.

214 Cf. *Yatīmah*, 4:392 (attributed to Abū l-Ḥasan ʿUmar ibn Abī ʿUmar al-Sajzī al-Nawqānī).

215 Cf. *Yatīmah*, 4:476 (attributed to Abū l-Muʿallā Mājid ibn al-Ṣalt). The reasoning seems to be that the concept of "life" is meaningful only because death renders it finite, and therefore scarce and valuable. In principle, then, lengthening one's life subtracts from its significance.

216 Cf. *Yatīmah*, 4:322–23.

217 Cf. *Yatīmah*, 3:76.

218 Cf. *Yatīmah*, 3:453 (attributed to Ibn Nubātah al-Saʿdī).

219 Al-Thaʿālibī, *al-Iʿjāz*, 268 (attributed to the judge Abū Aḥmad Manṣūr ibn Muḥammad). "Wine of the mouth" renders "wine of saliva,"—saliva being widely treated as erotic in classical Arabic poetry.

220 Cf. Ṣarradurr, *Dīwān*, 238.

221 Cf. Ṣarradurr, *Dīwān*, 254.

222 Cf. *Yatīmah*, 4:88. This poem makes frequent allusion to the *muʿallaqah* ("suspended ode") of the pre-Islamic poet Imruʾ al-Qays, including verbatim quotation in the final lines, taking up the familiar motifs of the lost love and the abandoned campsite in order to mock the secretaries for an exaggerated and greedy attachment to their patrons.

223 Cf. *Yatīmah*, 4:90 (attributed to Abū l-Ṭayyib Muḥammad ibn Ḥātim al-Muṣʿabī).

224 Cf. *Yatīmah*, 4:91–92.

225 Cf. *Yatīmah*, 4:98 (attributed to a Muḥammad ibn Mūsā al-Ḥaddādī al-Balkhī).

226 Cf. *Yatīmah*, 4:117 (attributed to quite a different person, Abū l-Ḥasan ʿAlī ibn al-Ḥasan al-Ḥarrānī, a contemporary of al-Thaʿālibī).

227 The *Yatīmah* offers a substantially different reading here: "O you who masters sins in her power."

228 Cf. *Yatīmah*, 4:146 (attributed to Abū l-Ḥasan ʿAlī ibn Hārūn al-Shaybānī).

229 Cf. *Yatīmah*, 4:159 (attributed to Abū l-Qāsim ʿAbdallāh ibn ʿAbd al-Raḥmān al-Dīnawarī). The numbers are obscure. Nine by nine (eighty-one) may refer to the number (in Eastern Arabic numerals) that can be read in the creases on the left palm, and three by four to the three segments in each of the four fingers. The miser's hand would have been created with the four fingers fused to the palm so that it never opens to offer its contents. While it is true that in Islamic cultures the left hand ought not to be used in giving gifts, the idea may be that the miser's possessions are retained in the left

hand, as far as possible from the right, with which gifts are given. I am grateful to Foued Kacimi al-Hasani al-Sharif for assistance with this line.

230 Cf. Ibn ʿAbd Rabbih, *ʿIqd*, 7:145, without the final line. Ziyād ibn Abī Sufyān was a prominent governor of the early Umayyad dynasty. Since he was an orphan, the Umayyads (here, "Ḥarb's clan") adopted him, but the move was widely mocked.

231 The poet is playing on the words *kharāj* (land tax), for which he substitutes *kharā* (shit), and *ḍiyāʿ* (estates), which becomes *ḍayāʿ* (ruin). The pseudo-secretary's incompetence, he implies, vitiates the precision that the administration should represent.

232 The Arabic plural *kuttāb* (secretaries), is a homonym of the word for "primary school."

233 Cf., for this and the preceding poem, Waṭwāṭ, *Ghurar*, 218. The last two lines differ entirely from those given by Waṭwāṭ.

234 Cf. al-Rāghib al-Iṣbahānī, *Muḥāḍarāt al-udabāʾ*, 1:105.

235 Not elsewhere attested.

236 The manuscripts of the present work have the erroneous reading "Ibn ʿAbbās ibn Mūsā," but the poet, al-Junayd ibn Muḥammad, originally referred to two people, Ibrāhīm ibn al-ʿAbbās al-Ṣūlī and Mūsā ibn ʿAbd al-Malik. Al-Junayd, nicknamed "Aubergine," was their contemporary (see source in next note).

237 Cf. al-Ṣafadī, *Wāfī*, 11:157, no. 2941. For explanation of the wordplay, see n. 231.

238 Not elsewhere attested. The word for "land tax" in the accusative case at the end of a line of poetry (*al-kharājā*), is homophonous with the phrase "the shit is out" (*al-kharā jā*).

239 Not elsewhere attested.

240 Only dots distinguish these letters from one another: *s* س and *sh* ش. ʿAmr and ʿUmar are distinguished by a silent letter suffixed to the former: عمرو and عمر. I have not found the poem attested elsewhere.

241 Not elsewhere attested. The letters *t* and *th* are distinguished only by dots (which, in professional secretarial hands, were often omitted): *t* ت and *th* ث.

242 This poem is not elsewhere attested. Something in this line is amiss, as it does not conform to an accepted poetic meter.

243 Not elsewhere attested. The meaning of the dungball reference is obscure.

244 What follows is a derisive presentation of Coptic bilingualism and the gradual, uneven adoption of Arabic in medieval Egypt. See Swanson, *The Coptic Papacy*, 71–74; Zaborowski, "From Coptic to Arabic in Medieval Egypt"; Parker, "Coptic Language and Identity in Ayyūbid Egypt."

245 On the cowl, or honorary hood (*ṭaylasān*), see the Glossary and Dozy, *Dictionnaire détaillé*, s.v. *ṭaylasān*.

246 The difference is between *waẓīfah* (task) and *waṣīfah*, literally "servant girl."

247 In the first instance, the secretary simply misspelt the word *muwāẓib* (diligent) as *muwāḍib*, a nonce word. In the second, he wrote *maṣrūr* (bound up) rather than the correct *masrūr* (overjoyed).

248 The secretary wrote *ukhṣiba*, literally "fecundated," when he should have written *ghuṣiba* (impelled).

249 The year 660 postdates both the composition of the present work and the reign of al-Malik al-Ṣāliḥ, and is close to the end of Ibn al-Nābulusī's life. This anecdote, which does not appear in manuscript T, must therefore represent an interpolation, either by the author himself or by a copyist.

250 Use of the Old French term "maréschal" (Ar. *al-marshān*) here reflects the Crusade-era setting of this anecdote; it refers to several European military offices. See Dozy, *Supplément*, 2:582; Godefroy, *Dictionnaire*, 5:170; Contamine, "Maréchal de France." Cf. al-Qalqashandī, *Ṣubḥ*, 8:300; al-Nuwayrī, *Nihāyah*, 30:197. Also, in the Arabic, the standard *-ān* termination for dual nouns and verbs is appended indiscriminately, to humorous effect.

251 The secretary wrote *ḥayḍah*, literally "menstruation," when he meant *hayḍah*, literally "cholera."

252 In Arabic the error is *jawzah*, literally "walnut," for the correct *zawjah* (wife).

253 Not elsewhere attested. In Arabic the mistake is *nāhiq*, literally "braying," for the correct *nāqih* (recovering).

254 Cf., e.g., al-Zajjājī, *Akhbār Abī l-Qāsim al-Zajjājī*, 20, with references to the *Sunan* of Ibn Mājah and al-Tirmidhī. The phrase the Copt intends to use literally means "on all four sides."

255 The correct form in Arabic is *bi-arbaʿ ḥadhāfīrihā*; the two nonsensical corruptions are *bi-arbaʿ ḥawāfīrihā* and *bi-ḥarādhīfihā*.

256 In the Arabic, the mistake is *al-ḥandarīs*, which is a nonce word, for the correct *al-khandarīs* (ancient).

257 "Nīsān" and *taysān* (Egyptian colloquial *tīs*) are distinguished by a single dot: نيسان and تيسان. The "Greek months" mentioned here are the Syro-Macedonian ones, the names of which derive from the ancient Babylonian calendar. By "Greek" the speaker means "of Christians using the Seleucid era," not "Byzantine," the term's usual meaning. The Byzantine Greeks did not use the Syro-Macedonian months, of which "Nīsān" is one.

258 "Dumbfounded" (*namih*) is a conjectural emendation of the manuscripts' meaningless *nah*. The speaker should have said *nahim* (avid).

259 The speaker said *manāḥis* (vices) when he meant *maḥāsin* (virtues).

260 The speaker said *majāz*, literally "metaphor," when he meant *mizāj* (mood or disposition).

261 He reads *qawwād* (قواد), literally "pimp," instead of the correct *fu'ād* (فؤاد) or "heart."

262 He reads *yashammu* (يشم, snuffles), for *shabimun* (شبم, is frigid).

263 He said *hāshim* (هاشم), literally "crusher," instead of the correct *hāmish* (هامش, margin).

264 Cf. al-Thaʻālibī, *al-Iʻjāz*, 152, attributed to al-Kumayt ibn Zayd al-Asadī (d. 126/743).

265 Not elsewhere attested.

266 The effect of the author's counsel here is to provide a broad and appealing justification for mulcting any state official without specific evidence of wrongdoing.

267 A well-known hadith; see, e.g., Muslim, *Ṣaḥīḥ*, 3:1463.

268 The identity of the narrator, ʻUmar's interlocutor, is not given here. In a shortened parallel version, it is the famous Companion and transmitter Qatādah ibn al-Nuʻmān. See Ibn Abī l-Dunyā, *Qiṣar al-amal*, 155.

269 The manuscript precisely replicates the name in the manuscripts of the *Futūḥ Miṣr* of Ibn ʻAbd al-Ḥakam (see Ibn ʻAbd al-Ḥakam, *History of the Conquest of Egypt*, 146 n. 5, 147 n. 1): Abū l-Mukhtār Qays ibn Yazīd ibn Qays ibn Yazīd ibn ʻAmr ibn Khuwaylid al-Ṣaʻiq al-Numayrī, but this is erroneous.

270 Cf. Ibn ʻAbd al-Ḥakam, *History of the Conquest of Egypt*, 147–48; al-Balādhurī, *Futūḥ al-buldān*, 541–42 (*Origins of the Islamic State, Part II*, 122–23); [Sulaym ibn Qays], *Kitāb*, 221–22.

271 The idea of the line seems to be that individuals who formerly possessed nothing suddenly turn up with attractive slave boys and women. There is also a moral critique: the word for "hares" (*al-khizzān*) is close to "silk" (*khazz*), forbidden to Muslim men, and "brightly bedizened" (*al-dumā*) refers most properly to decorated effigies or idols.

272 Cf. Ibn ʻAbd al-Ḥakam, *History*, 146; Ibn Kardabūs, *al-Iktifā'*, 1:310; al-Tawḥīdī, *al-Imtāʻ wa-l-mu'ānasah*, 2:95–96.

273 Abū Hurayrah's mother, Umaymah bint Ṣufayḥ. He attaches his descent to his mother, emphasizing his humble station, because his father died when he was very young. For the comparison to a "son of a prophet," cf. Amos 7:14.

274 Cf. Ibn ʻAbd al-Ḥakam, *History*, 148–49.

275 See §4.3.3 and n. 268 above.

276 Cf. al-Thaʻālibī, *al-Iʻjāz*, 102.

277 The syntax of the final full sentence of this section is difficult; the text may be corrupt. It is suggestive that the story begins with a quotation borrowed, as usual, from al-Thaʻālibī, which is then continued beyond al-Thaʻālibī's account in a manner that echoes Ibn al-Nābulusī's own life story, notably his flamboyant probity.

278 The author may mean that his historical account proper ends with Saladin's death (ca. 589/1193), or that his work refers to events down to his own present day.

279 Q Nūr 24:33.

280 Cf. Ibn Faḍl Allāh al-ʿUmarī, *Masālik al-abṣār*, 15:355, who gives a substantially different version attributed to ʿAbd al-ʿAzīz ibn ʿUmar ibn Nubātah al-Saʿdī (cf. the second poem in §3.3.20, attributed to the same tenth-century poet).

281 Q Baqarah 2:273.

The Fatimid Caliphs in Egypt

ca. 358–567/969–1171

al-Mu'izz li-Dīn Allāh, Abū Tamīm Ma'add ibn al-Manṣūr	d. 365/975
al-'Azīz bi-llāh, Abū Manṣūr Nizār ibn al-Mu'izz	d. 386/996
al-Ḥākim bi-Amr Allāh, Abū 'Alī al-Manṣūr ibn al-'Azīz	d. 411/1021
al-Ẓāhir li-I'zāz Dīn Allāh, Abū l-Ḥasan 'Alī ibn al-Ḥākim	d. 427/1036
al-Mustanṣir bi-llāh, Abū Tamīm Ma'add ibn al-Ẓāhir	d. 487/1094
al-Musta'lī bi-llāh, Abū l-Qāsim Aḥmad b. al-Mustanṣir	d. 495/1101
al-Āmir bi-Aḥkām Allāh, Abū 'Alī al-Manṣūr ibn al-Musta'lī	d. 524/1130
al-Ḥāfiẓ li-Dīn Allāh, Abū l-Maymūn 'Abd al-Majīd ibn Muḥammad	d. 544/1149
al-Ẓāfir bi-Amr Allāh, Abū l-Manṣūr Ismā'īl ibn al-Ḥāfiẓ	d. 549/1154
al-Fā'iz bi-Naṣr Allāh, Abū l-Qāsim 'Īsā ibn al-Ẓāfir	d. 555/1160
al-'Āḍid li-Dīn Allāh, Abū Muḥammad 'Abdallāh ibn Yūsuf	d. 567/1171

The Ayyubid Sultans in Egypt

ca. 567–648/1171–1250

al-Malik al-Nāṣir, Ṣalāḥ al-Dīn Abū l-Muẓaffar Yūsuf ibn Najm al-Dīn Ayyūb ibn Shādhī (Saladin)	d. 589/1193
al-Malik al-ʿAzīz, ʿImād al-Dīn Abū l-Fatḥ ʿUthmān ibn al-Nāṣir Yūsuf	d. 595/1198
al-Malik al-Manṣūr, Nāṣir al-Dīn Muḥammad ibn al-ʿAzīz ʿUthmān	d. 596/1200
al-Malik al-ʿĀdil I, Sayf al-Dīn Abū Bakr Muḥammad/Aḥmad ibn Najm al-Dīn Ayyūb (Saphadin)	d. 615/1218
al-Malik al-Kāmil, Nāsir al-Dīn Abū l-Maʿālī Muḥammad ibn al-ʿĀdil I Muḥammad/Aḥmad	d. 635/1238
al-Malik al-ʿĀdil II, Sayf al-Dīn Abū Bakr ibn al-Kāmil Muḥammad	deposed 637/1240
al-Malik al-Ṣāliḥ, Najm al-Dīn Ayyūb ibn al-Kāmil Muḥammad	d. 647/1249
al-Malik al-Muʿaẓẓam, Ghiyāth al-Dīn **Tūrān Shāh** ibn al-Ṣāliḥ Ayyūb	d. 648/1250
Shajar al-Durr, ʿIṣmat al-Dīn Umm Khalīl (wife of al-Ṣāliḥ)	abdicated 648/1250

Glossary of Names and Terms

This glossary gives basic information for individuals, places, tribes, battles, dynasties, and other noteworthy entities that appear in *The Sword of Ambition*. The entry for an individual is found by default under the personal name (*ism*), except for those generally known by some other name. Of the regnal dates, the latter is that of the ruler's death unless otherwise noted. English definite articles and the Arabic *al-* are disregarded for purposes of alphabetization. A question mark (?) following a name indicates that it has not been possible to identify an individual in any source other than the present one.

al-ʿAbbās ibn Muḥammad ? minor secretary to Hārūn al-Rashīd.

Abbasid caliphate (ca. 132–656/750–1258) the longest lasting and most prominent of the caliphal dynasties. Ascended to power in a revolt against the Umayyad caliphate. Ruled primarily from Iraq thereafter, but lost the greater part of its political and religious authority after the middle of the third/ninth century.

Abd al-Ḥamīd ibn Yaḥyā (d. 132/750) famous non-Arab secretary of later Umayyad caliphs. Pioneer of high literary Arabic style, particularly in the genre of advice literature.

ʿAbd al-Malik ibn Marwān (d. 86/705) Umayyad caliph who reconsolidated central authority after his victory in the second intra-Muslim conflict (*fitnah*), in part by the deft use of religious symbolism and ideology, illustrated in the reform of Arabo-Islamic coinage and of administration.

ʿAbdallāh ibn al-Abrash ? (mid-third/ninth c.) Christian government secretary and convert to Islam.

ʿAbdallāh ibn Yaḥyā ibn Khāqān (mid-third/ninth c.) grandee in the period of al-Mutawakkil. Brother of ʿUbaydallāh ibn Yaḥyā, vizier to al-Mutawakkil.

ʿAbdān al-Wāsiṭī (fl. mid-third/ninth c.) Christian secretary and convert to Islam.

ʿAbū l-ʿAbbās Aḥmad ibn Isḥāq the Secretary see *Aḥmad ibn Isḥāq the Secretary*.

Abū l-ʿAbbās Aḥmad ibn al-Rūmī the Secretary see *Aḥmad ibn al-Rūmī the Secretary*.

Abū ʿAbdallāh al-Ḥusayn ibn Ḥajjāj see *al-Ḥusayn (ibn Aḥmad) ibn (al-)Ḥajjāj the Secretary*.

Abū ʿAlī ibn ʿAbdallāh see *al-Sājī*.

Abū ʿAlī ibn al-Afḍal ibn Shāhān Shāh see *Kutayfāt*.

Abū ʿAlī ibn Muqlah, Muḥammad ibn ʿAlī see *Ibn Muqlah*.

Abū l-ʿAynāʾ, Muḥammad ibn al-Qāsim ibn Khallād (d. ca. 283/896) well-known poet and prosaist of Abbasid Iraq.

Abū Bakr al-Khwārizmī, Muḥammad ibn al-ʿAbbās (d. ca. 383/993) peripatetic secretary and literary eminence, particularly in epistolography and satire. Sparred with Badīʿ al-Zamān and al-Ṣāḥib ibn ʿAbbād. Spent most of his life in the northeastern reaches of the Islamic world.

Abū Bakr Muḥammad ibn al-ʿAbbās see *Abū Bakr al-Khwārizmī*.

Abū Bakr al-Ṣiddīq, ʿAbdallāh ibn Abī Quḥāfah (r. 11–13/632–34) early convert to Islam, close Companion of the Prophet, father of Prophet's wife ʿĀʾishah, and first caliph after the Prophet's death. Fought the Riddah ("apostasy") Wars to preserve the political union of Arab tribes that had paid allegiance to the Prophet.

Abū l-Faḍl Ibn al-ʿAmīd see *Ibn al-ʿAmīd*.

Abū l-Faraj ibn Zurʿah (d. ca. 585/1189) Saint Mark III, seventy-third patriarch of the Coptic Church. Selection occurred in 563/1167–68.

Abū l-Fatḥ al-Bustī see *al-Bustī*.

Abū l-Ḥasan Ibn al-Furāt see *Ibn al-Furāt*.

Abū Ḥumayd al-Sāʿidī (d. 60/680) Companion of the Prophet and hadith transmitter from Medina.

Abū Hurayrah, ʿAbd al-Raḥmān ibn Ṣakhr al-Dawsī (d. ca. 58/678) Companion. Major transmitter of reports about the Prophet's life.

Abū l-Hurṭumān ? a certain fruit seller.

Abū ʿImrān al-Sulamī see *al-Sulamī*.

Abū Jaʿfar Muḥammad ibn al-ʿAbbās see *Muḥammad ibn al-ʿAbbās*.

Abū Manṣūr Aḥmad ibn Muḥammad see *Aḥmad ibn Muḥammad al-Balkhī*.

Abū Manṣūr ʿAlī ibn al-Faḍl see *ʿAlī ibn al-Faḍl*.

Abū Manṣūr Ibn ʿAbdūn see *Ibn ʿAbdūn the Secretary*.

Abū Manṣūr Muḥammad ibn Aḥmad see *Muḥammad ibn Aḥmad*.

Abū Maryam ibn al-Muḥarrish al-Ḥanafī (fl. first/seventh c.) minor participant in the early Muslim conquests. Settled at Basra.

Abū Muḥammad al-Muhallabī, al-Ḥasan ibn Muḥammad (d. 352/963) vizier of the Buyid Muʿizz al-Dawlah. Patron of culture, *littérateur*.

Abū l-Mukhtār Yazīd ibn Qays see *Yazīd ibn Qays*.

Abū Mūsā al-Ashʿarī, ʿAbdallāh ibn Qays (d. ca. 42/662) Companion from South Arabia who later served as governor of Basra and Kufa under ʿUmar ibn al-Khaṭṭāb.

Abū Nūḥ ʿĪsā ibn Ibrāhīm (d. 255/869) high official under Caliph al-Mutawakkil. Christian convert to Islam. From a distinguished family of Christian lay elites with roots in the Iraqi town of al-Anbār.

Abū Nuwās, al-Ḥasan ibn Hāniʾ al-Thaqafī (d. ca. 198/813) towering figure in the history of Arabic poetry. Court poet, remembered especially for bacchanalian and erotic themes, and for hunting poetry.

Abū l-Qāsim Muḥammad ibn Muḥammad see *Muḥammad ibn Muḥammad ibn al-Jubayr the Secretary*.

Abū l-Qāsim al-Ṣāḥib ibn ʿAbbād see *al-Ṣāḥib ibn ʿAbbād*.

Abū l-Shīṣ, Muḥammad ibn ʿAbdallāh al-Khuzāʿī (d. ca. 200/815) Arab poet in circles close to Hārūn al-Rashīd.

Abū Tammām, Ḥabīb ibn Aws (d. ca. 231/846) eminent court poet and anthologist. Claimed descent from the Arab tribe of Ṭayyiʾ. Composed poetry on major historical events.

Abū Thābit see *Sulaymān ibn Quḍāʿah*.

Abū ʿUbaydah, ʿĀmir ibn ʿAbdallāh ibn al-Jarrāḥ (d. 18/639) important Companion and leading figure in the Muslim community after the Prophet's death. Led the conquest of Syria.

Abū Yaʿlā the Secretary ? official of rural extraction in Iraq.

Abū Yāsir the Christian (fourth/tenth c.) secretary in the employ of Muʾnis, according to *The Sword of Ambition*. An official of this name is sporadically attested in other sources of the period.

al-ʿĀḍid, Abū Muḥammad ʿAbdallāh ibn Yūsuf (r. 555–67/1160–71) last Fatimid caliph of Egypt. Brought to the throne by al-Malik al-Ṣāliḥ Ṭalāʾiʿ but generally prevented from exercising power during the tumultuous period of his rule.

Advice (naṣīḥah) venerable genre of Arabic literature, encompassing a wide range of moral and practical counsel. Often directed to rulers or other powerful persons.

Aḥmad ibn Abī Khālid (d. 210/825) secretary and vizier in the reign of al-Maʾmūn.

Aḥmad ibn al-Ḥusayn see *Badīʿ al-Zamān*.

Aḥmad ibn Isḥāq the Secretary, Abū l-ʿAbbās al-Jarmaqī (late fourth/tenth c.) secretary, poet, and mathematician. Patron was the Saffarid Emir Khalaf ibn Aḥmad (d. 399/1008–9).

Aḥmad ibn Isrāʾīl (d. 255/869) high official under Caliph al-Mutawakkil. Christian convert to Islam who became vizier after conversion. Originally from al-Anbār.

Aḥmad ibn Muḥammad al-Balkhī, Abū Manṣūr ? secretary and poet.

Aḥmad ibn al-Rūmī the Secretary, Abū l-ʿAbbās ? secretary and poet.

Aḥmad ibn Ṭūlūn (r. ca. 254–70/868–84) Turkic military officer of the Abbasids. De facto independent ruler of Egypt and founder of a minor dynasty there.

al-Aḥnaf ibn Qays al-Tamīmī (d. 67/686–87) significant tribal leader in the Muslim conquest of southern Iraq and Persia, notably in Khurasan.

al-Akhram See *Ibn Abī Zakariyyā the Secretary*.

ʿAlī ibn Abī Ṭālib (r. 35–40/656–61) cousin and son-in-law of the Prophet. Considered the fourth caliph by Sunnis, succeeding ʿUthmān ibn ʿAffān. His supporters formed the nucleus of the later Shiʿi sects. Upon ʿAlī's murder, power reverted to his Umayyad rival, Muʿāwiyah.

ʿAlī ibn al-Faḍl, Abū Manṣūr Ṣarradurr (d. 465/1073) Abū l-Faḍl ʿAlī ibn al-Ḥasan ibn ʿAlī ibn al-Faḍl. Secretary and poet of Baghdad who flourished under the Buyid dynasty. Described by many biographers as a Shiʿi or an unbeliever.

ʿAlī ibn Ibrāhīm ibn Najā al-Anṣārī, Zayn al-Dīn Ibn Nujayyah (d. 599/1203) maternal grandfather of Ibn al-Nābulusī. Influential scholar and courtier in late Fatimid and early Ayyubid Egypt.

ʿAlī ibn ʿĪsā ibn Dāʾūd al-Jarrāḥ, Abū l-Ḥasan (d. 334/946) secretary and vizier of the caliphs al-Muqtadir and al-Qāhir. Remembered for his piety and orthodoxy.

alms tax (zakat, ṣadaqah) one of the five pillars of Islam. Religiously mandated annual donation to worthy recipients (described in Q Tawbah 9:60). Assessed only on certain kinds of property.

al-Amīn, Muḥammad ibn Hārūn (r. 193–98/809–13) Abbasid caliph. Son of Hārūn al-Rashīd, and brother of al-Maʾmūn, against whom he fought and lost a devastating civil war for control of the empire.

al-Āmir bi-Aḥkām Allāh, Abū ʿAlī al-Manṣūr (r. 495–524/1101–30) Fatimid caliph. Reigned under the tutelage of the vizier al-Afḍal before having the latter assassinated in 515/1121. Ruled harshly thereafter, appointing the rapacious Monk Abū Najāḥ and thereby hastening his own assassination. A major succession dispute followed.

ʿAmmār ibn Yāsir (d. 37/657) Companion of the Prophet and one of the first converts to Islam. Suffered persecution for his faith. Later a staunch supporter of ʿAlī ibn Abī Ṭālib.

ʿAmr ibn al-ʿĀṣ (d. ca. 42/663) Companion of the Prophet from the tribe of Quraysh and a prominent commander in the early Muslim army. Led the conquest of Egypt, ca. 19/640.

al-Anbār district of Iraq west of Baghdad. In pre-Islamic times, an area of intensive Arab-Aramean-Persian interaction with a considerable Christian presence.

Ansina ancient Antinoöpolis, modern Shaykh ʿIbādah in Minya Governorate, Egypt.

ʿAnṭar(ah) ibn Shaddād (d. late-sixth c. AD) legendary pre-Islamic adventurer and poet.

ʿArīb al-Maʾmūniyyah (d. 277/890) noted courtesan and singer of Caliph al-Maʾmūn prior to his accession.

al-Aṣmaʿī, Abū Saʿīd ʿAbd al-Malik ibn Qurayb (d. ca. 213/828) Basran grammarian and philologist, and, like al-Kisāʾī, tutor to the sons of Hārūn al-Rashīd.

al-ʿĀṣ ibn Wāʾil (d. after 1/622) father of ʿAmr ibn al-ʿĀṣ.

ʿĀṣim ibn Qays ibn al-Ṣalt al-Sulamī (fl. first/seventh c.) minor participant in the Muslim conquests of southern Iraq and southwestern Persia.

al-ʿAttābī, Kulthūm ibn ʿAmr (d. 208/823 or 220/835) secretary and poet (esp. eulogist) in the circles of Hārūn al-Rashīd.

Ayyubid dynasty (ca. 567–648/1171–1250) Sunni rulers of Syria, Egypt, and parts of Arabia, who often formed a kind of confederacy of princedoms. Notwithstanding their frequent internal quarrels they intermittently carried forward the campaigns of their dynastic founder, Ṣalāḥ al-Dīn, against the Franks.

Badīʿ al-Zamān, Abū l-Faḍl Aḥmad ibn al-Ḥusayn al-Hamadhānī (d. 398/1008) Arabic prose writer and poet who pioneered the *maqāmah* genre, which cast tales of deception and adventure in ornate rhymed prose. Rose to fame by besting Abū Bakr al-Khwārizmī in a public contest of literary virtuosity.

Badr, Battle of (ca. 2/624) confrontation in which the outnumbered supporters of the Prophet, assisted by hosts of angels, dealt their pagan Meccan enemies their first defeat.

al-Baḥrayn region of eastern Arabia during the early Islamic period, stretching along the western coast of the Gulf.

Bamboo (Khayzurān) (d. 173/789) influential wife of al-Mahdī and mother of Hārūn al-Rashīd.

Banū Asad major northern Arab tribe in the early Islamic period.

Banū Ghazwān descendents of ʿUtbah ibn Ghazwān.

Banū Ḥabīb ? Samaritan family or tribe.

Barmakids prominent family of high officials in the early Abbasid state until their sudden fall during the reign of Hārūn al-Rashīd. Descendants of Buddhist priests at a large temple near Balkh. See also *Khālid ibn Barmak; Yaḥyā ibn Khālid; al-Faḍl ibn Yaḥyā; Jaʿfar ibn Yaḥyā.*

Basra important port city in lower Mesopotamia. Founded as a garrison town at the time of the Muslim conquest and particularly prominent in the first two centuries of Islam.

al-Bayḍāʾ elevation about seven miles southwest of Medina.

Bishr ibn al-Muḥtafiz al-Muzanī (first/seventh c.) Companion and minor participant in the Arab conquests of southern Iraq and southwestern Persia.

Book, the (al-kitāb) common term for the Qurʾan.

al-Buḥturī, Abū ʿUbādah al-Walīd ibn ʿUbaydallāh (d. 284/897) major Arab poet of the Abbasid era. Primarily a eulogist and panegyrist.

Būṣīr (al-)Sidr village near Giza in Egypt.

al-Bustī, Abū l-Fatḥ ʿAlī ibn Muḥammad (d. 400/1009) poet and prose writer of Iran and Central Asia. Noteworthy for use of paronomasia.

Calendar of the Emigration the Muslim lunar calendar that begins with the Emigration. Its twelve months are strictly tied to the phases of the moon, thus its 354-day cycle is not aligned with the solar year.

caliph (al-khalīfah) title of certain historical Muslim rulers, particularly in early Islam, who wielded a degree of religious as well as political authority. Understood variously as "deputy" (of God) or "successor" (of the Prophet).

Capella (al-ʿayyūq) star of yellowish hue in the constellation Auriga. Sixth brightest in the night sky.

Chosroes Anūshirwān (r. AD 531–79) famous Sasanian emperor. Became proverbial for wisdom in governance and patronage of culture.

Church of al-ʿAdawiyyah church, called al-Marṭūṭī, dedicated to Mary, in a place known as al-ʿAdawiyyah, about fifteen miles south of Fusṭāṭ.

Church of the Resurrection (kanīsat al-qiyāmah) the Church of the Holy Sepulcher in Jerusalem. Believed to be the site of Jesus's crucifixion and burial.

Commander of the Believers (amīr al-muʾminīn) standard title for the caliph.

Companion(s) term applied to those Muslims who associated with the Prophet during his lifetime. Ascribed a high degree of probity and exemplary moral uprightness in Sunni tradition.

cowl (ṭaylasān) shawl-like fringed garment worn over the head and shoulders. Sign of membership in the Muslim scholarly and secretarial classes of Egypt in Ibn al-Nābulusī's day.

Damascus Gate (bāb al-shām) one of the four gates of the original round city of Baghdad. Faced northwest.

Damietta (Dimyāṭ) port city in the eastern Nile delta. Historically vulnerable to attack from the sea, notably by Crusaders on multiple occasions in the thirteenth century.

Dhāt al-Salāsil, Expedition of (ca. 8/629) raid led by ʿAmr ibn al-ʿĀṣ against Arab tribes in the southern Transjordan.

dhimmi in Islamic law, a non-Muslim who is party to a Pact of Security (*dhimmah*).

Dhū l-Nūn al-Miṣrī (d. 246/861) important early Sufi mystic. From Ikhmim in Egypt.

Elephant, Year of the (ca. AD 570) year of the Prophet's birth according to some traditions. Named after an elephant that was sent (ineffectually) against Mecca by the Ethiopian ruler of South Arabia.

Emigrants (muhājirūn) those Companions who accompanied the Prophet Muḥammad in his Emigration from Mecca to Medina in 1/622.

Emigration, the (al-hijrah) the Prophet's journey or flight from Mecca to Yathrib (soon after renamed Medina) in AD 622. Marks the beginning of Muḥammad's political career and of the Muslim lunar calendar (see *Calendar of the Emigration*).

Emir Jāndār title of a high official in the Ayyubid state. Responsible for guarding the sultan and attending to such matters as executions.

Eternal Decree (al-qaḍāʾ wa-l-qadar) major Muslim doctrine concerning divine predetermination of events.

Example of the Prophet (sunnah) normative moral and legal example set by the Prophet, as his conduct was depicted in the Hadith.

faddān standard unit of land measurement in medieval Egypt. Conventionally defined as the area that can be worked by a yoke of oxen in a single day. Approximately 4,200 square meters.

al-Faḍl ibn al-Rabīʿ (d. ca. 207/823) vizier to the Abbasid caliphs Hārūn al-Rashīd and al-Amīn after the fall of the Barmakids. Son of al-Rabīʿ ibn Yūnus.

al-Faḍl ibn Sahl (d. 202/818) influential Iranian vizier, military commander, and adviser to the Abbasid caliph al-Maʾmūn during the latter's struggle with his brother, al-Amīn, for the caliphate. Convert to Islam from Zoroastrianism.

al-Faḍl ibn Yaḥyā ibn Khālid (d. 193/808) scion of the illustrious Barmakid family and influential administrator under Hārūn al-Rashīd, whose son Muḥammad, the future al-Amīn, he tutored.

Fakhr al-Dīn ʿUthmān ibn Qizil (d. 629/1232) powerful emir under the Ayyubid sultan al-Malik al-Kāmil.

Fars in the early Islamic period, large administrative province in southwest Iran. A hotbed of Zoroastrianism and anti-Arab sentiment, it was only gradually subdued.

al-Fatḥ ibn Khāqān (d. 247/861) Turkic officer, secretary, and adviser to the Abbasid caliphs al-Muʿtaṣim and al-Mutawakkil, he died defending the latter from assassins. Patron and practitioner of the literary arts.

Followers (al-tābiʿūn) generation of Muslims following that of the Companions.

Franks (al-ifranj) term applied to the peoples of Northwest Europe, usually in distinction to Greeks and Slavs. Standard term for the Crusaders among their Muslim contemporaries.

al-Furāt administrative district in the Sawad of Iraq during the early Islamic period.

Fusṭāṭ Arab garrison town founded shortly after the Muslim conquest of Egypt at the site of a Roman fortress. Located in a southern part of modern Cairo.

Gehenna (jahannam) in the Qurʾan, a place of fire and punishment for sinners.

al-Gharbiyyah administrative district in the western Nile delta.

Giza substantial town about twelve miles southwest of medieval Cairo.

Hadith (singular and collective plural) large corpus of reports about the Prophet's deeds and sayings. Each report is typically related by a Companion through a series of transmitters, who are usually named in sequence.

Revered as source of revealed law and moral guidance alongside the Qur'an.

al-Ḥāfiẓ, Abū l-Maymūn ʿAbd al-Majīd (r. 526–44/1132–49) Fatimid caliph of Egypt. Reign was marked by a series of disturbances and intrigues, such as the brief vizierate of the Christian Armenian Bahrām and the rise and fall of the latter's nemesis Riḍwān ibn Walakhshī.

al-Ḥajjāj ibn ʿAtīk al-Thaqafī (fl. first/seventh c.) minor participant in the Muslim conquests of Basra and southwestern Persia.

al-Ḥajjāj ibn Yūsuf al-Thaqafī (d. 95/714) powerful governor of Iraq under the early Marwānid Umayyad caliphs. Presented in the sources as a brutal and extraordinarily capable administrator.

al-Ḥajūn cemetery on the southeast side of Mecca.

al-Ḥākim, Abū ʿAlī al-Manṣūr (r. 386–411/996–1021) Fatimid caliph in Egypt. Politically astute and strong supporter of Ismāʿīlī missionary work. Idiosyncratic and inscrutable in his occasionally harsh policies toward, among others, non-Muslims and animals (notably, dogs).

Ḥarb ibn Umayyah (sixth c. AD) pre-Islamic progenitor of the Umayyad clan of the Prophet's tribe, Quraysh.

Hārūn al-Rashīd ibn Muḥammad (r. 170–93/786–809) Abbasid caliph of Baghdad at its height. Son of al-Mahdī and patron of the Barmakids until their sudden fall.

al-Ḥasan ibn Makhlad (d. late third/ninth c.) high official of the Abbasid state. Twice occupied the vizierate under Caliph al-Muʿtamid.

al-Ḥasan ibn Sahl (d. 236/850–51) high official of the Abbasid state, notably under al-Ma'mūn. Brother of al-Faḍl ibn Sahl.

al-Ḥasan ibn Wahb (d. 247/861) high official of the Abbasid state, particularly under Caliph al-Wāthiq. From an historically Christian family.

Ḥassān ibn Yazīd al-Nabaṭī (fl. early second/ninth c.) wealthy Christian official in Iraq during the later Umayyad period. Reportedly converted to Islam. Father's name varies in the sources.

al-Haytham ibn Khālid ? (fl. mid-third/ninth c.) Christian secretary in the reign of al-Mutawakkil.

Ḥayyān ibn Shurayḥ (d. early second/eighth c.) governor in Egypt under the Umayyad caliph ʿUmar ibn ʿAbd al-ʿAzīz. Attested in documentary sources.

al-Hishāmī, Abū ʿAbdallāh (fl. mid-third/ninth c.) major transmitter of traditions about music to Abū l-Faraj al-Iṣbahānī.

Ḥiṣn Ziyād town in present-day eastern Turkey, now Elazığ. Historically heavily Christian, particularly Armenian.

House, the see *Kaaba.*

Ḥumayd ibn Bishr ? aspirant to secretarial office from the Sawad.

al-Ḥusayn (ibn Aḥmad) ibn (al-)Ḥajjāj the Secretary, Abū ʿAbdallāh (d. 391/1001) Persian Shiʿi secretary, official, and poet.

Ibn ʿAbdūn the Secretary, Abū Manṣūr al-ʿAbdūnī (fl. early fourth/tenth c.) minor secretary and poet of Bukhara.

Ibn Abī l-ʿAlāʾ, al-Ḥārith Abū Firās al-Ḥamdānī (d. 357/968) pro-ʿAlid poet and official. Archrival of al-Mutanabbī.

Ibn Abī Zakariyyā the Secretary, Abū l-Karam al-Akhram Christian official of the Fatimid state. According to some sources, head of the office of financial oversight (*dīwān al-naẓar*) in the time of Caliph al-Ḥāfiẓ.

Ibn al-ʿAmīd, Abū l-Faḍl Muḥammad ibn al-Ḥusayn (d. ca. 360/970) famed secretary, military commander, and *littérateur* of Būyid Iraq.

Ibn Dukhān, Khāṣṣ(at) al-Dawlah Abū l-Faḍl/l-Faḍāʾil (d. 555–56/1160–61) Christian high administrator in the reign of the Fatimid caliph al-ʿĀḍid.

Ibn al-Furāt, Abū l-Ḥasan ʿAlī ibn Muḥammad ibn Mūsā (d. 312/924) renowned secretary and several times vizier to the Abbasid caliph al-Muqtadir.

Ibn Ghalāb, Khālid ibn al-Ḥārith ibn Aws ibn al-Duhmān (first/seventh c.) putative Companion of Muḥammad and participant in the conquests of southern Iraq and Persia.

Ibn Hablān (or Haylān, etc.) ? tax official in the reign of the Ayyubid sultan al-Malik al-Kāmil.

Ibn al-Hārūnī the Jew ? perhaps fictional. A mid-thirteenth century individual of the same name composed a noted dispensatorium, the *Minhāj al-dukkān* (*The Dispensary Manual*).

Ibn Ḥassūn ? (early seventh/thirteenth c.) governor of Damietta during the reign of al-Malik al-Kāmil. Perhaps identical with the emir Badr al-Dīn Ibn Ḥassūn who commanded a naval squadron against the Fifth Crusade in 616/1219.

Ibn al-Lutbiyyah man employed by the Prophet to collect the alms tax. Virtually nothing is related about him apart from the hadith in *The Sword of Ambition,* which is found in many other sources. The version found here places him among the Banū Asad, others among the Banū Azd.

Ibn Manārah, Yaḥyā ibn ʿĪsā (mid-third/ninth c.) minor secretary in Iraq. Satirized for incompetence.

Ibn Mufshīn (or Mafsīn, Hafsīn, etc.) ? tax official in the reign of the Ayyubid sultan al-Malik al-Kāmil.

Ibn Muqlah, Abū ʿAlī Muḥammad ibn ʿAlī (d. 328/940) renowned secretary and vizier of the caliphs al-Muqtadir and al-Qāhir. Pioneer in the field of calligraphy.

Ibn al-Nūrī ? (mid-seventh/thirteenth c.) overseer of finances in Damietta.

Ibn Rāshid ibn Isḥāq, Muḥammad ? (third/ninth c.) candidate for administrative appointment in Iraq.

Ibn Saʿīd ibn ʿAmr (or ʿAwn) ? (mid-third/ninth c.) Christian official of the Abbasid state in Damascus.

Ibn al-Ṣakhr al-Ibyārī ? (fl. early seventh/thirteenth c.) mid-level tax official in the Ayyubid state during the reign of al-Malik al-Kāmil.

Ibn Shukr, Ṣafī l-Dīn ʿAbdallāh ibn al-Ḥusayn (d. 622/1225) influential vizier under al-Malik al-ʿĀdil I and al-Malik al-Kāmil. Sometime colleague of Ibn al-Nābulusī.

Ibn al-Taʿāwīdhī ? possibly Abū l-Fatḥ Muḥammad (d. ca. 583/1187), a secretary and poet of Turkic extraction in Baghdad.

Ibn al-Tammār ? (late fourth/tenth c.) elite Christian, perhaps a state official.

Ibn Ṭūlūn see *Aḥmad ibn Ṭūlūn*.

Ibn Walakhshī see *Riḍwān ibn Walakhshī*.

Ibn al-Zanānīriyyah ? (early fifth/eleventh c.) Christian who was allegedly discovered with a Muslim woman in a church in Rāshidah during the reign of al-Ḥakim.

Ibn Zayn al-Dār ? (late sixth/twelfth c.) unsuccessful aspirant to the Coptic patriarchate ca. 563/1167.

Ibrāhīm ibn al-ʿAbbās al-Ṣūlī (d. 243/857) poet, prose writer, and secretary from an eminent Turkic family of Jurjān. Attached to al-Faḍl ibn Sahl. Great-uncle to the famous courtier Abū Bakr al-Ṣūlī.

Ibyār (or Abyār) town in the district of al-Gharbiyyah, Egypt.

Ikhmīm (or Akhmīm) town in Upper Egypt. It once boasted a large Pharaonic temple.

Imam (imām) literally "one who is in front." Term applied to leaders of the ritual prayer, and to the senior clerics in certain mosques. Shiʿah applied it to their spiritual leaders descended from ʿAlī ibn Abī Ṭālib, Sunnis somewhat later to their caliphs.

Imam Abū Bakr see *Abū Bakr al-Ṣiddīq*.

infidel (kāfir) standard polemical term for non-Muslims. In the Qur'an, a term denoting those who reject the message of Islam, with the connotation of ingratitude.

ʿĪsā ibn Nasṭūrus, Abū l-Faḍl (d. 387/997) Christian secretary and vizier to the Fatimid caliph al-ʿAzīz in 385–86/995–96. Continued briefly in high position until his fall under al-Ḥākim.

al-Iṣbahānī, Abū l-Faraj (d. 356/967) noted historian and collector of valuable poetry and anecdote in his major work, *The Book of Songs*.

Isfahan important city in central Iran.

Ismāʿīl ibn Ṣubayḥ al-Ḥarrānī the Secretary (d. after 195/810–11) prominent secretary in the chanceries of Hārūn al-Rashīd and al-Amīn.

Jaʿfar ibn Khālid ibn Barmak see *Jaʿfar ibn Yaḥyā ibn Khālid*.

Jaʿfar ibn Rabīʿah (d. ca. 136/753–54) scholar and transmitter of historical reports.

Jaʿfar ibn Yaḥyā ibn Khālid (d. 187/803) powerful Barmakid official under Hārūn al-Rashīd. Fell suddenly from grace and was executed.

al-Jāḥiẓ, ʿAmr ibn Baḥr (d. 255/869) famed theologian and *littérateur* of Basra. Patrons included Muḥammad ibn ʿAbd al-Malik al-Zayyāt and al-Mutawakkil.

Jamāl al-Dīn Aydughdī al-ʿAzīzī (d. 664/1265) Turkic emir under the late Ayyubids and early Mamluks. Particularly prominent under the Mamluk sultan Baybars.

Jamāl al-Dīn al-Jazzār, Abū l-Ḥusayn Yaḥyā ibn ʿAbd al-ʿAẓīm (d. 669/1270 or 679/1281) Egyptian butcher and poet (primarily panegyrist).

Jazʾ ibn Muʿāwiyah, al-Saʿdī al-Tamīmī (fl. first/seventh c.) participant in the Muslim conquest of southern Iraq and southwestern Persia.

Jundishapur major city in Khūzestān, southwestern Persia.

Kaaba, the cubic structure in Mecca controlled by the Prophet's tribe, the Quraysh, prior to his mission, housing idols of the Arab polytheists. Subsequently, a site of Muslim veneration toward which believers face during ritual prayer, and which is central to certain rites of the Pilgrimage.

Khālid ibn Barmak (d. 165/781–82) powerful administrator under the Abbasid caliphs al-Saffāḥ and al-Manṣūr. Father of Yaḥyā ibn Khālid, the famous Barmakid vizier of Hārūn al-Rashīd.

Khālid ibn Ṣafwān, Abū Ṣafwān al-Tamīmī (d. ca. 135/752) orator and poet of the late Umayyad period.

Khālid ibn al-Walīd (d. 21/642) noteworthy Companion, though at first an opponent of the Prophet. Later the most distinguished military commander of the early Muslim conquests.

al-Khaṭṭāb ibn Nufayl (late sixth c. AD) father of ʿUmar ibn al-Khaṭṭāb.

Khurasan Large and historically important region of northeastern Iran. Cradle of the Abbasid Revolution.

Khuwaylid al-Ṣaʿiq, ibn Nufayl (sixth c. AD) pre-Islamic chieftain of the Arab tribe of ʿĀmir ibn Ṣaʿṣaʿah.

Kipchak (qifjāq) large and ancient Turkic tribal confederation. Decimated by the Mongol conquests of the later thirteenth century.

al-Kisāʾī, Abū l-Ḥasab ʿAlī ibn Ḥamzah (d. 189/805) Iranian Kufan Qurʾan expert and scholar of the Arabic language. Tutor to Caliph Hārūn al-Rashīd and to his sons.

Kutayfāt (d. 526/1131) powerful Shiʿi vizier of the later Fatimid period; his Imāmī Shiʿism differed from the Ismāʿīlī Shiʿism of the rulers in recognizing a longer line of imams. Of Armenian extraction, his father (al-Afḍal) and grandfather (Badr al-Jamālī) had also been viziers; like them, he enjoyed virtually unchallenged authority in Egypt for a time.

Luxor (al-Uqṣur) town in Upper Egypt. Site of numerous ancient ruins.

al-Mahdī, Abū ʿAbdallāh Muḥammad ibn ʿAbdallāh (r. 158–69/775–85) third Abbasid caliph. Invested in building the religious legitimacy of the caliphate. Granted a great deal of power to the secretaries of his administration.

al-Malik al-ʿĀdil Sayf al-Dīn Abū Bakr Muḥammad ibn Najm al-Dīn Ayyūb (r. 596–615/1200–18) Ayyubid sultan of Egypt. Brother of Ṣalāḥ al-Dīn (Saladin). Known to the Franks as "Saphadin," al-Malik al-ʿĀdil was a capable commander, diplomat, and state builder.

al-Malik al-Kāmil Nāṣir al-Dīn Muḥammad ibn al-ʿĀdil Muḥammad (r. 615–35/1218–38) Ayyubid sultan of Egypt. Led resistance to the Fifth Crusade beginning in 1218. Sometime patron of Ibn al-Nābulusī.

al-Malik al-Ṣāliḥ Najm al-Dīn Ayyūb ibn al-Kāmil Muḥammad (r. 637–47/1240–49) last significant Ayyubid sultan of Egypt. Built up a corps of slave soldiers, unwittingly laying the foundation for Mamluk rule in Egypt. Ostensible dedicatee of *The Sword of Ambition*.

al-Malik al-Ṣāliḥ Ṭalāʾiʿ ibn Ruzzīk (d. 556/1161) powerful Armenian vizier of Egypt during the caliphates of the Fatimids al-Fāʾiz and al-ʿĀḍid, from 549/1154 until his murder. Remembered as refined, financially astute, and a foe to Christians.

al-Ma'mūn, Abū l-ʿAbbās ʿAbdallāh ibn Hārūn (r. ca. 204–18/819–33) seventh Abbasid caliph, son of Hārūn al-Rashīd. Fought devastating war of succession against his brother, al-Amīn, supported the Muʿtazilite theologians, and sponsored translation of Greek and Syriac learning into Arabic.

al-Manādhir district in southwestern Persia at the time of the Muslim conquests.

al-Manṣūr, Abū Jaʿfar ʿAbdallah ibn Muḥammad (r. 136–58/754–75) second Abbasid caliph following al-Saffāḥ. Responsible for many subsequent features of his dynasty's rule. Founded Baghdad in 145/762.

al-Marākibī, Aḥmad ibn ʿAbdallāh ibn Ismāʿīl (late second/eighth c.) superintendent (*ṣāḥib*) of the ships belonging to Hārūn al-Rashīd and owner of the slave girl ʿArīb.

Market of al-Ahwāz main city in the district of Khūzestān, southwestern Persia, at the time of the Muslim conquests.

Marwān ibn Abī Ḥafṣah (d. ca. 182/798) elegist and panegyrist of Arabian origin who strongly supported the Abbasids.

Marwān ibn Muḥammad ibn Marwān ibn al-Ḥakam (d. 132/750) last Umayyad caliph of Syria. Hard-bitten military commander whose power base was among the Arabs of the empire's northern marches. Killed in the course of the Abbasid Revolution by the Abbasid general Ṣāliḥ ibn ʿAlī.

al-Maṭariyyah suburb several miles northeast of Fatimid Cairo near the site of ancient Heliopolis.

Maymūn ibn Hārūn (d. ca. 277/890) minor secretary in the Abbasid government. Member of the powerful Banū Makhlad family.

mihrab niche in the interior wall of a mosque that indicates the direction of Mecca.

minbar stepped pulpit usually found near the mihrab of a congregational mosque.

al-Miqdād ibn al-Aswad al-Kindī (d. 33/653–54) Companion and early convert to Islam. Fought at Badr, participated in conquests, notably those of Syria and Egypt, and settled at an estate near Medina.

Monastery of Simon ancient monastic complex near Aleppo. Site of Simeon Stylites's pillar.

The Monk, Abū Najāḥ ibn Qannā (d. 523/1129) briefly high official to the Fatimid caliph al-Āmir. Despised by Egyptians of all religions for his rapacious confiscations.

Mosque of ʿAmr ibn al-ʿĀṣ first major mosque in Egypt. Established by ʿAmr at Fusṭāṭ ca. 19/641.

Mosque of the Messenger of God the mosque established by the Prophet in Medina.

Mosque of Tibr originally constructed northeast of Fusṭāṭ ca. 145/762. Renovated by an emir of the Ikhshīdid dynasty in Egypt, who was known as Tibr (d. ca. 360/971). Much in use during the Fatimid period.

Muʿāwiyah ibn Abī Sufyān (r. 41–60/661–80) Companion and first in the dynastic line of Umayyad caliphs. Fought ʿAlī ibn Abī Ṭālib in the first intra-Muslim conflict (*fitnah*), shifted the capital to Syria, and named his son Yazīd as successor, sowing the seeds of the second *fitnah*.

Muḥammad ibn al-ʿAbbās, Abū Jaʿfar (fl. late-fourth/tenth c.) secretary and *littérateur* patronized by Samanid kings in Bukhara. Son of a vizier to the Abbasid caliphs al-Muktafī and al-Muqtadir.

Muḥammad ibn ʿAbd al-Malik al-Zayyāt (d. 233/847) Persian vizier to the Abbasid caliphs al-Muʿtaṣim, al-Wāthiq, and al-Mutawakkil. Patron of Greek-to-Arabic translation.

Muḥammad ibn Aḥmad the Secretary, Abū Manṣūr (d. 370/980) philologist and grammarian of Herat, known as al-Azharī after an ancestor.

Muḥammad ibn Manṣūr al-Balkhī ? unidentified, possibly nonexistent poet. Though all of the poetry attributed to him in *The Sword of Ambition* is also found in the *Yatīmah*, none of it is attributed there to a person of this name.

Muḥammad ibn Maslamah al-Anṣārī (d. 43/663 or 664) Companion from Yathrib (Medina) who was closely associated with ʿUmar ibn al-Khaṭṭāb after the Emigration. Appointed a kind of inspector of state offices during ʿUmar's caliphate.

Muḥammad ibn Muḥammad ibn al-Jubayr the Secretary, Abū l-Qāsim (fl. late fourth/tenth c.) poet, prosaist, and secretary to the last Saffarid emir.

Muḥammad ibn al-Muntashir ibn al-Ajdaʿ (fl. early second/eighth c.) governor in Wasit under ʿUmar II and later Umayyad caliphs. Minor transmitter of Hadith.

Muḥammad ibn Mūsā (d. 259/873) polymath and prominent intellectual in Abbasid Iraq. Major patron of translations into Arabic from Greek and Syriac.

Muḥammad ibn Rāshid ibn Isḥāq (early third/ninth c.) obscure candidate for state office in Abbasid Iraq. Satirized by Abū ʿImrān al-Sulamī.

Muḥammad ibn Sulaymān Abbasid general who ended the Ṭūlūnid dynasty in Egypt in 292/905 on behalf of Caliph al-Muktafī. Replaced within months by a governor from Baghdad.

Muḥammad ibn Yazīd al-Anṣārī secretary in Umayyad Iraq during the era of al-Ḥajjāj ibn Yūsuf and ʿAbd al-Malik. The former recommended him to the latter as an ideal secretary, due to his discretion, intelligence, and trustworthiness.

Muharram the final month in the Muslim lunar calendar. Follows the month of Dhu l-Hijjah, in which the Pilgrimage is performed (see *Calendar of the Emigration*; *Pilgrimage*).

Muʾnis al-Muẓaffar, Abū l-Ḥasan (d. 321/933) eunuch official and general who gathered power to himself at the Abbasid caliph's expense.

Muqrān obscure contemporary of the poet Abū Tammām and target of his satire.

al-Muqtadir, Abū l-Faḍl Jaʿfar (r. 295–320/908–32) Abbasid caliph. Installed as a youth and generally ineffectual, notwithstanding the length of his reign.

Mūsā ibn ʿAbd al-Malik (fl. early third/ninth c.) high tax official under al-Mutawakkil.

Mushājiʿ ibn Masʿūd al-Sulamī (d. ca. 36/656) Companion and little-known Arab participant in the conquests of southern Iraq.

al-Mutanabbī, Abū l-Ṭayyib Aḥmad ibn al-Ḥusayn (d. 354/965) celebrated virtuoso court poet. Renowned for his panegyric and influential stylistic innovations.

al-Muʿtaṣim, Abū Isḥāq Muḥammad (r. 218–27/833–42) Abbasid caliph. Son of Hārūn al-Rashīd and brother of al-Maʾmūn. Accomplished military commander who built up a loyal corps of professional slave soldiers.

al-Mutawakkil, Abū l-Faḍl Jaʿfar ibn Muḥammad (r. 232–47/847–61) Abbasid caliph. Sought to built caliphal power, further developing the new capital at Samarra, appealing to influential Muslim traditionalists rather than to Muʿtazilites, and sidelining Turkic mercenaries, who responded by murdering him. First caliph to institute widely and consistently documented discriminatory measures against non-Muslims.

Muʿtazilite adherent of an early rationalist current in Islamic theology that enjoyed its heyday under the Abbasid caliph al-Maʾmūn and thereafter waned to numerical insignificance.

al-Muwaffaq ibn al-Khallāl, Abū l-Ḥajjāj Yūsuf ibn ʿAlī (d. 566/1170) high official and head of the chancery during the reign of the Fatimid caliph al-Ḥāfiẓ.

Nāfiʿ ibn al-Ḥārith, Abū ʿAbdallāh ibn Kaladah al-Thaqafī (d. mid-first/seventh c.) freed slave from Ṭāʾif. Companion and participant in the conquests of southern Iraq and southwestern Persia. Brother of Nufayʿ ibn al-Ḥārith and half-brother of Ziyād ibn Abī Sufyān.

Najm al-Dīn Ayyūb (d. 568/1173) Kurdish military commander and eponym of the Ayyubid dynasty as the father of its founder, Ṣalāḥ al-Dīn (i.e., Saladin). See also *Malik al-Ṣāliḥ, al-*.

Nīsān seventh month in the Syrian calendar, corresponding to April in the Roman calendar.

Nufayʿ ibn al-Ḥārith, Abū Bakrah ibn Kaladah/Masrūḥ al-Thaqafī (d. ca. 51/671) freed slave from Ṭāʾif. Companion and participant in the conquests of southern Iraq and southwestern Persia. Brother of Nāfiʿ ibn al-Ḥārith and half-brother of Ziyād ibn Abī Sufyān.

office (dīwān) standard term for a government bureau. In early Islam, the term *dīwān* referred to the register of conquest fighters who were to receive portions of the spoils.

Pact of Security (dhimmah) in classical Islamic law, an agreement concluded between Muslims and a group of non-Muslims that guarantees to the latter and to their descendants security and some freedom of worship in exchange for payment of a poll tax, political allegiance, and certain kinds of deference toward Muslims.

People of the Non-Muslim Lands (ahl al-ḥarb) literally "people of war." In classical Islamic law and political theory, non-Muslims whose status was not governed by a pact with the Muslims, a safe-conduct granted by the Muslims, or a truce with a Muslim sovereign. Liable in principle to attack and enslavement.

Pilgrimage (ḥajj) journey to Mecca prescribed once in the life of every Muslim capable of undertaking it. Involves a number of prescribed rituals and observances.

poll tax (jizyah) annual payment required of sane adult male dhimmis as a condition of the Pact of Security.

polytheist (mushrik) term applied, in its most proper sense, to the pre-Islamic Arab pagans, but also later, in polemical contexts, to non-Muslims generally.

al-Qāḍī al-Fāḍil, Abū ʿAlī ʿAbd al-Raḥīm al-Baysānī (d. 596/1200) close adviser and secretary to Ṣalāḥ al-Dīn. A Sunni, he began his secretarial career under the Fatimids.

Qudāmah ibn Ziyādah ? (fl. mid-third/ninth c.) Christian official of the Abbasid caliph al-Mutawakkil. Converted to Islam in order to retain his position. May be identical with the secretary Qudāmah ibn Zayd of some other historical reports from the period.

al-Quṣayr large monastery on the heights above Ṭurrah, to the south of Fusṭāṭ. Prior to its destruction by al-Ḥākim it contained as many as ten churches. Restored to some extent thereafter.

al-Rabīʿ ibn Yūnus (d. 169–70/785–86) emancipated slave and prominent servant of Abbasid caliphs from al-Saffāḥ to al-Hādī, bearing at certain times the ranks of chamberlain (*ḥājib*) and vizier. Father of al-Faḍl ibn Rabīʿ.

Ramadan eighth month in the Muslim lunar calendar, during which Muslims are obligated to fast the daylight hours.

Rāmhurmuz town and district in the southwest Persian region of Khūzestān.

al-Rashīd see *Hārūn al-Rashīd ibn Muḥammad.*

Rāshidah district on the eastern outskirts of medieval Fusṭāṭ near the cliffs of al-Muqaṭṭam.

Resurrection, Day of (yawm al-qiyāmah) day promised numerous times in the Qur'an (e.g., Q 75, Sūrat al-Qiyāmah) on which every individual will be resurrected and face God's judgment.

Riḍwān ibn Walakhshī (d. 542/1147) Sunni vizier of the Fatimids in Egypt. Revolted against the Christian Armenian vizier Bahrām, whom he replaced, taking the title of *malik* ("king"). Proceeded to bring government pressure to bear on the Christians of Egypt. Removed by al-Ḥāfiẓ in 533/1139.

Ṣadr al-Dīn, Abū l-Ḥasan Maḥmūd ibn Ḥamawayh (d. 617/1220) respected Shāfiʿī jurist and Sufi. Enjoyed high standing with al-Malik al-ʿĀdil I and al-Malik al-Kāmil.

Ṣafā small hill in Mecca near the Kaaba that plays a central role in the rituals of the Pilgrimage.

Safar second month in the Muslim lunar calendar.

al-Saffāḥ, Abū l-ʿAbbās ʿAbdallāh (r. 132–36/749–54) first Abbasid caliph. Consolidated the dynasty's power.

Ṣafī l-Dīn see *Ibn Shukr.*

Saḥbān Wāʾil (fl. first/seventh c.) renowned early Islamic orator whose name became proverbial for eloquence.

al-Ṣāḥib ibn ʿAbbād, Abū l-Qāsim Ismāʿīl (d. 385/995) prominent *littérateur*, patron, and vizier of the early Buyids.

Sahlān ? (fl. mid-third/ninth c.) Christian secretary and convert to Islam.

Saʿīd al-Dawlah al-Ibyārī ? (early seventh/thirteenth c.) accountant of the treasury (*mustawfī l-khizānah*) under the Ayyubid sultan al-Malik al-Kāmil.

Saʿīd ibn Ḥumayd ibn Saʿīd the Secretary (d. after 257/871) poet, prosaist, and mid-level official, notably under Caliph al-Muntaṣir.

al-Sājī the Secretary, Abū ʿAlī ibn ʿAbdallāh (ca. fourth/tenth c.) minor secretary and poet of Bukhara.

Saladin see *Ṣalāḥ al-Dīn*.

Ṣalāḥ al-Dīn, al-Malik al-Nāṣir Yūsuf ibn Najm al-Dīn Ayyub (r. 564–89/1169–93) Kurdish military commander and founder of the Ayyubid dynasty. Ruled over both Egypt and Syria. Great foe of the Crusaders, who knew him as Saladin. Dedicated supporter of Sunni Islam and its scholars.

Salamah ibn Saʿīd (mid-third/ninth c.) prominent Christian high official. Close to the Abbasid caliphs al-Mutawakkil and al-Mustaʿīn.

Ṣāliḥ ibn ʿAbd al-Quddūs the Secretary (d. 167/783) prominent non-Arab poet. Executed on the accusation of crypto-Manichean heresy (*zandaqah*). Poetry marked by moralizing didacticism.

Ṣāliḥ ibn ʿAbd al-Raḥmān, Abū l-Walīd (d. ca. 102/721) non-Arab Muslim finance official of al-Ḥajjāj ibn Yūsuf in Iraq, under whom he is closely associated with the adoption of Arabic as the language of administration. Rose to greater administrative heights after al-Ḥajjāj's death.

Ṣāliḥ ibn ʿAlī (d. ca. 152/769) commander loyal to the Abbasid caliphs during the war that brought them to power.

Salm al-Khāsir (d. 186/802) non-Arab Basran poet of the early Abbasid period. Skilled in many genres, in particular panegyric and elegy. Reputed libertine.

Samaritans small religious community bearing a close relationship to Judaism. Most adherents have historically lived in Palestine.

Samurah ibn Jundab (d. ca. 59/679) Companion. Took part in the Muslim conquest of southwestern Persia.

al-Ṣanīʿah ("the Protégé") (fl. early seventh/thirteenth c.) high official in the administration of al-Malik al-ʿĀdil I and al-Malik al-Kāmil. Probably the Christian al-Ṣanīʿah Abū Ghālib ibn al-Sukkārī, who also served under al-Malik al-ʿĀdil as superintendent of the administrative office (*dīwān*) of Alexandria. The same title was borne by other Christian officials, such as Ibn Abī Zakariyyā the Secretary, who was called Ṣanīʿat al-Khilāfah ("protégé of the caliphate").

Sarjūn ibn Manṣūr the Christian (fl. late first/seventh c.) influential administrator of Umayyad caliphs, most notably ʿAbd al-Malik. From a prominent Damascene family that had been involved in Byzantine administration. Features frequently in accounts of the change to Arabic as language of administration, representing the outgoing Greek-speaking regime.

Sawad rich agricultural region in lower Iraq, the alluvial lowland of the Tigris and Euphrates.

Sawwār ibn ʿAbdallāh ibn Qudāmah al-Tamīmī (d. ca. 156/773) judge in Basra under Caliph al-Manṣūr.

secretary (kātib, pl. kuttāb, katabah) literally, "writer." Term applied throughout Islamic history to persons performing a broad range of scribal and administrative functions, both official and private.

Shabīb ibn Shaybah, Abū Maʿmar al-Minqarī al-Baṣrī (d. ca. 170/786–87) Basran orator and pious advisor to early Abbasid caliphs.

Shāhawayh ? otherwise unattested official of the Abbasid state in the reign of al-Mahdī.

al-Sharqiyyah district in the eastern Nile delta.

Shāwar, Abū Shujāʿ ibn Mujīr al-Saʿdī (d. 564/1169) twice vizier of the last Fatimid caliph, al-ʿĀḍid.

shaykh ("elder") title of respect.

Shibl ibn Maʿbad al-Bajalī al-Aḥmasī (first/seventh c.) Companion and participant in the Muslim conquest of southern Iraq and southwestern Persia.

al-Sulamī, Abū ʿImrān (turn of second/eighth c.) minor poet in Iraq.

Sulaymān ibn Quḍāʿah, Abū Thābit ibn Saʿd al-Khushanī (late first/early eighth c.) non-Arab official under the Umayyad caliph ʿAbd al-Malik and his successors. Closely associated in many accounts with the change to Arabic as language of administration. More normally "Sulaymān ibn Saʿd al-Quḍāʿī," Quḍāʿah being the name of the Arab tribe with which he was affiliated.

Sulaymān ibn Wahb (d. 271/884–85) secretary and vizier under the caliphs al-Muhtadī and al-Muʿtamid.

Surraq district in Khūzestān, southwestern Persia.

Thumāmah ibn Ashras (d. 213/828) secretary and Muʿtazilite theologian close to circles of power in Abbasid Baghdad, especially those of al-Maʾmūn.

Tinnis important medieval port in the eastern Nile delta, near present-day Port Said. Razed during the lifetime of the author before the present work was composed.

al-Ubullah port town on the Tigris near Basra, conquered by the Arabs in the early conquests.

ʿUmar ibn ʿAbd al-ʿAzīz, Abū Ḥafṣ (r. 99–101/717–20) Umayyad caliph of Damascus. Celebrated for piety and uprightness. Maternal grandson of ʿUmar ibn al-Khaṭṭāb.

ʿUmar (or ʿAmr) ibn ʿAbdallāh al-Shaybānī ? attendant to Caliph al-Maʾmūn during his time in Egypt.

ʿUmar ibn al-Khaṭṭāb (r. 13–23/634–44) second caliph, succeeding Abū Bakr. Towering figure in the Muslim conquests and in the establishment of Islamic legal and administrative precedent. Portrayed by the sources as severe but just.

ʿUmar ibn Masʿadah (d. ca. 217/832) secretary and aphorist in the time of al-Maʾmūn.

ʿUmārah al-Yamanī, Abū Ḥamzah ibn ʿAlī al-Ḥakamī (d. 569/1174) important poet and prose writer of the late Fatimid period in Egypt.

Umaymah bint Ṣufayḥ Companion; mother of Abū Hurayrah.

Umayyad caliphate (41–132/661–750) the first caliphal dynasty of Islam. Descended from a prominent branch of the Prophet's tribe (Quraysh). Power rested on Arab tribal confederations based in Syria. Opposed by many, including Shiʿi partisans of ʿAlī ibn Abī Ṭālib's family, as well as Kharijites, and characterized as impious in much surviving historiography.

Umm ʿAbdallāh ibn Yaḥyā ibn Khālid (late second/eighth c.) wife of Yaḥyā ibn Khālid al-Barmakī.

Upper Egypt (al-Ṣaʿīd) roughly the portion of the Nile Valley in Egypt upstream (south) of Cairo or the thirtieth parallel.

ʿUtbah ibn Ghazwān, Abū Ghazwān al-Māzinī (d. 17/638) Noteworthy Companion and participant in the Muslim conquests of southern Iraq.

ʿUthmān ibn ʿAffān (r. 23–35/644–55) Companion and third caliph of the Muslim community, succeeding ʿUmar ibn al-Khaṭṭāb. Remembered for standardizing the Qurʾanic text, for his piety, and for nepotism toward his Umayyad family. His murder sparked the first intra-Muslim conflict (*fitnah*).

Yaḥyā ibn Khālid ibn Barmak (d. 190/805) leading member of illustrious Barmakid family of officials. Served as governor of Azerbaijan and then as powerful vizier under Hārūn al-Rashīd. Father of al-Faḍl and Jaʿfar, who with him fell suddenly from office in 186/802.

Yaʿqūb ibn Dāwūd, Abū ʿAbdallāh (d. 186/802) vizier of the early Abbasid caliphs. Sympathetic to the political claims of the descendants of ʿAlī ibn Abī Ṭālib.

Yazīd ibn Muḥammad al-Muhallabī (d. ca. 259/873) Basran Arab poet at the courts of al-Mutawakkil and his successors. Member of a prominent family of administrators.

Yazīd ibn Qays, Abū l-Mukhtār (first/seventh c.) Companion and minor poet of the early Islamic period.

Year of the Elephant see *Elephant*.

Year of the Emigration see *Emigration*.

Yūsuf, Prophet Qurʾanic Joseph, from whom the twelfth surah takes its name.

Zayn al-Dīn see *ʿAlī ibn Ibrāhīm ibn Najā al-Anṣārī*.

Ziyād ibn Abī Sufyān/ibn Abīhi (d. 53/673) prominent Arab governor of the early Umayyad period. Adopted into the ruling Sufyānid family despite his uncertain parentage, drawing the poets' derision.

Bibliography

Abele, Silke. *Der politisch-gesellschaftliche Einfluss der nestorianischen Ärzte am Hofe der Abbasidenkalifen von al-Manṣūr bis al-Mutawakkil*. Hamburg: Kovač, 2008.

Abū Dāʾūd, Sulaymān ibn al-Ashʿath al-Sijistānī. *Sunan Abī Dāʾūd*. Edited by M. al-Khālidī. 3 vols. Beirut: Dār al-Kutub al-ʿIlmiyyah, 1996.

Abū Hilāl al-ʿAskarī, al-Ḥasan ibn ʿAbdallāh ibn Sahl. *Kitāb al-ṣināʿatayn*. Istanbul: Maṭbaʿat Maḥmūd Bek, 1320/1902.

Abū l-Makārim, Saʿd Allāh Jirjis ibn Masʿūd. *Tārīkh Abī l-Makārim*. Edited by Ṣ. al-Suryānī. 4 vols. Cairo: al-Niʿām li-l-Ṭibāʿah wa-l-Tawrīdāt, 1984.

Abū Maʿshar. *On Historical Astrology: The Book of Religions and Dynasties (On the Great Conjunctions)*. Edited and translated by K. Yamamoto and C. Burnett. Leiden: Brill, 2000.

[Abū Ṣāliḥ the Armenian]. *The Churches and Monasteries of Egypt and Some Neighbouring Countries*. Translated by B. T. A. Evetts, with added noted by A. J. Butler. Oxford: The Clarendon Press, 1895.

Abū l-Shaykh al-Iṣbahānī, ʿAbdallāh ibn Muḥammad. *Kitāb al-ʿAẓamah*. Edited by R. Mubārakfūrī. 5 vols. Riyadh: Dār al-ʿĀṣimah, 1988–.

Abū ʿUbayd al-Qāsim ibn Sallām. *Kitāb al-amwāl*. Edited by A. Ibn Rajab. Riyadh: Dār al-Faḍīlah, 2007.

ʿĀlī, Muṣṭafā b. Aḥmet. *Naṣīḥatü/Nuṣḥatü s-selāṭīn = Muṣṭafā ʿĀlī's Counsel for Sultans of 1581*. Edited with a translation and commentary by A. Tietze. 2 vols. Vienna: Verlag der Österreichischen Akademie der Wissenschaften, 1979.

ʿAlī ibn Jahm. *Dīwān ʿAlī ibn Jahm*. Edited by Kh. Mardūm. 2nd ed. Beirut: Lajnat al-Turāth, 1971.

Alwash, Jawad Ahmad. *Umara Al-Yamani: The Poet*. Baghdad: Al-Maʿaref Press, 1971.

Antrim, Zayde. *Routes and Realms: The Power of Place in the Early Islamic World*. New York: Oxford University Press, 2012.

Arberry, Arthur J. *The Koran Interpreted*. New York: Macmillan, 1955.

Azdī, ʿAlī ibn Ẓāfir al-. *Badāʾiʿ al-badāʾih*. Edited by M. ʿAbd al-Qādir ʿAṭā. Beirut: Dār al-Kutub al-ʿIlmiyyah, 2007.

Baghdādī, ʿAbd al-Qādir ibn ʿUmar al-. *Khizānat al-adab wa-lubb lubāb lisān al-ʿarab*. Edited by ʿA. M. Hārūn. 4th ed. 13 vols. Cairo: Maktabat al-Khānjī, 1997.

Balādhurī, Aḥmad ibn Yaḥyā al-. *Futūḥ al-buldān.* Edited by ʿU. A. al-Ṭabbāʿ. Beirut: Mu'assasat al-Maʿārif, 1987.

———. *The Origins of the Islamic State.* Translated by Philip Khuri Hitti. New York: Columbia University Press, 1916; *The Origins of the Islamic State, Part II.* Translated by Francis Clark Murgotten. New York: Columbia University Press, 1924.

Balawī, ʿAbdallāh ibn Muḥammad al-. *Sīrat Aḥmad ibn Ṭūlūn.* Edited by M. Kurd ʿAlī. Cairo: Maktabat al-Thaqāfah al-Dīniyyah, 198–.

Berkey, Jonathan. *The Formation of Islam.* Cambridge: Cambridge University Press, 2004.

Bosworth, Clifford Edmund. "The Concept of Dhimma in Early Islam." In *Christians and Jews in the Ottoman Empire: The Functioning of a Plural Society*, edited by B. Braude and B. Lewis, 37–51. 2 vols. New York: Holmes & Meier, 1982.

Cabrol, Cécile. *Les secrétaires nestoriens à Bagdad (762–1258 AD).* Beirut: CERPOC, 2012.

Cahen, Claude. "Histoires coptes d'un cadi médiéval." *Bulletin de l'Institut français d'archéologie orientale*, 59 (1960): 133–50.

Cahen, Claude, and Carl H. Becker. "Kitāb lumaʿ al-qawānīn al-muḍiyya fī dawāwīn al-diyār al-miṣriyya." *Bulletin d'études orientales*, 16 (1958–60): 68–74.

Cameron, Alan and Jacqueline Long. *Barbarians and Politics at the Court of Arcadius.* Berkeley: University of California Press, 1993.

Catlos, Brian. "To Catch a Spy: The Case of Zayn al-Dîn and Ibn Dukhân." *Medieval Encounters* 2, no. 2 (1996): 99–113.

———. *Infidel Kings and Unholy Warriors.* New York: Farrar, Straus and Giroux, 2014.

Chadwick, Henry. *Origen: Contra Celsum.* Cambridge: Cambridge University Press, 1980.

Chamberlain, Michael. *Knowledge and Social Practice in Medieval Damascus, 1190–1350.* Cambridge: Cambridge University Press, 1994.

Cheikho, Louis and Camille Héchaïmé. *Wuzarā' al-Naṣrāniyyah wa-kuttābuhā fī l-islām.* Jūniyah: Librairie Saint-Paul, 1987.

Cohen, Mark R. *Under Crescent and Cross: The Jews in the Middle Ages.* Princeton: Princeton University Press, 1994.

———. "What was the Pact of ʿUmar? A Literary-Historical Study." *Jerusalem Studies in Arabic and Islam*, 23 (1999): 100–57.

———. *Poverty and Charity in the Jewish Community of Medieval Egypt.* Princeton: Princeton University Press, 2009.

Conrad, Lawrence. "A Nestorian Diploma of Investiture from the Tadhkira of Ibn Ḥamdūn: The Text and Its Significance." In *Studia Arabica et Islamica: Festschrift for Iḥsān ʿAbbās on His Sixtieth Birthday*, edited by Wadad al-Qadi, 83–104. Beirut: American University of Beirut/Imprimerie Catholique, 1981.

Contamine, Philippe. "Maréchal de France." In *Lexikon des Mittelalters*, edited by R. Auty et al., 6:230–31. 10 vols. Munich; Zurich: Artemis & Winkler Verlag, 1993.

Cooper, Richard. "The Assessment and Collection of Kharāj Tax in Medieval Egypt." *Journal of the American Oriental Society* 96, no. 3 (1976): 365–82.

Dalrymple, William. *From the Holy Mountain: A Journey in the Shadow of Byzantium*. London: HarperCollins, 1997.

Dhahabī, Shams al-Dīn Muḥammad b. Aḥmad al-. *Siyar aʿlām al-nubalāʾ*. Edited by Sh. al-Arnaʾūṭ, Ḥ. al-Asad. 30 vols. Beirut: Muʾassasat al-Risālah, 1981–.

———. *Taʾrīkh al-islām*. Edited by B. ʿA. Maʿrūf, S. al-Arnāʾūṭ et al. 64 vols. Beirut: Muʾassasat al-Risālah, 1988–.

Dimyāṭī, ʿAbd al-Muʾmin ibn Khalaf al-. "Muʿjam al-shuyūkh." MS Dār al-Kutub al-Waṭaniyyah al-Tūnisiyyah A-MSS-12909.

Dozy, Reinhart. *Dictionnaire détaillé des noms de vêtements chez les arabes*. Amsterdam: Jean Muller, 1845.

———. *Supplément aux dictionnaires arabes*. 3rd ed. 2 vols. Leiden: Brill; Paris: G. P. Maisonneuve et Larose, 1967.

el-Leithy, Tamer. "Sufis, Copts, and the Politics of Piety: Moral Regulation in Fourteenth-Century Upper Egypt." In *The Development of Sufism in Mamluk Egypt*, edited by R. McGregor and A. Sabra, 75–119. Cairo: Imprimerie de l'Institut français d'archéologie orientale, 2006.

Emon, Anver. *Religious Pluralism and Islamic Law: Dhimmis and Others in the Empire of Law*. Oxford: Oxford University Press, 2012.

The Encyclopedia of Arabic Literature. Edited by Julie Meisami and Paul Starkey. 2 vols. New York: Routledge, 1998.

The Encyclopaedia of Islam. Edited by M. Th. Houtsma, et al. 4 vols. Leiden: Brill, 1913–38.

The Encyclopaedia of Islam, Second Edition. Edited by H. A. R. Gibb, et al. 11 vols, Supplement, Index. Leiden: Brill, 1960–2009.

The Encyclopaedia of Islam Three. Edited by M. Gaborieau et al. Leiden: Brill, 2007–.

Ephrat, Daphna. *A Learned Society in a Period of Transition: The Sunni ʿUlamaʾ of Eleventh-Century Baghdad*. Albany, NY: State University of New York Press, 2000.

van Ess, Josef. *Chiliastische Erwartungen und die Versuchung der Göttlichkeit: Der Kalif al-Ḥākim, 386–411 AH*. Heidelberg: Winter, 1977.

Fattal, Antoine. *Le statut légal des non-musulmans en pays d'islam*. 2nd ed. Beirut: Dar el-Machreq, 1995.

Fleischer, Cornell. *Bureaucrat and Intellectual in the Ottoman Empire: The Historian Mustafa Ali, 1541–1600*. Princeton: Princeton University Press, 1986.

Frantz-Murphy, Gladys. *The Agrarian Administration of Egypt from the Arabs to the Ottomans*. Cairo: Institut français d'archéologie orientale, 1986.

Friedmann, Yohanan. *Tolerance and Coercion in Islam: Interfaith Relations in the Muslim Tradition*. Cambridge: Cambridge University Press, 2003.

Ghāzī ibn Aḥmad ibn al-Wāsiṭī, Shihāb al-Dīn. *Radd ʿalā ahl al-dhimmah wa-man tabiʿahum*. Edited by T. Āl Saʿūd. Riyadh: Al-Jamʿiyyah al-Tārīkhiyyah al-Saʿūdiyyah, 2010.

Gil, Moshe. *A History of Palestine 634–1099*. Translated by E. Broido. Cambridge: Cambridge University Press, 1997.

Godefroy, Fréderic. *Dictionnaire de l'ancienne langue française*. 10 vols. Paris: F. Vieweg, 1881–1902.

Goitein, S. D. *A Mediterranean Society: The Jewish Communities of the Arab World as Portrayed in the Documents of the Cairo Geniza*. 5 vols. Berkeley: University of California Press, 1967–88.

Goldenberg, David M. *The Curse of Ham: Race and Slavery in Early Christianity, Judaism, and Islam*. Princeton: Princeton University Press, 2009.

Goldziher, Ignaz. *Introduction to Islamic Theology and Law*. Translated by Andras and Ruth Hamori. Princeton: Princeton University Press, 1981.

Gordon, Matthew. "ʿArib al-Ma'muniyya: A Third/Ninth Century ʿAbbasid Courtesan." In *Views from the Edge: Essays in Honor of Richard W. Bulliet*, edited by N. Yavari, L. Potter, J. Oppenheim, 86–100. New York: Columbia University Press, 2004.

Gottheil, Richard. "An Answer to the Dhimmis." *Journal of the American Oriental Society* 41 (1921): 383–457.

Hillenbrand, Carole. *The Crusades: Islamic Perspectives*. New York: Routledge, 2000.

Hoyland, Robert. *Seeing Islam as Others Saw It*. Princeton: The Darwin Press, 1997.

Ḥusaynī, Aḥmad ibn Muḥammad al-. *Ṣilat al-takmilah li-wafayāt al-naqalah*. Edited by B. ʿA. Maʿrūf. 2 vols. Beirut: Mu'assasat al-Risālah, 2007.

Hutait, Ahmad. "Al-Aqbāṭ wa-l-idārah al-mamlūkiyyah fī ʿahd al-Nāṣir Muḥammad ibn Qalāwūn, Sharaf al-Dīn al-Nushū' namūdhajan" ["The Position of the Copts in Mamluk Administration—The Example of Sharaf al-Dīn al-Nushū'"]. In *Towards a Cultural History of the Mamluk Era*, edited by M. Haddad, A. Heinemann, J. Meloy, S. Slim, 29–40. Beirut: Orient-Institut Beirut, 2010.

Ibn ʿAbd al-Ḥakam, ʿAbd al-Raḥmān. *The History of the Conquest of Egypt, North Africa and Spain: Known as the Futūḥ Miṣr of Ibn ʿAbd al-Ḥakam*. Edited by C. Torrey. New Haven: Yale University Press, 1922.

Ibn ʿAbd al-Ḥakam, ʿAbdallāh. *Sīrat ʿUmar ibn ʿAbd al-ʿAzīz*. Edited by A. ʿUbayd. 2nd ed. Cairo: Maktabat Wahbah, 1983.

Ibn ʿAbd Rabbih, Aḥmad ibn Muḥammad. *Al-ʿIqd al-farīd*. Edited by ʿA. al-Tarḥīnī. 8 vols. Beirut: Dār al-Kutub al-ʿIlmiyyah, 1983.

Ibn Abī l-Dunyā, Abū Bakr ʿAbdallāh ibn Muḥammad. *Qiṣar al-amal*. Edited by M. Kh. R. Yūsuf. Beirut: Dār Ibn Ḥazm, 1995.

Ibn al-Durayhim, ʿAlī ibn Muḥammad. *Manhaj al-ṣawāb fī qubḥ istiktāb ahl al-kitāb*. Edited by S. Kisrawī. Beirut: Dār al-Kutub al-ʿIlmiyyah, 2002.

Ibn Faḍl Allāh al-ʿUmarī, Shihāb al-Dīn Aḥmad ibn Yaḥyā. *Masālik al-abṣār fī mamālik al-amṣār*. Edited by K. S. al-Jubūrī. 27 vols. Beirut: Dār al-Kutub al-ʿIlmiyyah, 2010.

Ibn Ḥamdūn, Muḥammad ibn al-Ḥasan. *Al-Tadhkirah al-Ḥamdūniyyah*. Edited by I. ʿAbbās, B. ʿAbbās. 10 vols. Beirut: Dār Ṣādir, 1996.

Ibn Ḥanbal, Aḥmad. *Musnad al-imām Aḥmad ibn Ḥanbal*. Edited by Sh. al-Arnāʾūṭ, N. al-ʿIrqsūsī. 52 vols. Beirut: Muʾassasat al-Risālah, 1993–2008.

Ibn Hishām, ʿAbd al-Malik. *Al-Sīrah al-nabawiyyah*. Edited by ʿU. Tadmurī. 4 vols. Beirut: Dār al-Kitāb al-ʿArabī, 1990.

Ibn al-Jarrāḥ, Abū ʿAbdallāh Muḥammad ibn Dāʾūd. *Al-Waraqah*. Edited by ʿA. ʿAzzām and ʿA. Aḥmad Farrāj. 2nd ed. Cairo: Dār al-Maʿārif, 1967.

Ibn Jubayr, Abū l-Ḥusayn Muḥammad ibn Aḥmad. *The Travels of Ibn Jubayr*. Translated by R. J. C. Broadhurst. London: Jonathan Cape, 1952.

Ibn Kardabūs, ʿAbd al-Malik. *Al-Iktifāʾ fī akhbār al-khulafāʾ*. Edited by Ṣ. al-Ghāmidī. Medina: Wizārat al-Taʿlīm al-ʿĀlī, 2008.

Ibn Kathīr, Abū l-Fidāʾ Ismāʿīl. *Al-Bidāyah wa-l-nihāyah*. Edited by I. al-Zaybaq. 2nd ed. 20 vols. Damascus; Beirut: Dār Ibn Kathīr, 2010.

Ibn Khallikān, Aḥmad ibn Muḥammad. *Wafayāt al-aʿyān wa-anbāʾ abnāʾ al-zamān*. Edited by I. ʿAbbās. 8 vols. Beirut: Dār Ṣādir, 1968–77.

Ibn Mājah, Muḥammad ibn Yazīd. *Sunan al-ḥāfiẓ Abī ʿAbdallāh Muḥammad ibn Yazīd al-Qazwīnī ibn Mājah*. Edited by M. F. ʿAbd al-Bāqī. 2 vols. Cairo: Dār Iḥyāʾ al-Kutub al-ʿArabiyyah, 1952–53.

Ibn al-Mawṣilī, Muḥammad ibn Muḥammad. *Ḥusn al-sulūk al-ḥāfiẓ li-dawlat al-mulūk*. Edited by F. Aḥmad. Alexandria: Muʾassasat Shabāb al-Jāmiʿah, 1996.

Ibn al-Nābulusī, ʿUthmān ibn Ibrāhīm. *Description du Faiyoum au 7ième siècle de l'hégire*. Edited by B. Moritz. Cairo: Imprimerie Nationale, 1899.

Ibn al-Naqqāsh, Muḥammad ibn ʿAlī. *Kitāb al-madhammah fī stiʿmāl ahl al-dhimmah*. Edited by ʿA. al-Ṭurayqī. Riyadh: Dār al-Muslim, 1995.

Ibn Qayyim al-Jawziyyah, Muḥammad ibn Abī Bakr. *Aḥkām ahl al-dhimmah*. Edited by Ṣ. Ṣāliḥ. 4th ed. 2 vols. Beirut: Dār al-ʿIlm li-l-Malāyīn, 1994.

———. *Rawḍat al-muḥibbīn wa-nuzhat al-mushtāqīn*. Edited by M. ʿA. Shams. Mecca: Dār ʿĀlam al-Fawāʾid, 1431 [2009 or 2010].

Ibn Qutaybah, ʿAbd Allāh ibn Muslim al-Dīnawarī. *ʿUyūn al-akhbār*. 4 vols. Cairo: al-Muʾassasah al-Miṣriyyah al-ʿĀmmah li-l-Taʾlīf wa-l-Tarjamah wa-l-Nashr, 1964.

Ibn Rajab, Zayn al-Dīn ʿAbd al-Raḥmān ibn Aḥmad. *Al-Dhayl ʿalā ṭabaqāt al-ḥanābilah*. Edited by ʿA. al-ʿUthaymīn. 5 vols. Riyadh: Maktabat al-ʿUbaykān, 2005.

Ibn al-Rūmī, ʿAlī ibn al-ʿAbbās. *Dīwān Ibn al-Rūmī*. Edited by A. Basaj. 3 vols. 3rd printing. Beirut: Dār al-Kutub al-ʿIlmiyyah, 2002.

Ibn Taghrī Birdī, Jamāl al-Dīn Abū l-Maḥāsin. *Al-Nujūm al-zāhirah fī mulūk Miṣr wa-l-Qāhirah*. 16 vols. Beirut: Dār al-Kutub al-ʿIlmiyyah, 1992.

Ibn Taymiyyah, Taqī al-Dīn Aḥmad. *Masʾalah fī l-kanāʾis*. Edited by ʿA. al-Shibl. Riyadh: Maktabat al-ʿUbaykān, 1995.

———. *Iqtiḍāʾ al-ṣirāṭ al-mustaqīm*. Edited by N. al-ʿAql. 4th ed. 2 vols. Riyadh: Maktabat al-Rushd, 1994.

Ibshīhī, Shihāb al-Dīn Muḥammad ibn Aḥmad al-. *al-Mustaṭraf fī kull fann mustaẓraf*. 2 vols. Beirut: Dār Maktabat al-Ḥayāt, 1992.

Iṣbahānī, Abū l-Faraj ʿAlī ibn al-Ḥusayn al-. *Kitāb al-Aghānī*. Edited by I. ʿAbbās, I. al-Saʿāfīn, and B. ʿAbbās. 25 vols. Beirut: Dār Ṣādir, 2002.

Jahshiyārī, Muḥammad ibn ʿAbdūs al-. *Kitāb al-wuzarāʾ wa-l-kuttāb*. Edited by M. al-Saqqā, et al. Cairo: Muṣṭafā l-Bābī l-Ḥalabī, 1938.

Khater, Antoine and O. H. E. Burmester, eds. and trans. *History of the Patriarchs of the Egyptian Church, Known as the History of the Holy Church: Volume IV, Part II*. Cairo: Imprimerie de l'Institut français d'archéologie orientale, 1974.

Khaṭīb al-Baghdādī, Aḥmad ibn ʿAlī al-. *Taʾrīkh madīnat al-salām*. Edited by B. ʿA. Maʿrūf. 17 vols. Beirut: Dār al-Gharb al-Islāmī, 2001.

Khaṭīb al-Tabrīzī, al-. *Sharḥ Dīwān Abī Tammām*. 2nd ed. 2 vols. Beirut: Dār al-Kitāb al-ʿArabī, 1994.

Lane, Edward William. *An Arabic-English Lexicon*. London; Edinburgh: Williams and Norgate, 1863–93.

Leiser, Gary. "The *Madrasa* and the Islamization of the Middle East: The Case of Egypt." *Journal of the American Research Center in Egypt*, 22 (1985): 29–47.

Levy-Rubin, Milka. *Non-Muslims in the Early Islamic Empire: From Surrender to Coexistence*. Cambridge: Cambridge University Press, 2011.

Madanī, Ṣadr al-Dīn ʿAlī ibn Maʿṣūm al-. *Anwār al-rabīʿ fī anwāʿ al-badīʿ*. Edited by Sh. H. Shukr. 7 vols. Najaf: Maṭbaʿat al-Nuʿmān, 1969.

Makdisi, George. *The Rise of the Colleges: Institutions of Learning in Islam and the West*. Edinburgh: Edinburgh University Press, 1981.

Makīn ibn al-ʿAmīd, Jirjis ibn Abī Yāsir al-. *Chronique des Ayyoubides (602–658 / 1205–6–1259–60)*. Translated by A. Eddé, F. Micheau. Paris: Académie des Inscriptions et Belles-Lettres, 1994.

Mallett, Alex. *Popular Muslim Reactions to the Franks in the Levant, 1097–1291*. Farnham, UK: Ashgate, 2014.

Maqrīzī, Aḥmad ibn ʿAlī al-. *Al-Mawāʿiẓ wa-l-iʿtibār fī dhikr al-khiṭaṭ wa-l-āthār*. Edited by A. F. Sayyid. 5 vols. London: Mu'assasat al-Furqān li-l-Turāth al-Islāmī, 2002–04.

———. *A History of the Ayyubid Sultans of Egypt*. Translated by R. J. C. Broadhurst. Boston: Twayne Publishers, 1980.

———. *Imtāʿ al-asmāʿ*. Edited by M. al-Numaysī. 15 vols. Beirut: Dār al-Kutub al-ʿIlmiyyah, 1999.

———. *Ittiʿāẓ al-ḥunafāʾ bi-akhbār al-aʾimmah al-Fāṭimiyyīn al-khulafāʾ*. Edited by J. Shayyāl and M. Ḥ. Aḥmad. 2nd ed. 3 vols. Cairo: Lajnat Iḥyāʾ al-Turāth al-Islāmī, 1996.

Marzubānī, Muḥammad ibn ʿImrān ibn Mūsā al-. *Al-Muwashshaḥ fī maʾākhidh al-ʿulamāʾ ʿalā l-shuʿarāʾ*. Edited by M. Shams al-Dīn. Beirut: Dār al-Kutub al-ʿIlmiyyah, 1995.

Mazor, Amir. "Jewish Court Physicians in the Mamluk Sultanate During the First Half of the 8th/14th Century." *Medieval Encounters*, 20 (2014): 38–65.

Muslim ibn al-Ḥajjāj. *Ṣaḥīḥ Muslim*. Edited by M. F. ʿAbd al-Bāqī. 5 vols. Cairo: Dār Iḥyāʾ al-Kutub al-ʿArabiyyah, 1955–56.

Nawājī, Muḥammad ibn al-Ḥasan al-. *Al-Shifāʾ fī badīʿ al-iktifāʾ*. Edited by M. Abū Nājī. Beirut: Dār Maktabat al-Ḥayāt, 1403 [1982 or 1983].

Noth, Albrecht in collaboration with Lawrence I. Conrad. *The Early Arabic Historical Tradition: A Source-Critical Study*. Translated by M. Bonner. Princeton: The Darwin Press, 1994.

Noth, Albrecht. "Problems of Differentiation between Muslims and Non-Muslims." Translated by M. Muehlhaeusler. In *Muslims and Others in Early Islamic Society*, edited by R. Hoyland, 103–25. London: Ashgate, 2004.

Nuwayrī, Aḥmad ibn ʿAbd al-Wahhāb al-. *Nihāyat al-arab fī funūn al-adab*. Edited by N. and Ḥ. Fawwāz et al. 31 vols. Beirut: Dār al-Kutub al-ʿIlmiyyah, 2004.

Owen, Charles A. and C. C. Torrey. "Scandal in the Egyptian Treasury: A Portion of the *Lumaʿ al-Qawānīn* of ʿUthmān ibn Ibrāhīm al-Nābulusī." *Journal of Near Eastern Studies* 14, no. 2 (1955): 70–96.

Papaconstantinou, Arietta. "Between Umma and Dhimma: The Christians of the Middle East under the Umayyads." *Annales islamologiques* 42 (2008): 127–56.

Parker, Kenneth. "Coptic Language and Identity in Ayyūbid Egypt." *Al-Masāq* 25, no. 2 (2013): 222–39.

Perlmann, Moshe. "Notes on Anti-Christian Propaganda in the Mamluk Empire." *Bulletin of the School of Oriental and African Studies* 10, no. 4 (1942): 843–61.

Qālī, Abū ʿAlī Ismāʿīl ibn al-Qāsim al-. *Kitāb al-Amālī.* 4 vols. Cairo: Al-Hayʾah al-Miṣriyyah al-ʿĀmmah li-l-Kitāb, 1975.

Qalqashandī, Aḥmad ibn ʿAlī al-. *Ṣubḥ al-aʿshā fī ṣināʿat al-inshāʾ.* 14 vols. Cairo: Al-Muʾassasah al-Miṣriyyah al-ʿĀmmah, 1964.

Qayrawānī, Ibrāhīm ibn ʿAlī al-Ḥuṣrī al-. *Zahr al-ādāb wa-thamar al-albāb.* Edited by Z. Mubārak. 4 vols. Beirut: Dār al-Jīl, 198?.

Rabie, Hassanein. *The Financial System of Egypt, A.H. 564–741/A.D. 1169–1341.* London: Oxford University Press, 1972.

———. "The Size and Value of the Iqṭāʿ in Egypt." In *Studies in the Economic History of the Middle East,* edited by M. A. Cook, 129–38. Oxford: Oxford University Press, 1970.

Rāghib al-Iṣbahānī, Abū l-Qāsim al-Ḥusayn ibn Muḥammad al-. *Muḥāḍarāt al-udabāʾ wa-muḥāwarāt al-shuʿarāʾ wa-l-bulaghāʾ.* Beirut: Dār Maktabat al-Ḥayāt, 1961.

Sadan, Joseph. "Some Literary Problems Concerning Judaism and Jewry in Medieval Arabic Sources." In *Studies in Islamic History and Civilization in Honor of Professor David Ayalon,* edited by M. Sharon, 353–98. Jerusalem: Cana, 1986.

Ṣafadī, Ṣalāḥ al-Dīn Khalīl ibn Aybak al-. *Aʿyān al-ʿaṣr wa-aʿwān al-naṣr.* Edited by ʿA. Abū Zayd et al. 6 vols. Beirut: Dār al-Fikr, 1998.

———. *Kitāb al-Wāfī bi-l-wafayāt.* Edited by A. al-Arnāʾūṭ, T. Muṣṭafā. 29 vols. Beirut: Dār Iḥyāʾ al-Turāth al-ʿArabī, 2000.

Saffārīnī, Muḥammad al-. *Ghidhāʾ al-albāb li-sharḥ manẓūmat al-ādāb.* 2 vols. Beirut: Dār al-Kutub al-ʿIlmiyyah, 1996.

Sakhāwī, Muḥammad ibn ʿAbd al-Raḥmān al-. *Al-Ajwibah al-marḍiyyah fīmā suʾila al-Sakhāwī ʿanhu min al-aḥādīth al-nabawiyyah.* Edited by M. Ibrāhīm. Riyadh: Dār al-Rāyah, 1418/1997 or 98.

Samir, Samir Khalil. "The Role of Christians in the Fāṭimid Government Services of Egypt to the Reign of al-Ḥāfiẓ." *Medieval Encounters* 2:3 (1996): 177–92.

Ṣarradurr, ʿAlī ibn al-Ḥasan ibn ʿAlī ibn al-Faḍl. *Dīwān Ṣarradurr.* Edited by M. ʿAbd al-ʿĀlī. Cairo: Maktabat al-Khānjī, 2008.

Sayyid, Ayman Fuʾād. *Al-Dawlah al-Fāṭimiyyah fī Miṣr: tafsīr jadīd.* Cairo: Al-Dār al-Miṣriyyah al-Lubnāniyyah, 1992.

Schmidtke, Sabine. "Moshe Perlmann (1905–2001): A Bibliography". *Jerusalem Studies in Arabic and Islam* 36 (2009): 33–61.

Sennott, Charles. *The Body and the Blood: The Middle East's Vanishing Christians and the Possibility for Peace.* New York: Public Affairs, 2003.

Sharīf al-Murtaḍā, ʿAlī ibn al-Ḥusayn al-ʿAlawī al-. *Amālī al-Murtaḍā*. Edited by M. A. Ibrāhīm. 2 vols. Cairo: Dār Iḥyāʾ al-Kutub al-ʿArabiyyah, 1954.

Shuʿaybī, Ḥamūd ibn ʿUqalāʾ al-. *Al-Qawl al-mukhtār fī ḥukm al-istiʿānah bi-l-kuffār*. Accessed February 9, 2016. http://www.saaid.net/book/open.php?cat=1&book=332.

Sirry, Munʿim. "The Public Role of Dhimmīs during the ʿAbbāsid Times." *Bulletin of the School of Oriental and African Studies* 74:2 (2011): 187–204.

Sivan, Emmanuel. "Réfugiés syro-palestiniens au temps des croisades." *Revue des études islamiques* 25 (1967): 135–48.

———. "Notes sur la situation des chrétiens à l'époque ayyubide." *Revue de l'histoire des religions* 172:2 (1967): 117–30.

Sprengling, M. "From Persian to Arabic." *The American Journal of Semitic Languages and Literatures* 56:2 (1939): 175–224.

———. "From Persian to Arabic." *The American Journal of Semitic Languages and Literatures* 57:3 (1940): 302–5.

Stewart, Devin. "The Doctorate of Islamic Law in Mamluk Egypt and Syria." In *Law and Education in Medieval Islam: Studies in Memory of Professor George Makdisi*, edited by J. Lowry, D. Stewart, and S. Toorawa, 66–78. [Cambridge, UK]: E. J. W. Gibb Memorial Trust, 2004.

———. "The *Maqāmāt* of Aḥmad b. Abī Bakr b. Aḥmad al-Rāzī al-Ḥanafī and the Ideology of the Counter-Crusade in Twelfth-Century Syria." *Middle Eastern Literatures*, 11:2 (2008): 211–32.

Stillman, Norman. "The Emergence, Development and Historical Continuity of the Sephardi Courtier Class." *Espacio, tiempo, y forma*, ser. III, no. 6 (1993): 17–30.

Stroumsa, Guy. "Tertullian on Idolatry and the Limits of Tolerance." In *Tolerance and Intolerance in Early Judaism and Christianity*, edited by G. Stanton and G. Stroumsa, 173–84. Cambridge: Cambridge University Press, 1998.

[Sulaym ibn Qays]. *Kitāb Sulaym ibn Qays al-Hilālī*. Edited by M. B. al-Anṣārī. Qom: Maṭbaʿat al-Hādī, 1994 or 95.

Ṣūlī, Abū Bakr Muḥammad ibn Yaḥyā al-. *Kitāb al-awrāq, qism akhbār al-shuʿarāʾ*. Edited by J. Heyworth-Dunne. Cairo: Maṭbaʿat al-Ṣāwī, 1934.

Swanson, Mark. *The Coptic Papacy in Islamic Egypt (641–1517)*. Cairo; New York: The American University in Cairo Press, 2010.

Synesius of Cyrene. *The Essays and Hymns of Synesius of Cyrene: Including the Address to the Emperor Arcadius and the Political Speeches*. Edited and translated by A. FitzGerald. 2 vols. London: Oxford University Press, 1930.

Ṭabarī, Muḥammad ibn Jarīr al-. *The History of al-Ṭabarī: Vol. XXI, The Victory of the Marwānids*. Translated by M. Fishbein. Albany: State University of New York Press, 1990.

———. *The History of al-Ṭabarī: Vol. XXXIV, Incipient Decline*. Translated by J. Kraemer. Albany: State University of New York Press, 1989.

Ṭaḥāwī, Aḥmad ibn Muḥammad al-. *Sharḥ mushkil al-āthār*. Edited by Sh. al-Arnā'ūṭ. 16 vols. Beirut: Mu'assasat al-Risālah, 1994.

Talmon-Heller, Daniella. "Arabic Sources on Muslim Villagers Under Frankish Rule." In *From Clermont to Jerusalem: The Crusades and Crusader Societies, 1095–1500*, edited by A. Murray, 103–18. Turnhout: Brepols, 1998.

Tanūkhī, Abū 'Alī l-Ḥasan ibn Abī l-Qāsim al-. *Al-Faraj ba'da l-shiddah*. Edited by 'A. al-Shāljī. Beirut: Dār Ṣādir, 1978; 2 vols. Cairo: Maktabat al-Khānjī, 1955.

Tawḥīdī, Abū Ḥayyān al-. *Al-Imtā' wa-l-mu'ānasah*. Edited by A. Amīn, A. al-Zayn. 3 vols. Cairo: Lajnat al-Ta'līf wa-l-Tarjamah wa-l-Nashr, 1939.

Tha'ālibī, Abū Manṣūr 'Abd al-Malik ibn Muḥammad al-. *Al-I'jāz wa-l-ījāz*. Edited by I. Āṣāf. Cairo: Al-Maṭba'ah al-'Umūmiyyah, 1897.

———. *Yatīmat al-dahr fī maḥāsin ahl al-'aṣr*. Edited by M. F. Qumayḥah. 5 vols. Beirut: Dār al-Kutub al-'Ilmiyyah, 1983.

Tillier, Mathieu. *Les cadis d'iraq et l'état abbasside (132/750–334/945)*. Damascus; Beirut: Institut français du Proche-Orient, 2009.

Timm, Stefan. *Das christlich-koptische Ägypten in arabischer Zeit: Eine Sammlung christlicher Stätten in Ägypten in arabischer Zeit*. 6 vols. Wiesbaden: L. Reichert, 1984–92.

Tirmidhī, Abū 'Īsā Muḥammad ibn 'Īsā al-. *Al-Jāmi' al-ṣaḥīḥ, wa-huwa Sunan al-Tirmidhī*. Edited by A. M. Shākir, M. F. 'Abd al-Bāqī, and I. 'Awaḍ. 5 vols. Cairo: Muṣṭafā l-Bābī al-Ḥalabī, 1937–.

Ṭurṭūshī, Muḥammad ibn al-Walīd al-. *Sirāj al-mulūk*. Edited by J. al-Bayātī. London: Riad el-Rayyes, 1990.

Tustarī, Muḥammad Taqī. *Bahj al-ṣabāghah fī sharḥ Nahj al-balāghah*. 14 vols. Tehran: Dār Amīr Kabīr li-l-Nashr, 1997.

'Umārah ibn 'Alī al-Ḥakamī al-Yamanī. *'Oumâra du Yémen, sa vie et son œuvre*. Edited with commentary and notes by H. Derenbourg. 2 vols. Paris: E. Leroux, 1897–1904.

Vajda, George. *Le Dictionnaire des Autorités (Mu'ǧam aš-Šuyūḫ) de 'Abd al-Mu'min al-Dimyāṭī*. Paris: Centre National de la Recherche Scientifique, 1962.

Wāḥidī, Abū l-Ḥasan 'Alī ibn Aḥmad al-. *Sharḥ Dīwān al-Mutanabbī*. Berlin: Mittler, 1861.

Waṭwāṭ, Muḥammad ibn Ibrāhīm ibn Yaḥyā. *Ghurar al-khaṣā'iṣ al-wāḍiḥah wa-'urar al-naqā'iṣ al-fāḍiḥah*. Būlāq: al-Maṭba'ah al-Miṣriyyah, 1284/1867.

Werthmuller, Kurt. *Coptic Identity and Ayyubid Politics in Egypt, 1218–50*. Cairo; New York: The American University in Cairo Press, 2010.

Wilken, Robert. *John Chrysostom and the Jews: Rhetoric and Reality in the Late 4th Century*. Berkeley: University of California Press, 1983.

Yāfiʿī, ʿAbd al-Fattāḥ ibn Ṣāliḥ Qudaysh al-. *Ḥukm tawliyat ahl al-dhimmah fī l-madhāhib al-arbaʿah*. Accessed 5 December 2014. http://muntada.islamtoday.net/t75045.html.

Yāqūt al-Ḥamawī. *Muʿjam al-udabāʾ*. Edited by I. ʿAbbās. 7 vols. Beirut: Dār al-Gharb al-Islāmī, 1993.

Yarbrough, Luke. "I'll not accept aid from a *mušrik*." In *The Late Roman and Early Islamic Mediterranean and Near East: Authority and Control in the Countryside*, edited by A. Delattre, M. Legendre, P. Sijpesteijn. Princeton: The Darwin Press. (forthcoming).

———. "The Madrasa and the Non-Muslims of Thirteenth-Century Egypt: A Reassessment." In *Entangled Histories: Knowledge, Authority, and Transmission in Thirteenth-Century Jewish Cultures*, edited by E. Baumgarten, R. Karras, and K. Mesler. Philadelphia: The University of Pennsylvania Press. (forthcoming).

———. "Origins of the *ghiyār*." *Journal of the American Oriental Society* 134:1 (2014), 113–21.

———. "A Rather Small Genre: Arabic Works Against Non-Muslim State Officials." (*Der Islam*, 93:1 [2016], forthcoming).

———. "Upholding God's Rule: Early Muslim Juristic Opposition to the State Employment of Non-Muslims." *Islamic Law and Society* 19:1 (2012): 11–85.

———. "ʿUthmān b. Ibrāhīm al-Nābulusī." In *Christian-Muslim Relations: A Bibliographical History*, edited by David Thomas et al. 11 vols. Leiden: Brill, 2012: 310–16.

Wasserstein, David. "Conversion and the *ahl al-dhimma*." In *The New Cambridge History of Islam*, edited by Michael Cook et al., 4:184–208. 6 vols. New York; Cambridge: Cambridge University Press, 2010.

Yūnīnī, Quṭb al-Dīn Mūsā ibn Muḥammad al-. *Dhayl mirʾāt al-zamān*. 2 vols. Hyderabad: Dāʾirat al-Maʿārif al-ʿUthmāniyyah, 1955.

Zaborowski, Jason. "From Coptic to Arabic in Medieval Egypt." *Medieval Encounters* 14:1 (2008): 15–40.

Zajjājī, ʿAbd al-Raḥmān al-. *Akhbār Abī l-Qāsim al-Zajjājī*. Edited by ʿA. Mubārak. Baghdad: Dār al-Rashīd li-l-Nashr, 1980.

Further Reading

Ibn al-Nābulusī and His Works

Cahen, Claude. "Histoires coptes d'un cadi médiéval." *Bulletin de l'Institut français d'archéologie orientale*, 59 (1960): 133–50.

Cahen, Claude, and C. Becker. "Kitāb luma' al-qawānīn al-muḍiyya fī dawāwīn al-diyār al-miṣriyya." *Bulletin d'études orientales*, 16 (1958–60): 68–74.

Catlos, Brian. "To Catch a Spy: The Case of Zayn al-Dîn and Ibn Dukhân." *Medieval Encounters* 2, no. 2 (1996): 99–113.

Owen, Charles A. and C. C. Torrey. "Scandal in the Egyptian Treasury: A Portion of the Luma' al-Qawānīn of 'Uthmān ibn Ibrāhīm al-Nābulusī." *Journal of Near Eastern Studies* 14, no. 2 (1955): 70–96.

The History of the Early and Medieval Islamic Periods, with Special Reference to Ayyubid Egypt

Berkey, Jonathan. *The Formation of Islam*. Cambridge: Cambridge University Press, 2004.

The Cambridge History of Egypt, Volume 1: Islamic Egypt (640–1517). Edited by Carl Petry. Cambridge: Cambridge University Press, 2008.

Humphreys, R. Stephen. *From Saladin to the Mongols: The Ayyubids of Damascus*. Albany, NY: State University of New York Press, 1977.

Lev, Yaacov. *Saladin in Egypt*. Leiden: Brill, 1999.

Walker, Paul. *Exploring an Islamic Empire: Fatimid History and Its Sources*. London: I. B. Tauris, 2002.

Non-Muslims in Islamic Societies, with Special Reference to the Copts

Atiya, Aziz Suryal. *A History of Eastern Christianity*. Enlarged and updated. Millwood, NY: Kraus Reprint Co., 1980.

The Claremont Coptic Encyclopedia (online): http://ccdl.libraries.claremont.edu/cdm/landingpage/collection/cce.

Cohen, Mark. *Under Crescent and Cross*. Princeton: Princeton University Press, 1994.

Fattal, Antoine. *Le statut légal des non-musulmans en pays d'islam.* 2nd ed. Beirut: Dar el-Machreq, 1995.

Goitein, S. D. *A Mediterranean Society: The Jewish Communities of the Arab World as Portrayed in the Documents of the Cairo Geniza.* 5 vols. Berkeley: University of California Press, 1967–88.

Lassner, Jacob. *Jews, Christians, and the Abode of Islam: Modern Scholarship, Medieval Realities.* Chicago: The University of Chicago Press, 2012.

Levy-Rubin, Milka. *Non-Muslims in the Early Islamic Empire.* Cambridge: Cambridge University Press, 2011.

Swanson, Mark. *The Coptic Papacy in Islamic Egypt (641–1517).* Cairo; New York: The American University in Cairo Press, 2010.

Werthmuller, Kurt. *Coptic Identity and Ayyubid Politics in Egypt, 1218–50.* Cairo; New York: The American University in Cairo Press, 2010.

Islamic Administration

Cahen, Claude. *Makhzūmiyyāt: Études sur l'histoire économique et financière de l'Égypte medieval.* Leiden: Brill, 1977.

Duri, Abd Al-Aziz. *Administration and Taxation from the Caliphate to the Umayyads and Abbasids.* Translated by R. Ali. London: I. B. Tauris, 2008.

Frantz-Murphy, Gladys. *The Agrarian Administration of Egypt from the Arabs to the Ottomans.* Cairo: Institut français d'archéologie orientale, 1986.

Intercommunal Conflict in Medieval Egypt

Gottheil, Richard. "An Answer to the Dhimmis." *Journal of the American Oriental Society*, 41 (1921): 383–457.

Gril, Denis. "Une émeute anti-chrétienne à Qūṣ au début du viie/xive siècle." *Annales islamologiques*, 16 (1980): 241–74.

Leithy, Tamer el-. "Sufis, Copts, and the Politics of Piety: Moral Regulation in Fourteenth-Century Upper Egypt." In *The Development of Sufism in Mamluk Egypt*, edited by R. McGregor and A. Sabra, 75–119. Cairo: Institut français d'archéologie orientale, 2006.

Perlmann, Moshe. "Notes on Anti-Christian Propaganda in the Mamluk Empire." *Bulletin of the School of Oriental and African Studies* 10, no. 4 (1942): 843–61.

Index

abase(ment). *See* humiliate, humiliation.
al-ʿAbbās ibn Muḥammad, §3.2.22
Abbasids. *See* caliphate, Abbasid.
ʿAbd al-Ḥamīd ibn Yaḥyā, §3.2.2
ʿAbd al-Malik ibn Marwān (Umayyad caliph), §0.3, §1.6.1
ʿAbdallāh ibn al-Abrash, §1.13.6
ʿAbdallāh ibn Yaḥyā ibn Khāqān, §1.13.1
Abū l-ʿAbbās Aḥmad ibn Isḥāq the Secretary. *See* Aḥmad ibn Isḥāq
Abū l-ʿAbbās Aḥmad ibn al-Rūmī the Secretary. *See* Aḥmad ibn al-Rūmī
Abū ʿAbdallāh al-Ḥusayn ibn Ḥajjāj. *See* al-Ḥusayn ibn Ḥajjāj
Abū ʿAlī ibn ʿAbdallāh. *See* al-Sājī
Abū ʿAlī ibn al-Afḍal ibn Shāhān Shāh ibn Amīr al-Juyūsh. *See* Kutayfāt
Abū ʿAlī ibn Muqlah, Muḥammad ibn ʿAlī. *See* Ibn Muqlah
Abū l-ʿAynāʾ, Muḥammad ibn al-Qāsim ibn Khallād, §3.2.10
Abū Bakr al-Khwārizmī, §3.2.15
Abū Bakr Muḥammad ibn al-ʿAbbās. *See* Muḥammad ibn al-ʿAbbās, Abū Bakr
Abū Bakr al-Ṣiddīq, §0.3, §1.4.1, §1.5.7
Abū l-Faḍl Ibn al-ʿAmīd. *See* Ibn al-ʿAmīd
Abū l-Faraj ibn Zurʿah, §2.14.5
Abū l-Fatḥ al-Bustī. *See* al-Bustī.
Abū l-Ḥasan Ibn al-Furāt. *See* Ibn al-Furāt
Abū Ḥumayd al-Sāʿidī, §4.3.2
Abū Hurayrah, ʿAbd al-Raḥmān ibn Ṣakhr al-Dawsī, §1.5.7, §4.3.8, 208n273
Abū l-Hurṭumān, §3.2.28
Abū ʿImrān al-Sulamī. *See* al-Sulamī
Abū Jaʿfar Muḥammad ibn al-ʿAbbās. *See* Muḥammad ibn al-ʿAbbās
Abū Manṣūr ʿAlī ibn al-Faḍl. *See* ʿAlī ibn al-Faḍl
Abū Manṣūr Ibn ʿAbdūn. *See* Ibn ʿAbdūn
Abū Manṣūr Muḥammad ibn Aḥmad. *See* Muḥammad ibn Aḥmad
Abū Maryam ibn al-Muḥarrish al-Ḥanafī, §4.3.5
Abū Muḥammad al-Muhallabī, §3.3.13, 204n210
Abū l-Mukhtār Yazīd ibn Qays. *See* Yazīd ibn Qays
Abū Mūsā al-Ashʿarī, §1.5.2, §1.5.6
Abū Nūḥ ʿĪsā ibn Ibrāhīm, §1.13.6
Abū Nuwās, al-Ḥasan ibn Hāniʾ al-Thaqafī, §3.2.8
Abū l-Qāsim Muḥammad ibn Muḥammad. *See* Muḥammad ibn Muḥammad
Abū l-Qāsim al-Ṣāḥib ibn ʿAbbād. *See* al-Ṣāḥib ibn ʿAbbād
Abū l-Shīṣ, Muḥammad ibn ʿAbdallāh al-Khuzāʿī, §3.2.4
Abū Tammām, §3.2.33
Abū Thābit. *See* Sulaymān ibn Quḍāʿah
Abū ʿUbaydah, ʿĀmir ibn ʿAbdallāh ibn al-Jarrāḥ, §4.3.4

Abū Yaʿlā, §3.2.28
Abū Yāsir the Christian, §1.14.1
Abyār. *See* Ibyār
al-ʿĀḍid (Fatimid caliph), §0.4, §2.14.3, §2.14.5
account(s) (*ḥisāb*), §§1.1.1–2, §1.9.1, §1.12.4, §1.13.1, §1.13.3, §1.15.3, §2.6.1, §2.14.3, §2.15.2, §3.2.21, §§3.2.35–36, §§4.2.21–22
accounting. *See* arithmetic
Adam, §3.2.10
administration, xx–xxii, xxviii, §1.1.2, §1.4.1, §1.6.1, §1.8.4, §2.2.1, §2.3.1, §2.4.1, §2.9.2, §2.13.1, §3.2.24, §§3.2.34–35, §4.2.2, §4.2.6, 206n231
Aḥmad ibn Abī Khālid, §3.2.9
Aḥmad ibn al-Ḥusayn. *See* Badīʿ al-Zamān
Aḥmad ibn Isḥāq the Secretary, Abū l-ʿAbbās, §3.3.17
Aḥmad ibn Isrāʾīl, §1.13.1
Aḥmad ibn Muḥammad al-Balkhī, Abū Manṣūr, §3.3.18
Aḥmad ibn al-Rūmī the Secretary, Abū l-ʿAbbās, §3.3.6
Aḥmad ibn Ṭūlūn, xxiv, §0.4, §2.4.1, 197n85
al-Aḥnaf, §4.3.5
Akhmīm. *See* Ikhmīm
al-Akhram. *See* Ibn Abī Zakariyyā
ʿAlam al-Dīn Ibrāhīm (father of the author), xix, §3.2.34
ʿAlī ibn Abī Ṭālib, §1.5.7
ʿAlī ibn al-Faḍl, Abū Manṣūr Ṣarradurr, §3.3.21
ʿAlī ibn Ibrāhīm ibn Najā al-Anṣārī, Zayn al-Dīn, xix–xx, xxxi, §§2.14.2–3, 200n116, 200n117
ʿAlī ibn ʿĪsā, §3.2.6
alms (*zakāt*, *ṣadaqah*), §3.2.3, §§4.3.1–2, §4.3.5
al-Amīn (Abbasid caliph), §§3.2.7–8
al-Āmir (Fatimid caliph), §0.4, §2.7.2, §§2.10.2–3, 199n105
ʿAmmār ibn Yāsir, §2.15.3
ʿAmr ibn al-ʿĀṣ, xli, §4.3.3, §4.3.6, 196n46
al-Anbār, §1.9.1
angel(s), §1.8.1, §3.2.1
Ansina, §1.12.1
ʿAntar(ah) ibn Shaddād, §1.12.4
apostasy, apostate(s), §2.15.4, 201n127
arab(s), §§0.1–2, §1.5.3, §3.2.1, §3.2.37
Arabic language, xiv, xxv, xxxii, xxxv–xxxvii, §1.6.1, §1.7.1, §1.13.5, §2.6.2, §2.8.1, §2.13.1, §3.2.1, §4.2.19, 198n87, 199n97, 199n106, 199–200n109, 202n146, 203n170, 203n179, 205n213, 205n219, 206n232, 206n244, 207n250, 207n252, 207n253, 207n255, 207n256
ʿArīb al-Maʾmūniyyah, §0.4, §2.8.1, 198n93
arithmetic, §1.7.1, §2.14.3, §3.2.1
army, armies, §1.12.3, §2.9.1, §3.2.9, §4.1.11
al-ʿĀṣ ibn Wāʾil, §4.3.6
al-Asʿad al-Fāʾizī, xxi
ascetic(s), §1.10.1, §2.7.1
ʿĀṣim ibn Qays ibn al-Ṣalt al-Sulamī, §4.3.5
al-Aṣmaʿī, Abū Saʿīd ʿAbd al-Malik ibn Qurayb, §3.2.6, 201n141
astrology, astrologer(s), §§2.9.2–3, §4.2.15, §4.2.17, 199n96; ascendant, §3.2.23
al-ʿAttābī, Kulthūm ibn ʿAmr, §3.2.7
audit, auditing, xx, §3.2.36
Ayyubid dynasty, xii, xviii, xxii, xxix–xxx, xxxv, 197n85, 203n184

Badīʿ al-Zamān, Abū l-Faḍl Aḥmad ibn al-Ḥusayn al-Hamadhānī, §3.2.16, §3.3.9, 202n155
Badr, Battle of, §1.2.1
Baghdad, xix, §3.2.7
al-Baḥrayn, §1.5.1, §4.3.8
Bamboo (Ar. *Khayzurān*), §3.2.7
Banū Asad, §4.3.2
Banū Ghazwān, §4.3.5
Banū Ḥabīb, §1.12.3
Barmakids, §3.2.5, 201n132
Basra, §1.10.2, §2.8.1, §4.3.5
bath(s), §1.8.2, §1.13.4, §2.6.1, §4.2.29
al-Baydāʾ, §1.2.1
belts, distinguishing (*zunnār*), §0.2, §2.10.3
bishop, Christian, xxvii, §2.14.4
Bishr ibn al-Muḥtafiz al-Muzanī, §4.3.5
bless(ing), xxxv, §2.10.3, §2.11.2, §3.2.31, §§3.2.34–35, §4.2.20, §4.4.2
blood, §1.5.6, 199–200n109; declared licit, §2.6.1, §2.15.4
book(s), xviii–xix, xxi–xxiv, xxvii, xxxiii, xxxvii, xli, §0.2, §0.6, §1.1.4, §1.7.2, §2.8.1, §2.10.3, §2.12.1, §2.15.1, §3.1.1, §4.2.15, §4.2.19, §4.2.26, §4.4.1, 202n146
brazen(ness) (*iqdām*), §2.6.3
bribe(ery)§1.9.1, §2.9.2, §3.2.20, §3.2.28, §3.2.33, §4.2.2, 202n159
Bridle, Land of the, §2.11.1, 199n99
al-Buḥturī, Abū ʿUbādah al-Walīd ibn ʿUbaydallāh, §2.15.1
Būṣīr Sidr, §3.2.2, 201n129
al-Bustī, Abū l-Fatḥ ʿAlī ibn Muḥammad., §3.2.20, §3.3.10
Byzantines. *See* Greek(s).
cadastral survey (*rawk*). *See* survey(or), surveying.
Cahen, Claude, xxiii, xxx, xxxiii, 193n3,
Cairo, xviii, xix, xxii, §2.6.1
calendar(s), §1.5.3, §4.2.17, 194n15, 207n257
caliph(ate), §0.3, §2.13.1, §2.15.1, §3.2.24, §4.4.1; Abbasid, xxvi, xxx, xli, §1.10.1, §§1.12.1–3, §§1.13.1–4, §2.8.1, §§3.2.2–3, §3.2.7, §3.2.11, §3.2.22, §3.2.33, §4.3.9, 195n37, 195n41, 196n54; Fatimid, xix, xxv, xxx–xxxi, §2.7.2, §2.9.2, §2.9.4, §2.13.2, §§2.14.2–3, 198n92, 199n105; Rightly Guided, xii, §1.5.1, §1.5.4; Umayyad, §1.6.1, §3.2.2, 194n21, 195n33
Capella (star), §1.12.4
casket(s), of the dead, §2.10.3
Catlos, Brian, xxxi, xxxvii
cattle. *See* cow(s)
Celsus, xxxii
Chamberlain, Michael, xxx
chamberlain(s) (ḥājib), §1.10.1, §1.13.2, §1.14.1, §2.13.2
chancery, §1.6.1, §2.9.1, §3.3.22
chess, §1.15.2
Chosroes Anūshirwān, §§3.2.24–25
Christianity, xiii, §2.6.1, §2.14.1, §§2.15.1–2
Christian(s), xiii, xxi, xxix, xxxii, §0.4, §1.1.3, §§1.8.2–3, §1.9.2, §1.12.1, §1.12.4, §2.1.1, §2.2.1, §2.5.1, §§2.6.1–3, §2.7.1, §2.8.1, §2.9.2, §2.10.1. §2.10.3, §2.14.1, §§2.15.1–4, 193n1, 196n45, 196n52, 197n79, 200n118, 207n257; beliefs, doctrines. *See* Christianity.; clergy, xxvii, §2.7.1, §2.14.5; official(s), state, xiii, xviii–xix, xxiv–xxv, xxviii–xxix, xxxi, xli, §1.5.1, §§1.5.5–6, §1.6.1, §1.7.1, §1.8.4, §1.9.1, §§1.10.1–2, §1.12.2,

Christian(s) (cont.), §1.13.1–3, §1.13.4, §1.14.1, §2.3.1, §2.7.1, §§2.9.2–4, §§2.11.1–2, §2.12.1, §§2.13.1–2, §§2.14.1–5, §4.2.8, 194n17, 198n92
Christians, Coptic, xviii–xix, xxi, xxv, §1.8.3, §1.12.4; description of, §0.4, §§2.1.1, §2.2.1, §2.4.1, §§2.5.1–2, §2.6.3, §3.2.37 ; history of, xxviii, §1.12.1, §4.4.1, 197n82, 197n85; mocked, xxiv, xxvi, §§4.2.8–13, §4.2.16, §§4.2.18–20, §4.2.26, §4.2.36, 206n244, 207n254; untrustworthy, xix, xxiii–xxiv, xxvi, xxix, §§2.6.2–3, §2.12.1, §4.2.2, §4.3.9, §4.4.2, 196n45
Chrysostom, John, xxxii
Church of the ʿAdawiyyah, §2.6.1
Church of the Resurrection, §1.12.4, 198n87
Church of the ʿAjūz, §2.6.1, 198n88
church(es), §1.8.3, §1.13.4, §2.6.1, §2.6.3, §2.15.1, 195n33, 198n88
Clear Book. *See* Qur'an.
clothes, clothing, §3.2.20, §3.2.23, §4.1.2, §§4.2.29–30, ; distinctive, for non-Muslims (*ghiyār*), xxiiii, xlii, §0.2, §§2.10.2–3. *See also ṭaylasān*; turban
coin(s), §1.15.3, §2.14.4, §4.2.28, §4.3.8; copper, §1.12.4, §1.15.3; gold, xviii, §1.7.1, §§1.13.1–2, §1.14.1, §2.6.1, §2.11.2, §3.2.34, §§3.2.36–37, §4.3.9, §4.4.2, 194n24; silver, §1.7.1, §1.12.4, §1.14.1, §2.5.1, §3.2.25, §4.2.28, §4.3.3, §4.4.2, 194n24
Commander of the Believers (title of caliph, *amīr al-mu'minīn*), §1.5.1, §§1.5.5–6, §1.6.1, §1.7.1, §§1.8.1–2, §§1.9.1–2, §1.10.1, §§1.12.1–2, §1.13.1, §1.13.3, §1.13.5, §1.14.2, §3.2.7, §3.2.9, §3.2.11, §3.2.22, §§4.3.4–5, §§4.3.8–9
Companion(s) of the Prophet (*ṣaḥābah*), xii, §0.1, §1.2.1, §4.4.3, 198n86, 208n268
confiscate, confiscation, §0.4, §1.14.1, §2.5.1, §§2.7.1–2, §2.9.2, §3.2.37, §4.3.1, §4.3.6, §4.3.8
convert, conversion, xviii, xxi, xxiv, xxx, §1.2.1, §1.8.2, §1.8.4, §2.5.1, §2.6.3, §2.14.1 ; effects of, §§4.2.9–11, §4.2.13, §4.2.16, §4.2.18, 201n127; feigned, xxi, §0.4, §1.12.3, §1.13.6, §§2.15.1–4, §4.2.2
Coptic language, §2.6.2, 206n244, 207n257
Copt(s). *See* Christians, Coptic
corrupt(ion), xix, xxi, §1.12.2, §2.1.2, §2.4.1, §2.9.2, §2.14.2, §2.15.1, §3.2.31, §3.2.37, §4.2.3, §4.2.19, §4.3.3, §4.3.9, 197n70, 199–200n109, 205n212, 207n255, 208n277
counter-crusade, xxix
country, countryside, xxii, §3.2.24, §§3.2.26–27, §3.2.33, §4.2.17, §4.2.30, §4.3.1. *See also* rustic(s)
court case(s), §0.4, §1.10.2, §2.10.1, §4.2.35
cow(s), §3.2.24, §3.2.33, §3.2.36
cross(es), §0.1, §2.6.1, §2.14.4
Crusade(s), xxviii–xxix, 207n250; Alexandrian, xxxiv, §2.6.3
curse(s), cursing, §1.8.1, §1.9.2, §1.15.3, §2.1.1, §2.2.1, §2.7.1, §2.10.3, §2.14.1, §2.14.4, §3.2.2, §3.2.33, §4.3.6

Damascus, §1.13.2
Damascus Gate (of Baghdad), §1.9.1
Damietta, §2.6.1, §§3.2.35–36, §4.2.7, §4.2.36
death, xix, §1.9.1, §2.8.1, §2.14.5, §3.2.7, §3.2.10, §3.2.32, §3.3.18, 197n81, 201n143, 205n215, 209n278

deceit, §1.13.5, §3.2.13, §4.1.2, 198n86. *See also* dishonest(y)
Delta of Egypt. *See* Egypt
Devil, the. *See* Satan
Dhāt al-Salāsil, Battle of, §4.3.6
dhimmi, xix, xxx, §§0.2–3, §1.5.2, §1.5.6, §1.8.2, §1.9.2, §1.10.1, §1.11.1, §§1.13.3–5, §§1.14.1–2, §2.6.1, §§2.10.2–3, 193n3
Dhū l-Nūn al-Miṣrī, §2.1.1
al-Dimyāṭī, ʿAbd al-Muʾmin ibn Khalaf, xx, xxiii, xl, xlii
disgrace. *See* humiliate, humiliation
dishonest(y), §1.6.1, §1.13.1, §§4.3.8–9. *See also* deceit
dismiss(al) (from employment), xix, xxiii–xxiv, xxvii, §1.6.1, §1.7.1, §1.9.2, §1.10.1, §1.11.1, §1.12.2, §3.2.28, §4.2.35
doctor(s). *See* medicine
donkey(s), §4.2.12, §4.3.6
drag, dragging; of caskets, §2.10.3; of people, §1.10.2, §3.2.36

Egypt, xix, xxii, xxiv–xxxi, xxxiv, §1.8.2, §1.12.1, §2.2.1, §2.4.1, §2.5.1, §2.7.2, §2.14.2, §2.14.4§3.2.37, §4.3.6, 196n46, 197n82, 198n91, 201n129, 206n244; Delta of, §4.4.2; entire land of, xxviii, xx, §0.4, §2.3.1, §2.6.3, §2.7.1, §3.2.35 ; Upper, xxii, §4.4.2, 196n45
Elephant, Year of the, §1.5.3
embezzle(ment), §2.12.1, §2.14.4, §3.2.35
Emigrant(s), Emigration (*hijrah*), xli, §§1.5.1–3, §1.6.1
Emir Jāndār, §3.2.36
employment, official, xx, xxiv, xxvi–xxvii, xxx, xli, §1.6.1, §1.9.1, §2.6.1, §§2.9.1–2, §3.2.11, §§3.2.24–25, §§3.2.30–31, §4.2.27, §4.3.2, §4.3.3; of non Muslims, xviii, xxv, xxvii, xxviii, xxx–xxxi, §0.3, §§1.1.3–4, §1.3.2, §1.4.1, §1.5.1, §§1.5.4–5, §1.5.7, §1.6.1, §1.8.4, §1.10.2, §1.12.1, §§1.13.4–5, §1.14.1, §2.14.3, §4.2.2, 194n12, 194n13
endowment(s), charitable (*waqf*), xxi, xxviii, §2.3.1, §2.15.2, §4.4.2
enemy, enemies, xxi, xxix, §0.2, §1.1.4, §§1.3.1–2, §1.5.2, §1.9.2, §2.6.3, §2.14.4, §3.2.21, §4.2.35, §4.3.8, 200n116
error(s), xxxiii–xxxiv, 193n1, 195n37; linguistic, xxxv, §§4.2.13–14, §4.2.26, 207n252; orthographic, §4.2.4, §4.2.19
estate(s), xxi, xli, §0.2, §§1.9.1–2, §1.10.2, §2.7.2, §4.1.1, §4.1.5, §4.3.9, §§4.4.1–2, 206n231
Eternal Decree, §0.1
Example of the Prophet (*al-sunnah*), §1.2.1, §1.6.1, §1.9.2, §2.14.3, §3.2.13
execution. *See* kill(ing)
eye(s), xxviii, §1.13.6, §2.9.4, §2.14.3, §2.15.1, §3.2.6, §§3.3.1–2, §§3.3.5–6, §3.3.13, §3.3.21, §4.4.2

al-Faḍl ibn al-Rabīʿ, §3.2.8, §3.3.3
al-Faḍl ibn Sahl, §§3.2.10–11
al-Faḍl ibn Yaḥyā ibn Khālid, §1.11.1, §3.2.7
Fakhr al-Dīn ʿUthmān ibn Qizil, §§3.2.36–37
Fars, §3.2.6
Fate, §1.5.6, §2.1.2, §2.14.4, §3.2.1, §3.2.6, §3.2.13, §3.2.19, §3.2.28, §3.3.16, §4.1.7
al-Fatḥ ibn Khāqān, §§1.13.1–2
Fāṭimah, orphan girl of Jaʿfar ibn Yaḥyā the Barmakid, §2.8.1
Fatimids. *See* caliphate, Fatimid
Fayyūm, the, xxi–xxii

ferry, ferryman, §2.11.1
Fleischer, Cornell, xxvii
flower(s); chamomile, §3.3.6; narcissus, §3.3.6, §3.3.20; rose, §3.3.6, §3.3.20
Follower(s) of the Prophet (*tābiʿūn*), §0.1, §4.4.3
folly. *See* fool(s), foolishness
fool(s), foolishness, §1.10.2, §1.12.4, §1.13.1, §2.11.1, §§3.2.30–31, §3.2.33, §4.1.8, §4.1.10, §4.1.12, §§4.2.23–24, §4.2.35
Fortune, §3.2.1, §3.3.9, §3.3.11, §3.3.24, §4.2.2, §4.2.8
Franks, xxii, xli, §2.10.3, §2.14.2, §2.14.4, §3.2.37
friend, friends, xviii, §§1.1.1–4, §§1.3.1–2, §1.8.4, §1.12.2, §1.15.3, §2.15.2, §§3.2.18–19, §3.2.21, §4.2.11, §4.2.13
fringes, on clothing, §0.2, 193n3
al-Furāt (Euphrates province), §4.3.5
Fusṭāṭ, §2.7.1

Gehenna, §1.12.4
al-Gharbiyyah, §3.2.35
ghiyār. *See* clothes, clothing.
gift, giving, §1.7.1, §§1.9.1–2, §1.12.4, §1.15.1, §1.15.3, §2.4.1, §2.9.2, §2.11.1, §2.14.2, §3.2.3, §3.2.6, §§3.2.9–11, §§3.2.18–19, §§3.2.22–23, §3.2.37, §3.3.24, §4.2.2, §4.2.7, §4.2.35, §§4.3.1–2, §4.3.6, 205–6n229
Giza, xx, §3.2.2
God, xxi, xxvii, §§0.1–2, §§1.1.1–4, §1.2.1, §1.4.1, §§1.5.1–2, §§1.5.6, §1.7.1, §§1.8.1–4, §§1.9.1–2, §1.10.1, §§1.12.1–3, §§1.13.5–6, §1.14.2, §1.15.2, §2.2.1, §2.4.1, §2.10.3, §2.14.3, §2.15. 4, §3.2. 2, §3.2.4, §3.2.10, §3.2.13, §3.2.26, §3.2.37, §3.3.5, §3.3.24, §§4.2.4–5, §§4.2.7–8, §4.2.22, §4.2.28, §4.2.33, §4.3.3, §4.3.5, §§4.3.8–9, §§4.4.2–3, 193n1, 195n33, 200n119
Goitein, S.D., xxix
gold, xviii, §1.7.1, §§1.13.1–2, §1.14.1, §2.6.1, §2.11.2, §3.2.16, §3.2.34, §§3.2.36–37, §3.3.9, §4.1.12, §4.3.6, §4.3.9, §4.4.2, 194n24, 202n157
governor(s), xii, §1.13.5, §2.3.1, §3.2.18, §3.2.27, §3.2.36, §4.3.6, 194n17, 206n230
grammar, grammarian(s), §1.12.2, §2.8.1, 196n48
Greek(s), xviii, §1.6.1, §1.7.1, §1.8.3, §1.12.1, §4.2.17, §4.4.2, 194n24, 195n32, 199n106, 207n257
Guidance (*hudā*), §1.6.1, §3.2.4, §4.3.6, 194n21

hadith, xii, xx, xxiv, §2.4.1, §3.2.1, §4.2.13, 193n2, 193n10, 197n80, 199n104, 202n153, 208n267. *See also* Example of the Prophet
hair, §3.3.10, §4.3.5; graying, silver, §3.2.24, §3.3.2
al-Ḥāfiẓ (Fatimid caliph), §0.4, §§2.9.1–3, §2.13.2
al-Ḥajjāj ibn ʿAtīk al-Thaqafī, §4.3.5
al-Ḥajjāj ibn Yūsuf al-Thaqafī, §0.3, §1.7.1
al-Ḥajūn, §2.15.2
al-Ḥākim bi-Amr Allāh (Fatimid caliph), xxxi, §0.4, §2.6.1, §2.6.3, §2.7.1
Ḥanbalī (legal rite), xix
hand(s), §1.10.2, §1.12.1, §1.13.5, §2.6.1, §3.2.10, §3.2.13, §3.3.24, §4.1.2, §4.2.22, §4.2.28, §4.3.2, 205–6n229; cut off, §1.7.1, §1.10.1, §2.6.2; stretched out, §1.8.1, §2.1.2, §2.7.1

handwriting, §1.13.1–2, §3.2.12
Ḥarb ibn Umayyah, §4.1.1, 206n230
Hārūn al-Rashīd (Abbasid caliph), §0.3, §1.11.1, §1.12.1, §§3.2.7–8, §3.2.22, §4.2.30, 201n143
al-Ḥasan ibn Makhlad, §1.13.1
al-Ḥasan ibn Sahl, §3.2.11
al-Ḥasan ibn Wahb, §3.2.12, 204n195, 204n196
Hasdai ibn Shaprut, xxviii
Ḥassān ibn Yazīd, §1.8.4
hate, hatred, §1.5.6, §1.13.5, §1.5.6, §2.14.2
al-Haytham ibn Khālid, §1.13.6
Ḥayyān ibn Shurayḥ, §1.8.2
Hebrew (language), §§2.13.1–2, 199–200n109
hire(ing). *See* employment
al-Hishāmī, Abū ʿAbdallāh, §2.8.1
Ḥiṣn Ziyād, §4.2.32
history, xii–xiii, xxiv, xxvi–xxviii, xxxii–xxxiii, §2.2.1, §2.8.1, §2.14.1, §3.2.2, 197n82
horoscope(s), §2.9.2
horse(s), xviii, §1.2.1, §2.10.3, §3.2.33, §4.2.19, §4.3.8, §4.4.2, 202n149
House, the. *See* Kaaba.
house(s), xx, §1.13.2, §2.3.1, §2.6.1, §2.7.2, §2.14.2, §3.2.29, §4.2.15, §§4.3.2–3
Ḥumayd ibn Bishr, §3.2.26
humiliate, humiliation, §0.2, §0.4, §1.5.6, §1.8.1, §1.10.2, §1.13.5, §1.15.3, §2.1.2, §2.5.1, §2.7.2, §2.9.4, §2.10.3, §§2.14.2–3, §2.14.5, §2.15.1, §2.15.4, §3.2.11, §§3.2.23–24, §3.2.26, §4.3.9, §3.2.32, §4.2.1, 196n52
al-Ḥusayn ibn Ḥajjāj the Secretary, Abū ʿAbdallāh, §3.3.20
Ḥusn al-sarīrah fī ttikhādh al-ḥiṣn bi-l-Jazīrah (another book by the author), xxii
Ḥusn al-sulūk fī faḍl malik Miṣr ʿalā sāʾir al-mulūk (another book by the author), xxii

Ibn ʿAbdūn the Secretary, Abū Manṣūr, §3.3.22
Ibn Abī l-ʿAlāʾ, al-Ḥārith Abū Firās al-Ḥamdānī, §3.2.23
Ibn Abī Zakariyyā the Secretary, Abū l-Karam al-Akhram, §§2.9.2–3
Ibn al-ʿAmīd, Abū al-Faḍl Muḥammad ibn al-Ḥusayn, §3.2.2, §3.2.17, §3.3.15, 204n211
Ibn Dukhān, Khāṣṣ(at) al-Dawlah Abū l-Faḍl/l-Faḍāʾil, xix–xx, xxix, xxxi, §§2.14.1–4, 200n116, 200n117
Ibn al-Furāt, Abū l-Ḥasan ʿAlī ibn Muḥammad ibn Mūsā, §1.14.2, §3.2.19, 202n161
Ibn Ghalāb, Khālid ibn al-Ḥārith ibn Aws ibn al-Duhmān, §4.3.5
Ibn Hablān, §3.2.36, 203n184
Ibn al-Hārūnī the Jew, §1.15.2
Ibn Ḥassūn, §3.2.36
Ibn Haylān. *See* Ibn Hablān
Ibn al-Lutbiyyah, §4.3.2
Ibn Manārah, Yaḥyā, §3.2.31, 203n180
Ibn Mufshīn, §3.2.36
Ibn Muqlah, Abū ʿAlī Muḥammad ibn ʿAlī, §3.2.21, 202n160
Ibn al-Nābulusī, ʿUthmān ibn Ibrāhīm, as character in his own book, xviii–xxii, xli, §§3.2.32–33

Ibn Nujayyah. *See* ʿAlī ibn Ibrāhīm ibn Najā al-Anṣārī, Zayn al-Dīn
Ibn al-Nūrī, §4.2.7
Ibn Qayyim al-Jawziyyah, xxxi
Ibn Rāshid, §3.2.23
Ibn Saʿīd ibn ʿAmr, §1.13.2
Ibn al-Ṣakhr al-Ibyārī, §3.2.34, §§3.2.36–37
Ibn Shukr, Ṣafī l-Dīn ʿAbdallāh ibn al-Ḥusayn, §3.2.35
Ibn al-Taʿāwīdhī, §3.2.29
Ibn al-Tammār, §2.6.1
Ibn Ṭūlūn. *See* Aḥmad ibn Ṭūlūn
Ibn Walakhshī. *See* Riḍwān ibn Walakhshī
Ibn al-Zanānīriyyah, §2.6.1
Ibn Zayn al-Dār, §2.14.5
Ibrāhīm ibn al-ʿAbbās al-Ṣūlī, §3.2.10, §3.3.5
Ibyār (or Abyār), §3.2.34, §3.2.36
Ikhmīm (or Akhmīm), §2.1.1
ill(ness), §§4.2.11–12, §4.2.31
Illustrious Book. *See* Qurʾan.
imam (title), §2.7.1
imprisonment. *See* prison(s).
infidel(s) (*kāfir*), §0.2, §§1.1.1–2, §1.2.1, §§1.3.2–3, §1.5.1, §1.5.4, §1.5.7, §1.7.1, §1.8.1, §1.8.4, §1.12.1, §1.13.1, §1.13.5, §2.7.1, §2.9.4, §2.10.3, §2.14.1, §2.14.3, §2.15.3, §3.2.33, 194n13, 200n116
injustice, §§1.9.1–2, §1.13.2
ink, xxxiv–xxxv, §4.1.1
inkwell(s), §4.1.12
intercession, intercessor, xx, §2.15.1
Iraq, §1.7.1, §3.2.28, §3.3.20, §4.2.29, 203n180
ʿĪsā ibn Nasṭūrus, §2.6.1, 198n92
al-Iṣbahānī, Abū l-Faraj, xxv, §2.8.1
Isfahan, §4.3.5
Islam, xii–xiii, xx–xxii, xxvi–xxxii, xliii, §§0.1–2, §0.4, §1.4.1, §§1.8.1–2, §1.8.4, §1.12.3, §§1.13.4–6, §1.15.2, §2.2.1, §2.5.1, §2.6.3, §2.9.4, §2.10.3, §§2.14.1–2, §§2.15.1–4, §4.2.2, §4.3.8, 194n15, 194n23, 194n24, 200n119, 201n127, 201n142, 205n222, 205–6n229
Ismāʿīl ibn Ṣubayḥ, §3.2.9
Iẓhār ṣanʿat al-Ḥayy al-Qayyūm fī tartīb bilād al-Fayyūm (another book by the author), xxii

Jaʿfar ibn Khālid ibn Barmak, 198n94
Jaʿfar ibn Rabīʿah, §4.3.7
Jaʿfar ibn Yaḥyā ibn Khālid, §2.8.1, §3.2.6
al-Jāḥiẓ, ʿAmr ibn Baḥr, §2.5.2, 198n86
Jamāl al-Dīn Abū l-Ḥusayn al-Jazzār, §4.2.36
Jamāl al-Dīn Aydughdī al-ʿAzīzī, §4.2.7
Jazʾ ibn Muʿāwiyah, §4.3.5
Jerusalem, §2.6.1
Jesus, §1.12.1
Jew(s), Jewish, xiii–xiv, xxix, xxxi, §0.3, §1.8.2, §§1.12.2–3, §§1.15.2–3, §2.1.1, §2.2.1, §2.6.1, §2.10.3, 193n1, 197n79; head of the Jewish community, §§2.13.1–2, 200n117; official(s), xiv–xxv, xxviii, §1.5.1, §1.10.1, §2.6.3, 194n17; traveling companion of Miqdād ibn al-Aswad, §1.15.1; trick played against by Christian associate, §0.4, §§2.3.1–3
jinn, §0.1, 193n2
Jirjis al-Jawharī, xxviii
John Damascene (John of Damascus), xxviii
Joseph, Prophet, §4.3.8

judge(s) (*qāḍī*), xix–xxi, xxviii, §1.8.3, §1.10.2, §2.7.1, §§2.9.2–3, §§3.2.34–35, §4.2.10, §4.2.18, §§4.2.32–36, §4.3.8, 195n33, 195n41, 205n219
judgment, §1.8.3, §1.12.3, §1.13.5, §2.3.1, §2.9.1, §2.14.3, §3.2.28, §4.4.3
Jundishapur, §4.3.5
jurist(s) (*faqīh*), xxii, xix, xxxi, xliii, §1.1.4, §4.2.14, §4.2.29, §4.2.35, 193n10
justice, §0.2, §1.3.3, §1.5.6, §1.9.2, §1.12.1, §2.9.1, §3.2.5, §3.2.22

Kaaba, §1.9.2, §1.13.3
al-Kāmil Nāṣir al-Dīn Muḥammad. *See* al-Malik al-Kāmil Nāṣir al-Dīn Muḥammad
Khālid ibn Barmak, §3.2.3, §3.3.1, 201n133
Khālid ibn Ṣafwān, §1.12.1, 196n46
Khālid ibn al-Walīd, §1.4.1, §4.3.4
al-Khaṭṭāb ibn Nufayl, §4.3.6
Khurasan, §1.11.1
kill(ing) ; of animals, §1.8.2, §2.14.5; of humans, §1.12.1, §2.10.3, §§2.13.1–2, §3.2.2, 199n104, 199–200n109, 201n129; deemed lawful, §2.15.4; execution, xx, §1.12.3, §1.13.3, §2.9.3, §2.14.4, 200n117
king(s) (*malik*, pl. *mulūk*), §0.2, §1.8.3, §1.12.1, §1.15.2, §2.14.3, §2.15.1, §§3.2.5–6, §3.2.11, §§3.2.23–24, §4.3.1, §4.4.1
Kipchak, §4.2.2
al-Kisāʾī, §1.12.2, §3.2.7, 196n48, 201n143
Kutayfāt, §2.7.2

land survey. *See* survey(or), surveying
land tax. *See* tax, taxation (land)
language(s). *See* Arabic; Coptic; Greek; Hebrew; Persian
law, legal reasoning, xii–xiii, xx, xxiv, xxxi, §2.3.1, §2.7.1, §2.15.4, §3.2.1, §3.2.35, §4.2.33, §4.2.35, 194n23
law college(s) (*madrasah*), xx, §2.3.1, §3.2.34
letter(s), Arabic, §3.2.12, §4.1.9, §§4.2.3–4, §§4.2.6–7, §4.2.19, §4.2.36, 198n87, 206n240, 206n241
letter(s), epistolary, §1.5.5, §1.8.1, §1.8.4, §1.10.2, §1.13.2, §§1.13.5–6, §3.2.9, §3.2.18, §3.2.35, §3.3.10, §4.2.1, §§4.2.3–4, §§4.2.7–8, §§4.3.4–5
liar(s). *See* lying
lie(s). *See* lying
literature (*adab*), xxvi, §3.2.1
love, xxiii, §1.1.4, §1.5.6, §1.13.5, §2.9.2, §2.15.1, §3.2.1, §3.2.6, §3.2.12, §3.2.19, §3.2.21, §3.3.1, §§3.3.4–5, §3.3.7, §3.3.12, §§3.3.21–22, §4.4.2, 205n222
loyal, loyalty, §3.2.2, §3.2.6, §3.2.11, §3.2.16
Lumaʿ al-qawānīn al-muḍiyyah fī dawāwīn al-diyār al-miṣriyyah (another book by the author), xx
Luxor, §1.12.1
lying, lie(s), liar(s) (see also deceit), §1.12.3, §1.13.1, §1.13.5, §2.3.1, §2.9.4, §2.12.1, §2.14.3, §3.2.4, §3.2.8, §3.2.10, §3.3.14

madrasah(s). *See* law college(s)
al-Mahdī (Abbasid caliph), §0.3, §§1.10.1–2, §§3.2.3–4, §3.2.8, §3.3.2, 195n41, 201n135
al-Malik al-ʿĀdil Sayf al-Dīn Abū Bakr (Ayyubid sultan), §0.2, §4.2.35, 203n185
al-Malik al-Kāmil Nāṣir al-Dīn Muḥammad (Ayyubid sultan), xx–xxi, xxix, §0.2, §3.2.34, §3.2.37, 203n185

al-Malik al-Ṣāliḥ Najm al-Dīn Ayyūb (Ayyubid sultan), xxi–xxii, xxiv, §0.2, 193n3
al-Malik al-Ṣāliḥ Ṭalāʾiʿ ibn Ruzzīk (Fatimid vizier-sultan), xix, §0.4, §2.14.3
Mamluks, xxiii, xxx, xli, xlii, 197n80
al-Maʾmūn (Abbasid caliph), §0.3, §§1.12.1–3, §2.8.1, §3.2.7, §3.2.11, 196n48
al-Manādhir, §4.3.5
al-Manṣūr (Abbasid caliph), §0.3, §§1.9.1–2, 195n37, 195n43
al-Marākibī, Aḥmad ibn ʿAbdallāh ibn Ismāʿīl, §2.8.1
maréschal (*marshān*), §4.2.8, 207n250
Market of al-Ahwāz, §4.3.5
Market of the Textile Merchants, §2.10.1
martyr, martyrdom, §0.2, §2.11.2, §2.14.1, §§3.2.34–35, §4.2.35
Marwān ibn Abī Ḥafṣah, §3.2.5
Marwān ibn al-Ḥakam (Umayyad caliph), §3.2.2, §3.2.5, 201n129
al-Maṭariyyah, §2.6.3
Maymūn ibn Hārūn, §1.13.1
Mecca, §1.9.2, §1.13.3, §2.15.2, §3.2.35, §4.2.29, §4.3.6
medicine(s), xlii, §1.12.1, §2.2.1, §4.2.23, 196n45
merchant(s). *See* trade, trader(s)
mercy, merciful, §1.4.1, §1.5.1, §2.10.1, §2.14.1, §3.2.2, §3.2.37
mihrab, §2.15.3
minbar, §4.3.2
al-Miqdād ibn al-Aswad al-Kindī, §1.15.1, 197n74
monastery, monasteries, §2.6.1, §§2.15.1–2, §4.2.32
Monastery of Simon, §2.15.2
money, xviii, xxiii, §1.13.1, §1.15.3, §2.5.1, §2.7.1, §2.9.2, §2.12.1, §3.2.5, §3.2.25, §4.3.1, §4.3.3. *See also* coin(s); wealth
Monk, the, Abū Najāḥ ibn Qannā, §2.7.1–2
monk(s), Christian, §2.15.2
moon(s), §3.2.16, §3.2.18, §3.3.4, §3.3.14, §3.3.20, 202n157, 204n194
mosque, xx, §1.10.2, §1.11.1, §2.3.1, §2.6.1, §2.7.1, §2.15.3, §4.2.30, 198n89
Mosque of ʿAmr ibn al-ʿĀṣ, §2.7.1, 198n91
Mosque of the Messenger of God, §1.5.6
Mosque of Tibr, §2.6.3
mother(s), §1.10.1, §1.13.1, §2.7.1, §2.15.1, §3.2.7, §3.2.23, §4.3.2, §4.3.8, 200n116, 208n273
Muʿāwiyah ibn Abī Sufyān, §1.5.5
Muḥammad, Prophet, xii, §0.1, §0.3, §1.2.1, §1.5.1, §1.5.4, §1.6.1, §§1.8.1–2, §1.9.2, §§1.13.4–5, §1.14.2, §1.15.1, §2.1.1, §2.10.3, §§2.15.3–4, §4.3.2, §4.3.4, §4.3.6, §4.4.3, 200n119
Muḥammad ibn al-ʿAbbās, Abū Bakr, §3.3.8
Muḥammad ibn al-ʿAbbās, Abū Jaʿfar, §3.3.7
Muḥammad ibn ʿAbd al-Malik al-Zayyāt, §3.2.13, §§3.3.4–5, §4.3.9
Muḥammad ibn Aḥmad the Secretary, Abū Manṣūr, §3.3.11
Muḥammad ibn Manṣūr al-Balkhī, §3.3.24
Muḥammad ibn Maslamah al-Anṣārī, §4.3.6
Muḥammad ibn Muḥammad ibn al-Jubayr the Secretary, Abū l-Qāsim, §3.3.16, 205n213
Muḥammad ibn al-Muntashir, §1.8.4
Muḥammad ibn Mūsā, §1.13.1
Muḥammad ibn Rāshid ibn Isḥāq, §3.2.23
Muḥammad ibn Sulaymān, §0.4, §2.5.1
Muḥammad ibn Yazīd al-Anṣārī, §1.6.1

Muharram (month), §1.5.3, 194n15
mule(s), xviii, 2.9.4, §2.10.3, §3.2.34, §4.1.4, §4.4.2
Mu'nis al-Muẓaffar, Abū l-Ḥasan, §1.14.1, 197n70
Muqrān, §3.2.33
al-Muqtadir Bi-llāh (Abbasid caliph), §0.3, §§1.14.1–2
Mūsā ibn ʿAbd al-Malik, §1.13.1, §4.1.5, 206n236
Mushājiʿ ibn Masʿūd al-Sulamī, §4.3.5
music, §0.4, §1.8.2, §1.12.1, §2.8.1, §2.14.5, §2.15.2, §3.2.12, §3.3.14, §4.2.24
Muṣṭafā ʿĀlī, xxvii
al-Mutanabbī, Abū l-Ṭayyib Aḥmad ibn al-Ḥusayn, §4.2.25, 204n209
al-Muʿtaṣim (Abbasid caliph), §3.2.33
al-Mutawakkil (Abbasid caliph), §0.3, §§1.13.1–5, 196n54
Muʿtazilite, §3.2.7
al-Muwaffaq ibn al-Khallāl, xxv–xxvi, §§2.9.1–3, 199n99

Nablus (al-Nābulus), xix
Nāfiʿ ibn al-Ḥārith, §4.3.5
Najm al-Dīn Ayyūb. *See* al-Malik al-Ṣāliḥ Najm al-Dīn Ayyūb
Napoleon Bonaparte, xxviii
natron, xxvi, §2.4.1
Nile river, xx–xxii, §2.7.2, §2.9.2
Nīsān (month), §4.2.17, 207n257
Nufayʿ ibn al-Ḥārith, Abū Bakrah, §4.3.5
Nūr al-Dīn (Zangid sultan), xix, xxi, xli
Nūr al-Dīn ibn Fakhr al-Dīn ibn al-Shaykh (Ayyubid emir), xxi, xli

office(s) (*dīwān*), xviii, xx, xxviii, §0.5, §1.6.1, §1.7.1, §1.11.1, §2.3.1, §2.6.2, §§2.9.1–2, §2.10.2, §§2.11.1–2, §§2.14.1–2, §2.14.4, §3.1.1, §3.2.9, §3.2.28, §§3.2.30–31, §§3.2.35–36, §4.1.1, §§4.1.5–6, §4.2.2, §§4.2.8–10, §§4.2.27–28, §4.2.35, §4.4.2, 200n118, 207n250
official, state, xx–xxi, xxiii–xiv, xxv–xxxi, xli–xlii, §1.7.1, §1.11.1, §§1.13.1–2, §§1.13.4–5, §1.14.2, §2.3.1, §2.6.2, §2.10.2, §2.11.1, §2.14.2, §§3.2.23–24, §§3.2.27–28, §§3.2.30–31, §§3.2.34–35, §4.2.6, §4.2.9, §4.3.1, §§4.3.8–9, 194n17, 196n54, 197n85, 198n92, 200n125, 203n177, 203n182, 203n184, 208n266
oppress(ion) (*ẓulm*), §1.8.1, §§1.9.1–2, §§1.10.1–2, §§1.12.1–2, §1.13.3, §1.13.5, §2.9.1, §2.11.1, §3.2.37
oud. *See* music

Pact of Security (*dhimmah*), xxxi, §2.6.1
patriarch, patriarchate, Christian, §2.7.1, §2.14.5
pen(s), §1.7.1, §1.10.1, §1.12.4, §2.2.1, §2.3.1, §2.9.2, §2.14.5, §3.2.2, §3.2.5, §3.2.9, §3.2.12, §3.2.20, §3.2.28, §4.1.10, 202n146
People of the Non-Muslim Lands (*ahl al-ḥarb*), §2.6.1
Perlmann, Moshe, xxxiii, xliv
Persia, Persian(s), §§1.5.1–2, §1.7.1, §1.12.1, §3.3.22, 194n24
pharaoh(s), §1.12.1, 200n116
Pilgrimage (*hajj*), xxvii, §1.5.3, §1.9.2, §1.13.3
poem(s), poetry, xvi, xx, xxiv–xxvi, xxxv–xxxviii, xlii, §§0.5–6, §1.6.1, §1.10.1, §2.14.3, §2.15.2, §3.2.1, §§3.2.4–5, §3.2.7, §3.2.28, §3.2.30, §3.2.33, §3.3.5, §3.3.25,

poem(s), poetry (cont.), §4.2.27, §4.2.32, §4.2.36, 196n51, 196n52, 196n53, 198n92, 199n99, 200n117, 201n133, 201n134, 201n135, 204n189, 204n198, 204n209, 204n210, 205n219, 205n222, 206n233, 206n238, 206n240, 206n242, 209n280
poet(s), xii, xvi, xix, xxiii–xxiv, §§1.12.3–4, §2.2.1, §2.9.4, §2.14.4, §2.15.1, §§3.2.3–7, §§3.2.10–11, §3.2.23, §§3.2.26–31, §3.2.33, §§4.1.1–11, §4.2.5, §4.2.11, §4.2.14, §4.2.27, §4.2.32, §4.3.5, §4.4.2, 195n33, 196n46, 199n99, 200n116, 201n139, 203n180, 204n190, 204n207, 205n222, 206n231, 206n236, 209n280
poll tax (*jizyah*). *See* tax(ation)
polytheist (*mushrik*), §1.2.1, §1.4.1, §1.5.7, 194n12
pray, prayer, xli, §1.8.2, §1.13.3, §2.7.1, §2.9.1, §2.10.3, §3.3.5, §4.2.3, §4.3.8
priest, Christian, §2.14.4, §2.15.2
prison(s), §1.9.1, §1.12.2, §2.6.1, §2.7.1, §2.9.1, §2.11.1, §2.13.2, §3.2.23
prisoner(s). *See* prison(s)
property, properties, xviii–xxi, xl, §1.1.2, §1.5.2, §1.5.6, §§1.9.1–2, §1.10.1, §1.12.4, §2.2.1, §2.4.1, §2.5.1, §§2.6.1–3, §§2.7.1–2, §2.9.2, §2.14.3, §2.15.1, §3.2.37, §4.2.32, §4.3.1, §§4.3.3–9, §4.4.1
protest, popular, §1.10.2, §1.12.1, §§1.13.2–3, §2.9.1

al-Qāḍī al-Fāḍil, Abū ʿAlī ʿAbd al-Raḥīm al-Baysānī, §4.2.3, §4.2.8
Qudāmah ibn Ziyādah, §1.13.6
Qurʾan, xii–xiii, xxiv, xxxi, xxxvii, §0.3, §§1.1.1–4, §1.5.3, §1.8.1, §1.8.4, §1.9.2, §1.12.2, §1.13.5, §1.15.2, §2.7.1, §2.10.3, §§2.14.3–4, §3.2.1, §3.2.13, §3.2.37, §4.2.2, 193n4, 195n33, 199n101
al-Quṣayr, monastery of, §2.6.1

al-Rabīʿ ibn Yūnus, §§1.9.1–2
Ramadan (month), §1.5.3, §2.4.1, 197n83, 204n194
Rāmhurmuz, §4.3.5
al-Rashīd. *See* Hārūn al-Rashīd
Rāshidah, §2.6.1
refinement, §3.2.1, §4.1.12, §4.3.9
register(s), xxiv, xxxvi, §1.5.1, §1.9.1, §1.12.3, §1.13.2, §2.4.1, §2.11.1, §2.14.2, §3.2.11, §4.2.34, §4.3.9
religion, xii, §§0.1–2, §§1.3.2–3, §1.4.1, §1.5.2, §§1.8.1–2, §1.8.4, §1.9.2, §1.10.1, §1.12.1, §1.13.5, §1.15.2, §2.14.3, §§2.15.1–3, §4.4.2, 194n18
Resurrection, Day of (*yawm al-qiyāmah*, *yawm al-dīn*), §1.12.4, §1.13.3, §4.3.2, 198n87, 199n104
Riḍwān ibn Walakhshī, §2.13.1
rural people. *See* rustics
rustics (*ahl al-rīf*, *ahl al-Sawād*), xxi, xxiv, xxix, §3.2.24, §3.2.26, §3.2.28, §§3.2.30–31, §3.2.33, §§3.2.36–7, §4.1.7, §4.2.27, §§4.2.29–31, §4.2.36

Sadan, Joseph, xxxi, xxxvii, xliv, 199–200n109
saddle(s), §1.8.2, §1.13.4, §2.9.4
Ṣadr al-Dīn, Abū l-Ḥasan Maḥmūd ibn Ḥamawayh, §4.2.35
Ṣafā, §2.15.2
Safar (month), §4.2.16
al-Saffāḥ (Abbasid caliph), §3.2.2
Ṣafī l-Dīn. *See* Ibn Shukr

Saḥbān Wāʾil, §4.2.14
al-Ṣāḥib ibn ʿAbbād, Abū l-Qāsim, §3.3.19
Sahlān ibn ʿAbdān al-Wāsiṭī, §1.13.6
Saʿīd al-Dawlah al-Ibyārī, §3.2.36
Saʿīd ibn Ḥumayd, §3.2.18, §3.2.36
al-Sājī the Secretary, Abū ʿAlī ibn ʿAbdallāh, §3.3.23
Saladin. *See* Ṣalāḥ al-Dīn
Ṣalāḥ al-Dīn, al-Malik al-Nāṣir Yūsuf ibn Najm al-Dīn Ayyūb (Ayyubid sultan), xx, xxv, xli, §2.11.2, §2.14.1, §4.4.1, 199n108, 200n117, 209n278
Salamah ibn Saʿīd, §1.13.1
Ṣāliḥ ibn ʿAbd al-Quddūs the Secretary, §3.3.12
Ṣāliḥ ibn ʿAbd al-Raḥmān, §1.7.1, 201n131
Ṣāliḥ ibn ʿAlī, §3.2.2
al-Ṣāliḥ ʿImād al-Dīn (Ayyubid prince), xxii
al-Ṣāliḥ Ismāʿīl (Ayyubid prince) , xxii
al-Ṣāliḥ Najm al-Dīn Ayyūb. *See* al-Malik al-Ṣāliḥ Najm al-Dīn Ayyūb
al-Ṣāliḥ Ṭalāʾiʿ ibn Ruzzīk. *See* al-Malik al-Ṣāliḥ Ṭalāʾiʿ ibn Ruzzīk
Salm al-Khāsir, §3.2.4
Samaritans, §1.12.3
Samurah ibn Jundab, §4.3.5
al-Ṣanīʿah, §3.2.36
Sarjūn ibn Manṣūr the Christian, §1.6.1
Satan (*al-shayṭān*), §1.4.1, §1.8.1, §2.13.3
Sawād, §3.2.24, §3.2.26, §4.2.29
Sawwār ibn ʿAbdallāh, §1.10.2, 195n41
Sayf al-Dīn Abū Bakr. *See* al-Malik al-ʿĀdil Sayf al-Dīn Abū Bakr
scandal, §2.12.1, §2.14.5, §3.2.31
school(s), §1.11.1, §4.1.2, 206n232. *See also* law college
seal, office of the, §1.6.1, §1.11.1
secretarial arts (*kitābah*), §0.5, §1.5.2, §1.5.6, §1.8.1, §2.2.1, §3.1.1, §3.2.2, §§3.2.24–25, §4.1.1, §4.2.2, 194n18
secretary, secretaries (*kātib*), xx, xxvi, §0.3, §§1.5.4–6, §1.6.1, §1.8.1, §1.8.4, §1.9.1, §§1.10.1–2, §§1.12.1–2, §1.13.1, §1.13.3, §1.13.6, §1.14.1, §2.2.1, §2.3.1, §2.6.3, §2.7.1, §§2.9.1–2, §2.13.1, §2.14.1, §2.14.3, §2.14.5, §4.3.9, 194n18, 196n45, 203n180, 206n232, 206n241; description of, xxvii, §0.5, §1.7.2, §3.1.1, §§3.2.1–22; excellence of, xxiv, xxvi, xxx, §0.5, §1.5.2, §3.2.23–28, §§3.3.1–25; of the army, §4.1.11; of the chancery, §1.6.1, §2.9.1, §3.3.22; of the land tax, §1.5.5, §2.11.1; unworthy pretenders, xxiv, xxvii, §0.6, §2.12.1, §2.14.5, §§4.1.1–12, §§4.2.2–17, 205n222, 206n231, 207n247, 207n248, 207n251
Seljuq, xxx
Shabīb ibn Shaybah, §1.9.2
Shāhawayh, §1.10.1
al-Sharqiyyah, §3.2.35
Shāwar, Abū Shujāʿ ibn Mujīr al-Saʿdī, §2.14.5
Shibl ibn Maʿbad al-Bajalī al-Aḥmasī, §4.3.5
Shiʿism, xxviii, xxx
silver, §1.7.1, §1.12.4, §1.13.1, §1.14.1, §2.5.1, §3.2.25, §3.2.34, §3.3.1, §4.2.28, §4.3.3, §4.4.2, 194n24
singing, singer(s). *See* music
Son of the Mouse, §1.12.4
slaughter. *See* kill(ing)
slave(s), slavery, xviii, xxii, §1.13.1, §2.1.1, §2.6.1, §2.8.1, §3.2.18, §4.2.2, §§4.2.7–9, §4.2.24, §4.2.33, §4.3.1, §4.4.2, 201n142, 208n271

star(s), §0.2, §1.12.4, §3.2.1, §3.2.16, §3.2.18, §3.2.23, 202n156, 202n157
stipend(s), xix, xxv, xxx, §1.11.1, §2.14.2, §2.14.4, §3.2.11, §3.3.22, §4.4.2, 200n116, 200n117
Sufi, xxviii, xxxiii, §1.10.1, §2.7.1, §4.2.35. *See also* ascetic(s)
al-Sulamī, Abū ʿImrān (poet), §3.2.23
Sulaymān ibn Quḍāʿah, Abū Thābit, §0.4, §1.6.1
Sulaymān ibn Wahb, §3.2.14
sultan(s), xviii, xx–xxiv, xxxv, xli–xlii, §0.2, §0.4, §2.3.1, §2.4.1, §2.11.2, §2.14.1, §2.14.3, §§3.2.34–37, §4.2.8, §4.2.35, §4.3.1, §§4.4.1–2, 197n80, 197n85
Sunni revival (See also Sunni shift), xliii.
Sunni shift, xxviii, xxix
Sunnism, xxviii–xxx, xliii
Surraq, §4.3.5
survey(or), surveying, xxii, §0.4, §2.11.1, §3.3.17
sword(s), §0.2, §1.10.1, §1.12.1, §2.2.1, §2.3.1, §2.7.1, §2.15.1, §3.2.16, §3.2.22, §3.2.33, §4.3.4
Sword of Ambition, The, xii; date of, xxiii, xlii; compared to other works of pre-modern literature, xxiv–xxv, xxvii- xxviii; contents of, xix, xxiv–xxvi, xxxi; edition of, xxxiii–xxxvi; genre of, xxiv–xxv; historical context, xviii–xxi, xxvii–xxviii; manuscripts of, xxxiii–xxxv, xl; past scholarship on, xxix–xxxi; reasons for composition, xxiii–xxv, §0.2, §§4.4.1–2; translation of, xxxvi–xxxvii; value as historical source, xiii, xxvi–xxviii
Synesius of Cyrene, xxvii
Syria, xviii–xix, xxviii, xxx, §1.6.1, §4.4.2

Taṣrīḥ al-Qur'an bi-l-naṣr ʿalā man istaʿāna bi-kuffār al-ʿaṣr (another book by the author), xxii
tax, taxation ; collecting, collection, xviii, xx, xxii, §§1.8.1–2, §1.15.3, §2.4.1, §2.9.1, §§2.11.1–2, §§3.2.36–37; farming, §3.2.24, §4.2.28; land (*kharāj*), §1.5.5, §1.12.3, §2.11.1, §4.1.1, §§4.1.5–6, §4.3.1, 206n231, 206n238; on firewood, §2.4.1; on fisheries, §2.4.1; on natron, §2.4.1; on pasture, §2.4.1; on ships, §2.11.2; poll (*jizyah*) , §1.5.2, §1.8.2, §1.13.4, §2.6.1, §2.7.1, §2.15.1; receipts, §2.9.2, §2.14.4, §3.2.5; deemed unlawful, §2.11.2, 197n85
ṭaylasān, xxxvii, §3.2.36, §4.2.2, §§4.2.9–11, §4.2.13, §§4.2.16–17, 193n3, 206n245, 206n245
temple(s), §2.1.1, §2.15.2, §3.3.21, 201n132
Tertullian, xxxii
al-Thaʿālibī, al-Manṣūr ʿAbd al-Malik ibn Muḥammad, xxiv -xxv, 204n209, 205n226, 208n277
Thumāmah ibn Ashras, §3.2.6
Tinnis, §2.11.2
tomb(s), §2.10.3
tongue(s), §1.6.1, §3.2.1, §3.2.8, §3.2.16, §3.3.22, §4.2.22; tied, stammering, §2.1.2, §2.15.1
torture, §2.7.2, §2.15.3
trade, trader(s), §2.7.1, §2.8.1, §2.10.1, §4.2.17, §4.3.5
travel, §1.15.1, §3.3.20, §4.2.2, §4.2.12
treasury, central (*khizānah, bayt al-māl*), §2.3.1, §2.4.1, §2.6.1, §2.6.3, §3.2.36, §4.3.1, §4.3.3, §4.3.9

Trinity, §2.14.3
trust, trusting, trustworthiness, xii–xiii, xxviii, §0.4, §1.1.2, §§1.3.1–2, §1.5.2, §1.5.4, §1.10.1, §1.13.5, §2.1.1, §2.9.2, §2.12.1, §2.13.3, §3.2.13, §3.2.18, §3.3.5, §4.2.32, §§4.3.5–6, §4.3.9
turban(s), §4.2.9, §4.3.4, 193n3
Turk(s), xxii, xxx, §4.2.2
tyranny, tyrant(s), §0.2, §1.3.3, §1.9.2, §1.12.1, §2.14.2, §3.2.5, §3.3.9

al-Ubullah, §4.3.5
Upper Egypt. *See* Egypt
ʿUmar ibn ʿAbd al-ʿAzīz (Umayyad caliph) , §0.3, §§1.8.1–4, 195n32, 195n33
ʿUmar ibn ʿAbdallāh al-Shaybānī, §1.12.1
ʿUmar ibn al-Khaṭṭāb (Rightly Guided caliph), §0.3, §§1.5.1–7, §1.7.1, §1.12.1, §§4.3.3–9, 208n268
ʿUmar ibn Masʿadah, §3.2.9
ʿUmārah al-Yamanī, xix–xx, §2.14.4, 200n117
Umaymah bint Ṣafīḥ, §4.3.8, 208n273
Umayyads. *See* caliphate, Umayyad
Umm ʿAbdallāh ibn Yaḥyā ibn Khālid, §2.8.1
unbeliever(s). *See* infidel(s)
ʿUtbah ibn Ghazwān, §4.3.5
ʿUthmān ibn ʿAffān (Rightly Guided caliph), §1.5.7
ʿUthmān ibn Ibrāhīm al-Nābulusī. *See* Ibn al-Nābulusī

vice(s), §2.14.1, §4.2.22, 207n259
virtue(s), virtuous, xxx, §1.3.1, §1.5.2, §1.6.1, §3.2.2, §3.2.11, §3.2.23, §3.3.21, §3.3.25, §4.2.22, 207n259
vizier(s), xix, xli, §1.7.2, §§2.13.1–2, §2.14.5, §§3.2.3–4, §3.2.8, §3.2.19, §3.2.21, §§3.2.23–24, §§3.2.26–28, §§3.2.33–34, §3.3.2, §3.3.5, §4.2.33, §4.3.9

war, 193n12, §2.6.1
wealth, xix, xxviii–xxix, xli, §0.6, §1.3.2, §1.5.1, §1.12.1, §2.3.1, §2.5.1, §2.6.3, §§2.9.1–2, §2.14.4, §2.15.1, §3.2.5, §§3.2.10–11, §3.2.22, §3.2.33, §3.2.37, §3.3.16, §4.2.2, §4.2.21, §4.3.1, §§4.3.5–6, §4.3.9, §4.4.2, 200n116, 205n213
weep, weeping, §2.14.4, §3.2.5, §§3.3.21–22
whiteness, whitewashing, §1.11.1, §1.13.4, §2.10.3, §2.14.3, §3.3.21
wine, §2.14.4, §3.3.4, §3.3.8, §3.3.11, §3.3.20, §3.3.24, §4.2.11, §4.2.15, §4.2.25, 204n192, 205n219
witness(es) (*shāhid, shuhūd*), §1.3.2, §1.8.4, §1.13.1, §2.10.2, §4.2.1, §4.3.3, §4.3.9
witness(es), professional legal (*ʿadl*), xix, §0.4, §2.7.1, §2.10.1, §2.12.1, §4.2.32, §4.2.35, §4.3.9, 199n100

Yaḥyā ibn Khālid ibn Barmak, §§3.2.5–6
Yaʿqūb ibn Dāwūd, §3.2.4, §3.3.2, 204n189
Yazīd ibn Muḥammad al-Muhallabī, §3.3.14
Yazīd ibn Qays, Abū l-Mukhtār, §4.3.5
Year of the Elephant. *See* Elephant, Year of
Year of the Emigration. *See* Emigration

Zayn al-Dīn. *See* ʿAlī ibn Ibrāhīm ibn Najā al-Anṣārī
Ziyād ibn Abī Sufyān, §4.1.1, 206n230
Ziyād ibn Abīhi. *See* Ziyād ibn Abī Sufyān.

About the NYU Abu Dhabi Institute

NYU
ABU DHABI
INSTITUTE

The Library of Arabic Literature is supported by a grant from the NYU Abu Dhabi Institute, a major hub of intellectual and creative activity and advanced research. The Institute hosts academic conferences, workshops, lectures, film series, performances, and other public programs directed both to audiences within the UAE and to the worldwide academic and research community. It is a center of the scholarly community for Abu Dhabi, bringing together faculty and researchers from institutions of higher learning throughout the region.

NYU Abu Dhabi, through the NYU Abu Dhabi Institute, is a world-class center of cutting-edge research, scholarship, and cultural activity. The Institute creates singular opportunities for leading researchers from across the arts, humanities, social sciences, sciences, engineering, and the professions to carry out creative scholarship and conduct research on issues of major disciplinary, multidisciplinary, and global significance.

About the Typefaces

The Arabic body text is set in DecoType Naskh, designed by Thomas Milo and Mirjam Somers, based on an analysis of five centuries of Ottoman manuscript practice. The exceptionally legible result is the first and only typeface in a style that fully implements the principles of script grammar (*qawāʿid al-khaṭṭ*).

The Arabic footnote text is set in DecoType Emiri, drawn by Mirjam Somers, based on the metal typeface in the naskh style that was cut for the 1924 Cairo edition of the Qurʾan.

Both Arabic typefaces in this series are controlled by a dedicated font layout engine. ACE, the Arabic Calligraphic Engine, invented by Peter Somers, Thomas Milo, and Mirjam Somers of DecoType, first operational in 1985, pioneered the principle followed by later smart font layout technologies such as OpenType, which is used for all other typefaces in this series.

The Arabic text was set with WinSoft Tasmeem, a sophisticated user interface for DecoType ACE inside Adobe InDesign. Tasmeem was conceived and created by Thomas Milo (DecoType) and Pascal Rubini (WinSoft) in 2005.

The English text is set in Adobe Text, a new and versatile text typeface family designed by Robert Slimbach for Western (Latin, Greek, Cyrillic) typesetting. Its workhorse qualities make it perfect for a wide variety of applications, especially for longer passages of text where legibility and economy are important. Adobe Text bridges the gap between calligraphic Renaissance types of the 15th and 16th centuries and high-contrast Modern styles of the 18th century, taking many of its design cues from early post-Renaissance Baroque transitional types cut by designers such as Christoffel van Dijck, Nicolaus Kis, and William Caslon. While grounded in classical form, Adobe Text is also a statement of contemporary utilitarian design, well suited to a wide variety of print and on-screen applications.

Titles Published by the Library of Arabic Literature

Classical Arabic Literature
Selected and translated by Geert Jan Van Gelder

A Treasury of Virtues, by al-Qāḍī al-Quḍāʿī
Edited and translated by Tahera Qutbuddin

The Epistle on Legal Theory, by al-Shāfiʿī
Edited and translated by Joseph E. Lowry

Leg Over Leg, by Aḥmad Fāris al-Shidyāq
Edited and translated by Humphrey Davies

Virtues of the Imām Aḥmad ibn Ḥanbal, by Ibn al-Jawzī
Edited and translated by Michael Cooperson

The Epistle of Forgiveness, by Abū l-ʿAlāʾ al-Maʿarrī
Edited and translated by Geert Jan Van Gelder and Gregor Schoeler

The Principles of Sufism, by ʿĀʾishah al-Bāʿūnīyah
Edited and translated by Th. Emil Homerin

The Expeditions, by Maʿmar ibn Rāshid
Edited and translated by Sean W. Anthony

Two Arabic Travel Books
- **Accounts of China and India**, by Abū Zayd al-Sīrāfī
  Edited and translated by Tim Mackintosh-Smith
- **Mission to the Volga**, by Ahmad Ibn Faḍlān
  Edited and translated by James Montgomery

Disagreements of the Jurists, by al-Qāḍī al-Nuʿmān
Edited and translated by Devin Stewart

Consorts of the Caliphs, by Ibn al-Sāʿī
Edited by Shawkat M. Toorawa and translated by the Editors of the Library of Arabic Literature

What ʿĪsā ibn Hishām Told Us, by Muḥammad al-Muwayliḥī
Edited and translated by Roger Allen

The Life and Times of Abū Tammām, by Abū Bakr Muḥammad ibn Yaḥyā al-Ṣūlī
Edited and translated by Beatrice Gruendler

The Sword of Ambition, by ʿUthmān ibn Ibrāhīm al-Nābulusī
Edited and translated by Luke Yarbrough

Brains Confounded by the Ode of Abū Shādūf Expounded, by Yūsuf al-Shirbīnī
Edited and translated by Humphrey Davies

About the Editor–Translator

Luke Yarbrough (PhD Princeton 2012) is Assistant Professor of Middle Eastern History in the History Department at Saint Louis University. His research is concerned with the history of the premodern Middle East and North Africa, including inter-communal relations, law and other prescriptive discourses, Arabic historiography, the oral transmission of knowledge, and comparative history. His articles on these subjects have appeared in *Islamic Law and Society*, the *Journal of the American Oriental Society*, and *Der Islam*, as well as in several edited volumes. He is currently working on a book about how non-Muslim state officials were represented in premodern Islamic thought.